MIZPAH

MIZPAH

The Bobby Dunbar Kidnapping Legend

ALLISON RAWLS BULLOCK

DEEDS PUBLISHING | ATLANTA

Letters, photographs, and legal documents are from the private collection of Hollis C. Rawls and Allison Rawls Bullock, including personal interviews, loaned photographs, and newspaper articles from the early 1900s. They are transcribed word for word for authenticity and character.

This book is as factual as extensive research will allow. Any errors are unintended and the author apologizes for any omissions or errors.

Printed in the United States of America
Published by Deeds Publishing LLC, Marietta, GA
www.deedspublishing.com

Printed in the United States of America

Library of Congress Cataloging-in-Publications Data is available upon request

ISBN 978-1-941165-06-5

Books are available in quantity for promotional or premium use. For information, write Deeds Publishing, PO Box 682212, Marietta, GA 30068 or info@deedspublishing.com.

Cover design by Allison Rawls Bullock and Saradel Rawls Berry

Typeset by Deeds Publishing

First edition 2014

10 9 8 7 6 5 4 3 2 1

Contents

Genesis 31:49 (KJV)

And Mizpah; for he said, The LORD watch between me and thee, when we are absent one from another.

"Each year, each age, leaves something. It gets compressed, of course, it disappears under the surface, but just a little of all that human life remains. A Roman tile, a coin, a clay pipe from Shakespeare's time. All left in place. When we dig down, we find it and we may put it on show. But don't think of it just as an object. Because that coin, that pipe belonged to someone: a person who lived, and loved, and looked out at the river and the sky each day just like you and me."

London by Edward Rutherfurd

Tinker, Tailor, Soldier, Sailor,

Rich Man, Poor Man, Beggar Man, Thief,

Doctor, Lawyer, Indian Chief.

Author's Note

This work of non-fiction is a compilation of: letters, photographs, and legal documents from the private collection of Hollis C. Rawls and Allison Rawls Bullock; personal interviews; loaned photographs; and newspaper articles from the early 1900s. They are transcribed word for word for authenticity and character.

I have included very little of my own commentary. The majority is taken directly from the above listed sources which were too numerous to fit in the book. I have also included a Mizpah Names chapter to help the reader keep track of the numerous characters.

I offer my apologies for leaving out anyone who wanted to be included, and including anyone who wanted to be left out.

For Hollis and Ben

Preface

When I was a child in the early sixties, my father, Ben Rawls, a lawyer turned banker, would often carry my two siblings and me back to work with him after hours or on the weekend to wrap up some unfinished business at Citizens Bank, a prominent two-story, turn-of-the-century structure at the intersection of Main and Second Streets in Columbia, Mississippi. Most likely our mother, Ann, with three children born within three years and three months, deserved a break.

The outing usually began with his returning phone calls at his desk up front while we played quietly behind the row of barred teller's cages, choosing our favorite booth and pretending we worked there. The rest of the time was dedicated to twirling on the tall cushioned stools above the mosaic tile floor. The inside of each regimented cubicle displayed a small shrine created by its daily occupant: family photos, a child's drawing, or maybe a postcard. When Daddy's work was complete, we were rewarded with a trip upstairs to the mezzanine for a soft drink in the building's employee lounge. Occasionally we would accompany him on up to the second floor of the building which consisted of a long hallway lined with darkened office spaces. At the extreme far end of the hall, he would unlock a door upon which the rectangle of textured glass was emblazoned with the painted names *Rawls and Hathorn*. The expansive front corner room had served as his father's, Hollis C. Rawls, law office for decades. It had fallen to my father, rather reluctantly at the time, as the youngest son to follow in Hollis' legal footsteps. He had graduated law school from his father's alma mater, the University of Mississippi, and had returned home to join his father's practice. After Hollis' death in 1960 at age 75, the room gently transformed into my grandfather's memorial as my father's interest turned toward a career in banking and an executive position downstairs.

Upstairs in Hollis' silent office, the walls were lined with towering glass-fronted Macey barrister bookcases, each one filled with dozens of thick legal volumes. A massive turn-of-the-century library table piled high with boxes and papers rested alongside a substantial arts-and-crafts mission-style oak partner desk. The desk's companion, a heavy Johnson Company swivel chair, could be pulled away from the desk, revealing a cavernous space where three children could create a fort. Above our heads sat an Underwood typewriter; an ancient telephone; several over-sized books; and an array of papers, pens, and glass organizers on the desk-top's faded green felt and thick glass. File cabinets, tables, lamps, and extra chairs vied for position in the crowded room. As Daddy rummaged about, we peered down at Main Street from our high vantage point and absorbed his permeating nostalgia. If only I had known then to pick his brain about the room's contents and the remarkable man to whom they had belonged. Hollis had died when I was only two and a half years old, but I grew up constantly hearing from kith and kin what a remarkable, well-loved gentleman he had been, serving three terms as our town's mayor.

In the seventies, as president of Citizens Bank, Daddy had been instrumental in building a much needed, larger bank two blocks north of the original one. Although the new, modern structure offered more space and convenience, to me it lacked the charm of the historic old building. Daddy transported Hollis' belongings to an unused second-story room at the new bank just down the hall from his office.

In 1987, after a year-long battle with colon cancer, our beloved father passed away at age fifty-nine. The city of Columbia grieved with us, for he was as revered as his father had been.

The following year, my husband's job was transferred from Columbia to Jackson, Mississippi, so we reluctantly packed up our two young daughters and moved. When given the opportunity to move back home in 1991, we gladly accepted.

My mother lived in the home Hollis and Adele Rawls had built in 1933. When Hollis died in 1960, Adele had a mother-in-law cottage built next door and deeded the house to my father. Mama had now determined that it was time to repeat the process with us, and after a lengthy renovation of the smaller house, she moved in.

The following year the bank contacted Mama, requesting that she empty Daddy's storage room which was badly needed for expansion. We had removed Daddy's desk and personal mementos from his office shortly after his death, and the bank had moved his remaining property into the room with Hollis' items. She and I gathered empty boxes, rolls of tape, and markers for the daunting task.

Mama began by disbursing Hollis' antique barristers among his nine grandchildren. Next, we tackled several file cabinets, reading, sorting, and boxing their contents. We frequently became engrossed in the seventy-five-year-old history we held in our hands and had to keep reminding ourselves to stay on track.

My brother had inherited Daddy's desk, so my sister and I got to choose between Hollis' desk and his library table. I chose the desk and was motivated to get it emptied for its journey home.

The contents appeared to have been left exactly as they were in the 1950's when Hollis became bedridden. The shallow middle drawer held a variety of writing implements: rulers, keys, combs, and other personal effects which we boxed, our reminiscing cut short by the magnitude of the job.

Each side of the desk appeared to contain three drawers, while in fact the right side consisted of one regular drawer above a deep, heavy file drawer concealed behind two drawer fronts. The double-sized drawer was filled to capacity with papers sandwiched between worn, drooping folders and dividers. While thumbing through the tightly packed contents, I discovered a section with several sepia-tinted photographs whose young subjects riveted my attention. The images had been inside a crumbling folder which barely contained seven to eight inches of documents, letters, and newspaper articles from 1912 through 1915.

I was immediately swept up in the chronicle of two tragic four-year-old boys, one named Bruce Anderson and the other Bobby Dunbar. An hour later I grudgingly set the file aside.

Throughout the next several days my mother and I distributed the bookcases, file cabinets, furniture, and mementos; packed up old law books; and consolidated the remaining papers into five or six labeled cartons which the bank offered to continue storing in the attic. I placed the one folder with the photos inside a cardboard box and carried it home for safe-keeping.

Over the next several years the file remained in the box on a shelf in my closet, being brought down whenever I could find a few quiet hours for reading. I was introduced to William Cantwell Walters, Julia Anderson, and the Dunbars through the words of Hollis Rawls—words I instinctively knew were of great significance.

The dilemma was easy to uncover: two mothers claimed one child. Percy and Lessie Dunbar had lost their four year-old son, Bobby, in a Louisiana swamp and eight months later had accused a traveling organ mender, Cantwell Walters, of having him. Cantwell, however, was traveling through Mississippi with his four-year-old nephew, Bruce, the son of his brother and Julia Anderson. Nevertheless, the well-to-do Dunbars took the child as theirs and had Cantwell arrested for kidnapping. My grandfather and his partner, Tom S. Dale, had represented Cantwell in his two-year fight to regain his nephew and his freedom.

As with any conflict, loyalties are pledged and allegiances sworn and I was no different, immediately siding with the legal team of Dale and Rawls.

In 2002, after the death of my father's brother, his widow, my Aunt Carol, came to Columbia for a visit. Out of the blue, she asked if I'd ever heard of the Dunbar case. I was shocked to learn that someone else was interested in the story. I went straight to the closet and pulled out the box.

Aunt Carol explained that Bobby Dunbar's granddaughter, Margaret, had contacted her son, discovering his connection to Hollis through his father's obituary. She was searching for information on the case, so I gave my aunt permission to give her my phone number.

When Margaret learned that I had a large collection of documents related to the case, she asked to come to Columbia to view them. Finding someone else with an interest in the story was thrilling, and I asked if she would be willing to share her research with our historical society. She agreed and the local paper advertised the upcoming event, inviting the public.

In the meantime, I commandeered a room in our house, pushed back the furniture, banished the nosy pets, and spent the next few weeks organizing the documents. Most of the letters and articles were dated, making putting them in chronological order fairly simple; but many of the items were obviously grouped together, so I came up with a system of keeping track of their original placement. This system proved to be invaluable for sorting out the story, although after being pressed together for almost ninety years, many of the pages were imprinted with an image of their neighboring page.

I assigned each document a number—five hundred and two in all, many of them multiple pages in length, for a total of over eight hundred pages. To protect the papers, I slipped each one into an archival page protector and placed them in five three-inch binders.

Margaret arrived with her father, Robert Dunbar, Jr., and we eagerly began to share information, but from two distinctly opposite vantage points. While she was adamant that Bobby had been reunited with the Dunbars, I was equally adamant that he had not. I brought up the obvious question of having DNA testing done to solve the mystery once-and-for-all, but she stated that her family had vehemently refused.

We looked at photos and newspaper articles she had copied from Lessie's scrapbook, and then she began flipping through the file searching for a transcript of the 1914 Opelousas, Louisiana, trial. It wasn't there. Supposedly, the State of Louisiana had requested that Dale and Rawls return their copy for correction, and it had never been returned. Every copy seems to have inexplicably vanished.

The following morning a small group of citizens gathered to learn about the "Trial of the Century," as the case had been known, and I had the honor of meeting Julia's two surviving children from Poplarville, Mississippi, Hollis E. Rawls, named in honor of my grandfather, and Jewel Rawls Tarver. They had read about the meeting in the paper.

From the moment I laid eyes on Mr. Rawls, I was astounded by his striking resemblance to Margaret's father. From their facial features, especially the eyes, to their bone structure and mannerisms, the two men appeared to be carbon copies of each other, twenty or thirty years apart. Julia's DNA had definitely marked each of these gentlemen, but no one acknowledged the similarities.

Margaret began her talk by describing her search for information concerning the kidnapping of her grandfather, Bobby. As she unfolded her story, a disparaging portrait of Julia and Cantwell emerged. Tom Dale and my grandfather Hollis fared no better and were described as having procured a kidnapper's release on a technicality after two years of legal scheming. I was mortified.

Afterwards, I apologized to Mr. Rawls and Mrs. Tarver, who were more than gracious. They briefly looked through the file, which was overwhelming; and we exchanged telephone numbers and addresses, promising to keep in touch.

Looking through the defense file that evening, I was reminded that these aging documents were not only treasured family heirlooms, they were likely the last remaining evidence of Cantwell's innocence and of Bruce's identity. The papers contained long-overdue redemption for the Walters, Anderson, and Rawls families; and I had been given the solemn responsibility of providing it to them.

I had only removed one file from my grandfather's papers and felt sure there was more information to be found, possibly the missing trial transcript, so I contacted the bank to get the last of my father's boxes out of storage. After several unsuccessful attempts, I was told that the remainder of his possessions had been discarded. The defense file could have easily disappeared with them.

Sitting down at our computer, I began to catalogue the documents. It had been almost thirty years since I had taken a typing class in high school, and my fingers fumbled over the keys. Eventually those fingers remembered what they had been taught.

On Margaret's second visit to Columbia, she brought several binders of typed newspaper articles from the period which heavily favored the Dunbars' position that the boy was theirs. She had marked through any portion that was in opposition to that stance, correcting it to her satisfaction up and down the margins.

"Walters cruelly beat Bobby," she told me. "And made him beg for food."

"My grandfather," I stated with conviction, "from what I know, would not have put up with a devious client for one day, much less two years. Just read the file," I said. "It *will* change your mind." She returned later with a flatbed scanner and asked to copy the file, "just for reading," she swore.

During this visit, Margaret noticed a small painting that was hanging in my den. I had painted the picture in 1995 from a photograph I took of a quaint, two-story house located on Highway 43 in Pearl River County.

I had been on my way to Picayune, Mississippi, and was following a winding two-lane road I hadn't traveled down since I was a child. When Interstate 59 opened in the late sixties, my father had opted for its more streamlined route to the Gulf Coast, but a friend had suggested that I take the scenic path down 43, known as Old River Road. As I drove through the rolling countryside, I tried to capture my curiously pleasant nostalgia on film. I pulled the car over many times that day, at old home-places under ancient oak trees or at quiet churches and cemeteries. They beckoned me to pause and take notice, so I did.

When Margaret saw the painting, she remarked that it looked a lot like Jeptha and Matilda Bilbos' house, where her grandfather and Cantwell had stayed for many nights sheltered under its tin roof. I assured her that the home was simply memorialized on canvas for its charm. Inquiring further about its location, we realized that the houses were indeed one and the same. **(See p. 322)**

Margaret had an old newspaper image of the house which showed a long-since-removed picket fence around the yard. In my painting I had left out the chain link fence that now bordered the yard and had added a picket fence. To say I was floored does not begin to describe my emotions. It was one of the more reassuring moments I have ever experienced, and for days afterward I struggled to convey to my family and friends its significance.

Margaret and her father were ensconced in two rooms of an immaculate, two-story Victorian bed and breakfast inn two blocks down the street from my house. The innkeepers were out of town but had arranged for their guests' usual breakfast to be prepared and brought in to the formal dining room each morning. Margaret showed me the visitors' living room, which was adjacent to the dining room, and led me upstairs to see their two cozy guestrooms. Back downstairs, we passed a hallway leading to the back of the house. "That's the owners' private area. Strictly off limits," she tutted. My tour ended on the large wrap-around porch where we enjoyed the swings and rocking chairs provided for the boarders.

During the mornings, Margaret would come over and look through the file as my two grandchildren played on the floor. In the afternoons when the children went home, she and I would sit on the porch of the inn and discuss the case though she remained closed to any scenario other than the one in which her grandfather was born Bobby Dunbar.

Margaret's uncle and aunt traveled to Columbia for a brief visit to view the file, and she invited me to supper while they were there. I arrived at the inn with a mental list of our local eateries; however, Margaret led me down the hall and into the back of the house where she and her family were lounging in the owners' den, frying sausages on their stove. I took a step backward only to hear, "Well they didn't mean *us.*"

I purchased a scanner and began transferring the documents into our computer. Many of the pages were legal-sized and too large to fit on the bed of a conventional scanner. They were also too fragile to run through the feeder, so I spent the next few months splicing the images together with a panorama program.

Several months later, I was at home by myself, sitting outside on our patio when I noticed the sound of a woman quietly sobbing. Looking around to see who was in distress, I realized I was completely alone. The soft, steady sound was easily within my reach, surrounding me, but it wasn't the least bit frightening or alarming. I looked around once more, making sure that I was indeed alone and then simply listened. It was pure anguish, broken open and spilling forth, all-consuming and unrelenting, immeasurable, insatiable sorrow. A mother was crying for her lost child. The sound continued for about a minute, stopping as suddenly as it had started. I got up, renewed in purpose, and returned to the computer.

Piecing together this story grew into an obsession that occupied a large percentage of my free time, but I had been assigned this task and would not be deterred.

With almost one third of the documents being written by hand, many barely legible, I learned to decipher each writers' unique script and began typing the 153 handwritten letters. My index alone filled another three-ring binder.

I made copies of Julia's letters for her children, including her parents' sworn affidavit, and delivered them to their house in Poplarville. Private family gifts. Both siblings recounted how the ordeal had affected her, causing her to remain sickly and fearful for the rest of her life; but they assured me that she had found happiness, raising seven children in a loving, Christian home. We discussed my plans for publishing the file, and I assured them that it supported their mother.

When Margaret finished reading Hollis' file and realized that the truth would come out, she convinced her family to have DNA testing done. She and her father announced the results at a prearranged press conference during the 2004 Walters' reunion in Barnesville, North Carolina, and then in Poplarville. I had recently undergone spinal surgery and couldn't travel.

In the spring of 2005, I traveled to my first Walters' family reunion in Barnesville, North Carolina, and met Michael Walters, a descendant of Cantwell and their family's leading historian. Five minutes after we met, he told me that Margaret had pointedly asked him not to invite me to the 2004 reunion. "She said you would be too distracting along her journey."

The 2005 annual gathering was held at Princess Ann State Park on the Lumber River, approximately one mile from where Cantwell was raised. I walked upon the land he had called home, the land taken from him. A small birthright, but a birthright nonetheless. The area is a place of tangible serenity and is beautiful beyond words.

The Walters family had heard the infamous story of their ancestor, W. C. Walters, who'd been charged with kidnapping Bobby Dunbar. A palpable twinge of embarrassment surrounded his name. I introduced them to the file and its basic message—the Dunbars were the kidnappers, not Cantwell. The Dunbars' tale was and is still a hoax.

For the first time, I saw photos of Cantwell's parents, his brothers and sisters, nieces and nephews. The solemn figures in the photographs came alive through the stories their family shared. Faded images began gathering flesh and bone and voice through their offspring. Their descendants deserve to know the simple truth.

When Michael explained that Bullock is a surname of William and Celia Walters, Cantwell's grandparents, I brushed the information aside, assured it was not the same Bullock. He went on to say that these relatives had moved to south Mississippi, and I began to pay closer attention. When I got home and checked my Bullock genealogy, I found that it is indeed the same family. My husband's great-great-great-grandfather, Joel Bullock, came from Robeson County, North Carolina.

Another nudge, another connection intertwining my spirit with theirs.

Later that summer, Hurricane Katrina hit the Mississippi Gulf Coast. Our daughters' homes, one in Bay St. Louis and the other in Diamondhead, were completely wiped away, leaving only a slab and scattered wreckage to mark their existence. The Bilbo house was lost, and Columbia suffered tremendous damage from the storm as well. My mother and mother-in-law, who were both in failing health, spiraled downward. We grieved the loss of precious lives, possessions, jobs, and communities that vanished within one day; and it took an entire year before everyone relocated and we began to return to normal. The file rested patiently as it had for so many years before.

The following year, I began to catalogue all the names contained in the file, recording what I knew about them and listing the documents where they appeared. In 2006 I received a copyright for my entire collection, *William Cantwell Walters' Defense File*© by Allison Rawls Bullock. Margaret's response to my copyright news was that I would be hearing from her lawyer. She then hung up the phone. Margaret had become desperately possessive of Hollis' file, believing that it was hers to construe. Apparently she no longer intended to honor her promise to me that she would not share the file.

My lawyer suggested I condense *William Cantwell Walters' Defense File* into a more readable form, selecting the most elemental documents and adding narration to bridge the gaps. He also recommended that I change the names and write the story as fiction, but my conscience would not allow it. From the beginning I have felt a sense of direction and guidance that has not been easily dismissed or ignored. Besides, it is not my story to change.

A few months later, at a gathering of my mother's family, I was telling the group about my writing project and the trip to the Walters' reunion. I described the overwhelming emotional connection I felt while there, and my aunt interrupted me. She looked me straight in the eyes and said, "Your great-great-great-grandfather, Harmon Thompson, the man who settled this family land where we stand, was born in Robeson County, North Carolina, and owned land along Hogg and Ashpole Swamp." It was the same area where Julia and Cantwell had lived. My instincts had told me I was home.

Deciding on which documents needed to be included in my book and which could be left out proved to be challenging; for every person involved, every record, every testimony, left an impression, a footprint of sorts, along the story's trail.

On my way to the 2007 Walters' reunion, I retraced a portion of Cantwell and Bruce's journey through Georgia, stopping in Eastman, Baxley, and Surrency where three of Cantwell's siblings lived. I was hoping, without success, to find a courthouse record or tombstone that would reveal Cantwell's fate.

At one point when the task before me seemed daunting, my Aunt Dell shared a story with me about her father, Hollis, during his college days at Ole Miss. He was the business manager of the yearbook staff, and as such, had placed the large annual order with a publisher. Due to a delay in printing and shipping, the books were not delivered before summer break, leaving the young man with cases of unsold books. He worked at the post office in Columbia until he was personally able to reconcile the monumental debt. Hearing of his tenacity was uplifting and contagious.

Hollis, Tom, Julia, Cantwell, and Bruce, along with their faithful friends, are the spirits that strengthened me, each one trusting that what was right and good and equitable would eventually come to light.

Just north of Audubon Park in New Orleans on Freret Street, one block from where the Dunbars brought Bruce when they left Columbia, sits the Howard-Tilton Memorial Library of Tulane University. Inside, dozens of rolls of microfilm contain many of the aged newspapers that covered the story—over two years of coverage in three large daily papers. The tragic drama ebbs and flows alongside articles on women's suffrage and General Huerta's coup in Mexico. At times it consumes the front pages, accompanied by photos and sketches; and at other times it's a small paragraph tucked away near the back, waiting to be discovered. The articles are literally windows in time.

Prologue

Forty-year-old Bobby Dunbar poses awkwardly in the corner of the sofa. Nothing in his face or the faces of his three children holds any enthusiasm at being photographed for a full page-and-a-half feature "The Famous Case of Bobbie Dunbar" in the *Morning Advocate Magazine*, October 1948. The mother, Marjorie Byars Dunbar, is the only participant to show any animation in her face or posture. She sits forward, eyes alert and lips forming a pleasant smile. Four-year-old daughter Mary, bow in hair, is on her lap; and their two sons, twelve-year-old Bobby, Jr., and ten-year-old John, sit Indian-style on the floor. The lamp on a side table and a magazine rack nearby complete the cozy family portrait.

After the required photo session, journalist Lillian Bourdier begins to discuss the details of Bobby's kidnapping thirty-six years ago, an event that stirred the entire nation and caused a political rift between Mississippi and Louisiana. She begins writing.

"Dunbar was once the most celebrated child in the nation, but there is nothing about this quiet, unassuming man to remind his neighbors and friends of that — he has wiped out those eight months and the long years which followed when efforts were being made to bring his kidnapper to justice.

The Bobby Dunbar case was a famous one — probably the most talked of in America until the Lindbergh kidnapping. Aside from much other publicity, Mrs. O. J. Cauvin of Abbeville wrote a song, "I Have Found My Child at Last." But Bobby Dunbar and his family have almost forgotten it."

"Mr. Dunbar," broaches the reporter, pulling off her glasses, "have you ever thought of trying to contact Cantwell Walters to question him about the kidnapping? ...Why you? ...Why no ransom?"

"If Walters is still living," Bobby offers reflectively, "I would certainly like to see him."

"You sound as if you have a trace of affection for your kidnapper. How is this possible?" Mrs. Bourdier leans back in her chair, tablet in hand. "What do *you* remember Bobby, beginning with August 23, 1913?"

"I recall being led away from the railway tracks by a man," Bobby pauses rubbing his chin. "A few months later another child was brought to Walters by Julia Anderson. I called him Bruce, but he fell out of the back of the wagon and died. I remember Cantwell burying him in a small town in Mississippi."…Another lengthy pause. "My belief is that Walters took me for companionship, not ransom, while he traveled the country mending stoves. We moved around a lot but I remember he was good to me."

"Tell Mrs. Bourdier good-night," Mrs. Dunbar prompts the children, ushering them out of the room to prepare for bed. When the family is gone, the reporter turns back to Bobby. "But you had whip marks on your back when you were found."

"My parents told me that," Bobby answers, "but I don't remember it. What little memory I have is of him singing. I do remember watching his knobby hands working the keyboard and stops of an organ and laughing as our legs pumped furiously to supply the air. I wasn't heavy enough to press the pedals down by myself." Momentarily lost in thought, the man silently mouthed …one …two …three …four …one …two …three …four.

"I remember being very afraid for a long time after Father and Mother found me and brought me home. They couldn't convince me I would not be stolen again. Gradually, with my family's help, my terrors ceased and my earlier memories returned."

Mrs. Bourdier marvels at the modest gentleman sitting before her. There is nothing in his countenance to suggest that he had once been the most fought over child in the country. For another hour she and Bobby cover the highlights of his kidnapping and recovery. Then with the interview over, Mrs. Bourdier closes her tablet and offers her hand to Mr. Dunbar, thanking him for his time and patience. "I will send you one of the first copies," she offers as she steps through the door and into the night.

Bobby locks the door, turns out the light, and stands quietly as the sounds of his house diminish around him.

ALLISON RAWLS BULLOCK | XXIX

The children are finished bathing and are in bed when their father comes in for a kiss. Marjorie is in her nightgown at the dressing table brushing her hair. His saving grace had been in marrying this resilient woman and creating a family of their own. Before that could take place, however, she had insisted Bobby make peace with his past. He began with the catch-phrase, "It doesn't matter who you are; what matters is how you choose to live your life."

Bobby sits on the side of the bed and begins to undress. Pockets are emptied; watch is laid on the nightstand; trousers, tie, and belt are hung on the valet stand. In the bathroom, shirt, socks, handkerchief, and underwear go into the clothes hamper. Naked, he reaches to adjust the drain and tap. "I will not look tonight," he thinks. "I will not look tonight… I will not look tonight…but tonight may be different."

While the tub fills, Bobby sits on the toilet seat and brings his left ankle across his right thigh. He slides his thumbs and forefingers up and down the outside of the left great toe, examining the even skin and the perfectly shaped nail, lifting the appendage to check the smooth underneath. It is an annoying thirty-six-year compulsion, but a fairly harmless one.

Chapter One
August 1912

The palm-sized perch hung motionless at the end of a four-foot section of fishing line. Sixteen other short baited lines in various states of use were securely tethered three feet apart on the heavier fifty-foot trot line running diagonally across a portion of the oxbow lake. The latest catch, the perch with the barbed end of a hook protruding from its jaw, had just renewed its efforts at freedom one last time, circling and diving until its eyes began to cloud over. The fish went limp, unable to efficiently pass water through its gills, and sank backwards toward the bottom of the lake where it hung in open water, perpendicularly suspended in the murky half-light of Swayze Lake.

The surface of the water rippled every few moments as one of the main lines was tugged from below. A paddle broke the surface of the water with barely a splash, silently propelling a pirogue along the bayou between other trees and logs that held similar setups. Once all of the lines had been placed and baited, the fishermen relaxed until it was time to return to the water and hopefully collect their bounty. In the distance, children could be heard laughing, but along this section of the lake, serious, muddy-booted men and older boys gathered silently along the bank, serenaded by the ever-present drone of cicadas.

In one swift sideways motion, the gar struck the soft underbelly of the perch, its needle-like teeth ripping away the entire lower half of the body. As the smaller fish bled out, the gar struck again, hitting higher up this time, and in its frenzy swallowed the same hook that had provided its meal.

The surface of the lake erupted as the huge fish jumped and rolled, flipping its body violently, and yanked upon the main line until it suddenly snapped. Blindly heading for the nearest cover, the gar, trailing a loaded portion of line, entered the complex branches of a large cypress that rested underwater near the bank. Once again the fish's movements were impeded by the tug of the line, and it gave a great surge forward and to one side, and then began rolling over, encountering the other shorter lines and other fish thrashing wildly in the network of limbs. Within a matter of seconds the great gar was hopelessly entangled just inches below the surface.

On the bank a great rush of activity occurred. Paul Mizzie shoved a small wooden skiff away from the shore, jumping in at the last second and paddling towards the commotion. "It snapped!" he yelled. "Another damn gar! *Merde!*" At this rate the display case in his butcher shop would be empty come Monday morning, for his customers invariably preferred river trout or white crappie to the bony gar. Pulling out a pistol, he ended the life of the tightly trussed predator.

More boats pushed away from the shore to help empty the line and access what could be salvaged, but it soon became clear that their efforts were futile in saving this line with its hooks and weights and unreachable fish, so they abandoned the entire mess, out of sight, underwater, and forgotten. The group headed to shore to begin the tedious process of tying another set of lines.

The resident flock of children had come running at the sound of the shot and watched from the top of the steep bank. Two of the older boys, followed by the children, raced back to the cabins to retrieve the needed supplies. Soon the men were bent to their task, determined to get another line back into the water. Once it was assembled, they scrambled down to the water's edge and their waiting boats. One of the smaller children, four-year-old Bobby Dunbar, was right behind them. Being the first grandchild and an older brother had given Bobby a healthy sense of entitlement in his world. He was charming, but spoiled rotten by his family.

As Paul straddled the water between his skiff and the bank, the little boy lost his footing and slid butt-first into the man's ankle. Caught off guard, the lanky fisherman instantly began to heave and contort his body in a frantic attempt to avoid the water and the startled child directly under him. When Paul miraculously regained his footing, he snapped at the boy, telling him to get back.

The pack of children watching from above laughed at the rebuke, and with one singsong voice chanted, "*Couillon! Couillon!*" The taunt caused Bobby's smooth olive complexion to become mottled by hot, red splotches that spread across his cheeks.

"That's enough!" the butcher barked, narrowing his eyes at the group. They quickly scattered, racing off to seek their next adventure.

Grabbing the boy by his mud-stained rompers, Paul pushed him upwards towards the path, telling him to go find his mama, and for the second time that morning the little boy's feelings received a serious bruising. He began to sob as he crawled up the bank.

* * *

Yesterday afternoon, the group of campers from Opelousas, Louisiana, had piled into the passenger car of the Half Moon train for a short ride to their favorite fishing site, a cluster of small rustic cabins beside Swayze Lake, thirteen miles to the east.

The two-mile-long, hundred-feet-wide, oxbow lake is similar in character to a bayou and is one of two large, dead lakes in the area, remnants of the Mississippi River's ancient course. Swayze Lake lay in the center of a vast, uninhabited cypress swamp fed by the nearby Atchafalaya River and its network of rising and falling bayous that stretched to the Gulf. Because the area is regularly inundated with floodwater, no navigable roads ventured into the dense twenty-square-mile section of low-lying marshland. Traversing this bayou meant walking or riding a horse along the raised railroad track, pumping a handcar over the steel rails, or catching the train. If the track and its bridges were underwater, nothing passed.

The Half Moon train cut through the heart of the swamp, running along a massive man-made berm of earth and rock with high trestles spanning Swayze and Second Lake. Smaller bridges crossed the network of bayous that snaked between them. The rail line had opened up a direct logging route from Opelousas to Melville on the western bank of the Atchafalaya and provided access to the rich fishing grounds it crossed. A cluster of drafty, unoccupied cabins near the two major bridges was the only sign of civilization between the two towns. The track had just reopened after months of heavy flooding and the repair work that followed.

Earlier that spring, high waters from the Ohio, Cumberland, and Tennessee rivers and the Mississippi River above Cairo, Illinois, had converged to produce record flooding above Memphis, crowding the already swollen Mississippi River channel. Standard three-foot-high dirt levees built and maintained by each land owner were useless, and entire communities vanished in the deluge. Dead bodies, both animal and human, littered the landscape, while the living swarmed ant-like onto high ground.

The misery roared downstream, aiming for Memphis and leaving nineteen thousand refugees there. The river wasn't navigable; roads and rail lines were underwater; factories flooded and closed; and mail service to the affected areas was halted indefinitely.

As the floodwater surged southward, it was reinforced by high water flowing in from the St. Francis and White rivers, creating an additional fifty thousand evacuees. When the Mississippi reached southern Louisiana, it spread to the West; crossing the narrow terrace of lowland and separating it from where the Red River flowed into the Atchafalaya. Swayze Lake lay a mere twenty miles south of this point. The trail of destruction was beyond our country's measure or imagination.

Relief camps sprang up every few miles and were managed by local committees charged with housing refugees, doling out supplies, and overseeing work crews. Each board divided the monies as they saw fit. Inevitably some members lined their own pockets or funneled resources and jobs toward their friends and families. The residents of hard-hit southern Louisiana were seething.

Inside the small excursion train, thirty-eight-year-old real-estate agent Percy Dunbar, along with his twenty-seven-year-old wife, Lessie, and their sons, Bobby, and two-year-old Alonzo, traveled with several other prominent families from Opelousas—his cousin Wallace Dunbar's family, his uncle Preston King, Lessie's sister Lorena, friends Paul Mizzie and his family, and a Mr. Richards. Everyone looked forward to a long weekend getaway at their fish camp in the remote location. Several men and boys followed on horseback.

The train stopped just short of the trestle crossing the lake beside a narrow trail that disappeared into the thick undergrowth. Preston King led them down the half-mile path to the campsite with Mr. Richard following behind, everybody packing in the groups' heavy gear. Sebe Frilot, the black caretaker and guide at Swayze and Second Lake, had been around the place since yesterday, mucking out the muddy cabins and ridding them of unwanted rats and snakes.

The men began the task of running the lines that would catch their supper while the women set up housekeeping. The children gathered firewood, and soon there were fish and potatoes frying in the skillet.

The next morning, August 23, family friends Dr. Daly and his son, along with the wealthy planter, attorney, and politician John Oge, joined the group. Percy announced he would be riding up the track toward Half Moon Bayou and Second Lake before heading into Melville on an errand as Notary Public.

"Can't you take one of the boys with you?" Lessie pleaded, envisioning her day singlehandedly corralling two rambunctious children. Alonzo had slept fitfully beside her in their small bunk, startling with each noise that pierced the darkness. She had spent half the night rubbing his back so his crying wouldn't wake the others. He would probably nap for a few hours.

Bobby tugged at his daddy's leg, "Me, Daddy, me, me! I wanna go with you!"

"Not today, Bobby," he answered, pushing back from the child's grasp. "I'm in a hurry. You stay here and play with Lonzo." Percy, who was known for having a wandering eye, had visions of relieving his cravings this afternoon.

"Noooooo!" Bobby screeched, appalled by the refusal. "I wanna go!"

"Percy, please," begged Lessie, "He just wants to spend some time with you, and I am exhausted."

"I said no," Percy answered sharply. "I have to head to the relief camp in Melville to sort out a nasty disagreement." Percy served on the board of the refugee camp at Melville, though the lines of begging humanity created little empathy within him. "Besides, I will get back sooner if I am riding alone."

When he went to kiss her, she leaned away, studying his face. "You're coming *straight* back?"

Percy brushed her off. "I'll be back later this afternoon and will take the boys off your hands."

He rode out around ten o'clock, with Bobby chasing after him at the last second, crying and screaming to go. Percy's cousin, Wallace Dunbar, caught the furious little boy and brought him back. To divert his attention, he took his young son, along with Bobby and Alonzo, to watch Paul shooting at any gar that approached their lines. At first the child refused to be placated, but the excitement over the broken line finally distracted him.

The fishermen ran the lines often, having extraordinarily good luck in the freshly stocked lake. Only a few hooks were empty or held translucent jelly-like eels.

"Bring me one!" Bobby shouted, searching for a stick with which to poke the gelatinous mass. John Oge pulled up a giant foul-hooked paddlefish and drew it into his boat with a net.

"I wanna see!" Bobby demanded. "Bring it to me, please!" He hopped from one leg to the other until the bizarre creature was before him. He studied the huge paddle, rubbing its bristled texture with a finger. His small backside had met a similar paddle, owing to his feisty character.

Following the men to a wide plank table, the boys watched and learned as the men dissected their catch. Bobby held out a waiting palm and Oge placed a small, still-pumping red heart in it. Percy had a budding outdoorsman.

* * *

Bobby had learned to climb out of his crib at an early age and soon began walking. Lessie was nearly run ragged trying to keep up with the energized and now-mobile baby. He studied how people got outside and then fidgeted with the door's knob until he achieved his goal.

"Robert Dunbar!" Lessie screamed in panic, heading for the street out front. "Bobby! You come here this instant!" When she reached the roadway in tears, a young neighborhood girl had Lessie's son securely by the hand.

Unlike Lessie, Percy simply viewed his son as outgoing and resourceful, aggressive at times like himself. "He will make his way in this world, Lessie. He's a Dunbar. You need to stop babying him and worrying so much."

Alonzo came along shortly thereafter and, being of a more even temperament, gave Lessie plenty of time to keep her eyes on Bobby. Until one day...

She had both boys outside in the back yard, the baby on a quilt in the warm sun and she and Bobby were kicking a rubber ball back and forth. When his interest drifted, they would pluck a dead flower from a potted plant or gather a bundle of twigs and toss them into their smoldering trash pile. Lessie picked up Alonzo just as Bobby decided to remove his shoes.

"No sir!" she snapped. "It's too cold out here." Bobby looked at his mother, grinned sideways, and took off running barefooted. He made several laughing loops around the yard, passing just out of her reach. He could tell she wasn't really mad. The child spied the ball which had been forgotten and began to kick it wildly. Lessie went to lay Alonzo back down to deal with Bobby.

"Aughh!" Bobby screamed. "No!"

When Lessie turned around she saw Bobby staring at his rubber ball, which lay at the edge of the fire pit and was just now beginning to flame.

"It's OK baby; we will get another one tomorrow." And she walked toward his crumbling frame. In an instant, Bobby charged forward, kicking the ball out of the fire. The rubber's jolly red color was gone, turned into thick flaming black goo which coated his left big toe and spread back into the rise of his arch and onto the side of his foot below the ankle. Bobby howled with the pain from a third-degree burn on the toe.

Bobby spent days in the hospital while the doctors surgically removed the rubber and then many months with the foot wrapped in cotton wadding saturated with linseed oil and lime-water—Carron Oil. At times doctors applied cotton wool with melted butter or local honey. Fortunately the burn healed and Bobby managed to keep his toe. Once the scar toughened, it did not slow the boy down one bit.

* * *

Back at the campsite, lunch was announced, and as everyone gathered at the cabins, they realized that Bobby was not there. Paul recounted the earlier incident to Lessie and then headed back up the trail to where they had been fishing. Lessie checked inside the cabins, but their search turned up nothing.

Bobby had not been seen around the cabins, so they assumed he had turned north on the path instead of south, heading deeper into the wilderness. Several searchers hurried off in that direction, but after a lengthy hike with no trace of the boy, they returned to the camp, hoping to find him there. The look on Lessie's face told them he had not returned.

Lessie joined the search and headed south on the trail toward the railroad tracks and the looming trestle that spanned the lake. On the far side of the tracks, they discovered a small set of footprints in the mud. Lessie dropped to her knees to examine the area, running her finger over the impressions. "They're his!" she cried out, scrambling to her feet. "Bobby!"

"Yep. It's him all right," Cousin Wallace agreed. The big toe of every other print was pitted and misshapen on one side. It was the imprint's defining characteristic. "Now we know where to look."

With a new surge of enthusiasm, they followed the impressions down a trail through the underbrush that led to a rail spur. There, thankfully, the footprints turned west, away from the lake, toward where the spur rejoined the main line forty yards away. They hurried along the spur, calling as they went, but found no further sign of the child. When they reached the main line, Lessie turned east looking toward the trestle in the distance. Her countenance began to crumble and she raced in that direction. Sebe left on horseback to locate Percy.

A railroad crew working a mile and a half down the track toward Opelousas was the first to hear of the missing child.

"Have you seen a little boy? Four years old—about this tall." Wallace marked the air with his flattened hand. "He wandered off from the fish camp a little while ago, and his mama's pretty upset."

"Mister, ain't nothing come by here today, not even a breeze. We've got another crew above the lake at Half Moon. Maybe they snagged him."

They left their tools and hurried toward the lake, gathering information from Wallace along the way: light hair, blue eyes, barefoot, blue rompers, straw hat, goes by Bobby or Robert. The crew working above the lake to the east reported that he had not come their way. Meanwhile, Sebe had located Percy at the home of a female friend. When Percy happened to catch the man's condescending look, he held up one finger to Sebe's face in warning. Riding back, guilt clutched at Percy with each passing mile, but he sloughed it off. "Bobby is fine," he thought.

As word spread, dozens of volunteers from Opelousas, Port Barre, and Melville were shuttled to the site. City and parish officials, businessmen, farmers, laborers, as well as the Dunbars' family rushed to help. A tracking dog was brought to the spur and led them westward to the main line, then turned right, leading them back to where they had begun. Bobby had made a complete circle.

The dog continued past the trail toward the bridge, never slowing or turning until the solid rail bed fell away beneath its paws. It gingerly scrabbled from plank to plank, obeying its master's command before stopping midway across, indicating the trail's end by baying out over the water. Lessie's screams, punctuated by the harsh crack of gunfire, signaled for everyone to gather at the bridge.

"You should have taken him with you!" she shrieked, clawing wildly at Percy's chest and face. "That's all he wanted!"

"He's not in the water, Less. They've already looked!"

"Remember, O most gracious Virgin Mary," Lessie sobbed as she was carried back to the cabin, "...that never was it known that *anyone* who fled to thy protection...implored thy help, or sought thine intercession was left unaided." Once inside the cabin she slid to her knees on the floor.

Walking along the water's edge just south of the bridge, Percy poked around in the overhanging bushes with a branch. He dropped to the ground as his mind registered a foreign object in the water, an object he recognized. It was Bobby's straw hat. He fished it out and, without thinking, he quickly shoved the evidence under his jacket and out of his sight. "It couldn't be!" his mind screamed. "It just couldn't be!" He clutched at his jacket and staggered away, vomiting behind the first available tree. "If only I had taken him," thought Percy, remembering his son's pleading face.

If Bobby was dead, he would be to blame. Percy whirled around to see if anyone had witnessed the action. Sebe, searching nearby, instantly looked away, but not before their eyes met. He dared not delve into the affairs of Percy Dunbar. And Percy was rumored to have had many affairs.

Percy made his way to the fire, and when no one was looking, he threw the hat into the flames. He then made his way outside the circle of light and did something he had not done since he was a child—he cried like a baby.

Clusters of men with lanterns and torches beat and hacked their way into the unforgiving swamp, half-swimming, half-crawling in the thick, sucking mire. They stumbled through reeking hog wallows, probed the mouths of alligator dens, looking for signs of fresh kill, and followed animal trails through palmetto flats and dense thorny thickets, shouting, cursing, and praying as they went.

When morning arrived, the lake was dragged and then dynamited to dislodge anything trapped below the surface. Alligators were shot and gutted to check the contents of their stomachs. Despite their efforts, no trace of the child was found. No body. No blood. No clothing—other than a lingering rumor that Bobby's hat had been found in the lake.

Lessie was inconsolable. She drifted in and out of a drugged delirium as family and friends offered words of hope. Whispers drifted toward her ears intimating that Percy's earlier mission involved a dalliance with one of her friends, but he maintained his steely composure and tirelessly directed the search.

When someone suggested that the boy had been lured away and kidnapped for ransom money or possibly for retribution over his flood allocations, Percy latched onto the idea. "Lessie," he whispered in his wife's ear, "I'll find him for you." The local newspaper shifted its coverage from a drowning to a kidnapping.

A reward was offered for the boy's safe return, and when the New Orleans newspapers picked up the story, it quickly spread statewide and beyond. Pictures of the boy rolled off the presses, and a sympathetic public strained to memorize his face. The reward grew to an astounding six thousand dollars from the influential and well-known family, but no one was able to produce the child and claim the money.

For months, Percy followed numerous leads from all over Louisiana and the adjoining states, relieved to be away from his depressing home. Bobby was identified as having been seen in Mobile and then supposedly heard crying in a tramp's shack in Lucedale. A lady from Poplarville told of a tramp with a crying child that matched Bobby's description. Percy's brother, Archie, headed to Poplarville but found that the child was not his nephew. Anyone with a small boy resembling Bobby was viewed as a possible suspect, and if he was not able to prove the boy's identity, he was detained until the Dunbar family could arrive. Each sighting fueled Lessie's hopes, but the outcome was always disappointing, sending her further into despair.

Percy, unable to stop searching for the child he had convinced Lessie was alive and well, grew wearier and more disheartened each day.

Chapter Two
December 1912

The old man and little boy trundled along in the buggy, the old man singing heartily and the child humming, their frosty breaths visible in the winter air, "Away in a manger, no crib for His bed, the little Lord Jesus lay down his sweet head." The four-year-old's cap bobbed dramatically to the rhythm; brows furrowed in concentration. Bruce Anderson sat between the man's legs, one bent normally and the other awkwardly jutting out, gripping the reins in his small gloved hands as they traveled through the countryside bordering the Pearl River in south Mississippi. They were heading to the home of Thomas Lumpkin, a local farmer who had recently hired William Cantwell Walters, commonly known as Cantwell Walters, to repair his pump organ.

Cantwell limped from the rig to the house, carrying in satchels of tools, rolls of canvas and strapping, coils of wire, and boxes of hooks and pins. A pot of hardened tallow or glue was placed on the stove to warm. Bruce carried in his thick tapestry floor cushion, well-worn from a small boy's burrowing, and plopped it down where Cantwell indicated near the stove. Its cotton batting shifted into a slight bowl which conveniently kept the child's small trinkets from rolling out of his reach. Bruce immediately began peeling off his shoes and socks.

"You wanna see my toes?"

"Oh no, Bruce," Mr. Lumpkin answered. "Keep 'em tucked in your warm shoes." Lumpkin knew this man and boy had been put through the ringer since the Dunbar child went missing and had been cleared each time. Besides, they came highly recommended by his neighbor, George Amacker. "The man is a hard worker and the kid's no trouble. Real polite." Cantwell had just finished a three-day repair job there.

Cantwell appreciated Lumpkin's hospitable gesture, adding, "My handicap, along with mine and Bruce's unpredictable routine, tends to cast our lot in with vagrants or beggars, sir, and we most certainly thank you for the opportunity of employment in your home." Cantwell was himself a well-educated, well-spoken man, but owing to a few poor business decisions and a crippling injury several years back, the majority of his holdings were sixty acres interest in his family's farm. Thankfully, he was able to practice an honorable, though humbling, occupation as an organ mender and fixer of instruments, fine and not so fine. He made a decent living while sending a portion to loved ones back home.

To many homeowners, Cantwell was nothing short of a wizard with his Sears and Roebuck manual of organ repair and a magical trunk of tools: miniature drawers with delicate latches, boxes and envelopes holding various reeds, and bundles of soft felt. His clients received double their money; for the man entertained as he worked, bringing news of his and Bruce's latest travels, reciting tongue-twisting limericks and animated stories, singing or quoting scripture from memory. He had long ago answered the bidding of the Holy Spirit and to a large degree pictured himself an opportunistic evangelist. His head never hit the pillow, nor a meal cross his lips, without returning gratitude.

Then there were communities and homeowners who were wary of any nomadic workers, viewing them as tramps, wanting them to hurry along. But these were few and far between, for Cantwell's good reputation preceded him from church to church and house to house.

The Lumpkin household included several children who inched ever closer to Bruce. Once they passed a smile between them and Bruce reached out and touched a fat little child's belly, the giggling children became instant friends.

Cantwell focused on his tedious and delicate work, at times sitting on the dusty floor, kneeling awkwardly on only one knee, or lying on his back. Occasionally he stopped, standing with some difficulty, and attempted to return the circulation to his damaged limb. The leg was as stiff as a post; the knee joint rigidly encased in scar tissue. He had recently had a length of silver wire removed from his once shattered kneecap. The foreign object, with its rough ends, had kept the area inflamed and painful, causing arthritis to set in, and several times a year he sought out a doctor to draw excess fluid from the joint.

Cantwell had begun his life in 1862 in the early stages of the Civil War. He was born in Barnesville, Robeson County, North Carolina, on a broad swatch of fertile lowland thirteen miles below Lumberton, along the Lumber River, for which the town is named. Nine miles further downriver was the border of South Carolina. Cape Fear and the port city of Wilmington lay seventy miles to the east.

His family owned a sizable chunk of farmland which they kept planted in cotton and tobacco, but the war brought production and distribution to a halt, crippling the area. Cantwell and his brothers and brothers-in-law and nephews struggled to get the farm producing again in the years following the war, but Reconstruction brought much higher property taxes, so they divvied up the land and opened some of it up for sharecropping. Their livelihood was devastated yet again in the Panic of 1873 when cotton prices fell by half, sparking a major depression.

Cantwell left the farm and went to work in the nearby lumber camps along the river and became known for his ability to coax music out of almost any instrument. His evening repertoire was varied and extensive, but he had a penchant for Baptist hymns. He married and fathered four children, but financial trouble rocked his marriage. His wife claimed he drank, was violent, and used profanity; all habits he abhorred, but the charge succeeded in getting her the divorce. The two had argued over custody of the children, but all four had stayed with their mother and returned to her family in Georgia. They remained distant.

Years later, while helping to build a blacksmith's shop in Louisiana, a heavy piece of steel fell on his leg, fracturing the kneecap. Surgeries and infections followed, and the leg never healed correctly, remaining frozen at an awkward angle.

Cantwell spent his lengthy recovery in Mississippi constructing a "thousand-stringed" musical instrument: a complex, box-like, tabletop harp that he dreamed of patenting and selling. The patent never materialized since very few individuals would devote the hours of time needed to master the instrument. A short time later, upon the suggestion of his childhood friend David Bledsoe, he enrolled in a trade-school course on organ repair and began to earn a modest but reliable living traveling a circuit of southern states from North Carolina to Mississippi. He also worked on pianos, violins, clocks, and other small machinery, ordering replacement parts by mail. Cantwell lodged with relatives and friends or in local boarding houses until his work in a community ran out and he moved on.

For five days and nights, Cantwell and Bruce bunked with the Lumpkin family while Cantwell worked on their organ and other minor items. The small home echoed with "Silent Night, Holy Night," along with Bruce's everyday favorites, "Take Me Out to the Ball Game," and "Oh! Susanna." On December 24, Cantwell finished the repairs and received five dollars for his work. He and Bruce went directly to a nearby store in McNeill to trade out their order, and Cantwell secretly purchased one of the child's Christmas presents, a small red umbrella that Bruce had fixated on.

The pair headed north, bound for Bilbo's Post Office, a rambling two-story boarding house at the well-traveled intersection of Ford's Creek Road and River Road. Jeptha and Matilda Bilbo, the elderly proprietors, also ran the area's post office from its interior. The couple was well respected in their community and church, and was known throughout several counties for their integrity. Cantwell and Bruce had stayed at the house several times since July 19, using it as their home-base while working in the surrounding communities. Mrs. Bilbo, a no-nonsense, banty-rooster-like little woman had instantly taken a liking to the affectionate little boy, once keeping him for an entire month while Cantwell recuperated in a New Orleans hospital after the surgery on his leg. She topped the list of Bruce's favorite *grandmas* he'd laid claim to between the Carolinas and Mississippi.

On their way, they passed through the town of Poplarville, thirteen miles north of McNeill. They stopped by the post office where they ran into the local sheriff, J. A. Moody. Moody questioned Cantwell thoroughly concerning Bruce's parentage.

"I'm the only Papa he's got," Cantwell assured the sheriff and turned towards the door. Assuming the role of Bruce's foster father at fifty years of age, and with a bum leg, was quite an undertaking, but he saw their paths as destined to cross. He'd been given a second chance at parenting, and as such, instantly began tutoring Bruce. The pair headed west for the thirteen-mile ride to the Bilbos' home, arriving just after dark on Christmas Eve. Homer, the Bilbos' young grandson, and Rambler, the resident dog, were anxiously waiting for their friend.

Bruce and Cantwell remained with the Bilbos, partaking in the Christmas celebrations. Mrs. Bilbo clucked over Bruce; herding him into her own flock, sewing for him, bathing him, and letting him help in the kitchen. Bruce loved lying sandwiched between Cantwell, with his hot water bottle on his aching knee, and Homer's small wiggling form, all pressed down by the heavy quilts covering them.

"God bleth Mama, Bernice, Grandma, Homer, me, Ugly Papa (his pet name for Cantwell), an everybody elth."

During the visit, Cantwell regaled the Bilbos and their boarders with his dramatic low-country-meets-Shakespearean storytelling and his music. He was their embodiment of "Roderick Darrel", from *Darrel of the Blessed Isles,* and the children were drawn to him; but despite the seasonal gaiety, the man seemed slightly distracted and kept a closer rein on the child.

The day after Christmas, Archie Dunbar showed up in Pearl River County, Mississippi, and located Sheriff Moody. He demanded to see the child traveling with W. C. Walters, so Moody sent Deputy Boyd and Archie to the Bilbos' home to examine Bruce and question Cantwell. Archie and the deputy reported back that the child was not Bobby Dunbar.

On December 30, D. F. Smith, postmaster at Carriere, a town three miles below McNeill, entered the Western Union Telegraph office and hurriedly scribbled out a message to be wired to the mayor of Opelousas.

Suspicious man here named Walters—cripple—has little boy four or five years old—Long light hair and blue eyed—might be Dunbar child—Wire me full description of child—answer quick

Signed D F Smith
William Cantwell Walters' Defense File© #310

The man paced the floor, waiting anxiously for the reply which followed shortly.

Dunbar child four years eight months—large round blue eyes—light hair—complexion fair—Rosy cheeks—short thick neck—big toe on left foot badly scarred from burn—if arrest is made advise at once

Signed T L Loeb. Mayor
William Cantwell Walters' Defense File© #311

Smith, his heart racing with thoughts of the well-publicized $6,000 reward, stuffed the message into his coat pocket and left in search of the area's sheriff, F. E. Brooks. The two men picked up local doctor H. G. Anderson to accompany them to the Bilbos.

Upon their arrival, Cantwell was questioned again about Bruce's identity. He stated that the boy, Charlie Bruce Anderson, was given to him in North Carolina by the boy's own mother ten months earlier.

"We have been in Pearl River County since mid-July," Cantwell answered, incensed by their accusations. "How could this boy possibly be the one you're looking for?"

"They *were* here in July," Mrs. Bilbo insisted. "I remember it well."

"Well, I have a job to do," stated the sheriff, "so…we can't leave until we talk to the child and examine him."

Bruce ducked behind Mrs. Bilbo.

"Is your name Bobby? Bobby Dunbar?" the men plied.

"Bruce, Grandma wants you to answer these men and just tell them the truth. That's all," Mrs. Bilbo urged.

"Are you Bobby Dunbar?" the men continued.

Bruce emphatically shook his head no.

"Where is your Papa, son? Is your Papa Percy Dunbar?"

"There'th my Papa," he announced, pointing to Cantwell.

The men thoroughly studied the child's face and feet, pointing out a small red area on top of his left foot.

"That's the smallpox," Mrs. Bilbo pointed out, pulling off his shirt and showing them another mark near the back of his neck. "He had a case in July when he first got here."

The disappointed trio departed.

Chapter Three
Ladies of Hub

The telegram addressed to C. P. Dunbar arrived at the house on Sunday morning, April 20, 1913. It was the second message Percy had received from Hub, Mississippi, a tiny community twenty miles north of Jeptha Bilbo's place and eight miles below Columbia. It was almost identical to the first message. The "Ladies of Hub" claimed to have found his missing child. Percy sighed and shook his head in disbelief.

Last fall the same group had wired him claiming they had seen a child who matched Bobby's newspaper photograph traveling with a suspicious tinker named Walters. Percy's twenty-five-year-old brother, Archie, had been sent to find W. C. Walters and the child; when he located them at the Bilbos, he took one look at the boy and declared that it was not his nephew.

Both telegrams said the man seemed evasive when they questioned him about the boy and would try to shield him from sight. Strangely, though, he seemed to have a real affection for the boy, and the boy returned it wholeheartedly. The chinwags were still convinced he was up to no good and managed to finagle Bruce away from Cantwell for a photograph. When the panicked Cantwell finally found the errant child, he deftly swatted the boy's backside for wandering off. The ladies noted to Percy that the child was whipped for almost revealing his true name, Bobby. Dr. Anderson was called upon again to examine Bruce but found no marks of abuse. No scar. The reason, they claimed; the boy's feet were so dirty that a major deformity could go unseen. They mailed the photo from Hub to Percy, but his brother, Archie, recognized it as the same child he saw at the Bilbo's, and it ended up in a bureau drawer with other photos of unrecognized little boys.

In today's telegram, the ladies were adamant that Percy find Walters and view the boy himself. They had done some investigating with the help of a man in their community, M. A. Cowart, who had recently hired the restorer to mend his organ. While Cantwell was conveniently occupied with a tedious repair, Cowart took the boy outside to view the cows. Cowart claimed that the child, on his own accord and without prompting, whispered a tearful message to him. "Bruce is my new name, but I've got an old name...it is Bobby. And I've got another papa who is a good papa and a good mama who is away off."

Cowart returned to the house holding Bruce and confronted Cantwell.

"Dat mean man," blubbered Bruce, reaching both hands toward Cantwell. "I din say it Papa." It was the first time the little boy had crumpled under a stranger's questioning.

The sobbing child leapt toward Cantwell, locking his arms and legs around him. Cowart, an officious resident of the area, failed to intimidate the man; so the duo packed up and left, heading toward Columbia.

Percy had received another photograph of that same child from Charlie Day, Marion County, Mississippi's sheriff, almost two weeks prior, but although he looked similar to his missing son, neither he nor Lessie recognized the boy. The eyes were not Bobby's. Percy walked over to the bureau drawer and retrieved the picture and read again about the beggar/tramp and the boy. He envisioned Lessie in the front porch swing with a giggling boy on either side of her, Lessie pinning two Christmas stockings to the mantle. If only Bobby would come home, Lessie could heal, returning the mother Alonzo grieved for. But more importantly, his wife might forgive him. Lessie had heard that he was unfaithful and his scarlet letter was draining.

Percy's cousin, Ola Dunbar Fox, and her husband, Harold Fox, had come up from New Orleans for the weekend to sit with Alonzo and the gaunt and unresponsive Lessie, giving Percy some relief. He showed Ola the latest letter and photograph and asked the visitors to stick around for a few more days.

For the second year in a row, the Mississippi River had left its banks and was once again devastating the region. Unable to cross the Atchafalaya delta, Percy had to take the train south to New Orleans first, and then head up into Mississippi. He arrived at Hub around midnight, exhausted from the long, circuitous journey. Dr. Anderson, John Fortenberry, the Marion County Deputy Sheriff, and Constable Walter Lott, along with various "Ladies of Hub" were waiting for him. Anderson, Lott, and Dunbar headed up to Columbia while Sheriff Day, Ott Pool, and Deputy Jeff Wallace were searching for Cantwell and Bruce north of town in a settlement called Newsom.

Percy waited in an all-night diner in Columbia where he described his desperate mission. When the other patrons learned that they could possibly be witnessing the resolution of the famous Dunbar kidnapping, their conversations ceased, meals were abandoned, chairs drawn closer, and plans forgotten.

If I do not find that child I do not know what will become of my wife. She has been as one demented for the last eight months and seems to grow worse all the while; she can not eat nor sleep and it is impossible for me to stay at home with her in this condition. I have become reconciled to the loss of the child, but I don't believe my wife ever will, and I do not know what I will do if I do not find that child.
William Cantwell Walters' Defense File© #153

Percy did not divulge to the group that Lessie blamed him for the whole incident. There would be no peace until he could return Bobby. He left to find a bed for the remainder of the night.

Day, Pool, and Wallace tracked Cantwell to a residence several miles northwest of town where Cantwell was working. They recognized his buggy outside. Waking the household around 5 a.m., Day ordered the startled gentleman to get dressed, telling him he had a visitor in town, Percy Dunbar. Day picked Bruce up, saying he needed a partner for the day, and pinned his badge on the boy's nightshirt.

"We will wait in the car."

Cantwell dressed hurriedly, assured that he was looking toward the end of their harassment.

On the way into town, Day made an unexpected detour, stopping by Deputy Wallace's home in nearby Foxworth. He announced that the child would remain there, telling the deputy not to let the child out of his sight.

"Don't worry," Cantwell whispered to Bruce, hugging him into his chest. "Eat yourself some breakfast and I'll be back to pick you up before you know it. I promise." He turned toward Day, "Afterward, I want a judge to make out some papers stating once and for all that this isn't the Dunbar boy!"

Although it was early, and Bruce had not yet collected his portion of the day's dirt, Mrs. Wallace set out a pan of soapy water for Bruce's bath. The four year-old splashed and she scrubbed. The couple picked up a foot and wiped it dry, then caught each other's gaze, Mrs. Wallace hiding a gasp with the back of her hand, and the deputy massaging his forehead with both hands. There was nothing there. No scar. A small fortune had slipped between their fingers along with the sudsy bathwater.

"Just get him dressed," Mrs. Wallace whispered.

Percy was furious when Day and Pool arrived in town with only Cantwell. The older man tried to direct the face-off, not unlike an evangelist leading a Baptist tent revival.

"Is this some kind of trick?" Percy demanded of the lawman. "I've come here to see a child, not some vagrant you managed to round up."

"Vagrant!" Cantwell hissed. "I have never in my life been…" but he was interrupted.

Percy's demeanor was belligerent and surly; he was used to calling the shots and played his part well. "Did you have my son, old man? God help you if you did! And if you have hurt him in any way…"

The meeting quickly digressed into a shouting match with Percy having to be physically restrained when Cantwell would admit no wrongdoing. It was decided that Cantwell would wait at the jail with Lott while Percy, Day, and Marion County Sheriff Stanley Hathorn headed to Foxworth.

In the meantime, word leaked out that Bobby Dunbar might be at the Wallaces' home, and a small crowd gathered to view the child being paraded about the yard. Bruce answered their initial questions with his name, his mama's name, and his sister's name, nodding or shaking his head in response. The barrage intensified as they probed to see if he had been brainwashed or threatened. The four year-old, barefooted and in his night dress, quickly tired of the inquiry and cried or pouted until he could be distracted.

Percy arrived and was finally shown the petulant little boy. "Bobby?" he asked. But when the child looked up there was no reaction. No spark of recognition. No embrace. Nothing. His determined expression looked similar to Bobby's; but the eyes were different, more pinched and puffy, and the lips were thinner. The nose wasn't right either; it was broader than Bobby's and his hair was lighter. Bruce returned to his activity with no emotion.

The consensus between Percy and Day was that Cantwell had bleached the boy's hair and that the eyes had changed shape, having acquired a squint due to constant exposure to the elements while living in a tented wagon and moving about to avoid detection. A tramp wouldn't have provided him a hat for protection. They decided he had stolen the boy to beg and that his wariness came from threats and abuse.

A bystander spoke up, "Wait just a minute. I know Cantwell and he is *not* the man you are portraying. Bruce is well-behaved and happy; Cantwell is gracious and well-spoken, although he talks too much. His work is dependable, and a he's a devout Christian."

"They're traveling in a one-horse buggy, not a tented wagon," said another.

"This is absolutely ridiculous," blurted an overall-clad farmer stepping to the forefront. "Mr. Walters had this child at my place twice this year, once in February and again in March, and I never had a moment's trouble with him. Bruce was happy as a lark. My children would have followed that man all over creation, with his endless whistling and storytelling. He never tried to lure any of *them* away, unless you count hauling the lot of them to church in his buggy."

Percy, along with Dr. Anderson, examined Bruce's feet. Both feet were dirty from walking around barefoot all day, but there was only smooth skin on the left toe where Bobby's thick scar should be. "I think I feel the remains of the scar," Percy proclaimed. Dr. Anderson's expression showed that he was puzzled. Percy, still holding Bruce's left foot, noticed a minor deformity of his two smallest toes; the first phalanx of each toe turned slightly inward, pulled tight by the unusual webbing between them. "Those toes are exactly like Bobby's!" Percy reached out to pick up Bruce, but the child kicked and screamed. He waited until the boy was pacified and called out Bobby's nickname, "Booboo," the nickname Cantwell also used for Bruce, and the child noticeably recognized the name.

Percy immediately demanded that Cantwell be arrested for the kidnapping of his son. Bruce renewed his frantic, high-pitched wailing. Part of the assembly cheered while others murmured among themselves and demanded more proof. Percy moved to leave immediately with Bobby, but half of the crowd rejected the idea and moved to block their exit.

Percy pulled several bills from his wallet and stuffed them into Wallace's hand. "I want you to take good care of him until I get back. Get him some decent clothes. Understand? And lock Walters up." He sent a telegram to Harold and Ola telling them he had found Bobby but needed Lessie to verify his identity. They were to bring her to New Orleans right away where he would meet them at the train station and then head back to Columbia. She would require sedation to make the journey. John Fortenberry of Hub would accompany Percy.

The *New Orleans Item* newspaper got wind of the discovery and sent one of their representatives, George Benz, to the station to meet the group.

"My God! Where is he, Percy?" choked Lessie. "Is he alright? Why did you leave him?"

Benz listened as Percy prepared his wife for what she could expect. "He is fine other than being scared to death and confused. Some tramp, a possible member of a kidnapping gang, had him living out of a wagon begging for food and we could never catch up to them because they stayed on the move, but we've got him now. The poor little fellow is convinced the old man is coming back to get him, but Walters will likely be hanging by a rope soon."

"It's him, Less! He's afraid to admit it, but I know it's him."

Percy's expression hardened. "He told the sheriff he'd get a whipping if he called himself Bobby, and… I couldn't bring him with me because they won't let him go just yet. They're holding out for the reward money. Actually they're squabbling over it, who found him first, and where."

"You know there is no reward money!" Harold whispered to Percy. "The reward expired in February."

"Exactly, and they're not too happy about it," Percy added. "That's why Lessie is coming. They won't dare try to stop her from taking Bobby home. There would be a riot!"

Percy explained the changes in their son's appearance—the different shape of the eyes, nose, and lips, the hair color, and the shrinking of the scar.

"Walters tried to make Bobby blend in, but he stood out like a sore thumb," Percy sighed, grinning. "You can't make a sow's ear out of a silk purse."

Percy, Lessie, Harold, Ola, Fortenberry, and Benz reached Columbia late during the night and were immediately driven to the Wallace's home, now swarming with curious onlookers. The well-respected Sheriff Stanley Hathorn was in attendance, as was Dr. Anderson. Bruce was asleep in bed.

By the dim light of a lantern, Lessie was escorted into a small bedroom where she stumbled toward the bed, sobbing, gathering the warm, sleeping child into her arms. Startled from his sleep, the boy began fighting and crying.

"Bobby? Bobby, it's Mama!" she choked. "Wake up."

Bruce's eyes flitted open and he struggled to free himself from the strange woman, whimpering as he turned away, returning to sleep. Lessie ran her hands over the small, tousled head. Her fingers rapidly traced the contours of his nose, eyes, and lips as she nuzzled in toward his face. She stiffened abruptly and sat back.

Slipping his feet from under the covers, she ran her fingers over his left foot, inspecting the toes. A keening shriek rose from her throat and she fell backward wild-eyed, leaping from the bed. Ola grabbed her by the shoulders. "You didn't get a good look at him, Lessie. Wait until he wakes up…" Lessie jerked free and pushed Ola out of her way, running past the gaping onlookers. Percy hustled his wife to the privacy of the automobile that had brought them.

"Bobby!" she screamed. "Bobby?! Where are you?! Mama's here." Lessie clawed at Percy's arms as he stuffed her into the car. She lunged across the seat, grappling for the opposite door handle.

Percy landed a hard slap across her cheek. "By God, woman!" he hissed, "Don't you know your own boy? It is him I tell you! He's right inside that house waiting for you." Lessie sat in stunned silence as Percy explained that the scar was there; it had just shrunk.

"It's too dark in there for you to get a good look," he insisted. "I saw him in broad daylight."

"Please…don't…lynch…Walters," she sobbed.

No one could convince the hysterical woman to go back into the house, so Percy announced via Hathorn that they would not make a statement that night "to prevent the kidnapper from being lynched." They would return in the morning. William Lampton, the son of a wealthy businessman in Columbia, offered to put them up for the night.

Those huddled at the jail were a bit more practical. When Hathorn returned to the jail, he told the loquacious Cantwell that he had no charges against him since Lessie had not claimed the boy. "If that kid is Bobby Dunbar, the open road is before you and you should take advantage of it." Cantwell held forth, comfortably perched in his seat of righteousness until nearly dawn when he would return to his ongoing repair.

After breakfast on Tuesday morning, the little boy was escorted outside into the Wallace's yard. He played with Sheriff Day in view of the large assembly that had remained overnight. The car carrying the Dunbars drove up.

From inside the automobile, Lessie cried out in broken tones, "Bobby, Bobby? Are you my little boy? Don't you remember your mother?"

At the sound of the name, the little fellow raised his head, and a puzzled expression came into his eyes, but the look quickly passed.

Percy got out of the car and offered the child an orange, while Lessie remained seated inside the auto. After thirty minutes of watching the boy from a distance, she was finally persuaded to get out. She examined the child's body again, looking him directly in the eyes, but after two examinations still was not sure.

Percy and the Fox's insisted on examining Bruce in private. The Lampton home would be ideal, but before that could happen, Sheriff Day insisted on getting a receipt for Bobby.

April 22nd, 1913

Columbia, Miss.

Received from C. A. Day, J. D. Wallace, and Ott Pool, the body of Robt. C. Dunbar, my long lost child and he is well and healthy as far as I can see. He was stolen from me at Swazye Lake near Opelousas, La. on Aug. 25th, 1912.

Signed C. P. Dunbar
Witness L. C. Wellborne Clerk Chancery Court
Courtesy of the Marion County Historical Society
and Jarvis Lowe

In Opelousas, former mayor Henry Estorage received word from his friend and business partner, Percy Dunbar, that Bobby had been found. As Deputy Clerk of the District Court and Clerk of the Police Jury, Estorage appeared before the town's city judge, calling for W. C. Walters' arrest. The judge sent a warrant for the man's arrest to St. Landry Parish Sheriff, Marion Swords, who immediately applied to Louisiana's governor, Luther Hall, for requisition of the fugitive. Swords asked that Estorage be appointed to collect him in Mississippi.

Percy and Lessie began to plead with the child to go with them to the Lamptons', but he vehemently refused. The promise of a fast ride in the car and a chance to blow the horn finally persuaded him.

As word of the Dunbar's discovery spread throughout Columbia, businesses closed and school was dismissed early. A crowd numbering in the hundreds gathered on the high green lawn surrounding the Lampton home where the little boy could be seen circling the estate's side yard in a pony cart. Toys lay scattered about the grass and a nearby table held a pitcher of cold lemonade and sandwiches.

Eventually the family worked its way towards the house, where an array of new clothing had been laid out in one of the upstairs bedrooms. Despite fierce protests heard throughout the house and yard, the women inside bathed the child and examined him further.

Chapter Four
April 22, 1913

Cantwell sat among the assortment of disemboweled organ parts that covered the church floor. The canvas patch on the bellows had cooled at last and it appeared to be holding. "Good thing," he thought, for the humidity was rising and he wanted to close up the instrument as soon as possible. When he finished, he would collect Bruce from the sheriff and they would be on their way, this time possessing an affidavit from Percy Dunbar himself.

He struggled to stand, and then hobbled to the door for a break, flexing his reluctant leg. His entire body hurt after a short two hours of tossing and turning as he replayed yesterday's disturbing events. First, the confrontation with Day and Percy, and then being detained for hours at the jail. He had heard the rumor that Percy thought Bruce could be his son, but he had also heard that Mrs. Dunbar had arrived during the night and was distraught when she discovered Bruce there instead of Bobby.

Just then Sheriff Day, along with a volatile Percy, arrived. In one motion Percy leapt out of the car and vaulted onto the porch, knocking Cantwell backwards into the wall.

"You lying son-of-a-bitch!" the man seethed, landing a punch on the older man's nose.

Cantwell slid to the floor. "You've lost your mind!" he stammered, trying to catch his breath. Blood poured from his nose.

"We have four members of the family saying it is Bobby," Day told him. "So you'd better start praying while you're down on your knees." He informed Cantwell that he was being officially charged with the kidnapping of Bobby Dunbar. The dusty, half-crippled gentleman, shaking his head as if to wake from an unpleasant dream, was placed in his own buggy and driven to the jail in Columbia.

* * *

Attorneys Tom Dale and his young partner, Hollis Rawls, the former mayor of Columbia, crossed Main Street heading for the busy courthouse square. The town was conveniently situated at the halfway point along the Pearl River between the state capitol of Jackson to the north and Pearlington to the south, where the river flowed into the Gulf of Mexico just above New Orleans. Its hotels, restaurants, and businesses were clustered near the steep, crowded, and somewhat seedy bluff along the east side of the heavily traveled waterway.

Hollis had spent much of his childhood in a boarding house along that bluff after the death of his mother, Sophie, when he was four years old. At the time his father, James, a rough-cut woodsman/river-man with an imperfect pedigree, owned a warehouse and pier at the water's edge. Sophie had been raised a short distance, but a world away, from James' domain. She was last in a long line of children born to her mother, Ruhama Atkinson Webb, the wealthy widow of the town's illustrious Atkinson founder. Sophie was not an Atkinson though. She was the overprotected only child of her father, Walter Webb, a much younger merchant the widow had married who was in business with her oldest son.

Walter was more than displeased when his daughter fell in love with the rowdy buccaneer James Rawls; and before he would agree to the marriage, he had insisted that James build Sophie a proper house in a proper neighborhood and allow Walter to furnish it in a proper manner. A humbled James reluctantly agreed.

The animosity between father and son-in-law waned with the birth of the couple's son, James Howard, but returned in force eight months later when the baby died after he was accidentally dropped by a roughhousing young cousin. Sophie was devastated, for she had been told by her doctor that James Howard would be her only child. When her crippling depression lifted, she searched for a way to fill her empty days and found it apprenticing at a millinery shop in New Orleans. Sophie then opened her own exclusive shop in Columbia.

Six and a half years later, the young woman awoke with a bout of morning sickness. Hollis' astonishing arrival rekindled a tenuous truce between his father and grandfather, but their relationship declined when his grandmother, Ruhama, died just one year later. Catastrophe struck the young family again just two years later when Sophie became ill. She died after a year-long illness.

Walter immediately petitioned for custody of his grandson, defining his worthiness with wealth and prestige. When James refused to give up his son, Walter attempted to force the man's hand. In the ensuing skirmish, Walter took back all of the elaborate furnishings he had provided for James' home; James countered by taking Hollis and returning to the boarding house where he had lived before his marriage.

The little boy quickly earned the nickname "Swamp Fox," for he spent the majority of his time in the waterways and backwoods along the river. He surveyed his kingdom from a fort perched high atop the bank near his father's pier, hailing the river traffic that passed by and mingling with the boisterous, sometimes unsavory, groups of men that traveled thereon. It wasn't unusual to see him swimming out to meet an approaching barge or paddling between the river's banks if the ferry was running too slowly. When he got back on dry ground, he hung his wet clothes next to his ever-present campfire to dry, a practice that rendered him somewhat sooty and rumpled.

His grandfather's store and the nearby courthouse and jail were also Hollis' home-away-from-home, keeping him up-to-date (although not always age-appropriately) on the activities of the populace. He often occupied a seat in the back of the courtroom with his nose pressed in a book, as the just and the unjust were expertly sorted and adjudicated. He relished the orderliness and decorum of the system.

When Hollis was thirteen years old, his father, James, married a local widow who had bought the millinery after Sophie's death. She had befriended the boy years earlier and, after the marriage, she "took Hollis in hand," smoothing out his rough edges and seeing to his formal schooling. He enrolled in Jefferson Military Academy, a college preparatory boarding school near Natchez, Mississippi, where he maintained the school's highest grades on record. Hollis went on to the University of Mississippi and dove headfirst into law school. He returned to his beloved hometown to practice his craft.

As the two lawyers neared the jail, Hollis thought of his own defining fourth year of life, when his mother died, and his thoughts turned towards the boy at the center of this tug-of-war.

The city's residents had emptied into the streets as news of the Dunbar's identification spread. A massive crowd had gathered a mile-and-a-half east of the jail at the Lampton's home, where Percy announced, "My wife and I found whip marks on Bobby's back." The effect was similar to dumping water onto a grease fire, and a surly band of men shuffled menacingly around the jail entrance. Percy came close to relieving himself of the stubborn old man right then as the group talked of lynching. The lawmen and officials inside the jail included Sheriff Hathorn and Columbia's Marshall Tom Ford, both friends of the lawyers who had contacted them on behalf of their prisoner. A ring of armed deputies circled the jail's entrance and windows.

When the lawyers entered, Cantwell rose from his chair with some difficulty, pulled himself upright, and with an air of distinction, bent at the waist, offering them a small bow. Extending his hand to each of the men, he thanked them for coming to his aid and apologized for his shabby appearance, explaining that he had been rudely accosted. A dried blood stain down the front of his shirt bore witness to the surprise attack.

Before the men had seated themselves, Cantwell looked directly at each of the lawyers. "Between you and me and God, I did not kidnap Robert Dunbar."

He quickly but politely got down to business, giving a brief synopsis of his troubles. Cantwell's workaday exterior, simple clothes that spent most of their time on a dusty floor, belied the articulate, self-possessed man sitting before them. He chatted openly, professing to be of the Baptist faith and asked them to contact a pastor.

"The child is Charlie Bruce Anderson from Barnesville, North Carolina; and his mother, Julia, who worked in my parents' home there, allowed me to bring him on my travels," he explained. "We have been together for over a year and never experienced any trouble until a few months ago. And no matter *what* the Dunbar's say, I *never* put welts on Bruce… though I did spank him occasionally when he was bad. I was strict *because* I liked him." He jerked himself back to the task at hand and began reciting last August's itinerary in detail, supplying names and dates to corroborate his story.

"Just ask him his name," stated Cantwell. "He'll tell you who he is. Percy Dunbar is who you should be arresting!"

"Mr. Walters," Hollis interrupted, "do you have any idea what would motivate the Dunbars to claim a random child as their own?"

"Well, I've heard several stories over the last few months…about Mrs. Dunbar's fragile condition. How she can't recover from the loss of her son and how Mr. Dunbar is desperate to find him." He paused.

"Go on, Mr. Walters," Hollis encouraged.

"Gentlemen, I am not one to judge any man for his actions, but I have also heard rumors that Mr. Dunbar was off visiting a lady friend when the boy vanished and that Mrs. Dunbar holds him responsible."

He continued, "Bruce does favor the Dunbar child, and he is sharp as a tack and friendly, too. Who wouldn't want Bruce as their son? My own sister asked me to leave him with her, said she would love to adopt him." Cantwell looked across the table to the men and then lowered his eyes.

"Mr. Dunbar is a powerful man in Louisiana, and I suppose I don't appear able to offer much resistance," he choked.

The lawyers assured him that if a crime had been committed against him, they would make every effort to see that it was rectified.

Not only was Cantwell anticipating complete exoneration, he expected Percy's forthcoming and well-earned apology as well as recompense for the expected attorneys' fees.

Sheriff Hathorn, who had been at the Wallace's home during Percy's examination the previous day, pulled Tom and Hollis aside and stated that he had not been convinced the man had found his son. He saw no emotional connection between them—no paternal feelings or actions from Percy.

"And why would Walters stick around if that child *was* Bobby Dunbar?" he questioned. Hathorn described Lessie's violent reaction last night when she saw the boy; and he voiced what many were thinking—that Cantwell was not physically able to navigate the desolate swamp in question, much less smuggle a child out of it.

Outside, the lawyers were approached by several people who said they knew the organ mender and his little boy. They vouched for his story.

Jeptha and Matilda Bilbo were two of the witnesses Cantwell had listed. The lawyers knew the couple and immediately placed a call to their residence, explaining the man's desperate situation.

They confirmed that the pair had come to stay with them last July and had returned several times since. "Cantwell is as honest and hardworking as they come, and a God-fearing man, otherwise I wouldn't have them staying in my home. He loves Bruce like a son, and Bruce loves him."

Mrs. Bilbo took the phone. "Bruce was actually sitting in my lap when we first read of the missing Dunbar child in the paper. I specifically told him that was what happened to naughty little boys who wander away."

Throughout the afternoon, the two lawyers traveled between their office, the Lampton home, and the jail, gathering information along the way. Dr. Anderson located the lawyers and recounted his two examinations of the child, declaring that, "there was no scar on his foot *or* whip marks on his back."

Local resident Jobie Sweeney voiced his doubts, maintaining that every time he asked the boy if his name was Robert or Bobby, his answer would be, "No, my name is Bruce." When asked if he had a little brother named Alonzo, he would shake his head in the negative and say, "No, got a little sister named Bernice."

William Cantwell Walters' Defense File© #151

At the Lampton home, Lessie and Ola tried repeatedly to comfort the agitated boy, but he grew more panicky as the afternoon wore on. Lessie collapsed, weeping with an intensity that matched the four-year-old's.

Approximately thirty-four hours after Bruce was taken from Cantwell, Percy hustled the boy into a bathroom and slammed the door.

When they returned twenty minutes later, the dazed, red-eyed child hesitantly placed his arms around Lessie's neck and whispered, "You are… mama."

Lessie fainted as the frightened lad, much to his displeasure, was taken out onto the second floor balcony and presented to the cheering crowd. The skirmish began to gather steam as the Dunbars scored their first shadowy victory.

Hollis sat down with Percy to discuss the conflicting facts, but the man was condescending and defensive. Percy dismissed the twenty-eight-year-old upstart lawyer and rose to leave. "He's my son and I am taking him home!"

Hollis explained that they had sent two cars to Pearl River County to pick up several witnesses who knew Mr. Walters and the child. Two of those witnesses were Jeptha and Matilda Bilbo, the esteemed uncle and aunt of Mississippi's fiery Lieutenant Governor. They would not arrive until morning and he, along with Sheriff Hathorn and a few other vociferous nonbelievers, insisted the Dunbars remain in town until then.

Percy answered, teeth clenched. "I'll wait for your so-called witnesses, but I'm warning you not to push me. You have no idea who you're dealing with." He emphasized his words by jabbing the young attorney's chest with his index finger. When Hollis didn't return the challenge, the deflated Percy turned on his heel and stormed out of the room.

The lawyer's everyday sang-froid remained unshakable, but his composure masked a near-constant churning in his gut. A ruptured appendix during his eleventh-grade year had doggedly tried to kill him for almost one year and had left him with chronic digestive trouble. Stress aggravated the condition. His partner, Dale, on the other hand, seemed to thrive on pressure and never shied away from a good fight. Hollis took a deep breath and went to find his bicarbonate of sodium.

Outside the Lampton home, cheers rose from the crowd each time they caught sight of the boy. With *Item* reporter Benz sequestered with the family and sending all their statements directly to the newspaper office in New Orleans, the daily newspaper laid an early claim to the sensational story.

The Hippodrome Theater in New Orleans, a theater that booked vaudeville acts, was right on the paper's tail, immediately wiring a proposition to the Dunbars for the rights to exhibit the child. Percy called the manager and made an appointment for 11 a.m. the following day.

Percy verified that he and Lessie had identified every scar and birthmark on their son's body. He took a position on the small upstairs balcony and proclaimed that Bobby had been brutally whipped into submission. As the one supposedly holding the purse strings on an exorbitant reward, Percy found many eager cohorts willing to say they had seen the whip marks and the scarred toe. He stated that Bobby was *forced* to call himself Bruce at the direction of the heartless old man. The reporters and townspeople hung breathlessly onto every word.

"Little Robert is afraid to speak of his past life, having been threatened into silence."

"A child garners sympathy for tramps, increasing their odds of finding food and shelter."

"The child was too refined and well-mannered to have belonged to a tinker."

The rumors gathered force and motion, twisting and overlapping until the unsuspecting little town was embroiled in a bitter dispute.

After the report that Bobby had recognized his mother, the citizens of Columbia were ecstatic. Mr. Lampton loaded the family into his automobile and, with an impromptu following of thirty other cars, paraded through the town. Dignitaries offered speeches of congratulations to the Dunbars while calling for restraint among the local vigilantes. Benz wrote:

> Harry Mounger, a prominent attorney of the county, stated that he would be ashamed of any man "that would profit financially through a mother's tears." This had the effect of stopping much talk concerning rewards for the finding of the boy. Jeff Wallace, who insisted that Mr. Dunbar give him a "receipt for the baby," had stated previously that he would not hand over the boy unless his portion of the reward was forthcoming. Most of those who declared Monday that they thought they should share in it have not said a word since.
>
> Other points brought out by Attorney Monger touched upon the necessity of deliberation in the case of Walters. He said he hoped nothing would occur to shame the county and the town, and declared Columbia could give him as fair a trial as anyone, and still inflict a heavy penalty if he were found guilty.
>
> The Item-April 23, 1913

As the sky darkened that evening, so did the crowd's disposition. Extra guards were posted at the jail's entrance.

During the night, Tom and Hollis were covertly informed that the Dunbars were preparing to leave town with the boy. The two lawyers drove to the depot at 4 a.m. and waited. Moments before the southbound train to New Orleans was scheduled to depart at 4:30, the Lamptons' automobile drove up with the Dunbars.

Bruce, having been awakened and dressed by strangers in the middle of the night, fretted and cried until placed in Sheriff Day's arms. Once he drifted back to sleep, he was placed in Lessie's lap for the ride to the station. It was there, with the sleeping child in her arms, where Tom and Hollis attempted to intervene, reminding Percy of his promise not to move the boy.

"To hell with that," Percy answered, "It's my boy and I'll ride a rotten rail to hell before I give him up!"

With no time to get a writ to stop them, the Dunbars, along with Benz, Lampton, Day, and Chancery Court Clerk Wellborne, boarded the train and left. Twenty miles south of the depot, the train carrying the Dunbar party left the state of Mississippi and crossed into Louisiana.

Benz wrote:

With a "baby jackknife" in his hand, and a big orange in the other, both the gifts of "big partner" Deputy Sheriff C. A. Day, Robert Dunbar, or "little partner" who was found after an absence of eight months, was lifted aboard the Great Northern train leaving here at 4:30 Wednesday morning, en route for home. His hastily given "dood bye" to those at the station meant no more to him than an incident of childhood. To them it meant the soldering of a strong bond of attachment that they had formed for the little fellow.

Ever since Day was placed in charge of Robert when he was found and given into the care of Deputy Sheriff Jeff D. Wallace, the man and the boy have been fast friends. That is when the names "big" and "little partner" first came to be used. When everyone else failed to make the boy obey or smile, Day was called and succeeded.

He was more like a father than a guardian. He aided in purchasing little gifts and giving him a "jetney" now and then. The jackknife was the crowning gift of all. Eight rails on the fence above the Wallace home and two cut thumbs are the sum total of the results achieved by the boy with this new possession.

Day was asked just why he had taken a fancy in the boy. "I had one about his age, and, well, he died," he said.

The Item-April 23, 1913

When Cantwell learned of the departure, he hastily wrote a letter to the couple, but for some unknown reason it was never mailed.

Columbia, Miss. Ap 23d 1913

Mr and Mrs C P Dunbar

Oppoluce La

I see that you Got Bruce But you have Heaped up trouble for yourselves I had no chance to Prove up But I Guess By now you Have Decided you are wrong it is vary likely I will Loose my Life on account of that and if I do the Great God will hold you accountable that Boys mother is Julia Anderson and He has A Little sister Named Burnece you ask him and He will tell you his Momma Name is Julia and His Little sister is Burnece Some peoepple Has Her at Chadburn NC you write to L F Brown at that Place and he likely knows If not you can find out and it look if you are able to take Bruce you ought to take the other one I took Poor Little Bruce almost A Lonely Little tot He had never Been Learned any Manners I Have Given so many statements and no one would Help me and you took my Little Boy Now if you will take him And go to Cerro Gordo NC and Enquire For E K Brown He will Carry you to His mother and Prove to you that he is Bruce Anderson and you need not Feel like you will Be Badly treated like I Have Been

Now Mr Dunbar If you had not treated me Like you Did I Could Have Proved to you that Bruce was not Robert Remember what Bad Befalls me From this you will Be Responsible to God that Boy is A Bastard No doubt and Dont contain one Drop of your Blood When you see your mistake it will maby Be too late to Do me any Good But you will Regret it as Long as you Live I Did not teach him to Beg or Bum But in as much as you Have him take good care of Him you will no Doubt Have your Hands Full

I never Learned the stait of it until just A Few Minutes Ago I would Have if I had Got any trace of you Poor Little Robert I should Have Done all For You I could But now I am where I Can Do nothing So you Have A Lost Robert and me A Lost Bruce May God Bless my Darling Boy Write me if I Don't Get Lynched How you are Geting Along with Him I think you will Be sad A Long time But Hope not too bad

William Cantwell Walters' Defense File© #7(3)

Chapter Five
Tug of War – Freret Street

C antwell's witnesses from Pearl River County arrived later that morning of the 23rd and met with the prisoner and his lawyers. Sheriff Hathorn, Deputy Sheriff Walter Lott, and Marshall Tom Ford had spent all night at the jail but were up with coffee ready for their guests. The Sheriff's desk had been cleared for the attorneys' secretary, Sarah Dale, sister of Tom Dale; and she was in place and ready. Extra chairs were dragged into the room for the Bilbos' and the lawyers and placed near Cantwell's cell.

"Mr. Dale," Mrs. Bilbo began eagerly, "Bruce wouldn't have gone with them willing, Lord knows, he would hardly let old Cantwell out of his sight."

Tom nodded, then turned to the secretary, "Miss Dale, are you ready?"

"Yes, Sir."

Tom began, "From what I gather so far is that Mr. Walters and this child, Bruce, were residing in this area before August 23, 1912, the date Bobby Dunbar disappeared. Am I correct?"

Cantwell nodded, "Yes, Sir."

"Do you propose to give us as true and accurate a record of events as best as you can remember?" Cantwell placed his hand solemnly across his chest covering the small Bible that rode in his breast pocket. "I do." Hollis had unearthed a calendar from last year and had it open on his lap. Tom told Cantwell to begin.

As if a spigot were turned, the old man opened his mouth.

"On July 12, 1912, I reached the home of Mr. Slade, five miles south-east of Purvis, Mississippi. His son was working in a blacksmith's shop across the railroad track and suggested my horse needed to be shod which he did the following day.

"*Afterwards I went to the Drug Store in Purvis and the boys made much over Bruce. I bought some medicine there. Maybe they have a receipt. Let's see,*" he thought a moment, rubbing his brow. "*Next we drove out to Mr. Mark Rayborn's house; his two grown sons were there, both school teachers. They will remember us. We spent two nights there, the 13th and 14th.*

"*On July 15, I fixed a machine at Mr. Davis' four miles south of Pinebur on the Columbia & Lumberton Road. Maybe he has some reference of the date. We spent that night at Mr. Rawls, six miles from Pinebur on the Columbia & Monticello road.*"

Hollis scribbled notes in each box, pausing to glance at Tom who had kicked back in his chair, physically moved by this unusual character before him. Cantwell was casually visualizing each date in his mind as if reading from a sheet of paper.

"*On the night of the 16th I went to the home of a Negro named Galloway, who keeps Post Office at Odile, Mississippi. He had a machine, clock, and an organ he wanted fixed. About dark we went up to Mr. Ham's and tried to stay the night with him but he was full up and couldn't take us. It was a long way to another white man's house, so we returned to Mr. Galloway's and made a pallet on their gallery. We worked there on July 17 and 18. I believe they took my payment out of the Post Office money and maybe their records show this.*" He paused for a moment, adjusting his seat.

"*On Friday, the 19, we showed up at the Bilbos' place.*" He looked toward the older couple and they gave each other a small nod. "*On the way there, Miss Dale, we passed Wash Lott, Bob Harvey, and Dan Holleman working on the road. They will have some record in their time book. Bruce was already asleep when we got there so I carried him in to bed.*"

"*I put them in the front corner bedroom,*" Mrs. Bilbo offered.

"*Go see Bill Stewart,*" Cantwell added, "*who lives with one of the Wheats. Stewart saw us at the Bilbos' in July and I know he keeps a record of his time. I saw it myself.*"

William Cantwell Walters' Defense File© #63

A box of sandwiches and fried chicken arrived at the jail, followed by a platter of cookies. Fresh coffee filled their cups and the prisoner's confidence rose.

"The Dunbars have likely realized their mistake by now and are on their way back," stated Cantwell.

He rolled off his itinerary of the four following weeks. Work at Fords Creek Church and the surrounding area. Time at the Bilbos'. The Springhill Church repair. Eventually, he arrived at the days surrounding Bobby's disappearance.

I spent Sunday the 18th day of August at the home of Levy Holleman four miles from McNeil. During the day there came to Mr. Levy Holleman's home the following people who will remember me and for whom I played my harp: Dan Holleman, Carlos Holleman, Orvis Penton and two of his brothers, Mrs. Jenkins, a Kentucky man and his wife, Mrs. Loveless, and Mr. and Mrs. Loveless and Mr. and Mrs. Boone.

Cantwell smiled at the memory, "Mrs. Jenkins knew almost every song verse for verse and fell into an easy tempo with me. We sang for two hours."

"Oh, pardon me for drifting, Miss Dale," he offered.

I spent Monday, the 19th day of August at the home of Levy Holleman, the same place where I had spent Sunday, spending that night there.

He continued:

"On the morning of the 20th of August, 1912, I left Levy Holleman's for McNeil about four miles away, and eat dinner on that day at Mr. Lost Smith's, reaching McNeil as I remember now after dinner. I got a shave while there and went into a store west of the depot and got a box to pack a fiddle in. I went to the express office, received a package and sent a package. I left McNeil and spent the night at Mr. Spears three or four miles southeast of McNeil.

"On August 21, we left Spears's and came by McNeil, by the home of Jeff Lott and eat dinner at the home of Wash Lott. We went by the home of Tom Lumpkin on our way to Ben Sones. We had to ask J. Q. Sones

the way after getting lost but we found it and spent the night of the 21 at Ben's house. I spent entire day and night of August 22 there as well."

Attention peaked as the lawyers inclined their bodies toward Cantwell, listening for hard, irrefutable evidence. The Bilbos were sitting behind the lawyers but had leaned forward between them. Miss Dale stretched her poised fingers and the lawmen passed looks between themselves.

"Let's see, we left Ben Sones on August 23, an ordinary day I remember, and went to young man Thigpen's one mile from Whitesand Church and in sight of George Amacker's. I worked on Thigpen's sewing machine all that day and spent the night of August 23, there.

The next morning, August 24, 1912, I closed up the repaired appliance and Bruce and I went by old man Thigpen's. We stopped at Holden's and I did a small repair for him and we doubled back and spent that night at old man Thigpen's.

Sunday, August 25, I went from old man Thigpen's to Whitesand Church and carried the Thigpen's dinner in my buggy. Bro. Holcomb preached at Whitesand on that Sunday and I played my harp and made a statement in public about fixing the organ. A good crowd was present and all the people that were there will remember me and Bruce. After preaching was over and the crowd left we went to Carl Bass's and stayed there overnight.

The next morning, August 26, 1912, I went to Al Goleman's at Poplarville, Mississippi, having little Bruce Anderson with me all the while."

William Cantwell Walters' Defense File© #64 & #87

With confidence, the lawyers began contacting these witnesses, asking each to make an affidavit as such. They planned to have the repairman and his boy cleared and on their way shortly.

However, even before Cantwell's lawyers had finished recording his testimony, the *Item* had declared that Bobby had been found and was on his way home. On April 23, they printed a photo of Bruce in Columbia labeled "Dunbar Boy." The Dunbars became instant celebrities. Their riveting drama provided a welcome diversion from two years of flood devastation, along with a growing instability in Europe and Mexico.

As word spread throughout the train that the family was on board, passengers worked their way toward the parlor car where the family was eating breakfast. They wanted to see the miraculous child and congratulate the parents. At each stop people clambered aboard hoping to meet the child silhouetted in the window. Outside the window, crowds of grinning, wide-eyed spectators chanted, "Bobby! Bobby! Bobby!"

More and more people packed into the car, shoving Bruce further into his seat. He sat in Day's lap, being dandled on the sheriff's thigh. The man's large arms encircled him. Lessie's trembling body pressed up against them and occasionally she reached out a thin white arm and pawed at him nervously. "We're almost home, Bobby; we're almost home," she repeated. Percy sat with one hip on the armrest covering the aisle entrance. Bruce routinely squeezed his eyes shut and wailed, which brought on more bouncing or petting from those in the seats around them.

"Papa!" Bruce screamed repeatedly, which resulted in Percy leaning in close to his face. Bruce smelled the man's greasy breakfast and the sour sweat running down his back. His hair oil rubbed onto Bruce's cheek, and its scent caused him to shiver.

Squeezing Bruce's narrow shoulders firmly, Percy gave him a little shake. "Bobby! I'm right here, Son."

Bruce hid his face against Day's chest after that and dozed for a short period.

Several of the Dunbars' relatives and friends joined the train along the way and heard a whispered first-hand account of the recovery; including a detailed recital of facts that the parents said convinced them they had their son. Certain moles, birthmarks, and characteristic traits were said to be seen.

"If the child has one mark of identification, he has twenty-five," Percy claimed.

When Bruce woke up, he was calmer. He removed his shoes and socks several times, presenting his feet; but when questioned about the kidnapper, Walters, or where he had been for the last eight months, he either completely shut down or had another attack of sheer panic. Percy laughed at the red-faced boy, saying his son had been known to have a healthy temper.

People catered to the boy's every whim, filling his pockets with coins and his mouth with treats. Along the route, women and children festooned the train in garlands and bouquets, attempting to make up for Bobby's eight months of trauma.

Upon their arrival in the city, they were taken to the *Item's* headquarters for an exclusive interview and photo session. A crowd of several hundred people had gathered outside the office's entrance and threatened to overwhelm the group on its appearance. Competing newspapers, including the *New Orleans Daily States* and the *Times-Democrat*, were present as well.

Once inside the office, the odd behavior of the child toward Lessie and Percy left many of the staff wondering whether the couple had indeed found their son, but the couple insisted that the boy was Bobby. The photographer eventually managed to capture several photographs of Lessie with the bewildered child sitting awkwardly on her lap. In a trembling voice Lessie faced the reporters:

"To the good ladies of Hub, Miss., I want to extend publicly through the Item my deepest thanks," said Mrs. Dunbar. "It is they who really deserve the credit for the return of my dear child.

"The Item has been mighty kind to us. It has stood by us and it is the publicity that has aided us greatly."

Mr. Dunbar too, was warm in his praise of the Item and declared that he owed a deep debt of gratitude to the newspaper for its assistance.

"I can look back at all my troubles and the strain of this last trip, but my joy is beyond explanation," said Mrs. Dunbar, happily, to a reporter for the Item, while the camera man got busy.

"Why, I haven't an enemy in the world. I'm so happy and it seems that everybody is my friend."

"He's a different child," cried the mother of little Robert Dunbar when the party was being taken in an automobile to the home of relatives here Wednesday morning soon after arriving in the city from Columbia, Miss.

She put her arms around the boy, hugged and kissed him and cried with joy. She seemed to be hurt when the boy pushed her hand down.

"He's so tired and worn out," said the mother, happily. "He'll be all right now, and won't the people be glad when he gets back home."

The child evidently has been taught to shun strangers by his captor. Few persons can form an acquaintance with the boy and he looks suspiciously at everyone.

The Item-April 23, 1913

Lessie's comment, "He's a different child," resonated loudly in the *Item's* staffs' ears. After the family slipped out by way of a side door, someone in the newspaper office commented that the child did not favor either parent, so their reporters decided to investigate further.

Lessie's unsuccessful attempts to comfort the child over the preceding days had drained what little physical and emotional strength she had, so instead of continuing on to Opelousas, they were taken to Harold and Ola's nearby home on Freret Street where their family doctor awaited.

Once they were settled, Percy headed to the Hippodrome. The theater's management related that they, as well as the Dunbars, could profit from the sensational story and guaranteed Percy two hundred dollars for a contract to show the child. Percy insisted on a one thousand dollar contract, which the theater promptly declined.

Back in Columbia, Tom was dictating four letters to Cantwell's family and friends trying to corroborate the man's account of his and the child's life.

He wrote to Cantwell's eighty-three-year-old father, James Pleasant, in Barnesville, North Carolina.

April 23, 1913

Dear Mr. Walters,

I write you in the interest of one W. C. Walters, your son, who is imprisoned here now and charged with having kidnapped a child from the State of Louisiana by the name of Dunbar, a child which was lost on the 23rd day of August, 1912. I am representing W. C. Walters as his Attorney, and I write you for such assistance as you can render in his behalf. In the State of Louisiana kidnapping is a hanging crime, and the feeling against your son, W. C. Walters, is bitter and excitement running high. On last Sunday Mr. Walters was arrested and he had in his custody a little child about the size and age and appearance of the missing Dunbar child. Both him and the child were held in custody until yesterday when Mr. & Mrs. Dunbar came here from Louisiana and identified the child as being theirs.

Mr. Walters tells me that the child which was in his possession and which is claimed by the Dunbars is in truth and in fact a child of Mrs. Julia Anderson. He calls him Bruce. That Mrs. Anderson gave the child

to him last December was a year ago, and that he left North Caroli-
na with him last February was a year ago. I am writing Mrs. Julia
Anderson also with reference to this matter. I understand that you are
a very old man and likely very feeble, but I am sure that you have the
interest of your son at heart, and if it is so that you can render him some
aid and assistance toward the making of his defense, you will be only
too glad to do so. I want you to write me, or have someone do so for you,
if you are too feeble yourself, and tell me if Mr. Walter's statement about
this child is true. Did Mrs. Julia Anderson give him a little boy by the
name of Bruce? If this is true, I want you to write me fully a history
of the child and of the woman. Make an affidavit to the correctness of
your statement before an officer, and by all means see that Mrs. Julia
Anderson, if this is her child, makes affidavit to the effect that she is the
mother of this little boy Bruce, and have her send me the picture of this
little child which Mr. Walters sent her some time since, together with
her affidavit to the effect that she is the mother of the child, the picture
of which she encloses with the affidavit.

Now Mr. Walters let me impress upon you the importance of this.
The situation is indeed critical and serious with Mr. W. C. Walters
here. As his lawyer, I believe him to be an innocent man. I believe
the Dunbars are mistaken in the identification of the child. They have
taken the child, but I believe they have taken the child of Julia Ander-
son and not their child, and if this be true, I want your sworn state-
ment to all that you know about it, and if you can furnish me with any
other information or with any sworn statements from other persons to
this effect kindly do so by return mail, as I need all of the help along
this line that I can get. I need it bad and I need it as quickly as I can
get it. I will try and postpone trial until I can hear from you and Julia
Anderson. Let me hear from you at once.

Yours very truly,
Thomas Dale

William Cantwell Walters' Defense File© #8

Four other letters of similar content were mailed: one to the justice
of the peace in Columbus County, the county neighboring Robeson
County where Cerro Gordo was located and where Julia's former husband was from; one to Cantwell's nephew, J. M. Walters, who farmed

the family's land in Barnesville; one to his sister, Synthelia; and one to Julia.

The following day in New Orleans, the Dunbars went shopping for some new clothes for the child.

Robbie Knows Just What Kind of Suit He Likes

Boy Displays Temper At Godchaux's While Selecting New Clothes.

"Robbie" Dunbar selected a new suit of clothes Thursday morning through the courtesy of Albert Godchaux, of the Godchaux Clothing Company. Little "Robbie," in company with his mother, grandmother, Mrs. Dunbar, and Mrs. Fox, visited the clothing establishment and immediately were the center of attraction. The boy displayed some temper while selecting a suit, which his mother declared further identified him, and left no room for doubt as to her positive identification.

Mr. Godchaux, accompanied by John Glass, advertising manager, and several of the Godchaux clerks took the Dunbar party to the children's department. It was there that little Robbie had things his own way.

No one dared suggest to him which was the prettiest, or which looked the best to him. He knew what he wanted. He made the clerk, Miss Eugenie Deck, understand too what he wanted.

He Didn't Want That.

First Mr. Godchaux showed the little fellow a beautiful sailor suit with red and blue trimmings, with stars and anchors, a great big blue string tie and an attractively decorated collar-the same kind worn by the sons of the rich.

But "Robbie" did not want that.

"No," he shouted, "I don't like that one. Take it away."

And Miss Deck and Mr. Godchaux obeyed the command. "Robbie" was the guest of the Godchaux house. He appeared to know it, too.

Miss Deck took charge of the youngster. She looked at the color of the old hat Robbie had worn. Holding it in her hand she caught Robbie throwing side glances at her. Finally the little fellow grabbed for the little headgear, saying, "I want my hat."

The hat was the color of Irish linen. Thinking that the favorite color of the little chap was Irish linen Miss Deck produced a suit of that material.

"I like that," said Robbie, as soon as he saw the new suit. "I like it." he repeated.

"Very well, little man," said Mr. Godchaux, "you shall have it or any other you may like."

He Was Stubborn.

Then it came time for Robbie to display his temper. He did not want to try the suit out in the store before all the people. No, he would not stand for that, and said so in just that many words. "Not here," he repeated several times. "I won't put it on here. Wait till we get home."

Everybody coaxed little Robbie to put on the brand new suit. But he was stubborn and obstinate. He wanted his own way about it. And he had his own way, too, for a while.

Finally, however, Robbie did not like the tan-colored suit. He wanted a white one, and to oblige him Miss Deck selected one of the choicest in the entire stock. It was a pure white uniform, beautifully embroidered: in fact, the prettiest in the store. Robbie knew it, for he held it tight when the clerk was exhibiting it before him.

"I like that one," he said.

"You shall have it," said Miss Deck, reassuringly.

Everybody thought Robbie was in the right frame of mind, and he was, too, until the elder Mrs. Dunbar, to whom Robbie appeared mostly attached, suggested that Robbie put the suit on.

Doesn't Like the Dark.

He would not stand for putting the suit on in front of everybody in the store. And he would not stand for going into the little dressing room.

"It's too dark," he shouted, as if reminded of some of the punishment he is supposed to have undergone while in the care of Walters. He cried and begged of his grandmother not to take him into the room.

"I don't want to go in there," he cried. "No, no, not there!"

He clung to his grandmother's neck and held on as if for dear life. He was finally coaxed into the room by Wharton Moony, the elder Mrs. Dunbar and Mrs. Fox, but throughout the performance of dressing the little fellow, there came from the dressing room screams of fear from

Robbie. He wanted to get out, and was not satisfied until he did get into the open.

Robbie clung closely to the elder Mrs. Dunbar during the entire period of his visit to the Godchaux store. He did not care to leave her side. Several times his mother called him, but he held fast to the elder woman.

"She reminds him so much of his grandma at home," said Mrs. Dunbar, smilingly. "He was perfectly attached to her."

Mrs. Fox called to Robbie several times also, but the little fellow wanted the elder woman, and he had his own way about it.

The New Orleans States-April 24, 1913

The elder Mrs. Dunbar, Ola's mother, held a great physical resemblance to Mrs. Bilbo. And perhaps their mannerisms or speech patterns were similar, for when Bruce met the woman for the first time he screamed, "Gramma," and bodily grabbed hold of the woman's legs and wouldn't let go.

The newspapers ran articles contradicting Cantwell's alibi that he was in Mississippi with Bruce when the Dunbar child had vanished, and reported Percy's discovery that a man answering Cantwell's description had been seen near Swayze Lake shortly after the child disappeared. Percy's reports of Bobby's abuse gained momentum.

Although Cantwell had spent time in Louisiana in previous years, the only time he had set foot in the state during 1912 was when he was a patient in Charity Hospital in New Orleans for surgery on his knee. The hospital first stated that they had never treated anyone by the name of W. C. Walters. After their statement was published, however, the hospital found his records and an employee remembered him for playing his harp for the hospitalized children.

The story caught the attention of a shipping agent in Eunice, Louisiana, twenty miles west of Opelousas. He alleged a trunk had arrived at his station over six months ago, supposedly consigned to William Walters, but it was never claimed. The agent said he retrieved the trunk from storage, finding it filled with clothes, books, and a man's photograph. He sent the photo to the *Item*, and the editors placed it on their front page. Below the man's scowling face, they added a sketch of the man obviously stealing a child with the caption, "William Walters. Is he a kidnapper?" Although the two men looked similar, it wasn't Cantwell's photo, or his trunk. **(See p. 298)**

After that picture was published, reports began pouring in from south-central Louisiana declaring that the man in the photo had been in their vicinity around the time of the kidnapping. They claimed he was living and traveling in a covered wagon with "W. C. Walters – Stovemender" painted on the side. It was then reported that the man had several kidnapped children in his possession, swapping them frequently to avoid detection.

"If you can locate where Walters hid the other children, you'll likely find Bruce Anderson."

A group in Mississippi insisted that William Walters had served time in the state penitentiary for shooting a man, and on his way to be incarcerated he had attempted to escape and jumped from the train. This was supposedly how Cantwell had fractured his kneecap. He was said to have taken part in a train robbery as well. Each of these reports was summarily proven to be false.

Lessie tried to soothe Bruce's frequent tantrums, but he continually rebuffed her advances. Various experts in psychology were quoted, offering their opinions as to why the child was having difficulty in recognizing his mother and father. They stated that it could take up to two weeks at home before the child recovered his memory.

Dozens of photographs of the child filled the papers, from his discovery in Columbia to his adventures in New Orleans. He was captured on horseback, peering from the window of a train, and in Lessie's arms at the newspaper office as she pressed in to kiss him. Instead of cuddling in towards the woman, the solemn little boy leaned away, placing his palm defensively against her chest.

Tom and Hollis sent a declaration to the newspapers insisting the Dunbars were mistaken in identifying their child. They reminded the public that Percy's brother had come to the Bilbos' home months ago to view this same boy and had declared that he was not his missing nephew. Mr. and Mrs. Bilbo had been shown a photo of Bobby taken before he disappeared, and they had confirmed that he was not the child they knew as Bruce Anderson.

Percy contacted Mississippi's Governor Earl Brewer, presenting dozens of reasons that he said proved the identity of the boy. Brewer hired the famous Burns Detective Agency in New Orleans to investigate the matter; and they sent their chief operative, detective Dan Lehon, to visit with the child. Lehon concluded that the Dunbars had made a mistake and did not know their own child. W. J. Burns, head of the agency, telephoned Brewer and assured him that it was a case of misidentification.

Governor Hall increased the pressure on Brewer to extradite Cantwell, but Brewer was receiving letters and phone calls from his constituents declaring the man's innocence. Hollis wrote to Governor Brewer.

April 25, 1913

Dear Governor,

We have refrained from indulging on your time in the matter of the requisition requested by the Louisiana authorities for W. C. Walters now in jail here charged with kidnapping the Dunbar child. We have not advised you personally in this connection, for the reason that it might appear to you that as Attorneys for Walters we were partisan, and perhaps saw the matter entirely through the eyes of our client, and we preferred to let you receive the information from other reliable sources in Columbia and adjoining counties.

It will require something like a week or ten days for us to secure the attendance of necessary witnesses now in North Carolina to establish thoroughly the innocence of our client. Mr. Walters, as you have perhaps noted, is practically without funds, and we have to depend to a great extent on letters to accomplish our investigation of parties and places in North Carolina. This, as you can realize, will be slow.

We give you every assurance as Attorneys and as your friends, that if the information which we now have at hand be correct, a grievous blunder has been made, and we feel that in justice to our client and to the public generally that he should be given every opportunity to test the truth or falsity of his statements.

People generally are complimenting very highly your present stand in the matter of the requisition, and we are absolutely confident that your position is dictated by good judgment and is unquestionably correct. No harm can come of the position you have assumed. The Dunbars have the child and if it is theirs they are satisfied. Walters is in jail here and there is no better Sheriff in the State than S. J. Hathorn, and you need not rest any uneasiness as to any likelihood of his escape.

We, therefore, desire that you give us sufficient time to get all of our witnesses here before re-considering the granting of the requisition pa-

*pers. If there is any further or other information that we can give you
we shall be pleased to have you advise us.*

*With assurances of continued personal esteem and regards, we beg
to remain, as ever,*

Your friends,
Tom Dale & Hollis Rawls
William Cantwell Walters' Defense File© #13

On the morning of April 25, the Dunbars left New Orleans for their triumphant return to Opelousas. Along the way the boy was obsessed with the idea that it was up to him to stop the train, so he persisted in pulling the bell cord. He kicked and cried when told not to do it, and while a man was holding him in his arms, he wriggled up to the standing position and grabbed the cord, pulling on it until the train stopped, which caused the brakeman to come running to see what the matter was.

At every stop crowds gathered to glimpse the boy and congratulate the parents. When the train reached Lafayette, the Dunbars headed to the Crescent News Hotel, with a huge crowd following behind.

*At the hotel Mr. and Mrs. Dunbar met little Alonzo, their second
child, who arrived from Opelousas this morning in the care of friends.
The father stood on the hotel gallery and raised the two children in
his arms. As soon as the children were seen, a stillness was noticeable
among the throng, everyone apparently trying to detect some resemblance between the children, but it soon was followed by a mighty cheer
as little Alonzo, who had seen his brother for the first time in eight
months, put his little arms around his brother's neck. "Bobbie," however, showed by no sign that he recognized his brother.*
The Times-April 26, 1913

Half of the crowd cheered for Bobby, while the rest were struck dumb by the unrecognizable boy.

NOT CAROLINA BOY

*Out of the maze of contradictory statements surrounding the identi-
fication of the boy recovered from William C. Walters at Columbia,*

Miss., as the missing Robert Dunbar, the Times-Democrat Friday succeeded in bringing out one fact of the greatest importance.

The boy the Dunbars claim as their son bears decided marks as a means of identification.

The boy taken from Carolina by Walters has NO marks of identification, according to the affidavit of his mother.

Therefore, the boy taken from Walters is not Julia Anderson's son, as she claims.

The Times-April 26, 1913

In Opelousas, preparations were being made for the family's arrival. Businesses and schools were closed, and the town was decorated with banners and flags. A brass band was assembled at the station, where several prominent citizens waited to welcome the group. A fire truck was parked nearby to carry Bobby home.

Despite a downpour of rain, three thousand people came to the station in buggies, wagons, autos, and on horseback to celebrate the memorable event and watch the procession on its way home. Members of the Masons, the Elks, the Woodmen, and the Odd Fellows were on hand. The newspapers verified that every member of the Dunbar and Whitley families recognized Bobby the instant they saw him.

Bruce screamed in fright at the spectacle playing out before him. The family explained away the tears, claiming a local woman had accidentally poked the boy in the eye with her umbrella.

Procession To Home

There was applause when the baby was carried into the house and placed for a minute in his highchair, which had been placed in the front hall arranged like a miniature throne and set with garlands of roses. The armloads of flowers which had been presented to him en route were spread at his feet, and the demonstration was so amazing that the boy became frightened and cried.

Lawyer Makes Address

John W. Lewis, prominent lawyer of Opelousas, spoke, in part, as follows:

"*The successful politician has stood before admiring thousands and heard his name mingled with shouts of gladness and praise, the returning soldier has seen reflected on his burnished blade the smiles of women and the proud glances of men, the advocate has swayed the judge and jury by his eloquence and force and linked his name with undying fame, but I would rather have it said in time to come that I was the honored mouthpiece of a people who to-day, with joy in their hearts and tears in their eyes, welcome home little Robert Dunbar, who Providence in His Mercy again has given into the arms of his parents.*

"*When word first went forth that little Robert was lost or stolen, every heart here for the moment was stilled, every eye bedimmed with tears, and the wails of the bereaved mother reached the very souls of men and women from one end of the continent to the other. As days lengthened into weeks, and weeks into months, and still no word came, hope gave way to despair, and a settled resignation to the dispensation of our Creator entered the hearts of all save the hearts of those fond parents, who thought by day and dreamed by night of a deliverance to them of their boy. Just as the last ray of hope had disappeared, and human effort seemed to be empty and futile, there flashed a word from the motherhood of Mississippi that little Robert had been seen and identified. With that rare instinct that comes with motherhood, these noble women insisted upon an investigation, and if to-day little Robert again diffuses the sunlight of his smile among us it is to the women of Hub, Miss., that offerings of gratitude should be made.*

"*And then, again, to the splendid citizens of Columbia we owe profound appreciation for the unselfish, noble and generous assistance given Mr. and Mrs. Dunbar in those trying moments which preceded the final identification of little Robert.*

"*But this investigation must not stop here. The people of this city, of this State, aye, of the entire nation, demand that those who are responsible for this heinous crime be brought to swift and sure justice. A thief may steal your wealth, a midnight assassin may steal the life that God has given you and go unwhipped of justice, but he who tears from the breast of the mother her child and plunges a whole State in tears can never be permitted long, to darken the civilization of the universe. Let justice be done, though the heavens fall, not through violence, not through those ebullitions of human wrath that disgrace a State and nation, but through the orderly processes of law, and it will be done. The citizens of Opelousas want law, want order, want jus-*

tice, and when the august chief magistrate of our sister State, in his own good time, delivers to the constituted authorities of Louisiana the suspected criminal not a finger will be raised to arrest the course of an orderly and impartial trial. When he hints at mob law in Opelousas we fling it back at him that for over 100 years only one instance has been recorded where summary justice was meted out in this city, and that here, in our temple of justice, the vilest criminal is accorded every constitutional safeguard. Not alone are the Dunbars and the people of this city interested in this issue. The fatherhood and motherhood of the country want it settled. They want to know whether their children can breathe the free and unrestricted air of heaven without feeling about their little bodies the tentacles of the kidnaper. They want to know if bodyguards and shotguns are to take the place of tops and marbles and toys. This is the fundamental question.

"Now, my friends, let us join in the festivities of this glad day, and make the world ring with the glad tidings that Bobby has been found, crying aloud in gladsome strains with that devoted mother and proud father, 'Eureka! Eureka!'"

The Times-April 26, 1913

As the Dunbar's friends and relatives swarmed their home, they stated that Bobby recognized his brother, Alonzo; his playmates Irma and Nathan Roos; and family friends, calling each one by name without any prompting whatsoever. Once again, Lessie collapsed from the strain.

Dr. F. C. Shute, the family's physician, came to the home to verify the child's identity. He had cared for Bobby since infancy; and after a thorough examination, acknowledged that although the scar on his toe had faded, it was still very much evident. The doctor also said that Bobby had a slight deformity of his penis, which he found on this boy, stating that it could not occur exactly the same way in two different children. With Harold and Ola Fox, John Lewis, and Dr. Shute in their pocket, the scales tipped evermore in the Dunbars' favor.

Percy sent his comments to Governor Brewer, sharing the letter's content with the *Times-Democrat*.

In a spirit of fairness and a desire to uphold the majesty of the law in the punishment of crime, I respectfully petition your Excellency to honor the requisition of Gov. Hall for the extradition of the prisoner, William C. Walters, at Columbia jail. I desire to assure your Excel-

lency that both myself and my wife are thoroughly satisfied with the identity of the child, and to say that if he were not our boy neither of us would want to keep him.

We desire to say further that in the presence of Mr. Lee Hawes, staff correspondent of The Times-Democrat; Mrs. Dunbar, Mrs. S. H. Fox, a cousin of my wife, and Mr. S. H. Fox, at the Fox residence, 7031 Freret street, New Orleans, a full physical inspection of the child was made to substantiate our claims as to his birthmarks, etc. We found the following totally identically with the claims of his parents: Curly cowlick on the forehead, scar on the forehead, mole on the lobe of the left ear, mole on the back of neck, mole on side of neck under right ear (identical with that on mother), two moles on right cheek, dimples in corners of eyes, strong resemblance of eyes to father, separated regular upper teeth, lower teeth like little brother, back and body covered with pinhead moles, dark spot in hair (identical with birthmark of father), deformity of penis, scar on forehead, cicatrice of burn on left big toe, malformation of two little toes on the left foot, the first phalanx of each turning inward slightly, cuticle of toes not clinging to nails, showing evidences of burn, familiarity of laugh and sob, recognition of and affection for mother, responds to pet name "Mr. Rabbit," playfully bites at father in "bear game," calls aunt (Mrs. W. M. Dunbar) "grandma" on account of facial resemblance to grandma in Opelousas, uses excellent English, free from grammatical errors common to hill country folk of North Carolina, where Walters claims to have been given him, and responds to his Christian name, Robbie.

Respectfully,
C. P. Dunbar.

The Times–April 25, 1913

The Dunbars pressed hard to portray Julia and Cantwell as illiterate tramps or beggars. The truth was, however, that it was Cantwell who was responsible for Bruce's excellent manners and proper speech. One of the most disturbing portions of Percy's letter is his weak explanation of Bruce's attempts to bite him.

On Saturday afternoon, April 26, thousands of Louisianans converged on the town square in Opelousas to officially welcome Bobby home. The screaming throng yelled out "Robert" or "Bobby" until Bruce obsessively started rocking back and forth. A small throne was erected for the boy on the speaker's platform so he could be seen by all. Despite the festivities, the guest of honor refused to enjoy the gala and cried loudly throughout several of the speeches. Only the gift of a new velocipede handed up to the child caused him to settle down. Afterwards, the children in attendance were treated to ice cream, cake, and lemonade.

New Joy Disperses All Gloom Once in Home of Dunbars

OPELOUSAS, La., April 26. If one were to search the world over, a happier family than the Dunbars here couldn't be found anywhere. The relaxation after the strain of disappointment and sorrow that they have undergone for the last eight months, ever since Robert was lost, is already apparent and the house, instead of being one of gloom, is the reverse.

Mrs. Dunbar showed the improvement Friday night. She laughed over some of the humorous incidents that had taken place in the few days preceding. At the time they occurred she was too busy with her own doubts and fears, but now she can see them in the other light.

As they put it, they "are on their own stamping ground." Mr. Dunbar laughingly declared he had had his own "gang" about him and had nothing to fear. The "gang," it might be mentioned, is a rather formidable one, too.

Friends of the couple here kept some one busy answering the telephone all Friday night. At intervals of two or three minutes a call was received from the surrounding country or from the town to ask how Robert or his mother was getting along. A friend of Mrs. Dunbar called up and stated she was very glad that it had turned out as it should.

"Yes," said the mother, "I've got my baby back and I'd like to see any one take him away from me again. Everyone who sees him is convinced as we are that there can be no mistake. I am so happy, I am almost afraid to wake up in the morning and find it all a dream."

Minutely visitors are shown to the house and offer their congratulations. A steady stream keeps going up the walk to the home, decorated both inside and out with bunting, flags and flowers. Opelousas has never been in such a fever of excitement nor had so much to talk about.

The Item-April 26, 1913

Chapter Six
Sifted to the Very Bottom

At their Columbia office, Tom and Hollis received a letter from Brewer's secretary responding to their request that the Governor withhold the extradition.

April 26, 1913

Gentlemen,

In the absence of Governor Brewer I acknowledge receipt of your letter in regard to Walters. The Governor will probably not return for a day or two, and at that time he will take up the question of honoring this requisition. On account of the seeming uncertainty as to the identity of the child, and the possible danger of lynching if taken to Louisiana he thought best to hold up action until he could get all the information available. Of course, he would wish this information as soon as he could get it, but he does not wish to see an innocent party taken to Louisiana and tried while his life might be in danger.

The whole matter will have the Governor's attention on his return.

Yours truly,
W. J. Buck
Private Secretary

William Cantwell Walters' Defense File© #14

While Tom and Hollis scrambled to sort out the details of Cantwell's story, newspapers around the nation reported on the remarkable recovery of Bobby. Despite the negative fanfare, sentiment in Columbia was rapidly turning toward Cantwell.

The *Daily States* out of New Orleans ruffled a few feathers when it published a letter from one of Cantwell's friends in North Carolina.

Saw Letter Opened and Read it Himself to Walters' Aged Father—Knew Anderson Boy Well.

William H. Murray, a rural letter carrier, of Barnesville, N. C., has made an affidavit, reproduced in this edition of the States, to facts which seem to prove that the boy now at Opelousas in the possession of Mr. and Mrs. C. P. Dunbar is Bruce Anderson, and not Robert Dunbar, Jr.

Murray knew little Bruce Anderson well and is a reliable man.

He saw the photograph of the boy sent to Walters' father by Walters from Hub, Miss., April 8. Murray swears that the photograph is that of Bruce Anderson. This is the same boy now in Opelousas. Murray saw the letter opened and the photograph taken out. He read the letter to old man Walters.

The photograph of the boy undoubtedly is that of the lad now in Opelousas. It is a tiny, foggy photograph that cannot be reproduced clearly for newspaper illustration. However, the original is clear enough so that all who have seen it since it reached the Daily States' office have agreed that it is the boy now at the Dunbar home. He even has crossed his feet in the same manner as is shown in a picture of "Robert Dunbar" printed in the Daily States.

This photograph could not be identified by Walters' parents as they had not seen Bruce Anderson for some time. The eyes of Walters' father are so bad that he cannot read.

Julia Anderson lives many miles from the Walters place and the picture of her boy never reached her. It was taken from the Walters' home and sent immediately to the Daily States after it was shown to Mr. Murray.

Part of the letter enclosed "For Julia," is reproduced.

The question as to whether Walters meant to write that he was having trouble over "a child lost," or "child I lost" is still debatable. The script reads, "I child lost." There is no doubt that the letter is a capital "I" and not an "a." It is the same kind of a capital "I" that he uses in other parts of his letter.

The letter and address on the envelope were written in pencil and it was necessary to trace the writing in ink to make newspaper reproduction possible.

The letter was mailed at Hub, Miss., at which town Walters was found with the child.

Walters' letter indicates that he had no doubt in his mind that the boy was Bruce Anderson. It seems hardly probable that he would have sent a picture to Julia Anderson, it is argued, of a boy other than her own.

'Mr. J P Walters
Barnesville, NC.
April the 8th, 1913.

Dear Father and Mother,

I will write you a few lines which leaves me as well as usual. Hope these Few Lines will Reach you well and Doing. I have no news to Write only we have been Having Lots of Rain But Have Been Several nice Sunshiny Days and the mornings are Very Cool. How Long Did F. H. stay with you all. So I will come to a close by saying Write Soon and all the News. Write to me at FoxWorth Miss. I will send you one of my pictures also one for Vinita. Will put in some for Julia. If she is not staying with you, Get it to her. I have decided to Buy me a Place out There and try the Poltry Business. I would be glad if you would sell out or pull out and come Live with me.

Your son as ever,
W. C. Walters.
this for Julia

Been trying to Get A good Picture of Him to send to you But I find it A Hard matter But I will Send the Best I Have Bruce appears to Love me Better and Better All the time I Have Been Given some trouble about Him on account of I child lost about His Age But you need not Be uneasy about Him He is one of the Happiest Little Boys you Ever saw so write to me soon and all the News

as Ever your Friend

W C Walters
Write to Foxworth Miss'

4/26ʰ/13

I do hereby certify to the best of my knowledge and belief that Photo with Bruce Anderson's name written across back of it is Photo of Julia Anderson's child and is same taken from here in Feb 1912 By W. C. Walters. Also Photo is same sent to J. P. Walters by W. C. Walters From Mississippi on April 8ʰ 1913.

W. H. Murray

The States-April 28, 1913

Cantwell's simple letter conveyed to Julia, "I Have Been Given some trouble about Him on account of I (one) child lost about His Age" and then the tender afterthought, "But you need not Be uneasy about Him, He is one of the Happiest Little Boys you Ever saw"

On the same day, the *Times-Democrat* out of New Orleans ran a contradictory article. A group of men working thirty-three miles west of Columbia reported having seen W. C. Walters with Bobby over four months ago.

McComb Men Encountered Pair Before Christmas.

McComb City, Miss., April 27.- Joe L. Johnson, B. L. Morgan and W. D. Holmes, employees of the Illinois Central shops here, are positive that W. C. Walters, alleged kidnaper, and Robert Dunbar, Jr., were in McComb last year just before Christmas, and they went before a notary here yesterday and made an affidavit to that effect. This they sent to P. C. Dunbar, the child's father, at Opelousas, La., and offered to do anything they could to assist the parents. The affidavit reads:

Before me, the undersigned, a notary public in and for McComb City, said county and State, personally appeared Joe L. Johnson, B. L. Morgan and W. D. Holmes, who, being first duly sworn, say on oath that they are now and were during the year 1912 employees of the Illinois Central Railroad Company in its shops at McComb City, Miss., and that on Wednesday, Dec. 18, 1912, about 6 p.m., they went into the passenger depot in said city, and that there was in said depot a man and a little boy, with high red-top boots on, and that in conversation with the man he stated to affiants in the presence of ten or fifteen others that his name was W. C. Walters, and that he was a detective, and that he had been out in search of the Dunbar child, and that on the day before he had succeeded in locating said child down in Louisiana, and that he intended to carry it back to its parents and claim the reward offered.

Affiants further state that the said Walters pulled from his pocketbook a photo, which he stated was a picture of Robert Dunbar, Jr., and which, in their opinion, was an exact likeness of the child he had with him, and which corresponds in every regard with the published picture of said child in the different papers, and affiants further state that they have looked carefully over the picture of Walters as it appears in print, and they are positive that he is the identical man that was in McComb that day. There were with Walters at the time another man and woman, who were with him very familiar, but with others exceedingly reticent.

JOE L. JOHNSON, B. L. MORGAN, and W. D. HOLMES.

Sworn to and subscribed before me this the 26th day of April, 1913.
E. P. WILLIAMS.
Notary Public.

The Times-April 28, 1913

As soon as the three men's statements appeared in the paper, Cantwell and his attorneys assembled once again with Miss Dale listing a detailed account of his exact location and whom he was with on December 18 and several days before and after.

On Sunday morning, December 15th, 1912, I was at George Cooper's Four miles East of Derby and Six miles from Poplarville, Pearl River County, Mississippi. I left there on the morning of the 15th and eat dinner at Mr. Tynes four miles West of Derby, this Mr. Tynes being a son of Warren. I traveled on West that afternoon and spent the night of the 15th at Cotton Joe Stewart's—14 miles West of Derby.

On December 16, I Left Cotton Joe Stewarts, went by Tom Stewarts, who lives 2 ½ miles from Buck Branch Church, fixed organ on a credit and eat dinner at Tom Stewarts. That evening I went to George

Amacker's 8 miles from Poplarville and one mile from White Sand Church and spent the night of the 16th at the home of George Amacker.

On December 17, I worked at the home of George Amacker on his organ, eating all of my meals there and spent that night there. On Wednesday, the 18th, I did the same thing, that is, worked on the organ of George Amacker, at his home—taking all of my meals there and spent that night there. While I was at George Amacker's his son-in-law, and his oldest son, Tom Amacker, together with Tom's wife, and their three grown daughters; also a lady school teacher were there. He had two Negroes at work on the place and I hired one of them to grease my buggy for me while I was there. Mr. Amacker was trying to get some cross-ties that he had got down on the Railroad and Mr. Mitchell—a neighbor came after some hogs while I was there.

On December 19, I left George Amacker's in the evening and went to the home of Thos. Lumpkin, one mile from McNeil, Mississippi, and spent the night of the 19th at his home.

William Cantwell Walters' Defense File© #65 & 87

Cantwell continued listing the days that he and Bruce had stayed with Tom Lumpkin repairing his organ and their journey to the Bilbo's on Christmas Eve.

Each side was increasing its claim on the boy, inundating Governor Brewer's office with calls and letters.

Tom wrote to Brewer once again.

April 28, 1913

Dear Governor,

We beg to write you again with reference to W. C. Walters who is in jail here now accused of kidnapping the Dunbar child.

So far you have declined to honor the requisition from the Governor of Louisiana, but we fear that it will probably be your disposition within the next day or two to honor the requisition.

We have practically concluded our investigation and Governor we are now in a position to know that Mr. & Mrs. Dunbar have made a great mistake. We can establish the fact that Mr. Walters had this child in his possession for more than a month before the Dunbar child was lost, and we can make this proof by a hundred reputable citizens of

Pearl River County; by people who knew the child then and will know it now. We will be able to produce its Mother, and others, if necessary, from North Carolina by whom we can also make this proof.

(Tom listed the alibis Cantwell had for his first days in Mississippi in July, and the August days surrounding Bobby's disappearance.)

If Mr. Walters is carried to Louisiana he will be so far removed from his witnesses that it will not be practical for him to make his defense, and will in all probability be tried, convicted and executed. There has been an awful mistake made by these people, and howsoever sure they may feel and regardless of what may be said to the contrary from Opelousas, we know that a mistake has been made. So let us insist Governor that you do not honor his requisition until first giving us a chance to go before you and show you what we have.
William Cantwell Walters' Defense File© #16

Support for Cantwell began pouring into Columbia from south Mississippi's merchants, farmers, and preachers. Twelve affidavits from his friends and family in North Carolina arrived, all containing the same basic message.

I saw W. C. Walters with the Boy name Bruce Anderson Several times and he told me he was going to take him off with him. Also Julia the boy's mother told me she had given the boy to Mr. Walters I Saw Julia Anderson with a letter from W. C. Walters Wrote in Mississippi Feb 1913 stating that Bruce was getting along Well and they had a nice time at Xmas also he sent Julia the boy's Picture

John Edwards
Sworne to before me this 28th day of April 1913
J R Lawson JP
William Cantwell Walters' Defense File© #18

Six individuals from Georgia, including Cantwell's friend and mentor, Professor David Bledsoe, verified that the man and Bruce were in Iron City during the first days of May 1912.

Governor Brewer wrote to Tom and Hollis.

April 29, 1913

Gentlemen:

This matter has certainly had me up in the air. The people at Opelousas strongly insist that the child is the Dunbar child, and they have written, wired and phoned me that the child was recognized by his playmates and the citizens there immediately on his return. I am also in receipt of letters from Georgia stating that Walters left North Carolina in 1912 with a child corresponding in age to this one, and insisting that the child taken by the Dunbars is not their child.

I am anxious to have all the proof of this matter presented as soon as possible, because the requisition should be either turned down outright, or honored. If you could get your proof together and fix some day for a habeas corpus hearing, giving the Louisiana people an opportunity to bring such evidence as they may have, the matter could be disposed of in that way by a Chancellor, and I would not be put to the necessity of acting as Judge and jury, and pass on evidence. What do you think of this?

In no event do I wish Walters turned aloose without my knowing it, because I have assured the Louisiana authorities that he would be held until the matter was sifted to the very bottom.

Yours truly,
Earl Brewer
Governor

William Cantwell Walters' Defense File© #32

As Brewer composed his letter on official stationary at the Governor's Mansion, one hundred miles to the south Joseph Galloway sat down in his modest kitchen and penciled a letter on two small sheets of lined note paper. He mailed it to the Columbia Marshall.

4/29/1913

Mr. Tom ford,

Sir I see in the pappers wheare they hav a man in gail charge with Kindnapping a Little boy the papper say the Father of the child said he lost his boy on the 23 of aug—this man & boy was at my place some whear about the 15 of July Now as I am a Negro you know what I say want do hin any good so I am just telling you so you want help mob him I will advise you to be very perttickler in the matter I feel that you would not to him harm if you knew better

Now this is a special notice to you If it don't consern me you know as I am who I am but if the suppose father of the child Lost his on the above date you hav the wrong man

Your servant as ever
Joseph Galloway
Odile, Miss

William Cantwell Walter's Defense File© # 31

The *Daily Picayune* out of New Orleans printed a malicious version of Galloway's letter.

I is ritin you dis leter to inform you dat dis man you is got in jail stayed at my house last July an dey is got de rong man, and fur de Lawd's sake don't let dem folds mob him, cause he is sho'not guilty.

Daily Picayune-May 1, 1913

Cantwell's older sister, Iredell, sent her affidavit to his lawyers.

Georgia, Dodge County.

Personally before the undersigned comes Mrs. Iradell Williamson, who on being sworn, deposes and says that she is a sister of W. C. Walters, and was raised in North Carolina, near Barnesville, but has lived in Georgia for the past twenty years.

Deponent further swears that during the month of July as stated, she had occasion to dress the said child for the said Anderson women while she was engaged in other work about the house, and in doing so, had occasion to note closely the person of said child. Deponent swears that the child was an exceptionally bright baby, fair, blue eyes, light hair slightly inclined to curl, cow-lick, rather small ears, slightly slue-foot-ed, and with the two small toes on the left foot grown together, and birth-mark on back of neck at root of hair.

Deponent further swears that she went again to the old home to visit her parents during the month of May, 1911, and that the same child was there and had grown into an attractive child, and that she, at the suggestion of the said Julia Anderson came very near adopting the child.

Deponent further swears that on the fourth day of April 1912, the said W. C. Walters, whom she had not seen in fifteen years, drove up to the home of deponent in Eastman, Ga., in a wagon, and had this same child with him. Deponent swears that the said W. C. Walters staid at or near Eastman for a period of three weeks, during which deponent kept the child, while Walters was driving around the County tinkering on machinery, watches, clocks, guns, etc., and that this was the same child as seen at the home of deponents father in North Carolina.

Deponent swears that the same marks were on the child when brought here as in the old home, and that when here, there were a few freckled across the face of the boy.

Deponent swears that when here during the month of April of last year that he for the greater part of the time called Walters "Ugly Papa", and that he was known and called by the name of Bruce, and that since leaving here deponent has received several letter from the said W. C. Walters, which she now has in her possession, which were written in the months of June and September, and later, and that in each of the said letters Walters mentions Bruce, and sends some word to deponent from Bruce.

Iradell Williamson

William Cantwell Walters Defense File© #33

After Marshall Ford received Joseph Galloway's letter he contacted Pastor G. W. Holcomb of Carriere, Mississippi, on Cantwell's behalf and received a reply three days later confirming Cantwell's earlier itinerary.

Dear Sir,

On the 4th Sunday in August 12, Mr. Walters was at Whitesand Church having just repaired the church organ…he had a little boy with him all the while…

It seems to be a tangl indeed.

Yours very truly,
G. W. Holcomb

William Cantwell Walters' Defense File© #34 & 87

The attorneys began replying to their stacks of letters supporting their client, thanking each one for information and requesting financial aid for the prisoner.

Chapter Seven
Julia

As the Dunbars were enjoying their celebrations in Opelousas, in North Carolina Julia Anderson's friend William Murray, the mail carrier from a neighboring community, handed her a forwarded letter incorrectly addressed to her former residence at the Walters' home. "City of Columbia, Columbia, Mississippi" was stamped in the upper left corner. As she sat down to read, she felt a sinking in her stomach.

April 24, 1913

Dear Madam:-

I write you in the interest of one W. C. Walters, who is now in prison here charged with the kidnapping of a Dunbar child from Opelusa, Louisiana. I am representing him as Attorney.

There was a child stolen from the Dunbar home on the 23ʳᵈ day of last August, and has ever since been missing. On last Sunday Mr. W. C. Walters was arrested here and there was found in his possession and charge a little boy about the same age of the Dunbar child, and evidently very much resembling the Dunbar child. Mr. Walters and the child were held until Mr. & Mrs. Dunbar could get here from Louisiana, and they claimed the child as being their own. Mr. Walters is charged with having kidnapped this child, which charge is pending against him both in Mississippi and Louisiana, and in the State of Louisiana kidnapping is a hanging crime, so you can see just how critical the situation is with Mr. Walters.

The image of Cantwell dancing beneath a noose caused Julia's stomach to heave, sending a warning burst of saliva into her mouth. She made it to a nearby bush in an effort at modesty.

Mr. Walters tells me that you are the mother of this child that was taken from him and claimed by the Dunbars. He tells me that his name is Bruce, and that you gave the child to him last December was a year ago, and that he left North Carolina last February was a year ago.

Julia remembered the day they left as if it were yesterday. The weather had turned out warmer than expected and the last bit of rain had moved on. She had prepared for this day, reminding herself to be grateful for it. She made Cantwell watch and learn as she filled a satchel with Bruce's assortment of clothing: numerous pairs of hand-me-down knickers and thick stockings, a wool jacket and cap that tied under the chin, two pair of knitted mittens, and several white middy shirts and gowns she had sewn. Cantwell showed up with a new pair of boots for his charge. The latest hand-me-downs were just too large. Julia sent an overstuffed floor cushion to soften the boy's journey and remind him of home. At the last second, Bruce grabbed a few precious items he couldn't do without and brushed her cheek goodbye. She grabbed the impatient child by the arm and scooped him up into an immense hug. "Your Mama loves you! Don't ever forget that."

Bruce smiled and smacked her on the lips. "I won't forget, Mama!"

In order that I may clear up this mystery I certainly want and certainly need your assistance. I want you to write me in answer to this letter whether or not Mr. Walter's statement about this child is true. Is it your child? If it is your child, how old is the child? When did you give it to Mr. Walters and when did he leave North Carolina with it? If it becomes necessary, and if Mr. Walters must be tried for his life on this charge, can you arrange in any way to come here in his behalf as a witness, if this is your child?

Mr. Walters tells me that he sent you a picture of little Bruce not long ago. I want you immediately upon receipt of this letter to go before a Magistrate (Justice of the Peace or Notary Public) show him the picture and make an affidavit to the effect that it is the picture of your child, Bruce, and that the same was forwarded to you by Mr. Walters from this State. If you have any letters from Mr. Walters in which he wrote you about little Bruce, I want you to kindly mail these letters to me. Remember that I need all the help that you can give me for this unfortunate man. As his lawyer I believe him innocent. I believe the Dunbars are mistaken and wrong in their identification of this child.

Julia suddenly bolted inside to retrieve a pan of biscuits from the oven. She returned in a moment, still obviously stunned.

Remember now Mrs. Anderson that this is indeed of much importance to Mr. Walters, and do not fail to let me hear from you by return mail, and if the little boy Bruce brought to this Country is your child say so to me in your letter. Make affidavit to that effect before some officer. Send me the affidavit and the picture which you have, and let the affidavit say that the picture which you inclose me is the picture of your child Bruce. Give me also date of birth, and tell me in a way as much as you can about the history of the child. This I will treat in strictest of confidence.

Hoping that you will feel kindly enough disposed toward Mr. Walters to give me the information which I am asking you for, and giving you the assurance that I am sincere in my efforts as a lawyer to establish his innocence. I hope to hear from you soon, and beg to remain,

Yours very truly,
T. S. Dale
William Cantwell Walters' Defense File© #12

It took twenty-nine-year-old Julia several minutes for this catastrophic news to sink in. As the daughter of struggling dirt farmers with little to show for a life of hard work and disappointment, she had seen her life turning around; but this letter brought her hurtling back to reality.

At seventeen she had married Elisha Floyd who had tried to end her life with a bullet on their wedding night. They separated after five months with Julia pregnant, but she lost the fetus to miscarriage. In January of 1908, at twenty-four years old, Julia fell for a traveling shoe salesman, Jim Cowan, whom she had met while cleaning and cooking in the logging camps and hotels along the lower end of the Lumber River. Julia was not divorced from Floyd, and the gossip sent her searching elsewhere for work. She found it as the live-in domestic for Cantwell's elderly and infirmed parents, Alice and James Pleasant Walters.

Julia was well-known as an excellent nursemaid and had a knack for sewing which she had learned from her mother, but she also had the stamina to work in the fields or turn an aging body four times a day. Though none of the elder Walters would have ever admitted it,

Julia was the good-natured sergeant of the household, keeping them all clean and fed.

The young woman soon became enamored with D. B. (Bunt) Walters, one of Cantwell's brothers. When it became evident that Julia was pregnant, the brother promptly left town to avoid the law after confiding to Cantwell that the baby was his. Julia's affair with Jim Cowan might have explained the pregnancy except the months did not quite add up correctly.

When Julia gave birth to her son, Bruce Anderson, in December of 1908, the Walters' household, excluding Cantwell and Bunt, believed the baby was Cowan's. They and the public looked on the still-married woman as tainted. Despite the stigma, the elder Walters allowed her and the baby to remain at their home, not knowing Bruce was their grandchild. Julia held out hope for D. B. to return. And he did eventually.

Bunt and Julia reunited and she became pregnant again. And again he fled the scene. When Bruce was around two years old, Julia gave birth to a little girl that she named Bernice Anderson. Whether the elder Walters knew she was Bunt's child is unknown, but they surely suspected.

Two years later the authorities investigated Julia after word got out that she had delivered a still-born baby by this same man. Her relationship with Bunt was considered open and notorious cohabitation. Bunt skipped town to avoid prosecution, and Julia and the children were taken to jail. She was accused by Cantwell's brother, Frank, a troublesome and feisty man who blamed Julia for Bunt's departure, of murdering the baby. Its tiny body was exhumed. When tests confirmed that the baby had died of natural causes, Julia and the children were released.

Amid the scandal that followed, Julia was pressured to find a suitable home for Bernice. A couple in neighboring Chadbourn wanted to adopt a daughter, and she made the heart-wrenching decision to give Bernice a fresh start.

Shortly afterwards, in November of 1911, Cantwell returned to Barnesville, North Carolina. Like Julia, he had suffered his share of heartache, having lost much of his life's savings and his family as well. And like Julia, he had picked himself up and forged ahead. He ruffled a few feathers on his return home when he left home one morning with one of two loads of seed cotton. He used the load to stave off the creditors wanting to take the farm, but the other family members had personal plans to spend the windfall.

Cantwell and Bruce became instant companions. The man gently encouraged the shy little boy and began working to correct a speech impediment that plagued him. Bruce was soon riding throughout the settlement with the man as he went about his business.

The rosy-cheeked, blond-haired boy began calling Cantwell "Papa;" and when the man jokingly replied that he was too ugly to be his papa, the child promptly renamed him "Ugly Papa," and the name stuck.

Julia marveled at the transformation in her son. Instead of shrinking back shyly, he stood proudly at mealtimes and offered the blessing as the older gentleman had taught him. He memorized his ABC's and so far had learned to count to thirty. Where he was prone to balk at his mother's direction or scolding, he thrived under Cantwell's discipline. Like Julia, Cantwell held high hopes for the boy's upbringing.

By mid-February, Cantwell's work in the area was complete and he began planning his departure. He would leave at the end of the month in his buggy heading for Georgia and the home of his sister. After three months of constant companionship, he asked Julia for permission to carry Bruce with him, and the child begged to go.

They would work their way down to Iradell's house over five or six weeks, lodging in boarding houses, hotels, or with friends and then stay with her and her husband, Milton, for a month in April. Iradell could take Bruce back home in May if he or his mother was unhappy. If things went well, they would continue working on into Alabama and Mississippi.

Now, fourteen months later Julia learned that Cantwell was locked up and Bruce had been kidnapped. The last letter she had received from them was just after Christmas, but there was no picture with it as Mr. Dale had stated. Cantwell's letter said they were getting along fine, but she found it strange that he asked her for Bruce's birth date again. Cantwell knew the date well.

William Murray reached out to touch Julia's arm. "There is more you need to know. Yesterday I received an inquiry from the *New Orleans Daily States* directed to Cantwell's parents. It described the trouble Cantwell was experiencing and asked for any information they could share to help clear up the mystery."

He continued, "When I delivered the message, the Walters produced the last letter they received from Cantwell, along with a note and a picture for you which they hadn't gotten around to forwarding. Julia," he spoke solemnly, averting his eyes, "they asked me to send the items straight on to the paper, and so I went to the justice of the peace and swore out an affidavit and mailed the documents that afternoon. The problem is, this morning I delivered a letter to the Walters, very similar to yours from T. S. Dale. Cantwell's attorneys requested the same letters and picture that I had sent to the *States* yesterday. I'm so sorry," he paused. "I sent them to the wrong person."

Murray and Julia hurriedly organized what little information they had and left for the post office, where a justice of the peace made out her affidavit.

That same afternoon Julia received an urgent telegram from the *Item* offering her one train ticket to come to Louisiana and view the child taken from the tinker, the child the Dunbars claimed as their own. The telegram hinted that Cantwell had lost her son and kidnapped Bobby as a replacement. F.M. Stephens, Cantwell's nephew and the postmaster in nearby Boardman, along with Cantwell's sister Synthelia, bolstered Julia for the journey. "Don't be afraid. You get down there and straighten things out for Cant." They saw her as a contributor to the controversy. The newspaper had made all the arrangements, including a chaperone, James Edmunds, who would intercept her in Alabama; and they would cover her expenses there and back, but she must leave at once. Without hesitation the woman left, alone, on the next train.

The *Item* warned her of the danger she faced in coming to Louisiana and instructed her to maintain a low profile until she was met by their representative. If their suspicions were correct, they were sitting on top of a phenomenal story, and they didn't want the *States* or the *Times* to scoop their witness.

Despite their efforts, rumors emerged that the "other mother" was coming to claim her son, and scouts were contacted along the route to watch for her. From North Carolina to Louisiana, they scuttled up and down the length of every southbound train in hopes of securing an interview or photo with the woman.

When Percy learned that Julia was on her way to Opelousas for a clandestine viewing of the child, courtesy of the *Item,* he was infuriated and conferred with his attorneys, John Lewis and E. P. Veazie. Lewis stated that they must permit the woman to see Bobby, but it would be on their terms and under their direction. He and Veazie arranged the details.

"The boy will only be taken away over my dead body!" Percy answered unequivocally. He cancelled all outings for the town's favorite son, keeping him sequestered inside the house or backyard.

James Edmunds and another *Item* associate joined Julia and assumed control of the woman. "Madam, we are here to assure you that the paper will protect your every interest, but you must realize that you will experience fierce animosity in Opelousas." Tucked away inside a private compartment, they interviewed her in great detail, quizzing her on her distressing past. Hearing the elaborate descriptions in the Dunbar's identification, Julia found herself momentarily questioning Cantwell. Had he lost Bruce? Her voice rose slightly when she told them the seed cotton story with Cantwell stepping in and making a decision for the household, leaving them fuming for a week. The more riled up Julia got, the more spark the reporters had to add to the story.

"Julia, didn't you want Bruce to be adopted, just like Bernice?"

"No, I just thought Cantwell was going to bring him back sooner," Julia defended.

As they neared New Orleans, a reporter from the *States* caught up with the pair and managed to interview the woman in spite of her chaperone. The *Item* called the following story false, as they claimed to be the only reporters to have interviewed the woman.

BRUCE'S MOTHER TO SEE IF SHE CAN IDENTIFY BOY IN OPELOUSAS; UNAFRAID

Arrives In New Orleans Early This Morning and Stops At Local Hotel—Will Probably Leave for Opelousas Tuesday Night—Insists She Will Know Boy and Is Unafraid.

Julia Anderson, mother of Bruce Anderson, arrived in New Orleans Tuesday morning on her way to Opelousas from her North Carolina home.

Julia Anderson holds the key to the mystery as to whether or not the Dunbars have misidentified the boy taken from W. C. Walters, the stove-mender.

At Opelousas she will be given the opportunity to see the lad that all Opelousas believes to be Robert Dunbar, Jr. She will be asked to pick him out of a score of other children.

She will be given every protection possible.

If the boy recognizes her, the whole mystery will be ended. He did not recognize Mrs. Dunbar when she went to Columbia, Miss., to get him.

If Julia Anderson, whose character is anything but good, identifies the boy, and if the citizens believe she is lying in an attempt to protect her friend, Walters, there is no way of predicting what will happen to the woman. They may, metaphorically, stone her out of town.

But Julia Anderson isn't afraid.

"If it is Bruce who is at Opelousas, I will know him," she said firmly. "I don't care what the people there try to do to me. I will tell the truth. I haven't seen my boy for a little more than a year, but I am positive that I could pick him out from a thousand boys. I hope they do put him among a lot of other children. I would know him anywhere."

Julia Anderson is not a woman of prepossessing appearance. When she descended from the Louisville & Nashville train at Lee Station Tuesday morning, she was heavily veiled and dressed in the clothing of a country woman. Her hands are rough and her face has been cut by the North Carolina winds. Her life has been a rough one, and every hardship that she has suffered has left a mark on a face that once was attractive.

She speaks the language of the country women, and her grammar is not of the best.

But she impresses one as being in earnest, and she is as fearless as any amazon.

She talks about the case readily, but she has little to tell.

"Walters took my boy away in February, 1912," she says. "He said he was going to bring him back soon. He never did."

That is the tenor of nearly all her statements.

"It must be my boy; he can't be any other," she told a reporter. "Walters wouldn't kill my boy, and if Bruce died, Walters wouldn't be afraid to tell me. There was no reason for him to substitute another boy."

"As a matter of fact," the reporter said, "you didn't care much whether Walters took your boy or not, did you?"

Julia Anderson started back, hesitated a moment, then evaded with: "What difference does that make?"

"But you have had three or four other children and you never showed any particular affection for them," the reporter persisted.

Julia Anderson was silent. She began to breathe heavily. She lifted her veil and rubbed her eyes with a hard finger.

"You don't know—" she began, slowly in a low voice. She almost whispered it. "You don't know—it's—I never had a chance—I—"

She choked. Her voice broke and she sobbed; "I want my boy. I want my boy."

She soon recovered and explained; "They're all against me up there. Everybody. Everybody calls me names as I pass by. The children know what I am. They want to arrest me every chance they get—the women abuse me. The men stand by and laugh. The men want—" She stopped suddenly and shook herself like a small boat coming out from under a huge wave. She steadied herself, threw up her chin.

"I'm going to see this boy," she declared stoutly. "Nobody can stop me. And if he's my boy, I'm going to take him away with me. I know my reputation is bad. But—"

A sudden terrifying idea stuck her. She looked about blankly.

"What if it ain't my boy?" she gasped; "What if it isn't Bruce? Where, then, can my boy be?"

"You're not afraid that a mob in Opelousas will attack you?" the reporter asked.

"Attack me?" she seemed surprised at the question. "Why should they attack me?"

"Because the people in Opelousas believe you are going there just to identify the child as yours so as to save Walters."

"I haven't any reason for saving Walters." She thought a moment. "What would the people do to me?"

The reporter replied that he didn't know.

"Let them do anything," she replied fiercely. "I'm going there to tell the truth and if they don't treat me square they'll be sorry. But they will treat me square, won't they? Don't they treat folks square down here? Or don't—oh, I don't know," she said, helplessly. "I don't know. I don't care much what they do."

Julia Anderson says that her boy had hair that was almost white, his eyes were grayish blue, he was 5 years old December 18, 1913, fair complexion, had a cowlick on his forehead and his baby teeth were even. She remembers that he had a mole on one of his legs above the knee, but says there were no marked blemishes on him and that if there were any other moles than the one she located, or any scars, she does not remember them.

In charge of persons who seek to prove that the Dunbars have made a mistake in identifying the boy as their son, the Anderson woman was taken from a Louisville and Nashville train at 6:50 Tuesday morning at Lee Station and brought into New Orleans in an automobile.

She left Chadbourn, a little country town of the Raleigh and Charleston Railroad, Sunday evening. She traveled over the Seaboard Rail Line, via Lumberton, Savannah and Montgomery.

At Lee Station, twenty miles from New Orleans, an automobile was awaiting the arrival of the L. and N. No. 3 from New York, on which a berth had been reserved for the North Carolina woman at Montgomery. The train was stopped and Miss Anderson and her escort boarded the automobile for town.

The Daily States-April 29, 1913

The exhausted woman was taken to a secret location and allowed to rest. Rumors concerning her moral character had arrived in town before she did, but she was resigned to endure another public inquest by the *Item* reporters if it cleared Cantwell and returned Bruce.

The reporters found her surprisingly modest and self-respecting, polite but candid. Julia listened again as Cantwell's supposed sins were listed: kidnapper, child abuser, thief, and possible murderer. She professed, "The Bible guides my life and I vow to tell the truth, no matter who it hurts." The paper's account of the interview predicted that although the woman might be mistaken or deluded, she appeared to be honest.

On Wednesday night, Julia was slipped out of New Orleans under cover of darkness, driven to a secluded spot along the rail line, and placed aboard a secured Pullman car bound for Opelousas. Attorney John Lewis joined Mr. Edmonds and the woman there. Fifty miles south of Opelousas they were spirited off the train and driven the rest of the journey. They arrived around four a.m. on Thursday, May 1, 1913, Julia's 30th birthday.

In a panting red automobile, Julia Anderson, thoroughly tired out, arrived in Opelousas early today. She was so exhausted by her all-night journey that she had to be helped from the car when it drove up to the residence of John W. Lewis, of counsel for the Dunbars.

She was hurried into the house and immediately retired. Crowds of curious persons made their way to the Lewis home, but Mr. Lewis assured them all that he had seen nothing of Julia Anderson and did not

know where she was. Julia slept until 9 o'clock, when she was awak-
ened to talk with the attorneys.

(The reporters present stated that she looked as if she had aged sev-
eral years after her nap.)

The word that she was actually in town spread rapidly over
Opelousas and business immediately was suspended. Crowds gathered
on every street corner.

Wild rumors were circulating, and the town was in a perpetual
state of commotion.

The Daily States-May 1, 1913

The blinds and curtains in the house were tightly drawn to prevent outsiders from witnessing the proceedings. Before Julia was allowed to see Bruce, she was interrogated in a closed back bedroom for several hours by Lewis, Veazie, and Edmonds. From time to time, Mrs. Lewis arrived with a tray of tea and cookies.

Shortly after the men left the room, Julia's head began to throb and she needed to use the rest room down the hall. When the bedroom doorknob wouldn't turn, the skin on the back of her neck began to crawl. Julia knocked twice, "Excuse me!" then instinctively turned toward the window. The room spun as she turned her head. Outside the window thirty to forty men had gathered in the yard whose attention she had just captured. She fell back away from the window.

The woman is almost a nervous wreck. The events of the last few days
have been so different from any she has heretofore experienced that
she is bewildered and now and then makes incoherent statements. She
follows meekly all orders that are given her and sometimes acts as if she
does not know just what she is doing. She is thoroughly worn out and
talks most of the time as if she were in a dream.

Sheriff Swords rushed to the Lewis home upon hearing that the
boy had been taken there. When Mr. Swords ran up on the porch, Mr.
Dunbar stuck out his head, told the sheriff that he couldn't come in, and
slammed the door in his face.

A man would come running down the street to say that Julia had
confessed that she and Walters were in a plot to kidnap the Dunbar
boy. This would be immediately denied by another man who would
assure the crowds that Julia had just identified the boy as hers. This
would immediately start a wrangle, for by this time the group would

be joined by the man who was close to a man who had once worked for the Dunbars and who had stated positively that Julia had been in town for two days and had seen the boy and had said it wasn't hers.

Nobody knew anything for sure, and everybody was guessing everything.

There was considerable feeling against the attorneys who held the woman all morning. Citizens of Opelousas felt that the affair should be settled as soon as possible.

The Daily States-May 1, 1913

A committee of local men, Doctors Charles F. Boagni, J. A. Haas, and J. P. Saizan, along with Mr. Leon Dupre and Henry Estorge, all friends of the family appointed to oversee the test, arrived and were admitted into the home. Two more cars pulled up and their occupants were quickly hustled inside. Julia heard chairs scrapping across the floor and the clinking of dishes. She strained to make out words from the low murmuring voices.

Unknown to Julia, Bruce and three other boys who resembled him were gathered in the dining room. Just before she was brought in, Bruce was removed.

The key turned in the lock, and Julia was escorted into the darkened dining room. As her eyes adjusted, she saw the little boys, each approximately the same size and coloring as Bruce, nibbling bits of cake from the table. The children reacted immediately to her presence, for they were aware that something dreadful was happening. The cake was forgotten as their eyes squeezed closed, each face skewed in fear, and involuntary wails rose from their throats. Around the perimeter of the room, the committee watched in stony silence.

"Bruce? Bruce, are you here? It's Mama!" She stumbled around the room looking back and forth into the faces of each child. The boys averted their eyes and refused to converse with the weeping, pleading stranger. Julia faced the committee. "Could you please turn up the lights?" Then, "My child is not here."

John Lewis erupted with vigorous, loud applause, booming, "She says her son is not here!" The room filled with clapping and cheering as the noisy display spread well out into the yard, across their streets, and was broadcast throughout town. During the commotion the children were removed.

"Wait! Wait!" she begged through her tears. "Where is the boy from the newspaper—the boy taken from Cantwell?" Julia heard her voice becoming shrill and distant as if it belonged to someone else, and she felt herself losing control.

In the meantime, the children's clothes were swapped and the boys, including Bruce, were briefly returned to the frightful gathering. None of them would stop crying and face her except Alonzo who laughed and called her "Old Cockcaw." Julia begged for more time, quiet time to sit with the one boy she couldn't take her eyes off, but she had no influence here. Lewis announced that the test was over, causing the woman's knees to buckle.

At that point, District Judge B. H. Pavy and District Attorney R. Lee Garland arrived and were told by those assembled outside that Miss Anderson had failed to identify the boy. Pavy and Garland had been assured by Lewis that the examination would not start without them.

"For God's sake, John," rumbled Pavy, pounding on the entrance. "Unlock the damn door."

With Julia collapsed in a heap on the floor, the climax of the stirring drama was presented when Lessie rushed into the room and clasped Bruce to her breast. Pale and trembling with emotion, she steadied herself against a little side table and then placed the boy in Julia's lap saying, "Madam, this is *my* child, and *I* am its mother. You have failed to identify him, and he is mine. Mine!" She reached down and snatched the crying boy away.

Julia sobbed, "I haven't seen my Bruce in fifteen months and I need some time to examine him and talk with him quietly before I can be sure. I want to do what is right and fair. Give him back to me! I believe the boy you're holding is my son." In the chaos that ensued, Lessie and the child were rushed out as Julia screamed, "Don't take him away just yet! I want my boy, my Bruce!"

Judge Pavy pacified the woman by telling her that the child was in town and she could see him later if she desired. Julia was ushered from the house and taken to a local hotel.

(Identification Test details are compiled from *The States*, *The Times Democrat*, and *The Item* May 2, 1913)

ONLY CLOSE FRIENDS OF DUNBARS ADMITTED WHEN WOMAN SEES BOY

...the county officials do not like the way the identification was carried on in secret. They are not anxious to prove that the boy is not the Dunbar's. They believe it is the Dunbar boy. But they want the identification to be regular and according to law.

Julia Anderson probably will be arrested as a material witness in the Dunbar case, and will be held in Opelousas under bond until the entire affair is settled.

District Attorney R. Lee Garland, E. P. Vezay and John W. Lewis, attorneys for the Dunbars, decided today that, under the circumstances, they must take immediate steps to get the Anderson woman into their custody. They will not allow her to be taken out of Opelousas except by their consent.

They fear that the persons who brought her here may attempt to take her out of Opelousas and send her back to North Carolina immediately. The Dunbar attorneys are determined that she shall be forced to give her testimony in court and before a jury.

The Daily States-May 1, 1913

Julia was visited at her hotel that afternoon by one of Lessie's sisters, who pleaded with her to give up her claim on the child, which she refused to do.

"This may very well kill my sister, for which you will be responsible. I want you to know that."

Despite being threatened by Garland, Lewis, and Veazie with arrest for perjury, Julia worked up enough courage to demand a second look at the child and was told by Judge Pavy that she would be given a chance early the following morning.

After Good Night's Rest "Other Mother" Undresses Lad and Believes She Has Found Her Son—Dunbar, Tired of All Trouble, Threatens Violence If Attempt Is Made To Take The Child From Him

BY F. S. TISDALE,

Staff Correspondent The Daily States.

OPELOUSAS, LA., May 2. Julia Anderson today announced that she believes the boy now in the possession of Mr. and Mrs. C. P. Dunbar is her son, Bruce Anderson.

She undressed the lad this morning in the office of Dr. John A. Haas, one of the Dunbar family physicians, and, after examining the lad, turned to the dozen men who were around her and declared:

"Gentlemen, I believe from the bottom of my heart this this is my child."

The boy gave no sign of having recognized her.

Julia Anderson had objected that the test made Saturday in John W. Lewis' home was too severe and not fair to her. R. Lee Garland, the district attorney, saw that today's trial was made under her own conditions.

It was only after a long examination of the boy that Julia Anderson drew herself up, looked squarely into the eyes of the grim circle of men about her, and said with deliberate emphasis that she believed she had found Bruce Anderson.

She could not say, when the prosecutor asked her, that she had found one mark on the boy's body to bear her out. She simply believed that he was Bruce Anderson, instead of Robert Dunbar, Jr.

After a good night's rest, Julia Anderson was feeling more like a normal woman this morning.

Immediately after breakfast she left the Florence Hotel with Mr. Garland and Judge B. H. Pavy. Without the boy seeing them, they went into the garage of Dr. John Haas.

The garage has a window that opens on the Dunbar lawn. It is screened by a little hedge of rose bushes. The woman took a chair to the window and sat, leaning her face on her hand, as they brought the unsuspecting Robert in the front yard.

It took a banana, Alonzo and Billy, the goat, to keep him there. Robert was humming a little tune. He busied himself with his favorite pastime of making the goat's life miserable. He alternated between pushing the four-legged unfortunate and dragging him about by his rope. It is a very durable goat.

And Julia Anderson watched as the little unsuspecting mystery played in his clean, white rompers.

In the garage with her were Dr. Haas, Mr. Garland, Judge Pavy, newspaper men and other witnesses.

Mrs. Dunbar, with a white, pinched face, watched from her porch. Mr. Dunbar watched the boy with a steady eye from the front gate. As he watched, he whittled a piece of shingle. It is a habit that he has when anything worries him.

Julia Anderson followed the boy with her eyes. A little gesture he made deepened the pathetic lines about her trembling lips. No one said anything. For minutes she gazed out through the little blind of rose bushes.

Then Alonzo butted in. He was playing near the fence, and a cough from the garage called his eyes to the faces in the window.

"Hello!" yelled Alonzo, running up to the fence.

Julia Anderson looked down in the smiling face of the little boy and tried to smile back.

It was a cheerless smile, and one that brought her plain linen handkerchief to her eyes. She turned from the window.

"Bring him in here," she said in a low tone. "I want to undress him."

"Which one?" asked Garland, watching her keenly.

"The one with the goat."

The one with the goat was Robert.

Mr. Dunbar nodded his head, and Harold Fox lifted the complacent Robert and his banana to his shoulder. It was a good thing that Robert happened to be in good humor. If Robert's temper had been working it would have taken the whole neighborhood to carry him into Dr. Haas' office.

Robert got in first and Julia Anderson, by another door, came around in front of him. She stretched up her hands to where the boy perched on Mr. Fox's shoulder.

"Come to my arms," she pleaded. "Won't you come to me?"

But Robert stuck both of his hands behind him and buried his face in Mr. Fox's shoulder. The woman bit her lip to keep back her tears.

"Come," she said, "take him into the doctor's private office. I want to take his clothes off."

Mr. Fox carried the boy into the next room. The same silent jury went with them. Mr. Dunbar stood in the doorway.

Julia Anderson put her big hands up and began deftly to un-button the white rompers. The prospect of being disrobed before all these people horrified Robert. Again he tried to hide himself in Mr. Fox's shoulder.

"Stop 'em," he said in a loud whisper. "Don't let 'em take off clothes before all these men."

"There, there, darlin'," the big woman soothed and Robert sub-mitted as she unbuttoned his union suit and exposed half of his fat, clean little body.

With nervous fingers she held back his clothes and looked at his left hip. She said her boy had a mole there. Without comment, she pulled off his shoes and stockings.

"How about the scar on the toe?" someone asked.

"That is my boy's foot. I haven't seen him for months. He could have got lots of scars in that time."

Robert is somewhat puzzled to know why his toes are of such engrossing interest. He leaned over and watched them with the rest. He even wriggled them a bit to add variety to the occasion.

Finally Julia Anderson stood up with her hands on her hips. One of them held a little white silk stocking. They could see by her face that something big was coming.

"Gentlemen," she said, shaking her head to emphasize every syllable. "I believe from the bottom of my heart that this is my child."

There was silence for one half second.

"What proof have you found?" asked Mr. Garland at last. "Did you find any marks?"

"No."

"Then what makes you think he is yours?"

"By his general features (which she described) and his actions."

Mr. Dunbar, standing in the door, cleared his throat and every eye was on him when he spoke.

"How about the mole behind the ear?" he asked.

"I did not look for that. I didn't know about it."

After this she tried to get the boy's recognition by calling him "Bruce." He made no sign of remembering the name. They let Julia Anderson go then. She left for New Orleans on the Southern Pacific's 9:20 train.

"It is my boy," Mrs. Dunbar said as she leaned against the rail of the porch. "I could never let him go. I don't care what Julia Anderson says.

Mr. Dunbar whittled a stick. There was a sinister light in his eyes.

"Somebody," said he, "is going to get their head shot off if this doesn't stop. It is Robert. We will keep him."

With the same plaintive monotone she used in questioning the boy, Julia Anderson talked about it all afterwards.

"I've lost children in death," she said, "but there never was a pain that hurt my heart like this. I believe he is my boy. I could never have left without giving him a fair examination.

"He didn't recognize me. No. He didn't recognize the Dunbars, either."

When asked whether she would take steps to gain possession of the child she believed is her own, Julia Anderson said;

"I can't say yet because I don't know. I'm going to let the Lord guide me in this as He has all along. I will do what He tells me."

As Julia Anderson got out of the carriage at the Opelousas station, several women of the town did a very graceful thing, they broke the ostracism to which she has been subjected and introduced themselves and talked with her. Their names should be remembered but they would not give them.

The Daily States

Assured that Bruce was in no immediate danger, Julia managed to remain calm and leave for New Orleans before she found herself arrested. The woman had become a pariah to her handlers from the *Item*. They openly mocked her imperfect speech and simple manner of dress, insinuating that she was ignorant and opportunistic. One claimed, "Of true mother love, she has none."

Because her train out of New Orleans would not depart until the following evening, the *Item* arranged a sightseeing tour of the city to keep Julia busy and prevent Tom and Hollis from locating her. Afterward, the reporters accused Julia of being so dazzled by the big city that she forgot about her child. She begged to be rerouted through Columbia on her way home, but the request was refused. The mood in Columbia was grim as the attorneys tried to ascertain what had occurred in Opelousas.

Amid the growing deluge of hatred that was spreading across Louisiana, a few brave souls dared to express their doubts about the identity of the child. A Louisiana citizen using the moniker "A Wellwisher," wrote to Governor Brewer stating that many people in Opelousas doubted that the child was Bobby.

Gov. Earl Brewer,

It is certainly a relief in these times when people are so easily influenced by popular prejudice to find one man who can stand aloof, clear sighted, view the situation and do his duty as you have done in this exciting Dunbar case.

We want to congratulate you. You who have won the admiration of all clear headed people. Not one-half the population in Opelousas believes the child to be the missing boy, particularly the women who knew him best, his mother's best friends, those who lived in the neighborhood, who saw him daily play with their children. Ladies are certainly the closest observers. The great trouble is, so many say if they think it is their child, let them have it.

I don't believe it lies in their power to give Walters a fair trial and you have acted wrongly in holding him. Twenty-five people told me there was not one trace of resemblance, but they believed he was Robert. They can't understand it. We only want justice and congratulate you on your noble stand.

A Wellwisher

The Daily States-April 30, 1913

Following Julia's assertion that the child was hers, a cousin of Bobby's, Edwin T. Bercier, was interviewed by the *Times*.

"There's no question as to the child held by the Dunbars being their own Bobbie," Bercier continued, "for he has asserted traits noticed before he was kidnaped. One that the reporters overlooked is that of his aquatic bent. Before Bobbie was kidnaped he used to come every afternoon and play and scare the gold fish in the fountain by the courthouse in Opelousas. Consequently he got wet every afternoon; he invariably fell in and was as invariably fished out by Charles Chachere, a deputy sheriff, who got so used to fishing him out of the shallow water and

taking him home that it grew to be a habit and part of his duty. He used to wait every afternoon until after Bobbie had fallen in before closing his office.

"No sooner was Bobbie back in Opelousas, and away from the throng that minutely watched him, so the deputy sheriff told me a day or so ago when he was in New Orleans, than he made for his old playground — and fell in as usual. Coincident with the procedure, the deputy sheriff was sitting in the window and saw the accident as of old. And as of old, he sauntered out, fished Bobbie out, and took him home, just as it were but the day before that he had gone through the usual course.

"Chachere of course grew to love the child and remembers him well. There is not a doubt in his mind that the child is Bobbie; for aside from the fountain escapades, the child talked to him of things that took place before he was kidnaped. He also asked about the gold fish in the fountain. He fell in on arrival the other day and didn't have time to see the frightened little creatures before he was fished out of the agitated waters in which they had quickly scurried to shelter under part of the fountain. The deputy sheriff promised to bring him some time when he had dry clothes on and let him see them again.

"My mother, Mrs. A. J. Bercier, who is in Opelousas, my home town, is positive that the child is Bobbie, and she has been ever since its return," he concluded.

The Times-May 2, 1913

Hollis sent a letter to Brewer after Julia's trip to Opelousas, asking for his patience.

May 2, 1913

Dear Governor:

There are so many contradictory statements as to how the identification occurred, until no one can be sure as to what really transpired, they only claim that the Anderson woman could not identify the child. However, all of the accounts agree that no one was present at this meeting but Mr. & Mrs. Dunbar, the Dunbar lawyers and Julia Anderson. As to what she said or done we have to rely entirely upon their statement, and we submit that this in no sense was a fair test; that the same consideration was not given her as that given to Mrs. Dunbar when she was in Columbia, as she spent practically a day and night with the child here, alone and to herself, before she reached her decision.

The representative of the Daily States has just called us and advised that Julia Anderson has given a statement to the public in which she says that she saw her child and that it was hers beyond question and beyond mistake.

We are asking the Dunbars if they will permit Mr. & Mrs. Jeptha Bilbo and Mr. & Mrs. Goleman, of Pearl River County, Mississippi, to inspect the child if we will bring these parties to Opelousas. We will bear the expenses of this trip, and one member of our firm will accompany them to Opelousas.

We are relying upon your promise to give us a hearing before you in Jackson before taking up again the granting of this requisition. If possible, we would like to start tomorrow for Opelusas, and earnestly insist that in no event requisition be granted until we can have these Pearl River County people inspect this child in Poplarville, or in Opelousas.

For your continued fairness and broad-minded actions in this case, we desire to extend to you the heartfelt appreciation of the old man in jail, as well as our own thanks.

Yours very truly,
DALE & RAWLS
William Cantwell Walters' Defense File© #41

A. J. McMullen, a reporter from the *States* who was sympathetic to Cantwell, was stationed in Columbia to intercept Julia. He wrote the following letter to Cantwell's lawyers.

Mr Dale,

Late tonight I was instructed by phone to come in on the 4.45 a.m. train tomorrow. They do not think Julia is on her way here and in consequence there is no further need of my remaining for the present.

Send a bill to The States for the spin today and also for a New Orleans phone call. I went to the Central office to put this call in and pay on this end. I could not get our editor then and told the girl to call me at your office.

I am leaving a copy of the story for Monday. It reads convincingly. I think, Mr Ross told me over the phone that they did not run my introduction today as they were afraid someone would accuse us of undue prejudice. He was glad to know I was impressed.

Say 'au revoir' to Mr Rawls for me. I enjoyed my stay here immensely and I will be back for the trial. Keep me Posted on our plans and I will help you from our end. Scoops would be doubly appreciated.

Thanking you for your kindness,
(Will leave Mr R's keys at hotel.) Truly,
J. McMullen

William Cantwell Walters' Defense File© #44

This *States* reporter uncovered several inconsistencies in the Dunbar's story. He mailed an interesting article to Tom and Hollis.

REAL DUNBAR CHILD DROWNED

As the kidnapped child of Mr. and Mrs. C. P. Dunbar, of Opelousas, La., has been the chief topic of interest in both Louisiana and Mississippi for several weeks past, the following letter received by a prominent Lexington lady from a friend at Opelousas will prove of particular interest at this time. The almost unanimous opinion of the people of Lexington has been that the child in question was really the Dunbar child, the mother, father and family physician having positively declared him to be. Julia Anderson's equally positive averment that the boy is her own child renders the settlement of the case a most difficult one and will require the judgment of a Solomon. Following is the letter:

'Opelousas, La., May 5, 1913.

My Very Dear Friend: I was overjoyed this morning when your letter was handed me, and in compliance with your request, hasten to reply.

This Dunbar case is indeed a mystery. While I cannot understand how the mother could not identify her own child, at first sight, I think that she really and truly believes that the child is hers. I could never have been so conservative.

She claims, that she would not say he was hers, when she first saw him, because her husband had warned her that the people would lynch the kidnapper. Such may be true, but it is hard to believe.

For my part, I see no resemblance whatever between the two children, except in badness. The features of this child are absolutely different to what I remember of the lost child.

I did not see the real Dunbar boy very often, for, while I have known the mother since she was a child, we rarely visited. She came to my house with her boy just one week before he was lost. On that occasion he was simply outrageous, and since I have seen this child, he also is outrageous. Apart from that, I see nothing in common; even the eyes are different-color and shape.

Honestly, I do not think this is the same child, but as I say, a mother should know her child.

She claims that she could identify him by a burnt toe, or rather deformed nail, caused by a burn.

The child seems to have no recollection whatever of his life in Opelousas; never mentions anything of his past; and when any questions are asked regarding the old man who stole him he fights and screams like he is wild.

I saw his mother attempt to dress him one afternoon, about a week ago, and he fought her like a tiger.

She told me with her own lips that he gave no sign whatever of recognizing any of the family, and never mentions one word of his past life. If you ask him a question, his lips are sealed.

A cousin of his father, a Mrs. Dunbar, from New Orleans, came in while I was at the Dunbar home. She never knew the child until he was brought from Mississippi to her home in New Orleans, but it appears she is the only one he will have anything to do with. On this occasion, he was screaming and fighting his mother. When she came in, he jumped up, rushed to her, crying: "There is my 'Dramma,' and I am going home with her, too." Immediately, he ran to the dresser drawer, began pulling out his clothes and piled them in my daughter's lap. That was the only time he smiled the whole hour that we were there.

In my heart, I really believe that child was drowned-the real Dunbar child-but, as I say, the mother should know her child better that I.

Public opinion here is somewhat divided. A great many think as I do.

I send you today a copy of the New Orleans States. The account in there is pretty true.

Do write me again real soon, and tell me something about the opinion of the Mississippi people regarding this Dunbar case. What do you think of it?

With much love and good wishes, as ever,

Devotedly yours,
M'
Lexington Advertiser.

The Lexington Advertiser &
William Cantwell Walters' Defense File© #47

The letter was attributed to Douce Mornhingveg, a friend of Lessie's. Other individuals refused to be swayed by public sentiment. Dr. A. J. Strange, of Opelousas, sent the men an account of the day Bobby was lost in the swamp.

Independence LA
Tangipahoa Ph. 5/3/13
Messrs Dale and Rawls
Columbia, Miss.,

Gentlemen:

In a few words I wish to say and give reasons that "Walters the man in jail is as innocent as the day is long."-

Reasons, I am originally from St. Landry and practiced medicine in Section that child was lost for over Ten Years and I know every foot of that section and the day that the child was lost I was one of the party that was on the scene a few hours later and helped to made a due & diligent search and taking everything into consideration myself as well as a good many of prominent citizens of St Landry amongst whom were some of the Parish officials and our deductions were that the child is in the bottom of Swayze Lake.-

If I had the time granted I could have a map made of that section and show any disinterested or fair minded person that its nothing but a swamp and chain of lakes and a physical impossibility for a man to get through without a great loss of time and being seen.-

Further I can take The Crowd that was on the Lake that day and get some of your officials and I will at a moment's notice and bring them on the spot and show them that the child was no doubt drowned in the lake and for a person to steal in must have been on the inside or else it could not have been done by an outsider without being seen and caught as his avenues of escape were limited and people would have certainly seen him unless he went straight up and landed in Mississippi between the suns.-

If you will pardon length I will attach a rough sketch and try to explain a few things.- **(See map p. 285)**

The Party of Dunbar & Co when going for their outing stopped at letter B and walked out to G where the camp was.= the trail on both sides is full of undergrowth, briers & C. at letter G. Mr. Mizzi was shooting garfish and little Robbie got where he was and he ran him back & told to go in house and in about 5 minutes dinner was announced and as party assembled around table Bobbie was missing and an immediate search was made and they started on another trail going north a short distance and not finding any trace they started back south and you will see at letter A they found a little barefooted tract characteristic of his foot and more particularly his left toe and they traced said tracts clear to main line of O. G. & south of it about 10 yds on a spur thence westerly for about 40 yds there northerly back to main line and the question arises which way did he go E or W.= If he would have gone West section crew would have seen him a couple of miles which was at letter H. and if he went East he would have fallen in the Lake as he would have to cross a long tressle.-

We got a Dog that was supposed to be O. K. that twice took up those steps & followed it to the lake & bayed & bayed & there is no doubt in my mind that he is there all newspaper talk & everything else notwithstanding.-

The papers have said a whole lot pro & con on the situation and the more they say the worse it seems but if a party of Reliable & level headed men will go over the scene and get a few that was out there that they will form the same opinions as its impossible to steal a child and only have a 15 minute start and get through that country and make his escape unless he does as I said before.-

The child only had a few minutes start and could have easily made it to the R. R. which was about ½ mile from the camp & went down in lake.-

I am not after any notoriety and don't want to get this into any newspaper but I would like to see a party made up and I'll head it and go over the ground with you or any representative of the Governor and have a map made and will go a longer way to clear up than reading newspapers.

Hoping I am not taking too much of your time and give this your careful thought and keep that man in Miss and also keep this out of the paper till you can verify my statements and link it with balance of your testimony.

Yours at your service for Justice
A. J. Strange M. D.–
Lately of Opelousas La

William Cantwell Walters' Defense File© #42

Julia returned to North Carolina with a newspaper photo of the child the Dunbars claimed was Bobby.

Boardman N. C.
May 7—13
Dale, Henington & Rawls

Dere Ser

I just Returned from La I seen the child and it was mine every Person I have showed the Photo too they Reconized it as soon as I Showed it W. G. Lawson & wife will swere to it evey time I did Pick him out from Dunbar I will close write to me just as soon as you get this

Yores truley
Julia Anderson

William Cantwell Walters' Defense File© #55

Chapter Eight
A Square Deal

For two weeks, Cantwell had been expecting the kidnapping charge to be dropped and Bruce to be returned, along with a sizable and well-earned apology. His patience was rapidly wearing thin. A man of whom it was said would still be "talkin in his coffin," Cantwell passed the time by sharing his plight from his prison window overlooking the courthouse square and bustling riverfront. He prayed fervently and openly for Lessie's sanity. He drew daily crowds, his fragile spectacles resting in place for reading his orations—part Bible study and sermon, part lecture and storytelling, and part concert. The majority of townspeople now supported Cantwell, but the reporters and hecklers, annoyed by his confidence, generally used his enthusiasm to ridicule him or trip him up.

Due to the kindness of the jailor and sheriff, various personal items, most notably the gentleman's harp, were allowed into the tiny cell. His well-worn Bible, when not in his hand, lay open on his cot, ready for edification. The bulk of his and Bruce's possessions were stored nearby.

The attorneys provided Cantwell with the latest newspapers out of New Orleans and Opelousas, along with a writing tablet, pencils, and stamps to keep him in contact with the outside world. A generous ration of chewing tobacco helped soothe his jangled nerves, but the stream of brown spit was distracting. Every other day he was allowed a bath and a razor to shave all but his lengthy mustache. Along one of the walls, a large collage made up of newspaper photos and articles, letters from friends, and numerous lists of names, places, and dates, chronicled the events that had derailed his life.

When word came from Julia affirming his story, he was elated; but that elation was short-lived. The headlines from Louisiana continued to report that the reunited family was gradually returning to normal. Several times a day another revelation reached the eager public. Only two weeks into Bruce's abduction, with a tempting banana just out of reach, he had claimed, "The old man took me from the lake that day. I was on the railroad tracks." However, even with underlying threats and skillful enticing, it took more than a month for Bruce to call Percy "Daddy." Lying, for which he once would have been punished, became the child's best ally, but each of those lies stung Cantwell like an angry hornet. And they kept multiplying.

Cantwell had difficulty getting his statements noticed at all. Like Julia, he was consistently portrayed in the negative, though both were honest, hardworking, and well-liked among their acquaintances.

When Tom and Hollis read McMullen's article "Real Dunbar Child Drowned," they saw an opportunity to get the truth before the public. They offered the reporter an exclusive chance to interview their client. The world would glimpse into the soul of their client.

Tinker Retraces His Wanderings With Boy For Readers Of States

BY ALBERT J. McMULLEN

William Cantwell Walters, alleged kidnaper of Robert Dunbar, Jr., today gave his first authorized newspaper interview. He talked to a reporter for The Daily States and gave in detail the evidence which he expects to use to prove his alibi.

Walters gave names, addresses and dates to prove that he was nowhere near Swayze Lake at the time the boy was kidnaped, and that he had Bruce Anderson with him at the home of Mr. Thigpen, five miles from the White Sand church, near Carriere, Miss., the day Robert Dunbar, Jr., was kidnaped. He remembered the dates by referring to letters and receipts and memoranda of work he did.

When Walters was interrupted today to be given an opportunity to tell his story through The States, he had just laid aside his Bible and was engaged in writing a story of his wanderings that he is preparing for posthumous publication in the event of an untimely end to his declining years.

"Let me tell my story," he began. "I have been misrepresented and misquoted so much that I feel it is the best way."

He paused and then went on, choosing his words carefully. Walters then traced his course down to the day of the alleged kidnaping, giv-

ing names, dates and other corroborative information that has been checked up by his attorneys.

"Never in my life was I west of the Mississippi river after I took Bruce from North Carolina," he declared with vehemence.

Many people talked to me and to little Bruce, who, by the way, was having the time of his life, as he did everywhere.

Walters continued his story to the time he went to the Charity Hospital in New Orleans and left Bruce with the Bilbos. At the hospital, he says, he occupied bed 969, in ward 69, and that Dr. Payne was his doctor.

"While in the hospital," he added, "they found out I could play the zither harp, and they had me play for the patients. I like to play for the children, especially for those who had no one to look after them, for it made me think of little Bruce, whom I love."

"There must be some mistake, God knows that. You know I cannot harness the wheels of evolution, but the boy in Opelousas, no matter what they find, is Bruce Anderson. All will come right, I know, for truth crushed to earth shall rise again."

"How do you feel toward the Dunbars?" he was asked.

"I feel deeply for them, but they are making a great mistake. If Mr. Dunbar would only have listened to me, I know he would have thought differently, but he would not and if the Dunbars send me to my grave, God knows they will be doing a great wrong. They will have lost their Bobbie and I my little Bruce."

Here Walters was shown a photograph of Robert Dunbar taken before he disappeared, and a recent picture of the boy taken from him. He was asked for his opinion.

"Can't they see," he replied, "that there is not one iota of favor to Mr. Dunbar's boy? I don't see the least expression in favor. Look at the hair of the Dunbar child, how it is trained up. I could never get Bruce's hair to stay like that, and I tried to. I always had to part it in the middle.

"I heard that Bruce called Mrs. Dunbar 'mamma.' He would call any lady who was not too old 'mamma,' and if a lady was too old, he would call her grandma. He called me 'Uncle Sam' at first, but lately he called me papa."

All through the interview Walters bore himself like a man who was confident that a mistake had been made and that he would prove it to the community. He is not an illiterate man, nor of the criminal type. He has read a great deal and has a good memory and a keen mind.

He is not given to profanity, and even in the funny stories he de-lights in telling, he does not use language the slightest bit offensive. His concluding remark was: "If they hang me they will hang an innocent man, and God knows I would rather be hanged for a crime I did not commit than for one I did commit."

The States–May 4, 1913

Tom, Hollis, and McMullen spent an entire day driving around Pearl River County, questioning individuals who had contact with Cantwell and Bruce over the last year, especially near the time Bobby disappeared. The majority characterized the man as jovial and light-hearted, an incessant talker who tutored his charge with care if not perfection. They were mutually affectionate with each other, and the boy was quite well-behaved. The older man allowed the mothers of the homes to bathe Bruce along with their own brood, which was customary; and he usually left each home with a child's outgrown jacket, a larger pair of shoes, or some personal knitted items. A few of the better seamstresses created whole outfits for the boy if he and Cantwell were around long enough.

"Did you ever see whip mark across the child's legs or back?"

"No marks, but Bruce did receive the occasional swat on his fanny same as my children, nothing more." Each affirmed that his chubby body was perfectly normal except one or two women mentioned that the two smallest toes on one foot had slightly more webbing between the digits.

Carl Bass, the timber cruiser from around Poplarville, produced his diary, or log book, for the lawyers, showing his daily activities for the entire year of 1912. In July he had documented a visit to the Bilbos' home where he met their two new boarders, Cantwell and Bruce. Bruce was the same child now shown in the newspapers. He later saw them at Whitesand Church on August 25, where Cantwell had just repaired the church organ. Bass, also the church clerk, had noted the repair in his diary; he then hired the man to come to his home and repair his personal organ. They stayed overnight with his family.

Allen Goleman and his wife of Poplarville had also met the pair at the Bilbos' on the same date. On August 26, the man and little boy arrived at the Golemans' house and headquartered there for almost two weeks, during which time Cantwell began constructing another elab-orate harp. Mrs. Goleman and Mrs. Bilbo had each cared for Bruce in their own homes for extended periods of time and would easily be able to recognize him. Goleman and Bass made out affidavits for the lawyers.

Hollis sent a letter to Governor Brewer asking that the Bilbos and the Golemans be permitted to "accompany us either to Opelousas or New Orleans to inspect the child." He went on to say that his request in this regard to Opelousas District Attorney Garland resulted in a telegram stating, "Will arrange for examination of Robert in New Orleans. Can't fix date. Will wire when."

William Cantwell Walters' Defense File© #46

Afterwards, they planned to carry the couples straight to Jackson to meet with Governor Brewer. The trip would cost nearly one hundred and fifty dollars, and Cantwell's witnesses for the most part were hard pressed to pay for their part of the travel and lodging. Cantwell certainly did not have a large amount of cash at his disposal, and the lawyers were working *pro bono*. They had already dipped into their own pockets attempting to free the innocent man, and Hollis had written to Brewer stating, "…we assure you now Governor that if they will consent to this inspection that we will bear the expenses of this trip, and one member of our firm will accompany them to Opelousas."

William Cantwell Walters' Defense File© #41

Cantwell put up his only collateral, one fourth interest, fifty acres, in his family's farm back in North Carolina. He began negotiating to borrow money against the land, estimated by his older brother to be worth one thousand dollars.

Tom Dale walked into his office May 7, 1913, to discover a letter from Stephen McIntyre, R. C. Lawrence & James Proctor of McIntyre, Lawrence, & Proctor—Attorneys at Law, Lumberton, North Carolina.

We understand that you have been retained to defend William C. Walters now in prison in your town upon a criminal charge. At the request of his brother, Mr. R. R. Barnes has agreed to loan him certain money for the purpose of assisting in his defense. We prepared the papers and at his request we forward the same to you so that you may have same executed and returned to us. We therefore enclose the note and mortgage for $325.00. Let Mr. Walters sign the note and also the deed and *let him acknowledge the execution of the mortgage deed before a notary public.*

As soon as these papers are returned to us we will place same on the record and notify Mr. Barnes and he will send you check for the amount.

William Cantwell Walters' Defense File© #48

After various fees were removed, Cantwell and his attorneys received a check for only three hundred dollars, but it gave oil to the engine.

In Opelousas, Lessie and the two boys only ventured out with chaperones in tow, designated to whisk Bruce away if needed. The boy's demeanor could harden into steel one moment and turn to a weeping fearful puddle the next.

As they shopped one day in town, a reporter hung with the crowd following the celebrated mother and her children. "Mrs. Dunbar," he shouted, "could we get a photo of you and the boys?"

"Not just now, thank you."

"Could you just show us his foot? We won't ask for any more of your time, just a quick peek at the scar."

"Sir," she reddened, "I do not have time for that now. He has already been examined numerous times by professionals." She grabbed the children and began to move away.

"Madam," he queried, "what about the Mississippi people who are coming here to examine him?"

Lessie turned to the newspaper man, her eyes narrowing dangerously, "On the advice of my attorneys, there will be *no* further examinations of Bobby!" Her party headed for their car and left in a cloud of dust.

Hollis wrote again to District Attorney Garland concerning this latest rumor.

May. 7. 1913

Dear Sir:

We have, of course, learned long since to pay but little attention to the sensational stories published in the papers regarding the Dunbar-Walters case, but we are advised from many sources that Mrs. Dunbar says that there will be no further inspection of Robert, and this in the light of the promise that we have from you to meet us in New Orleans at an early date for this purpose.

Having failed to hear from you as to the time for this meeting, we thought it well to address you this letter. We are resting, therefore, Mr. Garland absolutely upon your promise to us and to the Governor of our State that this inspection will be allowed in New Orleans. Any day that you see fit to name will meet our convenience, if you will advise us two days in advance of the day designated.

Very respectfully yours,
Dale & Rawls

William Cantwell Walters' Defense File© #54

The next day, Hollis wrote to Governor Brewer.

May 8, 1913

Dear Governor:

We are advised by the New Orleans papers that Mrs. Dunbar and her Attorneys do not propose to permit any further inspection of the boy now in their possession.

We have gone to considerable expense by making a personal visit over the northern portion of Pearl River County rounding up our witnesses and arranging with them to make the trip to New Orleans for the purpose of this inspection, relying exclusively on the promise of Mr. Garland that the child would be brought there for this purpose. We received from him the following telegram;

"Will arrange for examination of Robert in New Orleans. Can't fix date. Will wire when."

We advised Mr. Garland both by telegram and letter that we were ready for the inspection in New Orleans at the earliest possible date, and we do not feel now Governor that they should be permitted to back down and prevent an inspection of the child.

In other words Governor, could you advise them that you expect them to fulfill their promise and permit this inspection, and that the demand for requisition will not be considered by you unless they live up to their agreement solemnly made. We feel that if they refuse to do this they concede the weakness of their case, and that the old man in jail should be exonerated and discharged if they are afraid to let us and our witnesses see the boy. Knowing you as we do, and your well-known reputation for fair play and a square deal, we do not believe that you will permit any such high-handed procedure as this.

We are now in a position Governor to convince them that a mistake has been made, if they will only give us an opportunity. We are now in all things ready Governor and place ourselves absolutely in your hands.

Yours very truly,
Dale & Rawls

William Cantwell Walters' Defense File© #56

Harold Fox, the relative of the Dunbars, and Lee Hawes, the reporter from the *Item*, partnered up in Mississippi as self-appointed investigative agents for the Dunbars and the State of Louisiana. Traveling extensively throughout Mississippi and Louisiana, they pieced together an intricate network of stumbling blocks for Cantwell's alibi and the identification of Bruce. Their methods must have been very persuasive, for they gained reams of misinformation about the pair.

In response to pressure from Mississippi, Garland and Veazie, the Dunbars' attorneys, decided to have their own identification test. The men rounded up the McComb City witnesses who had testified that Cantwell and Bobby were in their city last December, and they headed to Columbia demanding to be shown the prisoner.

Before a crowded courtroom, each witness proclaimed that Cantwell was indeed the man they had seen in December, drawing cheers from many in the audience. Garland hired John Fortenberry of Hub to gather signatures on a petition demanding Governor Brewer's action on the requisition, while reporters hurried to publish this latest tidbit.

Undeterred, Hollis wrote to Brewer once again.

May 13, 1913

Dear Governor:

There has been so much said in the public press that the issue is becoming badly complicated. We do not possibly see though Governor how an honest and fair-minded public could possibly expect the old man in jail to have a fair deal without his witnesses being permitted to see the child in dispute.

It seems that we are going to have to depend entirely upon your good graces to arrange for this inspection, as we have practically exhausted every means within our power to bring the same about. We have interviewed Mr. Garland personally, and he gives us no positive assurance that we will ever be permitted to see the child. We are yet confident that a mistake has been made, and if given an opportunity before a fair-minded tribunal we are confident that we can make this proof.

A petition was being circulated in Columbia yesterday by one Mr. Fortenberry who has been here for several days as an employee of Mr. Garland, that this petition was being generally signed, asking that you grant the requisition papers without further investigation. We, of course, Governor paid no attention to this, for the reason that we felt sure that you would not.

Sentiment from the first locally has been strong in the Dunbar favor, and the signing of this petition only goes to show you that public sentiment has run high against Walters and leaves him now, as he has been all the while, a friendless old man in jail, practically without funds and with no one to speak for his interest. Public sentiment when stirred goes in one direction, oft times without reason, justification or excuse, and innumerable signatures generally can be secured to any kind of petition where the signers are absolutely ignorant of the merits of the controversy, or the truth or falsity of the accusation made.

We are confident that you will use all honest means within your power to secure for us an inspection of this child, and then at your convenience, the other parties having notice, we are ready to appear before you on the granting of this requisition.

Awaiting your advice in the premises and with expressions of continued esteem and regards, we beg to remain,

Very respectfully,
Dale & Rawls

William Cantwell Walters' Defense File© #68

One week later, Tom wrote again to Brewer.

On last Friday evening we learned that Mr. & Mrs. Dunbar had accepted an invitation to attend some Carnival occasion in New Orleans with "Robert," and we immediately made arrangements to have some of our Pearl River County witnesses go to New Orleans and thereby get a chance to see the child. After we had gone to this expense and while our witnesses were en route to New Orleans, it then developed for some reason or other that Mr. & Mrs. Dunbar declined to bring the child to New Orleans, acting under the advice of District Attorney Garland. We have to-day sent District Attorney Garland a telegram, which telegram was as follow, "Can we expect to see Robert in New Orleans and when. Answer definitely."

If he answers that we cannot see the child in New Orleans, then it shall be our purpose to ask permission to see the child at Opelousas, and if this they decline to do, we feel like there is nothing further that we can do and it would then be evident to the world that our client is not getting a square deal.

William Cantwell Walters' Defense File© #83

Hollis wrote to his cousin Allen Rawls in Poplarville who had helped set up the secret viewing, "The whole matter appears now to have been a Wild Goose Chase, and such it was, but our man in New Orleans had absolute accurate information that the Dunbars would have the child there on Saturday afternoon."

William Cantwell Walters' Defense File© #85

The spies Harold Fox and Lee Hawes, had been successful in cancelling the Mississippi witnesses' viewing, smugly standing on the train platform on their return and then publically labeling it as an underhanded gesture from Dale and Rawls.

Brewer finally answered Tom and Hollis, stating that he had contacted Garland about the examination.

In the meantime, E. G. Brown, an attorney and cousin of Cantwell's in Whiteville, North Carolina, offered his help. If Cantwell was brought to trial, he would come, bringing Julia with him. Brown wrote to his cousin, "I want to assure you that none of your relatives are going to sleep and allow the family name that you bear and your family connections to be humiliated with such innocent and frivolous charges as have been advanced against you…"

William Cantwell Walters' Defense File© #70

To Dale and Rawls he wrote, "…it is the family that wants to show that they are not brutish as some of the newspapers have in a sense intimated."

William Cantwell Walters' Defense File© #71

Brown met with Julia, advising her, and then carried her to make an affidavit.

As Justice of the Peace for Columbus County, E. K. Brown, another of Cantwell's cousins, took Julia's sworn affidavit stating that she gave Bruce to Cantwell with the understanding that he was to return him to her at her request. She further stated that she had seen the child held by the Dunbars, and he was definitely her son.

Two days later, ten citizens of Pearl River County, those discovered to have the most vital evidence of Cantwell's innocence, swore affidavits to that effect. Some had actual physical evidence: a dated receipt with Cantwell's signature on it written in the company of Bruce two days before Bobby was lost and a signed order taken in a Pearl River County store dated December 24, 1912, when Cantwell was reportedly spotted in Louisiana.

On May 22, exactly one month after Lessie claimed Bruce as hers, Tom and Hollis finally heard from Garland.

The difficulty which confronts me, as the prosecuting officer of the State of Louisiana, is this: Mrs. C. P. Dunbar responding to a fear in every mothers' breast, that something may happen to her child if carried away from her home, absolutely declines and refuses to remove the child out of the Parish, either to New Orleans or elsewhere for any purpose whatever, and she is so firm in this resolution that nothing short of a court order, in my opinion, could take the child from her and carry it beyond the limits of this city. As stated before to the Governor there is no such legal process obtainable under any law in Louisiana.

As everything touching the identification matter seems to be settled except the place and as Opelousas is objected to only on the ground of additional expense, in order to make sure, and to guarantee you a right to which you are clearly entitled, I personally will guarantee your expense bill out of New Orleans to this place, my liability not to exceed One Hundred Dollars.

Should this be acceptable you can come here on the day appointed, bring your witnesses, the identification will take place under the supervision of our District Judge, in your, and our presence, and in the presence of our most prominent citizens, and I am sure that your clients interest will get neither more nor less consideration here that it would receive in New Orleans.

Trusting that this proposition will prove acceptable, I am,
Yours very truly,
R. Lee Garland

William Cantwell Walters' Defense File© #88

Residents of Louisiana and Mississippi remained riveted to the drama that consumed their daily newspapers. All eyes were scanning Opelousas looking for the family to study them for any resemblances. Percy sent Lessie and the boys to stay indefinitely at his parents' plantation away from any clandestine observers. They lived out there with Percy's younger sister and brother who helped slip countless layers of Bobby Dunbar over Bruce's body and soul. Despite an overwhelming bias towards the Dunbar family, inconsistencies in the family's stories regularly surfaced, prompting many individuals to contact the Mississippi attorneys.

May 24/13
New Orleans. La
Messers., Dale and Rawls, Attorneys,
Columbas, Miss.

(Kindly pardon me I am ill in bed but this matter has just worried me is the reason I took the liberty to write to. Respelfully A Christian Woman)

Dear Sir,-

In view of human justice to Julia Anderson and Walters I am prompted to write to you—Walters may be morally bad and perhaps a degenerate) I think though he is inocent of the kidnapping of the Dunbar boy and also he should be given full justice and the Anderson woman also, Everything seems to be against them on account of their morals which I judge is wrong I do not think Walters know anything about the Dunbar boy only what he has heard and possibly read and perhaps seen the picture at the time of his disapearence—I sincerely believe The Dunbar have Bruce Anderson and not their boy and Gov. Brewer made a grave mistake by turning the child over to the Dunbars before it had been proven beyond a doubt that it was Robert, now they are in possession of the child which is a bad thing for the other side as the Dunbars will no doubt coax, or threaten the boy into saying many un-true things, so as to make their points another thing if this is their child why are They afraid for anyone to see or interview him privately—I would see nothing to fear and this seems strange I really believe the Dunbars know that the child is not their Robert but having lost their child & found this one are trying to keep him possibly for some mer-cenary purpose motive best known to them-selves. Robert Dunbar is call after old man Robert Dunbar his grandfather. The Dunbars claim that if the child was Julia Andesons she would not have to have seen him the second time to recognize him and that the child did not rec-ognize her either—now Julia A. did not have the advantage that the Dunbars had she had not seen her child in fifteen months nearly twice as long as the Dunbars had and she had to pick her boy out of a roomful of other boys and still she knew him under all these difficuties—and she was not allowed to take him privately & speak to him as they seemed to be afraid to allow this for fear he might recognize Julia as his mother (and if this be the Dunbar boy why should they be afaid of Julia Andeson, or the Bilbos either—This boy was not recognized by either of the Dunbars at first Mr. D- said he could not tell but wanted his wife to see him first and on Mrs D- seeing him the first time she failed to recognize him saying the childs eyes were too small to be her boy—but after she & Mr D- had spent the night togather away from the boy they both had another look at him even undressed him and suddenly discovered the moles & scars that they recognized and this seem the only thing that they did recognized about him (If this had been their own child and he had only been gone 8 months,) Do you think his featues would be so changed that they would not know him only by moles & scars This is a farce. I am a mother with only one child, and, she has scars & moles by which I would not under oath recognize her—I would not for-get my child features were she gone for years nor any good mother There is not one mother out of ten thousand who could tell you the exact location of moles on there children much less identify them. This is absurd. If the Dunbars do not know their child (who has only been gone 8 months) by his featues why they dont him at all. Why did not the Daily papers put the other pictue of R. Dunbar taken before he was lost the picture that was in the papers at the time of his diapearance with the one just taken it would give the Public a chance to see & compare the difference—I notice this was not done for some reason = I have never seen personally any of these parties therefore I judge by pictues I do not see in this little boy the slightest resemblance to the Dunbars or to the other Dunbar child while on the other hand I see a stricking resemblance to Julia Anderson and the boy whom they now claim as Robert. I firmly believe that Mr Dunbar & Mr Fox are not searching for Bruce Andeson at all but are trying learn all the particulars in the case so as to know how to act or perhaps they are trying to bribe witneses to prove that the child is Robert., I was speaking to a party from Opelousas who told me that there a lots of people there who solemnly believe that Robert Dunbar has been devoured by alligators or some wild beast and have no idea that the child now with the Dunbars is Robert of course the Dunbars do want to hear from these people. Please keep this private but I wanted you to have these particulas & hope you will successful in proving the facts in this case & restore J. A. & child (if it be hers

P. S. Sunday morning May 25/13

I wanted to add that I wonder what makes Julia Anderson so quiet and if the Dunbars have threatened her to silence—I am sure there must be some people where she lives who could identify her child why not get them even at the expense of the State—and I would like to say that there are very few people in Opelousus if any who could take an oath that the child is Robert Dunbar—and from what I have heard from there that there are lots and lots of the Citizens of Opelousas who don't believe that the child is Robert. Of course Mr Dunbar is going to say this if he wants I think he is a great bluffer and It was no one but Mr Dunbar who stopped the Bilbos by telegram and if the Mississippi people think Mr Dunbar is spending his own funds searching for the child they are mistaken when The boy first disappeared his friend and some of the townspeople felt sorry for them and put up all necessary money both for reward & expenses—I got this from Opelousas People who live & own property there—The very idea of Mr Dunbar trying to explain how the supposed Robert had his eyes reduced in size, It is perfectly silly to say that Walter doctud him for this purpose—Why I doubt if a thorough Doctor could so such a thing without injuring the childs health. Oh he will resort to all kinds schemes to make his case strong—I pray that you may pardon me for thus addressing you and you may be able to do your duty to your client and also the other parties concerned—Thanking

I am A Christian Woman, and a Louisianian
William Cantwell Walters' Defense File© #91

Governor Brewer sent a stern ultimatum to Garland.

May 24, 1913.

Dear Sir:

I will state that Mr. C. P. Dunbar took this child out of Mississippi before this defendant could get his witnesses in from the country, notwithstanding they had been sent for in an automobile, and over the begging, imploring and pleading not to leave until the witnesses, who had seen the child with Walters before the 23 of August, 1912, could get there, he took the child and left with it.

I am advised that this defendant is wholly without means to pay the expenses of his witnesses to Louisiana, besides the report has been industriously circulated in Mississippi that if the witnesses from Mississippi should identify this as the same child in Opelousas that they will be immediately arrested for perjury and detained in jail there, and this, of course, intimidates and frightens the witnesses from here, and tends to the obstruction of justice and fair play.

This matter has been going on for about six weeks and a failure of the numerous witnesses from Mississippi to have an opportunity to observe this child is brought about by its hasty removal by Mr. Dunbar from this state. I am going to require Mr. Dunbar to bring this child back to New Orleans, and in the presence of Dan S. Lehon, or John M. Parker, permit the witnesses from Mississippi to see the child,—having a free, fair opportunity to look at it and examine it.

I will refuse to honor the requisition unless they give him a square deal. So I suggest that within fifteen days from this date they present the child at the office of John M. Parker, or the office of Dan Lehon, for an inspection by the witnesses from Mississippi. Both of the gentlemen mentioned are men of integrity and ability, who are not interested, and will give both sides a fair, impartial opportunity. If they decline to do this, let me know. With kindest regards, I am

Your friend,
Earl Brewer
Governor

William Cantwell Walters' Defense File© #94

Hollis responded to the Governor, thanking him for his insistence.

They say that a man deserves no credit for doing the right, but there are circumstances and occasions which makes the performance of a duty doubly hard, and we feel that too much praise can not be given one who does his whole duty in the face of embarrassing and annoying circumstances. For the old man in jail, therefore, as well as for ourselves, we desire to thank you most heartily for standing as the man that you are. With the excitable and hot-headed part of our citizenship flooding you with petitions and unconfirmed rumors as they have been, it is indeed refreshing to find a man big enough to search for the truth and plant himself thereon, even though he sacrifices the good will of some who would readily join the mob.

We know Governor, as well as one can know anything from human testimony that the Dunbars have Bruce Anderson, and if they will only play half fair with us we will convince the world of the correctness of this proposition.

The Dunbars and their Counsel seem under the excitement of the moment to have lost all sight of right or justice and it is to you that we have to look to have the scales held evenly and justice done.

William Cantwell Walters' Defense File© #99

When reports began to surface of the way the Dunbars had handled the identity test in Opelousas, a woman from New Orleans wrote to Tom and Hollis concerned that they might try the same deception again. Tom answered, "…we very much fear that if Mr. Dunbar thought he could furnish a child at this identification other than the real one and do so successfully, he would not hesitate to do so…"

William Cantwell Walters' Defense File© #102

As Cantwell's attorneys fought to get one look at Bruce, they discovered that Percy had been in contact with several theaters; Lou Rose's in particular, attempting to get a high-priced contract to show the child to the public. They hired John Blank, an investigator out of New Orleans to look into the matter.

New Orleans, May, 28, 1913.

Messrs Dale & Rawls, Attorneys,

Gentlemen-

In answer to your request of me to procure certificate or affidavid from Lou Rose, He refused to let me have certificate stating that he had no time to spend in courts on this matter and it was of no interst to him to give certificate or make affidavid He seems to favor the Dunbars, But I will swear that he told me just what I have written to you, I think I can find the daily paper that quoted the proposition in question between Rose and the Dunbars

Yours truly,
John Blank

William Cantwell Walters' Defense File© #101

Blank mailed the attorneys the article, placing Percy uncomfortably on the defensive.

Theater Manager Says Dunbar Asked $1,000

Incensed because The States in an exclusive story Monday quoted Attorney Dale, of Columbia, Miss., as saying that the manager of the New Orleans Hippodrome confirmed the report that Mr. Dunbar had been trying to obtain a contract to show Robert, the father of the kidnaped boy issued a statement to the public Wednesday in which he branded this statement as a vile and conscious falsehood.

The following is a signed statement from Lew Rose, manager of the Hippodrome, sent to The States Thursday:

"Regarding the controversy in relation to the Dunbar child and the Hippodrome management, allow me to say this:

The day I heard the child was found in Columbia, Miss., I wired, via Western Union, a proposition to Mr. Dunbar, the father of Bobbie. Several hours later I got him on the long distance 'phone, and he said he would be in town the next day and made an appointment to see me at 11 o'clock in the morning.

He arrived the next morning, somewhat late, came into my office and heard my proposition. After which he asked me the seating capacity of the Hippodrome.

I then said to him, "What do you think it is worth?"

He replied, "One thousand dollars."

My partner, Sol Myers, was present at the time. He showed Mr. C. P. Dunbar our weekly expense book and explained that we could not pay that price and also engage seven other first-class vaudeville acts.

I proposed to Mr. C. P. Dunbar to give him 50 per cent of all over a certain amount and agreed to guarantee him $200.

He asked me to put that in writing, which I did, and he said he would take same home and consult his wife. This ended my dealings with Mr. C. P. Dunbar.

Very truly yours,
LEW ROSE
Manager Hippodrome.

Mr. Dunbar, in his public statement, also took occasion to brand as untrue a report by a States correspondent saying "It is known also that the manager of the New Orleans Orpheum has been approached."

With regard to this Walter Kattman, press agent for the Orpheum said Thursday:

"Hamlin and Benz of the Item staff approached me some time ago and said they had the exclusive stage rights to the Dunbar boy and that they wanted to arrange for an Orpheum contract. I told them it was useless for them to try any further as the Orpheum would not stake 'freak' acts."

The States-June 6, 1913 &
William Cantwell Walters' Defense File© #328

Blank suggested bringing Cantwell to New Orleans to ensure that the child the Dunbars produced was the same one taken from him, but

Cantwell could not remove himself from the jurisdiction of Mississippi because he would immediately be arrested in Louisiana. Tom and Hollis finally received a copy of Julia's affidavit.

STATE OF NORTH CAROLINA

COLUMBUS COUNTY.

Julia Anderson, being duly sworn, deposeth and says:
That she is a resident of North Carolina and has always during her life remained and held North Carolina as her home. That she is the mother of one Bruce Anderson, a child five years old, and the said Bruce Anderson is now, or was 30 days ago, in the possession of the Dunbars. That the said child held now in the possession of the said Dunbars is her child, Bruce Anderson.
That during the year 1912 she gave the body of her son, Bruce Anderson to one W. C. Walters, a native of North Carolina, with the understanding that Walters was to take said child and return same to her upon her request. She further says that she has seen the child held by the Dunbars and that the child held by the Dunbars is the child she gave Walters in the presence of Neil Stone, and this was the last time she had seen Bruce Anderson until she saw him in possession of Dunbar.

This 30ᵗʰ day of May, 1913.
Julia Anderson
William Cantwell Walters' Defense File© #104

As May rolled into June, Cantwell and his attorneys heard that the Dunbars had finally consented to an examination of the child. It was to be held on Saturday, June 7, at the Monteleone Hotel in New Orleans. Brewer requested that either John Parker, Chairman of the Board of Trade and Cotton Exchange in that city, or Dan Lehon, the investigator Brewer had sent to examine the child the Dunbars had when they first arrived in New Orleans, serve as mediator. Parker and John Lewis were political allies, and Lewis assured the chairman that the Dunbars were reputable people. On the other hand, Investigator Lehon didn't stand a chance as being chosen by the Dunbars after his deduction that the boy was Bruce Anderson.

As Cantwell eagerly awaited June 7, he received a letter from his nephew, J. M.

Barnesville NC
June 2d 1913

Dear Uncle

Your letter of recent date to hand and contents noted replying will Say that I will try to See Mr. Neill Stone & wife and Secure their affidavits one day this week and forward them to your attorneys.
   am pleased to note from the inclosed clippings that the Situation is progressing nicely in your behalf I am verry grateful to Gov Brewer for the clost attention he has given your case I think him a noble gentleman and trust that he will Secure you a Square deal.
   I regret to have to inform you of the death of your father whitch occurred on the morning of the 29th inst but as you no he had bin in poor health for the past 2 years So I presume the anouncement will not be unexpected to you he was confined to his bed only 12 days his remains was laid to rest in the old Daniels Cemitary

With Best Wishes for your Welfair I am
Your nephew
J. M. Walters

William Cantwell Walters' Defense File© #109

In the midst of fretting over Cantwell, the Walters family was now grieving the loss of its patriarch who had departed this world with a heavy heart.

Chapter Nine
The Dunbar Investigation

With the investigation looming and Cantwell's alibi continuing to be corroborated, the Dunbars' self-appointed detective force hastily announced that there had been *two* children and *two* abductors: Bruce with Cantwell originally and Bobby with Cantwell's look-alike, one of his brothers they surmised. The two kidnappers had reportedly swapped those boys in a Mississippi restaurant leaving Bobby with Cantwell, so said Miss Kate Collins who worked therein. According to the Dunbars, the boy they possessed bore the tell-tale scars on his foot. The gumshoes then announced that Bruce had likely been lost or killed and that Cantwell took Bobby to replace him.

Meanwhile, Julia was fielding offers from a Louisiana agent, Mr. Frank, wanting to make a contract with her to show Bruce on tour if she received him back.

Boardman N. C.
June 7—1913

Mr T. S. Dale,

Deare ser yes I Put all confidence in you as I think you will Do all you can for myself and W. C. Walters I Believe you will Do me right as fare as you can If you think it Rite for me to take up the offer with Mr. Frank nothing to Bother me from giting my child I will do just as you say I no it is my child and I want it I dont want the Dunbar to have the child I will write to Mr Frank today the 7 and tell Him to take it up with you and then you must see through all write I am depending on you for the write thing and Believe you will do me right find out if you can if Dunbar have got the Child with them I have got a lock of the child Bruce Hair would it Bee nessery for me to fetch it with me.

Mr Dale I want you to send me the witness names that has got to go out to Miss from North Carolina

so I remain yer trulery Friend
Julia Anderson

P. S. if you think it will Bee eney Harm in doing so I will not take up with it

Julia Anderson
William Cantwell Walters' Defense File© #116

The defense attorneys, along with Julia, were hesitant to accept any offer to exhibit Bruce, especially one coming from Louisiana. "Lord knows we could use the money though," they thought.

Ten witnesses from Pearl River County traveled south to New Orleans in three cars with Tom, Hollis, and T. R. (Doc) Willoughby, another Columbia attorney who had heard Percy say that "his doctor had advised him to find a replacement for Bobby." One of their witnesses was a young girl who had frequently played with Bruce in Mississippi.

Percy, incensed by evidence from Tom Dale that he had tried several times to exhibit Bobby for large sums of cash, refused to attend the examination, sending instead, his brother Archie, Mr. Fox, and Sheriff Swords to guard Lessie and the boy. Lessie collapsed in their train compartment before they reached Baton Rouge. The Opelousas contingent was armed with a new statement from Bobby's schoolteacher aunt, Katie Dunbar, Percy's sister, recalling another of Bobby's remembrances. "Don't get in the freight car! If you do, the ugly old man will get you."

Under Katie's care Bruce had begun speaking more often, repeating snippets of the kidnapping story he had heard about day and night for the past month. When he repeated what he was taught, everyone cheered.

Once all of the parties had arrived in New Orleans, had checked in, and had eaten a bite of lunch they made their way to a luxurious double suite arranged for the exam. Fifty-year-old John Parker sat in a plush director's chair at a head table with a podium and gavel situated to his right should he need it. A crisply dressed stenographer, Abraham Oliveira, sat to his left.

Two smaller tables were set up with three chairs each, one for Tom, Hollis, and Doc Willoughby, the other for Lewis, Garland, and Veazie. Mr. A. L. Yates, another attorney from Columbia claiming to be Brewer's representative, said he had forgotten his credentials at home and was not allowed in. The witnesses were seated in two rows of chairs set up for their comfort. Bruce, who had been brought to the hotel two days earlier with his face covered, and Lessie waited in the adjoining hotel room.

Parker's official "Dunbar Investigation—the investigation and testimony of witnesses in the matter of the identification of the child Robert Dunbar" began promptly at two p. m.

"Gentlemen, I am going to open this matter with a very brief statement," Parker began. "The first I knew officially about this case was on Tuesday afternoon, June 5, when I received this telegram from Governor Brewer:

'Much controversy has arisen as to the identity of the Dunbar child. The Dunbars will be in New Orleans on Saturday morning to submit to an examination by Mississippi witnesses at your office, if satisfactory to you. I wish you would be present and see that the Mississippi witnesses are accorded a fair deal, and I would be glad to hear from you as to what you think about it afterwards. I do this on account of my confidence in your absolute fairness.

Earl Brewer'

"I had never met or known any of the parties to this controversy and, until the receipt of Governor Brewer's telegram, had no knowledge whatever that I had been selected except from the notices in the press. I would unhesitatingly have declined to serve had it not been for the fact that some of you were already on your way to New Orleans. My first meeting with the attorneys was in my office this morning, where we outlined the method of procedure, and they asked me to act as referee. I am not a lawyer and would only take part provided they announced what their witnesses would testify to and permitted me to do *all* of the questioning." He paused, eyeing each participant. "The witnesses and the child."

Mrs. Bilbo and Mrs. Goleman looked at each other, incredulous that they would not be able to pick Bruce up or speak to him directly.

Parker continued, "I must admit I have heard some rumors as to the credibility of the witnesses and informed the attorneys of this fact, but I do not believe it will affect my judgment."

"I believe there is no question of the presence of the child who is introduced here today as having been at the various points named in Mississippi, from September until the time that he was recovered, and the essential feature to be developed is to prove the presence of this identical child in Mississippi prior to the 23rd of August, 1912, the time at which he disappeared."

The Mississippi lawyers cringed at Parker's intimation, *"The time at which he disappeared,"* instead of, *"the time at which Bobby disappeared."*

"Mr. Parker," stated Lewis, rising from his chair, "we took the position at the beginning of this controversy that we have no case; and we want it distinctly understood that at the request of Governor Brewer we are here today."

Parker raised his hand to silence Lewis. "We are now going to produce the child taken from Columbia, Mississippi, by Mr. Dunbar, so that he may be identified. Do you want the child in here? Let me see if I can bring him in."

Parker left the room and brought in Bruce, standing him on the head table facing the audience. The boy jumped into the waiting arms of Lewis and tossed a ball back and forth with Parker.

"Where is the man that give me this ball?" Bruce asked. "Where is the man?"

Lewis answered, "There he is—Mr. Parker." Lewis then carried the boy out of the room and returned him to Lessie.

The first witness, Deputy W. W. Lott, was questioned by Parker as to when he first saw the boy. He replied that he had examined Bruce for a scar in February 1913 and again two-and-one-half weeks before Percy took him, but he had not met Bruce before the crucial date of August 23, 1912.

Lott left the room and went to tell Jeptha Bilbo that it was his turn to testify.

When Bilbo was seated, Parker asked Tom and Hollis what they expected to prove by Mr. Bilbo. Hollis answered, "We wish to prove that W. C. Walters, along with Bruce Anderson, came to the Bilbos' home in Pearl River County on Friday before the third Sunday in July, 1912, and that they stayed there a little over a week. On the fourth Sunday of July, 1912, the two of them attended Ford Creek church with Mr. and

Mrs. Bilbo. They saw this child a second time, on the second Sunday in August, 1912, and have seen him at many times and places since then."

Parker asked for the child to be brought in and then began questioning the witness. "Mr. Bilbo, do you know this baby?"

"Of course I know that baby. He is Bruce Anderson."

"When did you first see this child?" Parker asked.

"I first saw him on the 19th of July. I remember the date for we had a church organ out of fix and we had a baptism, so we got the old gentleman Walters to fix the organ. He had it ready by the fourth Sunday in July."

"Was this the identical baby that was with him at that time?"

"Yes. That's the boy."

Parker asked how he knew that fact.

"By looking at his face."

"Was there any peculiarity about this child?"

"No, nothing unusual at all."

"How long did this child stay at your house?"

Mr. Bilbo thought a few moments. "All together he stayed there about six weeks."

Parker turned and addressed the child who was quietly playing with Veazie. "Do you know who this is, Bobbie?" Bruce timidly tucked his head into Veazie's shoulder.

"Tell me in my ear," Veazie suggested.

"Dat's old Bilbo." Bruce was then taken out of the room.

"Mr. Bilbo, when was the last time he stayed at your house?"

"The last time he was there was Christmas. They came on the 24th and left on the next Sunday."

Parker got down to brass tacks. "Was the child who came to your house in December with Walters the identical child who was at your house in July?"

"Yes, Sir."

"Are you positive that the date was in July and not in August?"

"Oh, I remember that all right."

"What makes you remember that date so particularly?"

"On account of our church meeting on the fourth Sunday in July."

"After eight months how are you able to identify the day and date? I want to know whether or not you are absolutely positive that that was the particular time and day when you first saw this child?"

Mr. Bilbo drew himself upright, cleared his throat loudly, and answered, "I am positive. Ask Homer Moody, he's here and he saw Bruce then. On the 29th there was a whole crowd."

"Has Homer Moody seen him since the finding of this boy?"

"No, Sir. But I am positive about the date and I'm just as positive that this is the same boy. I have seen him too many times to be mistaken. He knows me, too."

"He said he knew you."

Tom Dale interrupted. "Carl Bass said the date he met Cantwell and Bruce was the 29th of July. He has it in his record book."

Parker returned to Mr. Bilbo. "Did you have to look up his records to find the date?"

"Bass was at our home on the 29th of July, and the boy was there the night he stayed there. He had it on his day book."

"Then, Mr. Bilbo, it is not of your own knowledge that you have any recollection of the day? When you first testified you said the 19th, and now you say the 29th?"

"This man and boy came there first on the 19th, and Carl Bass came on the 29th."

"I do not want the attorney to show me a date, but I want what you know, yourself, and not what you know from somebody else."

"That's all right," Mr. Bilbo said irritated, and he was dismissed.

Mrs. Bilbo was called next, and Bruce was brought in to the room. Parker asked, "Madam, is this the child you knew as Bruce Anderson?"

"Yes, this is Bruce Anderson." Bruce was taken out of the room.

"Mrs. Bilbo," Parker asked, "when was the first time you ever saw this child?"

"It was on Friday before the third Sunday in July, the 19th."

"Is that the same child you saw the first time?"

"That is the same child. He stayed at my house several days. He was backwards and forwards, and he stayed there for two months alone. He stayed there four weeks at one time to a day."

"Do you mean he lived at your house?"

"Yes; he stayed there with me."

"Do you remember what time that four weeks was?"

"Yes, …it was somewhere about the middle of September when Walters got back to our house… about the middle of October when he came back from the hospital…and I kept the child four weeks when Walters came."

"How did it impress itself on you as to the first day that you met this child?" Parker asked.

Mrs. Bilbo frowned. "Because it was before our preaching and the organ was out of fix."

"We are not trying to mix you up, but we are trying to fix the dates absolutely. You say you cannot tell what time in September he came back?"

"No, Sir. I did not say that. Old man Walters went to the hospital in September and came back to my house on the 12th of October. He left this child with me."

"Are you certain about the time he went to the hospital?"

"Yes, Sir."

"And he stayed there, you say, until…"

"After he came to my house, I know, on the 12th of October we all went to a burying."

Parker persisted, "How did you happen to remember the date of the month when he first came there?"

"I told you as plain as I could," the small wiry woman answered, annoyed. "It was on the Friday before the third Sunday in July, and our church organ was out of fix. He went down there the next day, it was Saturday, and cured the organ."

"Is there any possibility of your making a mistake in the month?"

"No, Sir."

"Did you notice any particular marks on this child?"

"There was one little scar where old man Walters said he fell and struck against the window sill."

"You are sure that this is the same identical child that was brought to your house in July?"

"Yes, the same child."

"But you do not remember what time that child was brought back there in September?"

"No, I didn't keep no account of it."

Parker persisted. "Pardon my insistence. How could you keep the account of the exact date of the first meeting, that is, the first time you ever saw the child?"

The county's reigning matriarch, though small and delicate to look at, was a force to be reckoned with when it came to keeping law and order around her household and post office. Obviously distressed at being doubted, she straightened her hat, adjusted her glasses, and turning her piercing eyes on the younger Parker, treated him to her best "watch your step, Sonny" look.

"Because I told you about the organ being out of fix, that was the Friday before the third Sunday."

Parker hammered on, unfazed. "But you do not remember the other dates at all when he came back or left?"

"He left him there when he first came over here. The first place he went to from my house he went to Charles Miley's."

"The first time how long did he stay?"

"From Friday to sometime about Tuesday or Wednesday the next week."

Parker continued, "And the second time how long did he stay?"

"I don't remember."

"And the third time how long did he stay, Mrs. Bilbo?"

"So many times I don't remember. I know he was there at Christmas time, but I don't remember how long they stayed afterward."

"Mrs. Bilbo, I am going to ask you whether there was any peculiarity about the child's hands or feet?"

"No more peculiarity than there is about lots of them. Just a little web between his toes, and if you will look you will find it that way?"

"On which foot or toe was that?"

"I don't remember."

Parker asked for the child to be returned to the room.

"Mrs. Bilbo, I have been asked by the attorneys on the Walters' side to ask you if anybody came to your house to see this boy while he was there?"

"Yes, lots of people. Mr. Jim Holden and Mr. Boyd—I don't know his given name. Percy Dunbar's own brother, Archie, came to see Bruce with Mr. Ozy Brooks."

The child was brought in, his shoes and stockings were taken off, and its feet exhibited to Mrs. Bilbo and others in the room who examined them closely top and bottom. With the exception of a small scar on the great toe of the left foot, no apparent distinguishing marks or malformations were noted.

"Now, Mrs. Bilbo, you say there is no possible chance of your making a mistake as to the month in which you first saw this child?"

"No, Sir. There is no mistake about it. It was in the month of July."

"Has anybody asked you to study up dates, because that is the only date that you remember, in the whole matter?"

"No, Sir!" she denied. "I remember about October 12th and December 24th. He came back in January also." At that point, had the pair gotten into a physical altercation, they might have been about equally matched.

Parker answered, "That is all I desire to ask this witness."

Hollis brought in Charley Myley while Lewis brought in Bruce. Parker continued his questioning.

"Mr. Myley, did you ever see this child before?"

"Yes, Sir. That is Bruce Anderson."

"When did you first see him?"

"First time I saw him was the third Sunday in July."

"What date of the month?"

"Well, I ain't positive about what date of the month. It was the third Sunday in July. I remember because I borrowed some money from the Sixteenth Section Funds of the County. I saw the child on Sunday, and on Tuesday I went and borrowed this money."

"When did you see this child after that?"

"I saw the child on Wednesday."

"What date was that, do you remember?"

"I haven't got exactly the date of the month. It was on Wednesday after the third Sunday in July. The next time I saw the child Mr. Walters brought him to my place. Monday or Tuesday in the next week, after the fourth Sunday. One of those days he brought the child to my place."

"You don't even remember the dates that he brought him?"

"No, Sir. He stayed there after he came to my place two or three weeks. I don't know the exact days that he stayed there."

"Is there a chance of your mistaking August for July?"

"No, Sir, no chance. My wife went and asked the Chancery Clerk when we got the loan from the County, and Mr. Charles Ralph told my wife it was the 23rd of July."

"Did you ever notice any peculiarity about the child?"

"No, Sir. I noticed he was pretty smart child. I live in a log house and he would climb up the log walls. He was always busy."

Mr. Myley was dismissed and Hollis Rawls called Mrs. Charles Myley.

Hollis announced, "Her testimony will be of the same character as Mr. Myley."

Further into Mrs. Myley's testimony, Parker asked if she had any other way of knowing the dates except by guess work.

She answered indignantly, "You go to the Clerk's office in Poplarville. I'm as positive as I am sitting in this chair that the child was at Jeptha Bilbo's when we borrowed the money."

"Did this child look just as it does now?"

"Yes, of course. But he is older now."

Mr. Goleman took the stand next, stating that he was at the Bilbos' on July 21ˢᵗ when the pair came there the first time. When asked about the surety of the date, he answered, "I had two little nieces and a nephew that live in Alabama and they came to my place before the 4ᵗʰ of July and stayed four weeks. I carried those children in a team to the Bilbos,' and while we were there I first saw Walters and the boy. He came back in October and stayed with us ten days doing some repair work on our furniture and organ."

Parker asked, "Did you ever notice any peculiarities about this child, any malformation?"

"I never noticed any marks."

Mrs. Goleman testified that she remembered Cantwell and Bruce being at the Bilbos' when her little nieces and nephew were there during July. "He has stayed at my house many times and I saw him just four weeks before the Dunbars took him. He had no peculiar marks on him."

Homer Moody was called next. "I was staying at the Bilbos' home on Friday night July 19, when Cantwell and Bruce arrived."

Parker asked, "Were there any marks of any kind to distinguish the child?"

"I didn't pay much attention of course. I only played with him around the house. But I think there was a scar in one eye, the right eye."

Bruce was brought into the room and Homer pointed out the scar on the right eye that he had remembered. He then recalled that after the pair had been around the area for a few months some people became suspicious that he might have the missing Dunbar child.

Sheriff J. A. Moody took his turn next stating that he saw this same child on December 24 in Poplarville. "I heard that people were suspicious of this old man having this child, so I sent Deputy Boyd to the Bilbos' on December 26 to make an examination. He reported back that the child was not the Dunbar boy. On the 29ᵗʰ I had Deputy Brooks and a local doctor examine the boy once more. They were satisfied that it was not the child."

"What I am trying to get is facts," Parker announced. "Mrs. Dunbar is here with her little baby and we want to find out all we can about it. Do you think those people could remember the dates that they first saw this child this many months later?"

Moody answered, "I should not think so."

Bruce was returned to the room, and six-year-old Edna Myley was brought in. Parker asked if she knew the little boy.

"Yes, that's Bruce. He played with me at my house last summer."

When Parker asked Bruce if he remembered Edna, Bruce refused to answer.

Parker announced, "This closes the investigation, and I will make my report immediately and send it to Governor Brewer. You gentlemen shall also receive a carbon copy of same."

William Cantwell Walters' Defense File© #115

Parker trusted that the Dunbars' were credible, but it was well-known at the time that he had a long-standing distrust of Mississippi's fiery Lieutenant Governor, the self-proclaimed racist, Theodore Bilbo. Parker's animosity likely trickled down to the Lieutenant Governor's nephew, Jeptha Bilbo. That afternoon, Parker mailed his opinion to Governor Brewer, after giving a copy of the report to the *Item*.

In my opinion, the Dunbar child was undoubtedly around Ford Creek Church, and with the Bilbos from the time old man Walters went to the hospital in September and came back to their house October 12th, and that the witnesses are honestly mistaken in their opinion that the 'partly web-footed' boy that they saw in July could by any possibility be the same child identified by the mother who bore him, his father, the family doctor who brought him into the world, and by the many children who have played with him, and by men and women of the highest integrity who have known him all his life.

After today, seeing for the first time, the child with its mother, relatives and friends, and most attentively listening to the testimony of the Mississippi witnesses, I make this as my report, with a full appreciation of the responsibility involved, that in my judgment the child exhibited today is Robbie Dunbar.

The Item-June 8, 1913

Parker had judged the child's life according to legitimacy vs. identity, playing God in a bizarre twist, while John Lewis, the Dunbars' attorney, whined that Dale and Rawls had practically dictated the proceedings.

When Cantwell's attorneys saw Parker's report published in the paper the following morning, they were shocked and outraged. Before leaving New Orleans, Hollis took the opportunity to correct some of Parker's devastating misconceptions.

PARKER MISUNDERSTOOD, HIS OPINION FOR PUBLIC "UNCALLED FOR"— RAWLS

Walters' Attorneys Criticize Conduct of Examination Of Their Witnesses and Declare Governor Brewer Will Not Be Influenced.

Claiming that John M. Parker misunderstood his functions in the examination of the Dunbar boy held in the Hotel Monteleone Saturday, that he violated all precedent in making public his finding before the governor of Mississippi received it; that he has prejudiced the public mind against an innocent man, and that the judge, in Saturday's examination, occupied the position of a shrewd prosecuting attorney, and was so thoroughly convinced of Walters' guilt before the beginning of the testimony that he attempted in every way to reconcile that testimony with the guilt of Walters, was the charge made against John M. Parker by Hollis Rawls, of Dale & Rawls, the attorneys for William C. Walters, the alleged kidnapper.

"It was not an examination, it was a misunderstanding" cried Rawls, after making his attack on Parker.

"Walters cannot get a fair trial in Louisiana.

"To grant a requisition would be to authorize a lynching!"

Gov. Brewer Won't Be Influenced.

"Gov. Brewer is too big a man to be governed by the ex parte personal opinion of one man, even though that man be John M. Parker."

Before departing for their home in Columbia, the attorneys for Walters took a parting shot at the man selected by the governor of their state to hear the testimony of the examination. Parker answered

Gov. Brewers, "Glad to know what you think about it afterwards," by mailing the governor his personal opinion that "It IS Robbie Dunbar."

"The so-called opinion was ill-timed and took us by surprise," admitted Hollis Rawls at the Monteleone hotel before he and Mr. Dale left for Columbia, "as our understanding from Gov. Brewer was that the purpose of this meeting was to permit an inspection by Mississippi witnesses of the child in the controversy and procure their opinion—not that of John M. Parker or any other disinterested parties or spectators.

"We offered no testimony as to the guilt or innocence of W. C. Walters. We were permitted to ask no questions and tried in no way to influence Mr. Parker. We would ask a fair-minded and impartial public to read the stenographic report of the testimony and see if it is not true that Mr. Parker occupied the position of a shrewd prosecuting attorney and was so thoroughly convinced of Walters' guilt before the beginning of the testimony that he attempted in every way to reconcile that testimony with the guilt of Walters.

Offers More Proof.

"The people of Mississippi for the past two years have had opportunities to judge of the moral character of Gov. Brewer, and, knowing him as we do, we are confident that when he reads the official transcript that the private opinion of any one man cannot deter him from seeing justice done. We are now prepared to show by two communities, numbering perhaps 300 persons, that the child claimed by the Dunbars is Bruce Anderson and that they saw him in Pearl River county prior to August 23, 1912. Mr. Parker was frank enough to say that he doubted the credulity of our witnesses, especially the Bilbos, and that after spending an hour with Mrs. Dunbar and her friends he was confident she had her own child. He stated further that to brand the boy as an illegitimate child would be a crime, and this, taken in connection with the reason furnished by Mr. Parker in the conclusion of his opinion, should be sufficient to convince any fair minded person that he had formed his personal opinion before the meeting was ever held. The life of an innocent man is in the hands of Gov. Brewer, for we are confident that all fair minded people will grant that Walters cannot get a fair trial in Louisiana and the granting of this requisition will be the authorizing of a legal lynching.

Think Parker Misunderstood.

"We feel that to some extent Mr. Parker misunderstood his function in this identification meeting, as our information was that his sole duties were to see that each side was shown every courtesy and that the Mississippi witnesses were permitted to inspect the child in dispute. The request that he published from Gov. Brewer was, as we took it, a mere courtesy from the governor to Mr. Parker, and surely it was never intended that in violation of all precedent Mr. Parker's personal opinion should be given to the world in advance of the stenographic report on which this opinion was based, and in so doing, even though unintentionally, he has prejudiced the public mind against an innocent man. Mr. Parker stated at the conference that the witnesses would not be placed under oath, for the reason that it was no trial and did not smack of any judicial procedure."

The Item-June 9, 1913

On June 9, 1913, Parker answered this criticism with a telegram to the Item. "…he doesn't care a rap for the criticism that has been directed at him by the Walters' attorneys." Surprisingly, after Percy's latest published claim—that their Bobby had two webbed toes—Parker went on to say, "Now that Robbie Dunbar, with perfect feet, is found, it is time to look for poor little Anderson."

The Item-June 10, 1913

Chapter Ten
A Flying Machine

To denounce his critics, Parker substantiated his verdict with reports of a tramp traveling in a covered wagon with two disheveled look-alike children. His unnamed source had said they were headed to Poplarville. Cantwell's chance of receiving a fair trial in Louisiana continued to plummet. Tom and Hollis persuaded Brewer to withhold granting the requisition until they could personally appear before him in Jackson. They were granted a hearing set for June 17, giving them ten days to further substantiate their evidence.

On June 12, Pearl River County farmer Charlie Myley wrote to the attorneys.

> *As they have fell upon the Dates all together and say we are mistaken in them i have more Dates there corect The first is this card when i went to hospital aug the 19th 1912 When making redy to go Walters was at my home and me and my wife was a week trying to Deside Wheather to get the Old Man Walters to Stay with her or not and finly when the time come for me to go She Said She would not Stay with him and i went off upset about nobody to Stay with her This is my Reasons for knowing this Date i will Send you card Please take care of it and Return it Without fail*
> **William Cantwell Walters' Defense File© #125 (See p. 294)**

Pinned to the man's letter was his appointment card from the hospital in New Orleans, for the date of August 19, 1912. He included another letter.

> *This is another date that I Remember When W. L. Rushing Varnado, La., a insurance man was here i cared him around to get up aplications Walters and child was hear then and Rushing Saw him hear for a day*

or to and talked with Mrs Bilbo about the child you can Call him up on the phon at Varnado La this Date is aug. 7th 1912 i will Send you one of Receipt

William Cantwell Walters' Defense File© #129

Myley included the dated receipt from the Continental Casualty Company for a policy sold that day by Mr. Rushing to Hirriam E. Newman.

The lawyers also received an affidavit from J. J. Scarborough, the postmaster at Poplarville, Mississippi, who had a signed receipt from W. C. Walters for a money order dated August 7, 1912.

William Cantwell Walters' Defense File© #132 (See p. 307)

Marion County Deputy Sheriff W. W. Lott traveled around Pearl River County collecting eleven additional affidavits backing up the dates in Cantwell's alibi. Tom and Hollis emptied their pockets arranging this presentation of evidence and carrying it to the Governor's mansion in Jackson. The newspaper in Columbia published an account of the hearing.

The following is the opening statement of the Governor as he dictated it to his secretary, W. J. Buck:

"I have been of the opinion all the while that a mistake had been made and I am now thoroughly convinced that the child now in the possession of the Dunbars is Bruce Anderson and that W. C. Walters is innocent."

The above statement was objected to by Mr. Coutierie, legal adviser of Governor Brewer, and it was then withheld by the governor and the following was dictated and later given to the public:

"In passing upon this application for requisition I have done so with great care and caution in view of the fact that this case where a man is to be taken out of the jurisdiction of this State and removed far from his witnesses and to be delivered for trial in a State where they have no jurisdiction of his witnesses and where their attendance to testify for him cannot be compelled. I therefore refused to grant this requisition hastily until I could give the Louisiana authorities ample time to consider the question well, and as a practical man, knowing the popular excitement that attends such matters all over the country, and as there was some time to elapse before court would convene where

he was to be tried, I could see no harm that could come to anyone by a reasonable delay.

"There is a sharp conflict in the facts. Many good, reputable, disinterested witnesses in this state willing to swear positively that this man was in Mississippi, and that this child is Bruce Anderson and not Robert Dunbar. But this is a question of facts that I think should be decided by the court of Louisiana, and the courts of that state, it may be presumed, will give the man a fair and impartial trial.

"I have sufficiently delayed this matter to give time for the passions of the people to subside and for all parties to be heard and believe that this question is one that should be decided by the courts and not by me, and I therefore grant the requisition.

"All the questions of his guilt or innocence are matters of fact for the court or jury to decide, and which I do not undertake to decide. For instance, it is contended by his counsel that he was not in the state of Louisiana at the time of the commission of the offense. This question I do not decide, but simply hold that all questions involved in it as to his guilt or innocence are questions for the court and not for the governor."

Marion County Progress &
William Cantwell Walters' Defense File© #185

Tom and Hollis immediately applied for a writ of *Habeas Corpus*, ordering Cantwell to appear in a Mississippi circuit court to decide if his detention was legal, our country's most efficient way to safeguard the liberty of the subject. Judge A. E. Weathersby of the Fifteenth Judicial District would rule on the application. Their petition held that Cantwell was unlawfully imprisoned on a warrant issued by Brewer at the request of the Louisiana authorities. First of all, he was not subject to extradition for he was not a fugitive from the state of Louisiana and was not there when the crime charged against him was committed. Secondly, Cantwell had a charge of kidnapping pending in Marion County and was not subject to extradition until those charges were answered. Thirdly, the basis of the erroneous charge was due to the fact that he had in his possession legally a boy child named Bruce Anderson; since the child was Bruce not Robert, he could not have been kidnapped by Cantwell. Their client had violated no criminal law of Louisiana and was immune from extradition.

William Cantwell Walters' Defense File© #157

Sheriff Swords, who had come for his prisoner, bristled and postured at being denied. The Dunbars and their attorneys unsuccessfully attempted to have the Mississippi charges dropped, rendering the hearing unnecessary and sending Cantwell out into the open, but the Defense's application was granted and the hearing was scheduled for July 2 in Poplarville.

Hollis wrote to E. G. Brown about bringing Julia, instructing him to "come either to Columbia or direct to Poplarville."

William Cantwell Walters' Defense File© #163

Meanwhile, the Dunbar family was traveling throughout Louisiana as if they were members of visiting royalty. On one of the Dunbars' junkets to Alexandria, Mr. A. Koenig told Percy of "seeing Cantwell's covered wagon parked in a lot near his house in the winter after Bobby had disappeared." As expected, he claimed the man's brother and two little boys were with him.

Bruce was paraded through each town, likely holding an emblazoned jar with "Bobby Dunbar Fund" on the side. Donations overflowed each time he was placed on stage, obediently proclaiming his scripted question, "They don't have bad men here who steal children, do they?" Other than his coached lines, Bruce persisted in staying mostly silent. Percy surely felt he had found the hen that laid the golden egg, and he kept it under constant scrutiny, but the hen shivered in the dark with every four-year-olds' unacknowledged terror—abandonment. His waning impressions of riding high up on Julia's ample hip or the sound of her laughter made his heart lurch and his belly ache. Unexpected sounds and smells pricked his soul, for ever since they had left North Carolina, Cantwell had determined to keep Julia's memory fresh in the boy's mind.

Bruce cried for his Papa, whose music had charmed him to sleep most nights and cured many of his four-year-old tantrums, but he was furious at the man for leaving him. He instinctively searched for Cantwell in each crowd, but those moments likely ended with a voice in his ear declaring, "Old Man Walters will be locked up forever, Bobby. Daddy will shoot him in the head if he tries to take you away."

The child sat in his room with visions of young Bobby lost in the swamp, being snatched—by the devil himself. He imagined his ride in an open boxcar for the dramatic getaway and later being tied to a tree and whipped. He saw little Bobby, forced to beg, hands out, pitifully trembling for a crust of bread. He could almost remember it for he was told the stories repeatedly.

In Columbia, Tom and Hollis were again dipping into their own pockets for their client after unsuccessfully begging his friends and family for contributions. Cantwell had no choice but to sell the remainder of his North Carolina property. The man's dwindling economic status surreptitiously labeled him as ignorant and untrustworthy, though everyone who knew him personally acknowledged that he was both intelligent and of a good character. A fellow lawyer from Mississippi wrote to the men.

Gentlemen:

I have watched the progress of this case through the press with more than casual interest, because I believe that the decision of the governor in the disposition of the demand of Gov. Hall, will either put Mississippi in an attitude to say that she will protect her citicens, whether temporary or permanent and see that they have the benefit of every reasonable doubt; or she will calmly submit to a man being turned over to hostile hands, which in this case means certain death.

It may be that I am a little biased in the matter, but I may offer in justification that I have always taken the side of the underdog in the fight, and often working without fee or even expense money being advanced. In this case I believe they have the wrong man. The preponderence of the evidence is with the Dunbars, but certainly it is not of that class which excludes every hypotheses other than that of guilt. From all that I can gather, the Mississippi witnesses who have no interest in the case are just as positive of the identity of the child as the alleged Father and Mother are, and certainly their testimony is worthy of belief. They come from that class of humanity who know nothing but straight forward and honest dealings, and while probably poor in this worlds goods, they are rich in that quality which is worth more than money; to see fair play and honest treatment.

I have no criticism to offer of John M. Parker, who is my friend, but certainly Mr. Parker has not shown a judicial mind in passing upon this case. It seems to me that he would resolve the doubt in favor of the prosecution, rather than the poor fellow whose life hangs in the balance. I do not believe that Parker would wilfully attempt to influence

Gov. Brewer to do wrong, but evidently the demand of the Dunbars and their wealth and social standing must have had its effect.

It may be contended that the jury should pass upon the question of doubt. You and me know what that means in a criminal case where on the one side is wealth and influence, and on the other, poverty and helplessness. Our trial by jury is almost a farce in cases of this character, and to give this man over to the Louisiana authorities would mean a mere formality of a trial which would certainly result in the infliction of the death penalty; and in such case, the blood of the man would unquestionably be upon the state of Mississippi.

I do not believe in protecting a guilty man, but it seems to me that there is enough doubt in this case to warrant our Governor in liberating this unfortunate fellow, and I hope that your effort in his behalf, which I understand is without fee, may be fruitful.

I would write the Governor about this matter but for the fact that I have recently made so many recommendations to him in other matters, that I do not like to be constantly making suggestions, however, should you think it wise to do so, you are at liberty to present him with this letter.

Life is too sacred to be sacrificed to gratify the selfish desire of a few people connected with this matter, and while it is the duty of every man, whether in private or public paths to see to it that the guilty are punished, it is likewise his duty to see to it that an innocent man does not suffer. I hope the Governor will take this view of the matter and resolve all the doubt in favor of the helpless old fellow now in Columbia jail, and if he does so, I believe that his sense of justice and fair dealing will lead him to discharge the man. I have one great fear however, that in the event Gov. Brewer does release this prisoner, that the authorities will try the kidnapping stunt themselves as was done in the labor cases, and in the end get possession of Walters.

With best wishes for your success in this case, I am,
Yours very truly,
A. A. Hammond
Heidelberg, Miss.

William Cantwell Walters' Defense File© #155

Another letter arrived for the attorneys.

Brookhaven Miss June 26 1913
to Hon Rawles & Dale
Columla Miss

I haven Ben able to under stand why walters wood hafto go to Lou-
isana to Bee Tried for a crime Don in Missippi Eaven it was Baby
Dunbar Mr Dunbar his self through he was swap for in Missippi I
have Bin with govner Brewer all the Time and still with govner and
not only my self But others I no of here I Do think that Mr and Mrs
Dunbar are Perefectly honest and think they have there child I Dont
think any Body wood up hole a Kid napper it looks strange to me at
first site Bruce knew Mr Bilbo and call him By name only Being with
him a few weeks and July anderson say Bruce Bruce smiled at her it
seams that Bruce Baby Did not notice Mr and Mrs Dunbar at first
Eaven for sevel hours Befor Bruce woden notice them By coksen and
Doing all they Did to get him to notice them I have Bin Reding the
item Ever Day since walters was a Rested my Judgement is that Baby
is Bruce andersen
    it would Bee so Bad to Punish a man and him not guilty
    I think a miss stake has Bin made my self in Bruce Baby

your friend
William Cantwell Walters' Defense File© #184

On July 1, Cantwell arrived by train in Poplarville, escorted by Sheriff Lott and his deputy. Waiting at the jail were a drove of nosy reporters. Percy had planned to attend the hearing with his attorneys but changed his mind at the last minute due to his growing animosity toward Tom Dale. Bunt Walters arrived to support his brother and Julia. After all, the child at the center of the fight was most assuredly his. Unexpectedly, E. G. Brown from North Carolina did not show up with Julia.
William Cantwell Walters' Defense File© #218

On the morning of July 2, Tom Dale called G. M. Donald to the stand where they covered in detail his tenure during August, 1912. Yes, he was the agent for the Southern Express Company who received and forwarded express packages on the Northeastern Railroad line through McNeil.

Tom purposely waited to catch Judge Weathersby's eyes. Once done, he then shifted back to Donald for the *Pièce de résistance*.

"As agent of the company, did you keep a record of all shipments coming into and out of that point at McNeil, into the office?"

Donald rose to his full height and concentration, "Yes, Sir. And I have the book right here with me."

Tom continued, "Would you refer to your record of August 20, 1912, and state whether or not your record shows a package to have been shipped to W.C. Walters at McNeil."

"Yes, Sir, it does."

The Dunbar's lawyer, Garland, jumped to his feet, "Your honor, if the object of this testimony is to prove an alibi on behalf of the Relator, we desire to introduce a formal objection!"

"Just hold on a moment," Weathersby interrupted, "I can't tell yet what it is going to lead up to. I will over-rule the objection for the present and reserve the right to exclude it from the record if it becomes necessary. The Court *will not* consider evidence that is not admissible. I will let the record show that."

Tom returned, unfazed, to the subject, "What does your record show with reference to the shipment for W. C. Walters?"

Donald held the book slightly aloft for dramatic effect, "My record shows it was delivered to a man who signed W. C. Walters."

"Did you see that man?"

"Oh yes, Sir. Signed his own name, right here on 8-20-1912."

"I will ask you, Mr. Donald, to state whether or not you have had a letter from Mr. Walters since he was placed in jail at Columbia?"

Donald jumped as Lee Garland boomed, "Objection!"

Weathersby sustained the objection, as Tom turned to Garland, "It is merely our purpose to match the signatures."

"Objection is over-ruled as far as the question if he has had a letter from him," the judge injected.

"Mr. Donald," asked Tom, "how did the signature on the record and letter compare?"

Garland objected, as the witness was not an expert on handwriting, which Weathersby sustained.

Tom continued. "I will ask you, Mr. Donald, to check your records and see whether or not on the same day this man Walters shipped a package from McNeil, Mississippi?"

"Yes, Sir. It was left there on August 20 by this man, W. C. Walters. He shipped a boxed violin to W.H. Meeks."

Tom retired to his seat as Garland rose for the cross examination.

"Did you deliver the package personally?"

"Yes, Sir."

"We want to make a formal motion to exclude the testimony on the ground that it is attempting to prove an alibi for Walters."

"The motion is overruled for the present."

Garland returned to Mr. Donald. "Are you acquainted with the Defendant? Do you have any recollection of seeing him?"

"I saw him on the day he got the package."

"This man here?"

"Looked like him; I can't tell."

"Can't tell."

Tom redirected the examination. "Mr. Donald, I will ask you to state whether or not this is the only express package or shipment that came to your office during the month of August, 1912, addressed to W. C. Walters."

Donald checked his record book. "That was the only package."

Weathersby tapped his gavel. "The motion to exclude will now be sustained and you will let the record show that. This testimony doesn't pretend to show anything except an attempt to prove an alibi."

Levi Hollemon was next to testify. The tall, thin, bespectacled man first tipped his head toward Cantwell, and then on questioning by Tom, said he knew the man in August of 1912. When asked if he remembered going to McNeil with Mr. Walters to get an express package, he answered, "Yes, Sir."

Garland rose again, "We want to make the same objection."

"Objection is overruled for the present."

"When did you see Mr. Walters during the month of August, 1912?"

"He was at my place on the 14th and 15th of August. He had my organ tore up on the 14th, and I took his horse and buggy on the 15th and went to see one of my neighbors, me and my wife. I used his horse and buggy on the 15th."

"August 15, 1912?" Tom repeated.

"I think he stayed at my house or at Mr. Spiers. He come to my house the first week in August and he stayed there oft and on all through August. He would come and go. He was sick there three or four days and lay up there. I know he had been there once or twice before the 14th and 15th, and he was there from then on until he went to the hospital."

"At your house?"

"Yes, Sir. Backward and forward. I had a good pasture and plenty of corn, and he was crippled and I told him that he could make that his headquarters and work through the settlement, and he was there a whole lot.

"Is this the man, Walters, you refer to?"

"Yes, Sir, that is the gentlemen."

"Is this the same man you went to McNeil with when you went after the express package?

"Yes, Sir, same man."

Garland rose, "We move to exclude this testimony."

"I don't believe I will sustain the motion now, but will take the same into consideration. My idea is that to prove an alibi is not the proper thing to do, but I will over-rule this for the present," Weathersby sighed and rubbed his forehead.

Garland answered, "We reserve the right to except."

Tom approached the judge, "If the court please, I will say right here that in order to expedite matters, that all of our testimony will be to show that on the 23rd day of August, 1912, W. C. Walters was not in the state of Louisiana and for that reason was not subject to extradition, and if the court is going to rule that this is not admissible, all that we can do is to offer to introduce this testimony."

Judge Weathersby called all of the attorneys up to his desk. "My idea is that a *Prim facae* (Prima facae—at first sight) case is made out by the papers issued by the Governor, and unless there is something outside of this testimony that goes to the merits of the case that proves an alibi, I don't see the necessity of it myself. I don't know what you are going to prove, but just what we have heard is only to prove an alibi for Mr. Walters."

"That is exactly what we are trying to do," stammered Tom, his face darkening.

"My idea of the law," stated the judge "leads me to believe that I have no right to take that into consideration at all."

"It is our purpose of this trial," Tom repeated slowly, "to prove that Walters was not in the state of Louisiana, but was in the state of Mississippi on the 23rd of August, 1912, and if the court rules against us…"

"I am going to rule against you so far as the testimony already offered is concerned. I didn't sustain the motion but said I would take it into consideration before passing upon it."

"It is no idea of ours to foresee the ruling of the court," Tom replied sharply, "but we see now that the court is of the opinion that this testimony to show that Walters was not in the state of Louisiana but was in Mississippi is not admissible."

Both sets of lawyers returned to their seats.

Next, Reverend J. Q. Sones answered the prerequisite questions of where he lived, his occupation, and how and when he knew Cantwell.

"Well, the third Sunday is our regular meeting time and I had an appointment to go above Columbia at that time and I had my date down on my ledger. After the talk got up, I looked at my ledger and ascertained the date. I saw him later at my brothers."

Garland jumped in, "We make a motion to exclude the evidence on the ground of attempting to prove an alibi, and reserve the right to except."

"If it was going before a jury, I would sustain the motion," the judge answered, "but as it is I will over-rule the motion and try to remember these things when I go to pass upon it."

Sones had seen Cantwell on the third Sunday in August, 1912. When asked how he remembered the date, he replied that the following Friday he left for his regular annual meeting—Missionary Baptist—at Varnado, Louisiana. "It commenced on Saturday before the 4th Sunday. I don't remember the date."

"And that was a regular annual meeting."

"Yes, Sir."

Tom and Hollis had no choice but to continue.

Poplarville farmer J. S. Thigpen, with whom Cantwell and Bruce had spent the night of August 23, 1912, recalled the evening in question to Tom and the judge. Cantwell had repaired a sewing machine while there.

Garland cross-examined Thigpen with his same method of questioning the remembrance of dates. "Have any record?" he queried.

"Only the beginning of a singing school led by Wash Lee on the 26th following our meeting, which was on the 25th, and by that I remembered that it was in August."

Garland moved to exclude this testimony, and Weathersby overruled.

L. A. Thigpen, father of J. S. Thigpen, was called to testify next. He lived ten miles west of Poplarville near Whitesand Church, now and last August.

Tom asked if he knew Mr. Walters and if he saw him during August last year. He answered yes.

"Where?"

"At my home. He spent the night there on Saturday the 24th of August."

"Where did he go, if anywhere, the next day?"

"We went to church at Whitesand, where Brother Holcolm preaches. I rode in the buggy with him and Bruce. Cantwell had worked on the organ earlier."

Garland moved to exclude the evidence, and Weathersby sustained the portion that referenced the child.

Garland asked if there was any record of the services kept in some book by the clerk. Thigpen answered yes, and that Otho Stewart was the clerk last August.

Tom called Reverend G. W. Holcomb, who stated his profession and that he knew the Relator, Mr. Walters.

"Reverend Holcomb, I will ask you whether or not you preached at Whitesand on the 4th Sunday in August, and if you saw Mr. Walters in attendance that day?"

"Yes, Sir. And two or three days after that he came to Mr. Golemans near where I lived and stayed around there two weeks."

Tom asked what Cantwell was doing around that settlement, and Holcomb replied that he was fixing organs. Tom questioned him on the reliability of his dates.

Holcomb made a handsome, believable witness, for he dressed sharply and was extremely proper in mannerisms. He replied that they had a man that had come in to teach singing school to examine the organ to see if it was up to what Walters had claimed to do—to fix it as good as new. There was some doubt as to whether it was as good as new, but the man said there was some improvement. Mr. Walters made a talk contending that he had made his work thorough and perfect.

Garland replied, "We make our same motion to exclude and reserve the right to except."

Tom called W. C. Bass who lived nine miles southwest of Poplarville and who held a job for timber owner J. W. Blodgett.

"What position do you hold with Blodgett, please Sir?"

"I just look after their stuff—see that everything moves along all right around their timber. Keep up with conditions in Pearl River County. I don't do any estimating—I just look after the timber."

"I will ask you to state whether or not your employment with the Blodgett Company requires you to keep a diary or memorandum of your doings and whereabouts, and were you doing that during the months of July and August of last year?"

Bass answered, "They don't require it of me, but I have been doing it for a number of years."

Tom asked if he knew Cantwell. He said he did.

"I saw him at Whitesand Church on the 25th day of August, 1912."

"Now is there anything in your diary from which you can determine the fact that you were there at church on that day?"

"Yes, Sir, I had it marked church day."

Garland rose from his seat, "We want to make an objection here. The time testified to is after the commission of the crime."

"Objection is sustained."

"I will ask you, Mr. Bass," emphasized Tom, "if there is anything in your records to show that you had this work done on your organ on the 26th?"

"I had it marked on my book—work on organ that day."

"We want to make our former motion to exclude the testimony," repeated Garland.

"I sustain the objection."

Garland questioned the man, "Did you have his name on your diary?"

"No, Sir."

Tom called J. J. Scarborough to the stand. Scarborough said he lived in Poplarville and was living there during last August. He held the position of postmaster, he added. He adjusted his tie as he said it, proffering an air of responsibility on the jowly, pleasant faced gentleman.

Tom probed, "I will ask you, Mr. Scarborough, if your position as postmaster requires the keeping of a record of money orders?"

"Yes, Sir."

"Do you know this man, Mr. Walters?"

"Yes, Sir. He came in about 12 o'clock on August 7, 1912, and purchased a money order."

"We move to strike that out," Garland objected, "because the time in the first place—his presence outside of the state must be shown at the time or about the time of the commission of the crime."

"Overruled."

Tom called J. J. Amacker to the stand. The man told where he lived, seven miles west of Poplarville. He responded, "Yes, Sir," when asked if he knew the Relator, Mr. Walters. He stated that he had seen him at Whitesand Church on the 4th Sunday in August last year and that he had come to his home a week earlier to repair his organ.

Garland repeated, "We renew our motion."

"Motion over-ruled."

"You say he came to your house to fix an organ?" Garland asked.

"Yes, Sir. Said Jeptha Bilbo sent him there."

"He had fixed the organ previously?"

"Yes, Sir."

Tom called J. M. Tynes to the stand, asking his name and where he lived.

"I live 10 miles—9 or 10 miles west of here. About one mile from Whitesand Church."

"Were you living at the same place last year—in August, 1912?"

"Yes, Sir."

"Is that your church?"

"Yes, Sir."

"I will ask you, Mr. Tynes, if you saw this man, Walters, at any time during the month of August 1912.

"Well, I first saw him at my place the first week in August, then on the 25th day of August, or the 4th Sunday in August at church. He come back up there to collect for some work that he had done on our church organ."

Garland objected, "We make a motion to strike out the evidence on the ground that it is an attempt to prove an alibi for the Relator."

"Motion over-ruled."

Garland's cross-examination consisted of the usual rebuttal.

Hollis called Ben Alsobrook to the stand, having him state his name and address at McNeil. He continued with the usual questions: did he know Mr. Walters and had he seen him during August 1912.

"I saw him at Mr. B. J. Sones four miles above McNeil and about one-half mile from my house.

"What was the occasion of your being at Mr. B. J. Sones?"

"I was cutting some dogwood timber right back of Mr. Sones field that I had bought from him. We went around to the house to get water and found Mr. Walters there. That was August 22, 1912."

Hollis asked how he remembered the date.

"Well, I had a man hired by the name of Jones helping me and I give him time on that day, the 22nd day of August. My time book shows that."

Garland began his cross examination, "You recollect that date by referring to your time book?"

"Yes, Sir. My time book shows that Walters was there."

"What did Mr. Walters have to do with your time book?"

"I had a man hired by the name of Jones—Sam Jones—he was working with me in getting the dogwood and I give him time on the 22nd day of August, the day we commenced working.

"Was that the only time you saw Walters?"

"No, Sir, I saw him lots of times. I saw him at McNeil one time after the 22nd and I met him at Sones Chapel Church in October, the third Sunday in October. Then I saw him again on December 24th at McNeil in Lloyd Thigpen's store."

"When you met him the first time, the 22nd day of August, did you have a conversation with him?"

"Yes, Sir. I saw him five or six times that day. I was working right back of the field and I come to the house five or six times to get water and he was working on the gallery on some clocks."

"Have you refreshed your memory since this occurrence by looking at your book?"

"Yes, Sir. My book shows that he was there."

"You got your book with you?"

"No, Sir. It is at the house. But it shows that I went to work on that day."

Garland moved to exclude the testimony and reserved the right to except.

When court was reconvened, Tom called Cantwell to the stand having him state his name and asking if he was the one who petitioned for this writ of *Habeas Corpus*.

Cantwell answered yes. He then told that his native home was in North Carolina and that he had first come to Mississippi in 1910.

"Mr. Walters, where were you during the month of August of last year, 1912?"

"Well, I was around Bilbo, in Pearl River County."

"Were you in the state of Louisiana at all during the year 1912, except when you were in the hospital?"

"Not at all. I went to the hospital in New Orleans around the early part of September and stayed there about a month."

Cantwell recalled going to get the express package at McNeil on August 20, 1912, and spending that night at Mr. Spiers near McNeil.

"I went out around and come in among some of the Lumpkins and then in back by McNeil to Mr. Wash Lott's and eat dinner there, and then in the afternoon I went on down to Mr. Ben Sones and spent the night of the 21st there?"

"Where did you go on the next day, the 22nd?"

"Stayed there all day, with the exception of going over to his son's house. I stayed that night again at Ben Sones. The next day, the 23rd, I went over to Mr. Spiers—young man Spiers—then back in the road by Joe Lumpkins and then back to Mr. Sones again and then right around by Mr. Thigpen's. I stayed the night at L. A. Thigpen's."

"What did you do at Mr. Thigpen's?"

"Worked on a machine some."

"The next morning, Saturday the 24th, where did you go?"

Cantwell testified that he went over to Holman's to do some work on his machine and went back to the Thigpen's. Thigpen's unmarried son was there and two of his grown daughters and the old lady. He had spent the night there. The next day he, Bruce, and Mr. Thigpen's unmarried son had gone to church.

"We carried the dinner in our buggy. After church we went back to Tom Amacker's, the Thigpen's, and ended up at Mr. Bass's."

"Mr. Walters, when did you last leave your North Carolina home?"

"We left about the first of March, 1912, heading for Eastman, Georgia, where I have two sisters living. We were traveling with a horse and a light buggy. Bruce and I arrived about the first of April, but I was suffering all the time with my knee.

"We went down to Iron City and spent a few days with acquaintances. After I left there I crossed the Chattahoochee River and went out around by Dothan and Brewton, Alabama. I was trying to get to the hospital. We went by Atmore and Bay Minette and finally had to go back to get across the river around by Mobile, and a man by the name of Henderson performed an operation on me. This was around the middle of May."

"Where did you go then?"

"Around the first of June I entered into Mississippi, crossing the Chickasahey and Leaf River and I never took up to do anything until I got in near New Augusta to a man name Meeks. I put up with him and worked for him—fixed an organ, machine and clock—and there was a man on the place by the name of Yates and I fixed a machine for him. I carried him out to one of his appointments to preaching and went back out there and worked around and finally carried him back to another of his appointments and worked around through to Purvis."

"What time was it when you came to Purvis?"

"About the 13th of July. I went from there to the Bilbos,' arriving around July 19."

"How long did you stay there?"

"I made my home at Mr. Bilbo's. I would work around and go back there. When I fixed that organ at Whitesand, I came into Poplarville and sent a money order off and went back to Mr. Bilbo's, and then I went to Mr. Levy Holleman's. I had been told there was an organ there to be fixed. I did some work there, and besides that I had my instrument with me and they kept me busy playing all the time."

"At any time during the months of July and August, were you in the state of Louisiana?"

"Not at all. I was far from Louisiana. Six years ago I was staying in Louisiana at Elizabeth. Got hurt and went to the hospital. I left Louisiana at the end of 1910, crossing the river at Vicksburg. I went to the hospital there. I left there and came down to Dentville, and I made a musical instrument with 287 strings on it. It is at my old home in North Carolina."

"What about the musical instrument that you made in this county?"

"Before I went to the hospital, right here in Mr. Blythe's shop I made a frame of another one and I went to work at Mr. Al Golemans and made that on his gallery. I worked about two weeks there, and this little boy Bruce was there running up and down with the children and everybody knew Bruce and he was cared for and loved, and the ladies would take him and wash him and dress him, and he was one of the sweetest little boys I ever saw. I was just as happy as I wanted to be, except I was suffering all along."

"Where is the boy now?"

"Objection!"

"Sustained."

"Mr. Walters, were you in the state of Louisiana at any time during the months of July and August, 1912?"

"The only time I was in Louisiana in 1912 was around early September when I was in the hospital in New Orleans. I think if anyone had gotten over those rivers and swamps like they say, they would have had to gone in a flying machine. I know I didn't have one. I could hardly walk."

Garland eagerly asked him how he knew anything about those rivers and swamps, to which Cantwell replied, rolling his eyes, "I don't know anything about it, only from hearing people talk."

Cantwell straightened himself to a dignified a pose to prepare for the coming onslaught.

Garland asked him if he knew where Pineville, Louisiana, was and did he live there in 1911, to which Cantwell answered yes to the town and then no to the year. He worked there in a blacksmith shop with Mr. McLendon in 1909 or 1910.

"I couldn't do much the three weeks I stayed with him."

Garland eyed Cantwell, ready to strike. "During those few weeks you boarded with Mrs. McManus, did you not?"

"No, Sir, I did not. I know that lady. She ran a restaurant and I stopped in there and got some lunches.

In Pineville 1909 or 1910, Cantwell had traded McLendon a watch for a horse. He had never seen him since.

"Did you have a wagon at that time?" Garland pressed.

Cantwell grinned, "I had a nice little buggy I bought over there in Louisiana. It had been run away with and fixed up. I headed up to Widow Wainwright's, she lives beside Little River and runs the ferry. I worked there for her and ran the ferry for a while. I was down there Christmas of 1909."

"Have you been to Forrest Hill?"

"Yes, Sir. I think I fixed a clock when I was down there for a Mr. Mallett. He was in the livery business. Haven't seen the man in years I don't guess."

Garland straightened his tie and drew in a deep breath while moving to stand within a foot of Cantwell's face. He paused, "Have you ever been to Opelousas?"

Without missing a beat, Cantwell returned the charged stare, "No, Sir. Never was."

Garland made a motion to exclude all of that portion of the testimony of the relator, W. C. Walters, tending to establish an alibi.

"Overruled."

Tom approached the judge's desk with two sets of papers: Exhibit "F" was Mrs. L. A. Thigpen's affidavit stating that Cantwell and little Bruce were at her home on August 24 through August 25, 1912. Exhibit "G" was B. J. Sones' affidavit stating Cantwell and Bruce were at his house from August 21 to August 23, 1912.

Garland objected to each. The Court sustained each objection. The two affidavits were given to the stenographer.

J. A. McKinley, Justice of the Peace in Columbia, took the stand and Tom asked him if his court docket contained a kidnapping charge made against W. C. Walters. He answered yes. The affidavit was made on April 21, 1913. He was asked if a warrant was issued upon that affidavit, and McKinley answered yes.

"Was Mr. Walters arrested by virtue of that warrant?"

"Yes, Sir —now I don't know about that."

"Was the warrant returned?"

"Yes."

Tom asked if the charge was pending on the 18th day of June, 1913. McKinley answered yes. The lawyer then asked if the case was now pending in his court.

"No, Sir. It was dismissed on the 21st day of June, 1913."

Toxey Hall, the District Attorney in Columbia, rose up to cross-examine McKinley. He asked the Justice of the Peace if his constable, Walter Lott, was present and opened the court for him.

McKinley answered, "Yes, Sir."

Hall asked if a formal motion had been made to dismiss Cantwell's case.

McKinley again answered, "Yes, Sir."

"Do you have that motion?"

"Yes, Sir."

"Let me see it." He paused. "This is the original motion which was filed in that cause. We desire to introduce this motion, which is as follows:

State of Mississippi, Marion County. In the Justice Court of Beat Number Five. J. A. McKinley, Justice of the Peace. State of Mississippi vs. W. C. Walters—charged with kidnapping.

Comes now the District Attorney and County Attorney who prosecute the pleas of the State of Mississippi and move the court to dismiss this cause and discharge the defendant without bond. June 21, 1913.

Signed—Toxey Hall, District Attorney
B. A. Sylverstein, County prosecuting Attorney

"If the court please, we desire to introduce the judgment of the Court in the case of the State vs. Walters, which shows that affidavit was issued April 21, 1913, charging him with kidnapping."

Tom objected, for Hall and Sylverstein's motion was filed June 21, 1913, and should not have any bearing as to whether or not Brewer's requisition should have been honored on June 18. If the Mississippi charge was dismissed, Cantwell would immediately be arrested by Swords and carried to Louisiana.

Weathersby overruled. Hall continued reading.

This cause coming on to be heard on motion of the District Attorney and County Prosecuting Attorney to dismiss this case and discharge the Defendant, W. C. Walters without bond, and the court having heard and considered said motion and being of the opinion that said motion should be sustained; it is therefore hereby ordered and adjudged by the Court that said motion be, and the same is hereby sustained, and that this cause be, and the same is hereby dismissed and the defendant discharged without bond. Ordered and adjudged in open court, this the 21st day of June, A. D. 1913.

J. A. McKinley, J. O.

"We desire to introduce that judgment, if the court please," Hall requested.

Tom rose abruptly. "Objection."

"Overruled."

"Mr. McKinley, with reference to the warrant that was issued, which is not on your docket, was it ever returned to you?" When McKinley answered yes, Hall continued, "You have it in your possession now?"

"No, Sir, not the warrant. Somebody sent for that warrant and I sent it to them. It was never returned."

"Have you the affidavit?"

"Yes, Sir."

"So the warrant has never been returned to your court? Have you seen it since it was issued by you?"

"No, Sir."

(The Mississippi warrant had disappeared, leaving Cantwell subject to the Louisiana warrant.)

Garland's team was prepared. They delivered Henry Estorge's original affidavit from April 22, 1913, exhibit "A" stating to the Opelousas City Judge that Cantwell had kidnapped Robert Dunbar on August 23, 1913, and that he should be arrested and dealt with according to law.

Next, exhibit "B", the original warrant, was the City Judge's charge to Sheriff Marion Swords to arrest Cantwell and bring him forth to answer the charges.

Garland handed over the Application for Requisition, marked exhibit "C", Swords' request to Louisiana's Governor Hall stating that William C. Walters, kidnapper of Robert Dunbar, had fled the state and needed to be apprehended. Swords nominated Henry E. Estorge of the parish of St Landry to be appointed as the Louisiana agent to receive the fugitive wherever he is found and bring him into this state and deliver him to Sheriff Swords. Swords had asked Toxey Hall to issue a requisition to the Governor of the state of Mississippi for the apprehension and rendition of William C. Walters to Estorge.

The original Requisition, marked exhibit "D", came next. It was Hall's request to Brewer maintaining that William C. Walters stands charged with the crime of kidnapping committed in the parish of St. Landry and that he had fled from the justice of this state and taken refuge in Mississippi. It required that the said William C. Walters be apprehended and delivered to Estorge.

Last but not least came the original Executive Warrant issued from Governor Earl Brewer on June 18 to the sheriff of Marion County. It specified that Louisiana's Governor Hall had demanded of him the arrest and delivery of said W. C. Walters to Henry E. Estorge, whom he had appointed as agent to receive and convey said W. C. Walters to the jurisdictional limits within which he stands charged.

Garland now began with the Dunbars' witnesses. William Mallet went first, stating where he lived—twenty-two miles south of Alexandria, his occupation—livery and feed, and then he was questioned if he knew the Relator, W. C. Walters.

"I saw him at my place on two occasions last year," Mallet began. "First time was early June."

"Which way was he traveling?"

"In the direction of Alexandria. He was repairing stoves. I saw him again on July 22, 1912, at my place. On this occasion he had W. C. Walters written on the curtain of his wagon."

Garland pointed at Cantwell. "You recognize this man as being the same man that was there?"

"Yes, Sir. He stayed there until evening and hitched up his horse and drove out in front of my house and let his curtains down on his wagon and I saw his name written on the curtains. That was the first I saw of the curtains having his name on it. He asked me the way to Eunice, in St. Landry Parish."

Tom made a motion to exclude that testimony since it was not near the time of Bobby's disappearance on August 23.

"Overruled."

Weathersby stated, "The court will remember that we were not permitted to go further back than August 20."

Tom asked Mr. Mallet how long he had been living at Forrest Hill and how long he had been in the livery business. Both answers were 1897. Mallet told that he was both a Constable and Deputy Sheriff. He stated he "didn't recollect the gentleman until this evening. I remember an occasion when I saw him before."

"Now what brought that back to your memory?" Tom asked.

"Well, I just remember seeing the man—he was a watch tinker then. The first time he was at my place he was afoot. The second time was the 23rd day of July in his wagon with W. C. Walters—Stovemender on the curtain."

Garland called W. A. Stogner from Tylertown, Mississippi, to the stand.

"Are you acquainted with the Relator here, W. C. Walters?"

"Yes, Sir. He has been to my place. He was at my house about two weeks before he was arrested."

"Did he speak to you on that occasion about the Dunbar child?"

"Objection," called Tom, "If we can't testify as to the Dunbar child, you certainly can't."

"Overruled."

Stogner spoke slowly to make his point, "He told me that he was in that neighborhood about the time the child was stolen."

"Objection!"

"Overruled."

Mrs. McManus, an unhappy, bird-like woman of Pineville, Louisiana, took the stand.

"I've known Mr. Walters since 1910 when he worked in our town. He was there again in the fall of 1911 and when he left there, he was going down toward Lake Charles in a wagon, stove-fixing and selling his harps."

Tom made a motion to exclude her testimony, which was overruled.

Mr. A. B. Dantin of Alexandria, Louisiana, took his seat to be questioned by Garland. He stated he was a boiler maker and had seen Cantwell in his shop.

"He come into the shop where I was working on August 6, 1912. Said he wanted to buy a piece of Russian iron. The manager was out of town that day and the foreman was in the shop. This gentleman walks out with the foreman, J. J. Duffy, and come back and finally he went off without anything in his hand except a stick. He had his wagon on the outside, and I was working by the door at that time and happened to look out and saw on the wagon W. C. Walters—Stovemender."

Garland asked, "You remember him as being the same man you saw on that occasion?"

"Yes, Sir."

Tom approached the man, doubt written all over his face. He tediously grilled Dantin on the wagon curtain, the Russian iron, and the manager's absence. When he questioned him about the date he claimed to have seen Cantwell, Dantin replied that he had looked at the affidavit for surety.

"What affidavit? Who got you to make out this affidavit?"

"Mr. Dunbar asked me to make it out. I just met him that day—Mr. C P. Dunbar. I think it is his brother in Alexandria. I met his brother about a month ago."

"You remember that date by the manager being gone that day?"

"I remember that was the day that Walters was there. I remember that he was there the day the manager was out of town. We were talking about this man—the way he come into the place."

"Well, how did he—come into the place?"

"He come in there looking like an ordinary hobo, but I think he has cleaned up a little since the last time I saw him."

Tom and Hollis felt a shift in the room.

Veazie rose slowly, adjusted his stance in the room, and called Frank Ansley, a diminutive but wiry man of Port Barre, Louisiana, to present his statement. Ansley said he was working as a bridge carpenter for the

Opelousas G & N.E. about five miles from Swayze Lake on Saturday the 24th day of last August 1912. And yes, he recognized Cantwell as being the man he met that day on the right of way halfway between Melville and Port Barre. The room came to a standstill. When Hollis looked toward his senior partner, Tom's face wore a steely grimace.

Ansley continued, "I was one of the first to reach the scene on Friday when it was first learned that the child was lost. We were working nearby this same place, and on our return we had to pass along there. There was no other way of getting out except through the swamps. We learned of the child being lost about five o'clock in the evening, and we remained down there until 10 o'clock. We didn't have any lights and we put our car on the track and went home.

"It was on the next morning—Saturday—that we passed this man, Mr. Walters, on the right of way between Port Barre and Swazye Lake. I returned to Swayze on Sunday, and on my return to Port Barre, I was riding on the back of a passenger train and saw this man again. Then on Monday as we come out we didn't see anything of him until that evening he come to us at our works. We were two miles east of Swayze Lake, and he just came up told me that he was on his way to the Charity Hospital. He asked me about the reward for this child and I told him what the reward was and he said that that would be a pretty good stake for a hobo."

Tom covered much the same line of questioning as Veazie, honing in on the dates, the encounter at their work site, the asking of the size of reward for the child, and then he inquired, "Mr. Ansley, why didn't you report that?"

"I did report it. There have been others wise about that besides me. Others saw him the same day that was more interested than I was. The man didn't have anything. Wasn't anything to take him up for. We just suspicioned him, that was all."

"There was no effort made to take him up?" Tom asked.

"No, Sir."

Garland redirected the questioning, "What is the nature of that country between Port Barre and Melville?"

"A dense swamp for 14 or 15 miles."

"Anybody living in there?"

"One colored man living in there four miles from Melville. At the 8 mile post is a station and there is a colored family or two living there and that is all the inhabitants between those two places."

Garland called Percy's uncle, Preston King of Opelousas, to the stand.

King stated at the height of the search between 800 to 1,000 people, including himself, were searching for that child.

"Would you look at this man, W. C. Walters, and say whether you saw him and where?"

"Yes, Sir. I saw him near Swayze Lake about three quarters of a mile from where the child disappeared. He asked me if I was a sheriff, and I told him that I was hunting for a lost child and when I mentioned that, he said, 'Oh, Yes. I heard that a child had been lost' and I asked him where he was going and he said that he was going to Melville, and I told him if he found that child between there and Melville to let me know or bring him back to me and I would give him $250.00, and he said, 'as much as I need money I wouldn't charge you anything for finding the child, but you could give me anything you wanted to.'"

Dale began his cross examination, "You first saw him right close to where the child's tracks disappeared?"

"Yes, Sir, right at the bridge crossing Swayze Lake."

"You didn't see anything of this child with this man when you saw him?"

"He didn't have anything but a stick."

"Did he see you coming some distance before you got to him?"

"I suppose he did but he didn't make any effort to hide. I never thought of the child being kidnapped. I thought the child was lost in the swamp. If I had just thought for a moment that morning that the child was kidnapped, I would have taken charge of that gentleman."

"You just let this man walk around there and talk about this lost child, suspicious character as he was, and no one undertook to arrest him? Have you seen this man since?"

"Not until today," said King. "Only time I saw him was that day and today when he walked in the court room. I have seen his pictures in the paper though and studied them a good bit."

"Did you recognize him from the pictures?"

"Only one. The only picture that I thought looked like him was a large picture in the *Item*. This picture was just a large head and it looked a good deal like the man that I saw."

Tom took a deep breath and conferred with Hollis. He then called Cantwell to the stand. He began by asking if Mrs. McManus' statement was true about Cantwell living in Pineville during 1911 and 1912. Cantwell corrected the date; he was there until the last of 1909 about two months before Christmas, adding, "The woman must have been crazy."

"Mr. Walters, you heard what Mr. Ansley had to say about meeting you on the railroad track on August 24th, 25th and 26th. Were you ever there in Louisiana on those days?"

"I certainly was not. He must have seen some other man that he thought was me. I've never seen that man in my life. I was at Whitesand Church on the 25th where there were 200 people around who saw me. I couldn't have been at two places."

"Objection."

"Sustained."

"You heard what Mr. Dantin had to say about you going to the shop in Alexandria—some boiler works—and calling for some iron on the 6th day of August?"

"I was not there. I was last in Alexandria in 1909."

"You heard what was said about your having your name written on your wagon W. C. Walters—Stovemender?"

"Never had any kind of wagon in my life and never been in the business of stove mending. I work on clocks, machines and organs."

"Mr. Stogner said you told him about two weeks before you were arrested that you were in the neighborhood of Swayze Lake when the child was taken."

"I certainly never told him anything of the kind," Cantwell blustered.

William Cantwell Walters' Defense File© #200

(The *Habeas Corpus* hearing had ordered Cantwell to appear in a Mississippi circuit court to determine if his *detention* was *legal*. The alibis from each side would only be tested in a criminal trial.)

After the hearing, Judge Weathersby ruled, "that the petitioner was not, as alleged, unlawfully and wrongfully imprisoned and restrained of his liberty, but that on the contrary Petitioner was being rightfully and lawfully held to be carried into the State of Louisiana, there to be tried on a charge of kidnapping, and that the requisition of Governor Hall of Louisiana to Governor Earl Brewer, of Mississippi, was duly and legally honored."

William Cantwell Walters' Defense File© #202

Tom and Hollis immediately appealed to the Supreme Court of Mississippi, and the following day Cantwell was granted a stay of judgment. The attorneys would have to reach deeper into their own pockets, for Cantwell's payment for his land which had been promised at $350.00 had been shaved down to $200.00.

William Cantwell Walters' Defense File© #212

At the time of the *Habeas Corpus* hearing, the *Item* republished the photograph mentioned by Preston King during his testimony—a large head shot it had labeled as William Walters, the kidnapper. The Louisiana witnesses had seen the man in the picture, who was not Cantwell, around Opelousas during the time of the child's disappearance. While the two men did look similar, the added embellishments throughout their testimonies were either contrived or imagined.

Cantwell wrote a note to his attorneys about that mislabeled photograph and provided a correct photograph of himself. He included both pictures with his note.

Here you will see A Photo of me taken July the 1st 1913 and A Picture Purported to Be mine that Appeard in New orleanes Item July the 3d 1913 this (Item) photo looks vary much like some I had taken A Few Days Before I was Arrested By this you can see Part of what they are Doing to me

Yours Oft W C Walters Columbia Miss
William Cantwell Walters' Defense File© #204 #206

(See p. 298)

Tom and Hollis contacted Thomas Kleinpeter, a Louisiana attorney sympathetic to their case, to sort out this latest problem. He answered with a letter from Opelousas.

Get a picture from the "Item" and one from the States—of this morning. The States picture I find is a correct picture of "Walters" that of the "Item" is that of "Roderick."

The prosecution will attempt to prove by two or more witnesses that the picture shows the man who admitted the boy is the Dunbar boy.

T. K.
I knew "Roderick" & C. (Cantwell)
William Cantwell Walters' Defense File© #207
(See p. 299)

Chapter Eleven
A41084

While Tom and Hollis prepared Cantwell's appeal, Bruce remained in the hands of the Dunbar family, becoming the well-trained puppet they demanded. His routine eventually became second nature.

"I remember this place," he would proclaim, cautiously monitoring his audience. "I used to come here with Daddy and Lonzo long, long time ago, before the dirty old man got me."

"Bruce fell off the wagon one night and died. Ol' Man Walters buried him in a stump-hole."

These tidbits were fed to the press who passed them on to an eager audience. "Bobby Dunbar Thriving." Newspaper sales soared as sympathy for the Dunbars increased. Contempt for Julia and Cantwell rose as well.

Back in Columbia, the prisoner refused to be bowed and continued portraying his innocence with righteous vigor, sparking the occasional taunt from his various onlookers. If he reacted in anger, the outburst received top billing in the next day's papers. Cantwell spent his sleepless nights playing hymns above the deserted town square.

On July 5, Julia wrote to the attorneys from Wilmington, North Carolina.

mr. T S Dale

Deare sir

I will take the time in riting you a few words in ansure to youre Letter of Last week was aful sorrow that w c walters will half to bee turned over to LA form I don't have any ido that I will ever see my Deare baby any more it is giving me Lots of trouble it don't seame Like I ever will go throw with it it is aful fore me I have to and if you need me are want me to go you will half to send heare fore me I sure want to go it is aful hard fore me it seams Like it will nearly over come me I want you to do all you can fore me I no it is my child and I want it Please Dont fail to Let me heare from you at once I would of swore to the child when I was out there but I was afraid that they would kill me well the People told me they would kill me and Bruce did Look so good to me but O how my hart did ach to Just get him in my armes and get out of site with him well it brakes my hart I no he is my child and god noes he is so Let me heare at once I still Looking and wating on you

as ever your friend
Julia Anderson
tell Walters to still hold up fore me to bee there when the trial is bad.

William Cantwell Walters' Defense File© #208

Percy was contacted by "Wellwisher," the Louisiana informant who told Brewer that half of the citizens of Opelousas did not believe the boy was Bobby. Percy attempted by code to lure the secret writer into a meeting. New Orleans investigator John Blank discovered the message in the *Item* and mailed it to Tom and Hollis.

New Orleans, La., July 31th, 1913.
Messrs Dale & Rawls, Attorneys,
Columbia, Mississippi:

Gentlemen:

Enclose find a copy of letter taken from the New Orleans Item, said letter writen in figures and subsituted by letters which I presume you will be able to read as I have. The key of this letter is as follow. #1 represents A #2—B #3—C & c.

This may be of some benifet to you and for that reason I am sending it to you. This letter has been published twice in succession in the daily Item.

Yours truly,
J. B.

* * *

Item July 29/13

15 16 5 12 15 21 19 1 19 12 1

10 21 12 25 26th

23 5 12 12—23 9 19 8 5 18,

4 5 1 18 19 9 18,

9 23 9 12 12 2 5 9 14 14 5 23 15 18 12 5 1 14 19 15 14 1 21 7. 6th
1 14 4 7th. 1 20 20 8 5 3 15 19 13 15 16 15 12 9 20 1 14 8 15 20 5
12, 1 14 4 23 15 21 12 4 2 5 7 12 1 4 20 15 13 5 5 20 25 15 21 9 6
16 15 19 19 9 2 12 5.

23 8 1 20 16 1 19 19 5 19 2 5 20 23 55 14 21 19 23 9 12 12 2 5
19 20 18 9 3 20 12 25 3 15 14 6 9 4 5 14 20 9 1 12, 6 15 18 13 25
15 14 12 25 15 2 10 5 3 20 9 14 7 15 9 14 7 6 21 18 20 8 5 18 9
14—20 15 20 8 9 19 13 1 20 20 5 18 9 19 20 15 19 8 15 23 1 12 15
20 15 6 16 5 15 16 12 5 23 8 1 20 6 15 15 12 19 20 8 5 25 1 18 5.

9 6 25 15 21 3 1 14 13 55 20 13 5, 23 18 9 20 5 13 5 8 5 18 5 1 19
19 15 15 14 1 19 25 15 21 19 55 20 8 9 19.

25 15 21 18 19 20 18 21 12 25

3. 16 4 21 14 2 1 18.

Applying his key to decode the letter, Blank included this message:

Opelousas, La., July 26th.
Wellwisher,

Dear Sir:--

I will be in New Orleans, on Aug. 6th. And 7th. at the Cosmopolitan
Hotel and would be glad to meet you if possible. What passes between

*us will be strictly confidential for my only object in going further into
this matter is to show a lot of people what fools they are*
     if you can meet me write me here as soon as you see this.

Yours truly,
C. P. Dunbar

**The New Orleans Item &
William Cantwell Walters' Defense File© #221**

Wellwisher stood Percy up, increasing the man's irritation. Meanwhile, the two attorneys who were responsible for preventing Cantwell's requisition became targets for misguided vigilantes.

New Orleans La aug. 8. 1913

To the famous Kidnappers attorny Rawls & Dale

*We or watting for you to Come in october to defend Walters and we
will take a Shot at you and Dale we do not Say much but Look out
we don't get you Before then; you are watched every day in your place
in Columbia we know you are Stealing Walters money from him, they
is know chance for him getting out of opperlusses but the rope around
his neck*
     *for as Brewer is Concearn he is know good he is a big grafter like
your Self he is like the Bilbo famly we do not here any more from the
Liare the Said he had a web foot, when they found he had know web
foot they Said Some thing Else World Champion Liar*
     *in a few days you will recive a Photograph of you and Rowls taking
a Suck at Julia Anderson*

Your Sencerly
T J K & May gord Bless you amen

William Cantwell Walter's Defense File© #223 (See p. 301)

Tom Dale wrote, "...*public sentiment has so blinded and prejudiced
the people in this case until it looks now as if it is possible that...the
mighty truth, will never be known.*"

William Cantwell Walters' Defense File© #216

Cantwell's appeal to the Mississippi Supreme Court wouldn't come up for several months, and he felt that his attorneys had lost interest in his case. During the same time, his knee began to act up, swelling and aching, which added to his generally sour mood. His frustrations boiled over onto paper.

Aug the 18th 1913
Dale & Rawls

"Dear Sirs,"

He hurriedly scratched with his pencil.

"I guess you are too Busy to Come to see me And I will write. I sent A Letter to you to Be sent to the Papers and I Dont Hear any more of it."

He closed his eyes, imagining the letter lying on a crowded desk somewhere, forgotten.

"It Looks like if We Lie Still and say nothing the world will say I am Guilty. Have you Got out those Pictures yet and Do you Intend to? If you Dont and will say so I will no not to depend on it."

He stood up and hobbled around the room a minute. He continued,

"Your Reputation is as much at stake as mine. I Loose in this Case it will ruin your Reputation. It may Be that I Don't know what is Best But I Hate to Lie Idle & Be Branded A Criminal when you no the Crime Has been Comited Aganst me. You Have Failed to Advise now Come Around And If we are Plum Helpless we will Declare to the world so. So write soon,"

He pressed harder into the page,

"and Let me Hear From you.
As Ever yours obedient
W C Walters Columbia Miss
Aug. the 19th 1913 Ps. I Got another Clipping this Am"
William Cantwell Walters' Defense File© #228

Hollis sat down at his desk after lunch, picking up the envelope with the other letter Cantwell spoke of. The attorney was unusually worn out, so as patiently as possible, but with a touch of added formality he answered his newest critic.

August 19, 1913

Dear Sir & Friend:-

We have your note of yesterday and note carefully what you have to say. Our failing to come to see you at the jail was not intentional, but due to the fact that our Mr. Dale after returning to the office on Friday was called away again on Sunday on business and is still out of the City. As you understand, when only one of us are here, that one has to stay in the office continually and has absolutely no chance to get out. This, therefore accounts for our not seeing you for the last several days. However, it is the writer's intention to get down to the jail at the earliest possible date.

The writer went over carefully with Mr. Dale the statement that you had prepared for the papers, and after viewing it from every possible angle, we felt that it was not wise or proper at this time to publish the same. As you understand, the public generally pays absolutely no attention to what you say, or what we say, and invariably they transpose your remarks and make your own words condemn you instead of help you. At the suggestion of the writer, therefore, approved by the writer, we deemed it best at this stage of the game not to publish the piece, and we think that in the long run you will see where we were right.

Regarding the pictures, Mr. Dale assures me that they are being made, and just as soon as they are completed we will furnish you with some of them so that you can send them where you desire, and we will likewise distribute some.

Now, Friend Walters, we know that confinement in jail at this season of the year is bad, but we want you to bear it with the best fortitude that you can and believe always, if you have ever doubted it, that we are doing everything that lies in human power and skill for you. We believe that after the services we have rendered you, it is not necessary to tell you this, because if you do not appreciate it now you never will.

I am expecting Mr. Dale to return on Thursday of this week and if we do not get to see you before that time, we will both come down together and spend as much time as possible with you. Be careful as to what you say, and please do not send any stuff to the Newspapers now, as additional talk will hurt us instead of helping us, and we know that we are right when we advise you this way. Take it easy and use yourself as best you can and let us assure you that we are making the best fight of which we are capable in your behalf. With best wishes and kind personal regards, we are, as ever,

Your friends,
Dale & Rawls

William Cantwell Walters' Defense File© #229

Two days later, on the four-month anniversary of Bruce's kidnapping, Cantwell asked for several sheets of Sheriff Hathorn's personal stationary. "Forget the newspapers," he paused, patting the stack, "this is heading to the Acting Assistant Attorney General in Washington, D. C." Over the next several days he would fill eighteen pages top to bottom, some front to back, with several lengthy accounts of his ordeal, signing them as prisoner A41084.

Cantwell readied his small table for some serious writing, assembling around himself extra pencils, tobacco, and the mound of published reports he had collected concerning the Dunbar mystery. He thumbed through dozens of newspaper articles, positive and negative, arranging them by name and date. He reread and sorted each letter he'd received. The few photographs he had gathered remained stuck to the wall looking down on his fervent efforts. Everything lay before him as naked and vulnerable as the insides of an organ. "I can do this," he thought. "It just needs to be put in the right order."

Cantwell's head was swimming and his knee ached. He pulled up his trouser leg to find his injured knee fevered, red, and swollen. Within the hour a doctor had sterilized the knee, then using a large syringe began withdrawing several ounces of puss-filled fluid. Cantwell would spend the better part of a week with the leg propped up and wrapped with a poultice.

When his fever would break, he would write from his cot with a sacred, almost frenzied perseverance, recording the four-month disaster.

Cantwell used bits of language he picked up from his attorneys and word of mouth from friends and relatives.

A41084

W C Walters Au the 21st 1913

I Beleave that their is An organised Band of Criminal threw Miss And La And I Beleave C P Dunbar is their Chief And it was A Plan thy Had to take my Bruce and Put me out of the way and Put Him on the Stage He Has A Good while Ago mad some move in that Direction And there is A Great many Belong to it or they Have sold out or Sceared out I Have Located 2 more I Beleave Belongs to it. A man Name Herring and one Name Graham Near Angie La not Far From Here I think there Meen organizer Here is Bud Wall. I wrote some of this to the secret service Department From what I can Learn He is one of C P Dunbars Earnest workers Here is where one strong hold of the white cappers were Dr Anderson At Hub one of the men Hope Arrest me Had Examined Bruce And said He Knew he was not the Dunbar Child A Mr Barnes was in His office at the time He is A sawmill man An Ex Deputy says He will sware that Charlie Day said He Knew He was not the Dunbar Child But was Going to take Him Any How

E B Southerand says He will sware He Heard Dunbar say at Hub that He was Going to take Bruce And said He Asked Him what He was Going to Do about the Burnt toe & Dunbar said He was Going to take Him Anyhow Peoepple Had been writing to Him so much about me And the Boy Bruce Thom Ford Marshal Here at Columbia told me that these Peoepple At Hub wrote to Dunbar to Come And Get the Child whether He was His or not

I Dont see why thy should Have Done it unless it was Because thy Had treated me Like thy Did And was Afraid I would Prosacute them they Had their skeam well Planed shows it was not the First Skeam thy Ever worked

Dock Wiloughby at Foxworth told me He Asked Bruce what His Name was after thy Got Him And He said His name was Bruce and His MaMa was name Julia And His Little sister was Nam Burnice when I Had Him He would talk to any one And tell any thing He Knew and He has I Lot of sense But thy have Got the Poor Little Fillow Cowd he has never seen anyone that He loves like he Does me and He sees he Cant talk Good about me and He wont talk And I Am Perswaded to Beleave while I Dont no one thing about them Peoepple or Opelusas it is sevrel Hundred miles From Here But As I say I am Perswaded to Beleave C P Dunbar spirited his own Child Away so He Could take these Misterious trips I will send you A Copy of A Clipping sent to me By some one From Opelusas and After Reading it and studing it makes me more Firmly Beleave it And I Have Been told that C P Dunbar Belonged to the Blackhand And Am shure He Belongs to something Bad I no those witnesses he Brought From Pineville Belong to that Class the Rapiedes Parish Records will show that the McManuses Have A Bad Record and it Has been Claimed that Bobbie Dunbar Has been seen in Alexandra La A. Dunbar Has Kinfolks their

William Cantwell Walters' Defense File© #233

Cantwell numbered and folded the three sheets together and slid them to the side just as his supper arrived. His mind raced a mile a minute, causing him to ignore his food. He looked over at his workspace where the long narrow article "Real Dunbar Child Drowned" **(See p. 90)** stuck out like a flag. He bowed his head in thought, twirled his mustache with trembling fingers, then began another letter.

Here is Another Cliping you see Me and Bruce is vary Misterious over in La But over in Pearlriver County and From there Back to NC there is no Mystry At All

Was Real Dunbar Boy Drowned A New Eliment of Mystry Has Entred Into the Celibrated Controversy A New Phase of Mystry Enters the Controversy over the Chil in the Possession of the Dunbar Family At Opelosas whose Identity Alleaged to Have Been Kidnapped By W C Walters Now in Jail at Columbia Miss Some Persons at Opelusas whose Identity has thus Far not been Revealed writes A Letter to A Friend At Lexinton Miss Seting Forth the theory that the Real Dunbar Child was Drowned The Letter is Published In A Current Issue of the Lexington Advertiser And while it By no Means Clears up the Mystry The statements of the unknown writer Are Highly Interesting Here is A Portion of the Epistle

Staring at the cut out newspaper article, he copied, word for word, a portion of McMullen's article "Real Dunbar Child Drowned." The article told of how the child screamed and fought when asked about Cantwell, and then later refused to speak about his past.

You Can see the Dear Little Boy was cowed Because he knew he was among my Enemys and when with me he was the Happiest Little Boy you Ever saw and was Loved Peted & Caressed By Rich and Poor And Appeared to think the whole world was made of Love that woman knowes he is not hers He Does not Answr the Description of theres.

A41084

The States & William Cantwell Walters'
Defense File© #236

The old man's tears dripped on the four pages of paper as he folded them into another bundle. "If I had never taken Bruce, he would be safe at home." Cantwell pictured Julia's face, so far away, lined with worry. He put out the lantern to hide his wretched condition. "Dear God in Heaven, I'm truly afraid," he offered. "I'm afraid! Won't you help me?" He stifled his agonized sobbing with a ticking covered feather pillow.

In the morning his renewed mind leapt to a start. After he'd washed his face and his oozing knee was freshly dressed, he began his third letter. It took the better part of the day with short bursts of writing, fevered napping, praying, and expectorating.

A41084

you no a Child Can Be taught to say anything But this Don't Look Real to me Here It is, 'Bobbies Memory Geting Clearer Dunbar Child For second time Refers to Alleged Kidnaper As Walters.'

Cantwell rubbed his tense neck in disbelief. Why couldn't the public see what he saw? He answered the headline, underlining as he saw fit.

you see He Could not speak well and He would not speak at All He Caled me "PaPa."
'Daddy If you Had stayed Close By me And Hadnt Riddin off on the Horse, Just look that old man Walters wouldn't have Got me' this Assertion Made By Little Bobbie Dunbar to His Father Last week at

*their Home In Opelousas Gave what C Percy Dunbar the Father Be-
lieves is An Important Clue In the Link of Evidince in the solution of
the Kidnaping Mystey For the Second time the Child Had Refered to
the old man as Walters Mr Dunbar who Arrived here Wednsday with
Sherif Swords of St Landry Parish said the Child has Developed A
Fear that somebody means to steal him Again And is Afraid to Go Any
where in the Dark He is Growing more Comunicative to His Parents
And to members of the Dunbar Famly and the statement Fited with
things Comented on the Boy said that it Rained Hard the Night He
was stolen And He Got vary wet*

The tenderhearted old man cringed at the thought of Bruce being
afraid for four solid months. What repercussions would there be on the
four-year-olds' psyche?

*Mr Dunbar Came here to meet the Anonymous Letter writer who has
ben signing Himself well wisher the Letter Directed that thy meet at
the Cosmopolitan Hotell Aug the 7 at 10 oclock Mr Dunbar said He
Beleaves the Fellow is some sort of A Crank one of the Last Letters
said that the Cosmopolitan Hotell would Be Drenched with Blood If
there was Any Attempt made but Attempt was made to Apprehend
the Anonamous one the Opelousas man And Sherif Swords Called At
Police Headquarters Wednsday to Confer with Inspector Reynols Mr
Dunbar Denied that He Asked For Police Protection saying that He
Did not think it nesesay But he Did Receive A Permit to Arm himself
If he Deems it Nesesay Both of the Opelousas men Refused to treat the
Anonamous Letters seriously thy said thy Had not Decided wheth-
er thy would Go to the Cosmopolitan Thy Register at the Monteleon
Hotel*

Cantwell paused, wondering if he had included enough details.

*Now If you will study the matter Clost you will see it is there own
Clan or someone that knows He needs to Be Hacked But I Beleave C
P Dunbar Has some one in New Orleans Doing this to try to Hold
Public sentiment*

W C Walters

*Now is it Posable that A man Cant Be Protected From such outlaws
as these God forbid*

A41084

The States 7-1913 & William Cantwell Walters'
Defense File© #237

The man folded the two sheets of paper together and placed them
carefully with his other two letters. His knee was finally beginning to
get better, but his brain was tired and he grew more restless and claus-
trophobic with each letter. The writing, however, gave purpose to the
boredom of each day.

His fourth letter began as usual:

A41084
Says Opelusas Doubts Identity
Special to the states Jackson Miss April the 30th 1913
*Govener Brewer Received A Letter Opelousas La signed A well
wisher As Follows*

Cantwell inserted "Wellwisher's" April letter to Brewer. **(See p. 87)**

*Ps If they no it is not theirs and what will Become of me
All mothers Compaires Photos of their Children 4 years Apart And
the Likenesses were Identical Thy Cant understand it
Walters—Now C P Dunbar Knew He was not His His Brother
went and Looked at Him soon after He was supposed to Have Lost
his At Mr Jephtha Bilbos at Bilbo PO where Bruce Had been the most
of the time since the 19th of July 1912 Jephtha Bilbo is uncle to the
Lieutenant Govner of Miss*

Cantwell added that Archie Dunbar had traveled to the Bilbo's to
look at Bruce. The witnesses who were at the Bilbo's at the time declared that Archie said it was not his nephew and left. Despite the
Dunbars' constant searching and traveling to look at different children,
they claimed that this event never happened, that Archie had not gone
to the one place where Cantwell and Bruce stayed the most often. He
continued his letter:

And Dan Smith A Merchant of Carraire that saw me and Bruce at Levi Holemans Previous to Aug the 23d 1912 tol me that some one Had Corosponded with Dunbar about me And Bruce this was in Jan 1913

Will Give you the Names of A Few Peoepple visited Home in NC that surounded me & Bruce Anderson

Cantwell wrote as fast as he could remember the names. Big, crooked, loopy script that ran in four messy columns down two pages.

R R Barnes Merchant Walter Murray Mail Carier Jo Murray Postmaster J M Walters Farmer Mc D Walters Farmer Sidny Lee Farmer Quin Brett Farmer Barnesville NC Marion Stephens Merchant Rev Mathewel Stephens F H Walters Resident Boardman NC M G Williamson Merchant Jeth Williamson MG son Genova Williamson Evergreen E K Brown L F Brown Chadburn NC Doyle Bell Farmer James Bell Farmer J R Gerrald Farmer Arnold Bell Merchant Sims Allen Merchant Asbery Bell Merchant Bayboro SC J B Walters Barber Honce Walters Barber Baxly GA J I Pope Ice & Coal Dealer M M Williamson Farmer James Pope Resident and many other Eastman GA Prof D L Bledsoe & Prof Anderson & many others Iron City GA Sylus Fellows L Jones & Daughter Pinkerd Ala Dave Nichols Eastabetcha Miss D L Traylor Beaumont Miss Frank Beasly & John Yates New Augusta Miss

William Rabon Alengo Rabon Russel Raybon Mr & Mrs Parker Baxterville Miss John Davis Pinebur Miss Jo Galoway Odeal Miss Jeptha Bilbo Dolph Smith George Smith and 50 more Bilbo PO Miss Theadore Bilbo Deacon of the Church at Spring Hill G W Holcomb Paster John Davis Hilsdale

I Had Bruce at Meeting at Spring Hill on the 11th Aug 1912

He was at Preeching at Fords Creek Church on the 4 Sunday in July 1912

Had Him at Preeching at White Sand Church on Aug the 26

Could Prove Him By at Least 500 Peoepple in Pearl River County the Deacons of the Whitesand Church are J J Amaker James Tyines Poplarville PO Miss

I Had Him at Levi Holemans on Sunday Aug the 18th and He went out to the Church with Mrs Holeman and in the Evening not Less than 20 Peoepple were At Levi Holemans

Rev Lonnie Lee and others saw us the 19th of Aug 1912 Lonnie Lee Post Office in McNeil Miss

Cantwell inserted an almost identical copy of the note he had sent to Tom and Hollis concerning the incorrect photo labeled William Walters that appeared in the *Item*.

I will send you one of my Photos taken July the 1st 1913 look very much like some taken Before I was Arrested also I will send you A Picture Appeared in the New Orleans Itim of July the 3d 1913 Will Give you some Idia How thy are Butchering me up No Doubt But C P Dunbar thought He would take Bruce He was such A nice Bright Little Boy and Put Him on the stage after Geting me out of the way Him and His Clan and thy have Failed so Far Thy First Declared to the world I was An umbrela Fixer Next A stove mender Next A Burglar next A train Rober And Finaly An Instrument Fixer And Now thy Have Found that my Friends are the Peoepple I Have Been Among And the Best Peoepple in the Country Preechers Deacons of Churches and Church members I never Had any Enemys only Among the Crimnal Class near Every name I sent you are Church Members

W C Walters
William Cantwell Walters' Defense File© #238

Cantwell folded the letter's four pages, two front and back, and placed it in the stack with the other three letters. He was so exhausted that he rested for the remainder of the day. The following morning he was able to limp around his cell and call for a shave. After breakfast he began letter five:

A41084

Now you see He says & no doubt But it is His C P Dunbar Alone Note Carefuly
    'Dady if you Had stayed Close By me And Hadnt Ridden off the Horse that old man Walters wouldn't Have Got me'
    Now the Question Arrises what should this mean unless He took His own Child off For someone to Get him and He on Horseback And Left the Little Fellow to Be taken Further He say things Comented

on these Peoepple First Declared I Had Kidnaped their Boy and that thy Had Him then thy Declared I Had swaped For Him And now thy Have Bought out Everything or Got them scared I would not Be Afraid to Go to Opelusas and Be tried If I Could Get My witnesses But If you will Put watchers after them you will Find thy Are A Bad set not only Bad But Dangerous and Everyone that volunteers to Help C P Dunbar Belongs to that Clan I Guess Opelusas Must Be 3 or 400 Miles From where I was in Pearl River County At Pearl River And the Miss River and no telling How many more Lay Between And you no it would Have been Imposable For me to Have taken a strange child Right Fresh From Its Parrents and Had it at A Church where Any one Had nevr seen it Before And Fooled the Peoepple W C Bass was at the Meeting at Whitesand on the 25 of Aug 1912 And Had Previously Seen him at Jephtha Bilbos And we spent the Night of the 25th Aug 1912 At W C Basses Also the Day of the 26th and the Night of the 26th 1912 As Has ben Shown By Afidavit also By sworn Evidenc in Court

Respectfuly submited
W C Walters Columbia Miss

S J Hathorn & Dale & Rawls will sware that Every Statement I Made when Arrested Proved to Be true Dale & Rawls Has Pictures of the 2 Children Has Promised to Have some Reproduced For me to Circulate

William Cantwell Walters' Defense File© #239

Cantwell folded the letter's three pages together and added it to the stack. The prisoner ended the bundle of letters with one last page dated August 25, 1913.

I Have Learned From one Isaiah Peters that Dunbar Said He Knew nothing abut the Little Boy But if His wife Claimed Him He would Have Him or Ride to Hell on A Rotten Rail...

William Cantwell Walters' Defense File© #240

Cantwell placed the letters in a large envelope addressed to D. L. Carlton, Acting Attorney General, Washington, D. C. It was stamped with extra postage but never cancelled or sent. The jailor likely made a stop by the offices of Dale and Rawls on his way to the post office, for the jumbled packet of letters was found in an opened envelope with the Defense File.

Hollis opened a letter from Padgett and Watson, Attorneys and Counselors of Baxley, Georgia.

Messrs. R. J. and J. B. Walters, brothers of W. C. Walters, have employed us to make an investigation for them and ascertain through you gentlemen the status of his case.

We have seen some accounts in the papers as to the steps that have been taken by you gentlemen in your most earnest and laborious task in your endeavoring to free your client.

We would thank you gentlemen to write us at this time suggesting if there is anything that can be done by any of his relatives or us in helping you in your efforts to give this man a fair chance.

William Cantwell Walters' Defense File© #222

Hollis answered, "We sued out a writ of *Habeas Corpus* after we lost our fight before Governor Brewer to prevent the honoring of the requisition. This writ came on for hearing at Poplarville in July and after a two day trial the court held that Brewer was in his province when he honored the requisition. We immediately filed our appeal and are waiting the result from the Supreme Court of this State. Our Court is now in vacation and will not reconvene until the second Monday in October, and we expect to hear from the appeal between that date and Christmas."

The attorney got to the point quickly, "The greatest handicap in the case is the lack of finances."

He continued, "It has occurred to us that if Julia Anderson could institute *Habeas Corpus* proceedings for the recovery of her child in the Federal Courts of Louisiana, that this would have a bearing on the Walters case."

William Cantwell Walters' Defense File© #243

Tom received a letter from Julia, now living and working in Wilmington.

10 st north 102
wilmington nc

august 22 1913

Mr thomas s Dale

Deare sire Just a few Lines to Let you heare from me I have finly stop getting any hearing from you at all and cant find out a thing from w c walters are the child I have rote 3 or 4 Letters to you and cannot heare a word I sure want to hear heare what have been don but it Looks imposible some how farr me to get a hearing from you I want you to rite to me at once and Let me no what have been dun if walters is still in Jail are where he is and if the Dunbars have my child I have got some of Bruces heare if it is not settled if it will bee any benefit to you I will send it Please Let me heare at once how everthing is and what they are doing the Last hearing I got was June 23 and I do want to no so bad it seams Like I will go crazy if I cant heare now will you Please Let me heare from you at once yours as ever

miss Julia Anderson

PS I have shard the Picture of bruce to Lots of People in wilmington that new bruce and they say it is bruce and they would swere that it is bruce and will make out a List of names and send if you want them too Please let me heare at once

William Cantwell Walters' Defense File© #235

Hollis quickly wrote back to the frantic woman.

August 26, 1913
Miss Julia Anderson,
Wilmington, N. C.

Dear Madam:-

We cannot at all understand why you have not been hearing from us relative to the W. C. Walters case. We have written you a number of times since you say you received our last letter and it must be due to the fact that you have been changing your address and the letters have gone astray.

Hollis explained Cantwell's current circumstances, including the writ of Habeas Corpus and their appeal to the Supreme Court of Mississippi. He hesitated when writing that they wouldn't hear anything until mid-October at the earliest.

If we lose on this appeal we have an appeal to the Supreme Court of the United States, if we desire to take it. If we win on this appeal Walters will perhaps be tried in Mississippi, if tried at all, and not in Louisiana. We have before advised you, for him to go to Louisiana now would be certain conviction and almost certain death, and we are making the best fight of which we are capable to keep him away from Louisiana, with all the odds against us.

We are working hard on a plan to start proceedings to recover Bruce, but just at this time we are not in a position to advise you definitely as to this. During September, however, we will want to take this matter up more fully with you, and in the mean time we want you to keep us advised as to your address so that we can get you by telegraph, if it becomes necessary. The great trouble with W. C.'s defense now is the lack of money. If we had funds sufficiently large to transport his witnesses from North Carolina, Georgia and Mississippi to Louisiana, we would be in fairly good shape to go to trial in that state. But as he is without funds to pay the expenses of his witnesses, he could not hope for anything but a certain conviction and execution. Sentiment is still high regarding the case and the majority of it is yet favorable to the Dunbars. They have your child still in their possession and the newspapers say that he is fine, healthy and doing well. Let us hear from you all along with your correct street address. With best wishes and kind personal regards, we beg to remain,

Yours very truly,
Dale & Rawls

William Cantwell Walters' Defense File© #244

Julia immediately wrote back.

august the 29 1913

Mr Dales henington and Rawls

I recived youre Letter today was more then glad to heare from you all well I have rote a Letter to w c and I will ansure yourse I sure hope we will get the child all right fore it seams Like it will run me crazzie if we cant I am going to see how much I can get and if I can get somewhere 75 ore a hundard Dolers would it bee all rite fore me to fix up and go out there it seams Like if to go and see walters and not Let none of the La folks no anything about it I think if I could go and bee at the trile and wast to state how they dun me and the way they tryed to get me to give up my clame on the child Dunbars sister beged me to Just give up my clame and not clame the child untill they found the rest of the children that walters had and I knew that he had not had but one child and that it was mine well I hope to heare frome you again soon I have got some of the first heare was ever cut off of his head and it is the same coler of the child heare now and if it was not I would no it was bruce well Let me heare again soon I remain yours truly and Depend on and you fore all you can do in the recovery of my child I hope to soon get him back

Julia Anderson
William Cantwell Walters' Defense File© #246

After four months, Julia realized that Bruce might soon be lost forever, past the point of no return. She packed a bag and began making her way south, getting as far as the train depot in Savannah, Georgia, over two hundred miles away before her money ran out. After two days stranded at the station, she was discovered by the matron, penniless, hungry, and alone. A local charity organization provided funds to send her to the home of two of Cantwell's brothers, J. B. who lived in Baxley, Georgia, and Radford who lived ten miles away in Surrency. The two men took charge of Julia, informing Padgett and Watson of their decision. Padgett and Watson then informed Dale and Rawls.

Cantwell's brothers, along with Padgett and Watson hoped to raise sufficient funds, almost impossible within an economically hard-hit family and community, to assist Julia in filing legal papers for Bruce's return and then to push for Cantwell's release.

On September 9, J. M. Walters, Cantwell's nephew, challenged Tom and Hollis' plan of waiting on the Mississippi Supreme Court to rule.

I don't See why Some Steps can't be taken to recover the child.

If Mr Dunbar taken the child from Walters without due process of Law has not Walters produced as mutch Evidence to Show that the child is Bruce Anderson as Mr Dunbar has produced to Establish his clam to the child

William Cantwell Walters' Defense File© #249 🔵

On September 13, Hollis answered J. M. directly and to the point:

You are correct in your information that Mr. & Mrs. C. P. Dunbar, with the assistance of the officers and the public, took Bruce Anderson from the possession of W. C. Walters and out of the jurisdiction of the State of Mississippi by force and without due process of law.

We were retained in the case just a few hours before they carried the child away, and we thought then and think now that to have made an effort legally to deprive them of the possession of the child at that time would have resulted serious for Walters. That is, we are confident that he would have been severely dealt with at the hands of a mob. And too, we knew practically nothing of the facts of the case when the child was removed. In other words, we were not sure that the child was Bruce Anderson and had nothing to prove it except the bare statement of W. C. Walters. If we had known then, what we do now, we would have risked the danger of lynching and stopped the child by Writ of Habeas Corpus.

The writer agrees with you thoroughly that some effort should be made to recover possession of the child from the Dunbars, and I think that Julia Anderson would be the proper party to institute this proceeding. If a fund sufficiently large could be raised to bring her and her witnesses to New Orleans, Habeas Corpus proceedings could be instituted in the Federal Courts there for the recovery of the child, and I am confident that when this step was taken we will have gone a long ways toward liberating Walters. This matter would have already received our attention, but for the fact that W. C. has no funds and we have spent in his defense our time and some of our own money and are not able to finance a fight for the child.

It is my personal opinion that a better move could not be made than to institute immediate Habeas Corpus proceeding in the Federal Courts at New Orleans for the recovery of the child, and I think you are on the right track when you see his people and friends in your State, together with the kinspeople and friends of Julia Anderson looking toward this end.

As a legal proposition I cannot agree with you upon any court in your state having jurisdiction of the body of the child who is now detained illegally in Louisiana, and am confident that any Attorney in your State whom you consult will thus advise you.

You inquire as to Walters financial condition. You are correct as to the amount that has been sent us from North Carolina. In April we received $300.00 from a deed of trust and in July we received two donations of $20.00 each, making $40.00; and in August we received $200.00 balance due on his interest in the place, making a total of $540.00.

We have no accurate list of the money we have paid out in this behalf, but suppose that if it was necessary, by checking through the cancelled vouchers, check stubs and other receipts on file in the office, we could arrive at the amount. We estimate however, that we have spent considerably more than $500.00 in his defense to date, and I am sure that this amount is not under estimated.

You have no doubt noticed from the public press that Julia Anderson is in Savanah, Georgia, attempting, it seems to come to Columbia. They appealed to us for transportation for her. We answered promptly advising that there is no necessity of her coming here now, as there will be nothing doing in the case until after his appeal is disposed of in our Supreme Court. We do not know of any work that she could secure here, and we are not in a condition financially to support her. We think it best, therefore, that she stay with her people until the occasion demands her presence here. If there is further or other information that we can give you in this connection, feel no hesitancy in calling on us. W. C. is in good health and with his musical instrument seems to be passing the time as pleasantly as could be expected under the circumstances. We see to it all the while that he has the necessary clothing, medical attention, tobacco, newspapers and any other small luxury that he desired, paying for the same, of course, ourselves.

Your very truly,
Dale & Rawls

William Cantwell Walters' Defense File© #250

"It had to be done, Hollis," Tom assured his anguished partner with a firm pat on the back. "We cannot change the current state of events. You and I are holding onto Cantwell by the skin-of-our-teeth, and if we spread ourselves any thinner, the entire case may collapse."

Three days later Hollis opened another letter from Padgett and Watson.

Sept. 15th 1913.
Messrs. Rawls & Dale,
Columbia, Miss.

Gentlemen;

Mrs. Julia Anderson the mother of Bruce Anderson is here and will be here for a few days with the brothers of W. C. Walters. I have just had a consultation with her and she is anxious to take some steps for the recovery of her child which she declares most emphatically is now in possession of C. P. Dunbar in Louisiana. She desires to go and be at the trial of W. C. Walters and do everything she can to clear him, for she says that the Dunbars have her child. She has with her pictures of Mr. and Mrs. Dunbar taken with the child at New Oleans and also a picture of the Dunbar child which was not lost. I have carefully observed her and the pictures of the child and I am satisfied that she is correct in stating that the Dunbars have her child.

She is a lady of reasonable intelligence, fair complexion, light hair, blue eyes and in fact every feature compares favorably with the picture of the child which the Dunbars have. Upon the other hand I observe that both Mr. and Mrs. Dunbar are dark complexion with dark hair and the other little boy of theirs has dark hair and is dark. This it seems to me is a strong link in favor of her contentions and the contentions of Mr. Walters. The brothers of Mr. Walters here are poor men but they are very much interested in assisting their brother in establishing his innocence and I think they will raise sufficient funds to aid Mrs. Anderson in recovering her child if we can devise any way to do so. We are going to have her here with them for several days and in the meantime will get up whatever evidence we can to aid and assist in the trial of W. C. Walters and we will be glad to hear from you at once as to what you now think as to the advisibility of entering proceedings for the recovery of the child by Mrs. Ander-

son. She seems to be very much in earnest and is very much affected over the Dunbars having her child. In fact she says that she will fight for the child as long as she lives or she will not let the Dunbars keep her child.

There are many things which she suggests about the child and the circumstances connected with the Dunbars having taken him which seems to make her claim and contention that the child is hers absolutely bona fide. We shall be glad to hear from you further in this matter as we are anxious to do what we can for Mrs. Anderson, however, we desire and think best to cooperate with you gentlemen in what is done.

Awaiting your reply, we are

Yours truly,
Padgett & Watson

William Cantwell Walters' Defense File© #251

Tom and Hollis were elated but skeptical when Padgett & Watson wanted to enter the proceedings. Hollis wrote, "Our Mr. Dale expresses a desire to have a conference with one or both members of your firm, and, if it is so you can, we would like very much to have one of you gentlemen come to Columbia and we will see if we could not devise some means of instituting proceedings in the Federal Court."

William Cantwell Walters' Defense File© #252

Tom and Hollis remained focused on Cantwell's situation, trying to prevent his certain execution. They likely realized by now that Bruce would never leave the Dunbars; Percy had the power to prevent it. Three weeks later they received another letter from Padgett and Watson.

October 8th, 1913.
Messrs. Dale & Rawls,
Columbia, Miss.

Gentlemen:

Mrs. Anderson is here at this time having returned to remain here until needed upon the trial of her case or the Walters case. She says that she received a telegram from you stating that whenever you got ready for her to go you would send her a ticket, and desired us to notify you that she would remain at Baxley until advised about the trial.

Now with respect to her bringing proceedings for the child in possession of the Dunbars, we are still of the opinion that it would be advisable to bring a habeas corpus proceeding for her child and to do this before the trial of Walters.

The question we are considering at this time is whether we would be able to enter the proceedings in Mississippi where Walters had the child and where he was taken from him by Mr. Dunbar and thus enable us to have the trial in the locality where the witnesses could be forced to attend.

We will write you again in a few days more definite as to the result of our investigation and very likely will arrange to have a consultation with you looking toward entering the proceeding

As stated to you in our previous letter, Mrs. Anderson is a very poor woman and is unable to pay any attorney's fees or expenses, as doubtless you well know. Her friends here and in North Carolina could likely raise a small amount of money for the purpose of aiding her in recovering her child but the expenses, in our opinion, would be a great deal more than she or her friends here could raise to pay lawyers anything like a reasonable fee, and in this connection we desire to call your attention, for the purpose of only getting your opinion, to a proposition which we understand had been submitted to Mrs. Anderson and which she referred to you, as being made by some party in Louisiana offering to bear, or help bear expenses of the litigation for her child in the sum of $1,500.00 provided they were assured of getting possession of the child after she recovered him, for a while at least for the purpose of using him in moving pictures, etc.

Mrs. Anderson says she referred this matter to you and while she is absolutely unwilling to part with possession of her child and unwilling to accept payment from any concern for her child, I think that we, as attorneys, could handle the matter aside from her, that we could manage her so as to comply with any agreement made with any party furnishing money for this litigation.

We are merely suggesting this to you in a confidential way as we got an intimation of same from Mr. Walter's brother, with whom she is staying and would like to know what you think of the advisability of making such arrangements.

William Cantwell Walters' Defense File© #259

Though Padgett and Watson seemed to truly want to help the cause, Tom and Hollis agreed with Julia. As strapped as they all were for cash, they could not in good faith recommend making a deal to exhibit Bruce with some unknown source in Louisiana. They had to stay true to their course and trust the Mississippi Supreme Court to rule in Cantwell's favor. Then they could possibly attempt Bruce's recovery. It was their only chance to save the old man's life and there was no room for regret.

Cantwell waited in a cold concrete cell throughout October and November for the court to rule on his case. On November 22, the *Marion County Progress* in Columbia published a lengthy article from the beleaguered man.

A Revelation

My name is William Cantwell Walters. I am fifty-one years of age; was born in North Carolina near Barnesville, the year 1862, of humble though honorable parentage. No stigma has ever rested on the family name. I do not belong to the criminal class, as the newspapers would paint me to the wide, wide world; nor has my life been such as to cast the slightest shadow on the good name of my honored sire or sainted mother. My father has recently passed over the dark river, though if he could speak he would testify in my behalf. My dear mother, though bowed down with the weight of hoary age, knows I'm telling the truth, when I say I've been condemned and crucified, as it were, by public sentiment, without cause, and THAT mother is praying for me, that the blinded world may know the truth regarding my condemnation and crucifixion. Will there be no curcease to my suffering? Will the prayers of my mother, sisters and others never be answered? Can it be that the Almighty God will withhold the light from the eyes of the world until an innocent man has worn his life away behind the prison bars? Or will fate irrevocably still kiss to slumber the mighty populace and court decree my transfer to Opelousas to be tried for a crime of which I'm not guilty? Removed hundreds of miles from my witnesses, with no friends or funds to continue the fight for my life and liberty, afflicted from my youth with rheumatism and hookworms and for several years with hydrocile and a crippled knee, the knee-cap having been shattered, making my whole leg as stiff as an iron post; with all these afflictions and discomforts, like a wounded bird in a darkened cage, I continue to pray and sing for justice, life and liberty; the while challenging the world from the uncoveted couch of a dingy dungeon, to search the court records of the Carolinas and Georgia, where I have lived the most of my life, and see what my reputation is there. I have lived the simple life and had little to do in court houses and in the courts. But it seems that I must suffer now for an imaginary sin or crime that has never been committed. The generosity of a North Carolina servant woman in the home of my parents at Barnesville, by placing in my care and keeping her only son, Charlie Bruce Anderson, is the prime cause of my undoing. Oh, if we could just read the yet unwritten pages of the book of the future. But I loved the little boy and he loved me, and why should I fear when I knew not what to fear? If I had known that someone was going to lose a child several hundred miles away and claim Bruce Anderson as that child, without due process of law or anything else, many months afterwards and charge me with kidnapping and throw me in jail without giving me any chance whatever, why, of course, I would have left the child at my mother's home and, hence, would not be in any trouble. Mr. and Mrs. Dunbar have in their home in the place of the little boy they claim to have lost, Bruce Anderson, the son of Julia Anderson, and if I had to die that would be my dying declaration. I am sorry for Mrs. C. P. Dunbar and also Mr. C. P. Dunbar, if they are honest in contending that Bruce Anderson is Bobbie Dunbar. God knows it is strange to think that a mother would not know her child, and that is the reason PUBLIC SENTIMENT is so hard on me, but this is a case where the mother must be honest in mistaking the child of another for her own. I left Bruce Anderson with Mrs. Bilbo while I was in the hospital in September, 1912, and while in the hospital I learned of the disappearance of the Dunbar child. Until that time I had never heard of the Dunbars. Upon my return from the hospital to Mrs. Bilbo's they told me that someone had been there looking for the lost Dunbar child and examined Bruce and said that he was not the Dunbar child, Mrs. Bilbo telling the parties that Bruce had come to her home in July, 1912, over a month before the Dunbar child disappeared. No man can sympathize more with Mrs. Dunbar than I can, for I feel the loss of poor little Bruce almost as much as a real parent could. There is no one who would be more willing to help a parent who had lost a child than I, but as it now is, the Dunbars have Bruce Anderson and I may have to die on account of it. I have already had to spend my interest in my old home in Barnesville, N. C., besides my personal effects to fight for life this far and God only knows what the end will be. But one thing certain and sure, if the Supreme Court says that I must go to Opelousas for trial, I will go like a man, without a murmur, even though my witnesses are unable to attend court there. And if I am convicted and my life is taken for an alleged crime of which I'm not guilty and know nothing of, who, let me ask, who will be required to atone for my innocent blood? God will repay in his own good way, some day. I'm ready. I have suffered patiently a martyr to Public Sentiment and frenzied emotion. Though proud as the ancient Spartans by nature, a poor cripple beggar I am, made so by cruel circumstance. Living I yield to no spirit but the God-Spirit and the sweet music of the soul such as is made from the harps of angels. Dying I can look up through the Etheral blue of Heaven, thank God, and say my conscience is clear; the heart strings of weeping mothers bind not my withering limbs, and the crime of kidnapping stains not my humble threshhold door.

W. C. WALTERS,

Columbia, Miss.

As the year drew to a close, the traditional celebrations offered no joy, but served only to magnify Julia and Cantwell's loss. Each grieved for the child who had loved them.

Columbia Miss
Dec the 30th 1913

Hon T S Dale

Dear Sir at your Earleist Conveanance Pleas Call Around At the Jail and See your old Friend W C Walters And Lets Do some Planing

Respectfuly Yours
W C Walters
Columbia Miss

William Cantwell Walters' Defense File© #264

Chapter Twelve
A Dark Stream

In January the Mississippi Supreme Court denied Cantwell's appeal and ruled that he must be turned over to Louisiana. Cantwell decided to forego an appeal to the United States Supreme Court, considering that it could take from one to two years for a decision. By then, if he wasn't already, Bruce would have been irreversibly brainwashed.

Padgett wrote to Dale and Rawls:

Mrs. Anderson is here and is anxious to go to Louisiana and endeavor to recover her child. If the trial of Walters is set for the 16th, we think the habeas corpus should be presented to the District Judge on or about the 12th. This would necessarily postpone the criminal case until we could determine the civil case.
William Cantwell Walters Defense File© #271

Hollis answered Padgett:

As you know already, Walters is absolutely without funds or friends to make his defense at Opelousas, by failing to resist further and going on to Opelousas of his own accord, it appears to some extent that public sentiment is not so strong against him and that he has made some few friends in Opelousas. At any rate, we are advised that there is a movement on foot to have the Police Jury of St. Landry Parish to make a small appropriation to assist him in bringing his witnesses to his trial. We are confident, therefore, that a habeas corpus proceeding now be for the recovery of the child, that this movement would result disastrously to Walters. The Parish would immediately withdraw its offer of assistance and leave Walters helpless and stranded, without the slightest hope of securing the attendance of any of his witnesses. In other words, we think this movement now would inflame public sentiment against him and make his conviction almost certain.

We cannot help but feel that we are right in this proposition and that by far the better course would be for all of us to join hands in an effort to acquit Walters and then institute proceedings as outlined by you, for the recovery of the child.

William Cantwell Walters' Defense File© #276

On February 2 the prisoner, along with his harp, was released into Sheriff Swords' custody. Those who believed him guilty rejoiced when Cantwell finally crossed the Louisiana state line. Initially, he was taken into New Orleans to Royal Street in the heart of the French Quarter and into the lobby of the Monteleon Hotel where city officials and representatives of the press had gathered. Swords, towing Cantwell by the arm, had to elbow his way through the gathered throng outside. The older gentleman was allowed a stiff drink at the bar before officially being presented to the State.

The dastardly villain they had anticipated held the disposition of an affable country preacher, shaking hands and looking each person directly in the eye. Even after being plied with several on-the-house rounds of liquor, he never once faltered in his endless supply of stories and alibis; and his indomitable spirit remained unshakable, dampening their long-awaited celebration.

The entourage boarded the train to Opelousas, approaching the same swampland that entombed Bobby's remains. The car was filled to overflowing with a variety of key Louisiana dignitaries, buzzing report-ers, and tight-lipped lawmen. The Dunbars had sent a heavy presence as well. At each station, hardened faces searched the window for the kidnapper's likeness, pointing and shouting. The noise, commotion, and smoke were overwhelming. At one point Cantwell blocked out every sound assaulting his ears and was drawn to the window looking north over the seemingly endless Atchafalaya Basin. He sensed a stirring in his soul, a crossing of paths with the child he'd never met. The train continued toward its final destination, a stark jail cell in the belly of Opelousas.

With the trial immediately scheduled for February 16, the Colum-bia attorneys scrambled to have it delayed long enough to allow them to gather their witnesses. They had no funds to provide witnesses from Mississippi, much less North Carolina and Georgia. Hollis wrote to

Garland attempting "to secure an appropriation from the Police Jury of your Parish."

William Cantwell Walters' Defense File© #272

He then typed a letter to the Opelousas Police Jury, "appreciating the generosity of the Parish in this matter, it is our purpose to only call those (witnesses) who are absolutely material to his defense."

William Cantwell Walters' Defense File© #274

Next, Hollis wrote to Swords seeking a reputable attorney from Opelousas to join them in representing Cantwell. Judge Pavy assigned E. B. Dubuisson to assist them, and the Columbia attorneys began to familiarize him with the case.

William Cantwell Walters' Defense File© #'s 279 & 281

The trial date was pushed back until February 24. Hollis wrote to Dubuisson stating that there were many in Opelousas, including friends and relatives of the Dunbars, who recognized "that the child in possession of the Dunbars is not Robert Dunbar." He asked Dubuisson to "begin in a quiet way to make an investigation as to this."

William Cantwell Walters' Defense File© #'s 284 & 292

The lawyers hired Thomas Kleinpeter, the Louisiana attorney who had helped sort out the mislabeled photo of Cantwell in the *Item*, to investigate and pushed to delay the trial again in order to gather his information. The trial date was officially set for April 14, 1914, the Tuesday after Easter.

Kleinpeter wrote to Dale and Rawls, "You could not get an impartial Jury in the Parish or County of St. Landry.

"Our Juries in all cases where Death is the penalty have, under Section 1000 of our Revised Statutes, a right to qualify their verdicts, with a life imprisonment, thus leaving open a chance for pardon."

William Cantwell Walters' Defense File© #306

Kleinpeter added, "There is now, a state of astonishment bordering on protest, that the State should or the Parish should furnish funds necessary to produce evidence to prove the innocence of the accused." He further warned that the citizens of Opelousas were protesting the idea of providing any funds to help secure the defendant's witnesses.

William Cantwell Walters' Defense File© #307

As Cantwell was conversing with the crowd below his prison window, someone cried out, "You got a noose waitin' on you ole man. You afraid?"

Cantwell responded simply, "God will protect me," although his faltering words exposed the toll his ordeal had taken. He penciled a letter to his attorneys.

Opelousas La Mch the 10th 1914

Mess Dale & Rawls Columbia Miss

I Have Located A Good witness From China Grove the only one From there I Have been able to Locate He was teaching school there and me and Bruce Visited His school In July 1912 would Be Glad we Could Get Him I Have Had the Idia suggested to me to Have Enlarged Pictures of Bruce and Bobie Dunbar Mr Dale said He was Going to Have them Enlarged I would try to Have it Done But I Have none But Newspaper Pictures will you Do it let me no Dr T J Walters wrote me He would send you 25 Dollars and Advise you to Do As I said about it No doubt But you will need it to start one witnesses Has Mr Dubison Attended to Any Part of the Buiseness Has He Corosponded with you I am mystifide About Him I want Every thing Done wright It May Be Posable that I Have tried to Do too much But to try to Call Up all the Richeous Forces I Dont see How too much Could Be done I Dont see How nor I Dont Beleave the Good Peopple of Pearlriver Co Could Fail to Do all they Can. I Trust that God in his mighty Power will Reign in my Behalf I Have worked And worried until My Brain is tired I Have sung and Played Music And Been on my Feet until I am about Give out All over I Have tried in my Ignorant simple way to Get the Good Peoepple of Opelousas St Landry Parish & La Interested Dont no Just How But what I think to Be some of the Leading Citizens Has Assured me I should not Be Hurt I Have Learned From Mager sources that the Peoepple stood about 10 W to 1 D this school Teacher is Prof V B Easterling Hattiesburg Miss R # 3 Let me Hear From you Early I Likely will Get some mony at Court

William Cantwell Walters' Defense File© #299

Cantwell occupied his time by preaching, writing letters, and granting interviews. A few reporters printed discrepancies in the Dunbars' accounts, but they and their employers were ridiculed, swaying the majority of the Louisiana populace into accepting Lessie's mantra, "A mother knows her child."

The Dunbars successfully marketed a wanton cast of deprived and depraved characters to fit their needs, leading people to assume that even if the boy *was* Bruce, he was better off where he was. It was almost inconceivable that this family could have been mistaken in recognizing their child or taken such drastic measures to cover up the mistake, but it fascinated the citizenry nonetheless. A wild-eyed four-year-old had been methodically stripped to the bone and later reassembled according to the wide-ranging network of plot-twists coming from the Opelousas family. He could never be unbroken.

Cantwell met with Attorney Dubuisson, giving him a list of witnesses that he believed were crucial in his defense. Dubuisson wrote to Tom and Hollis stating that he believed sentiment in Opelousas was equally divided as to the defendant's guilt or innocence. The Mississippi attorneys assembled their massive amount of evidence and laid out their plan of attack.

Back in Pearl River County, Mississippi, on April 6, 1914, Justice of the Peace J. P. Mitchell heard rapping at his office door. He was not surprised to see longtime friend D. F. Smith, the Postmaster and Notary Public at Carriere, Mississippi, and H. G. Anderson, also of Carriere, come walking in. Their serious expressions caused Mitchell to take notice even though he had been expecting the men for a few days.

"We need to make out an affidavit concerning the search for the Dunbar child last year," Smith began remorsefully. "I've helped create a monster."

Mitchell pulled out a chair for each of his friends. Looking to Smith first, he held out a worn bible. "Place your right hand on the bible and repeat after me," he said. "I, state your name, do solemnly swear,"

"I, D. F. Smith, do solemnly swear,"

Mitchell continued, "to tell the truth in the matter upon which I am giving testimony,"

"to tell the truth in the matter upon which I am giving testimony,"

Mitchell looked the man in the eye, "so help me God."

"so help me God."

Smith slid two sheets of paper toward Mitchell. The first was a copy of the Western Union telegram from himself to Loeb in December, 1912, "Suspicious man here name Walters…"

The second, a copy of the Western Union telegram from Loeb to him, "big toe on left foot badly scarred…" **(See p. 278)**

With the affiant duly sworn, Mitchell began listening and typing.

The attached copies of the Telegrams which have been certified to by J. H. Horne, manager of the Western Union Telegraph Company of this place, also a reputable citizen of the Town of Carriere, Pearl River County, Mississippi, are a true and correct copy of the exchange of wires between himself and Mayor, T. L. Loeb, of Opelousas, La., and that he, Smith, caused an investigation to be made December, 30, 1912 of the child named in the attached Telegrams, by F. E. Brooks, at that time a lawful and legal Deputy Sheriff of Pearl River County, Mississippi, and Mr. H. G. Anderson, reputable citizens of the town of Carriere, Miss., and that after a close investigation of the child then in the possession of W. C. Walter, they decided that it was not C. P. Dunbar's child, which had been lost prior to that date at Opelousas, La. Smith further says that he often saw W. C. Walters with this same child prior to that date, and while he is not positive as to dates he states that he saw this same W. C. Walters and the same child at Levy Hollomon's place sometime during the month of August, 1912, and that W. C. Walters was in and around this neighborhood, in Pearl River County Mississippi from sometime in August, 1912 until sometime in January, 1913.

Smith felt a great burden fall from his shoulders.

Mitchell turned toward Anderson, "Place your hand on the bible and repeat after me," he began.

"I, state your name, do solemnly swear,"

"I, H. G. Anderson, do solemnly swear,"

Mitchell continued, "to tell the truth in the matter upon which I am giving testimony,"

"to tell the truth in the matter upon which I am giving testimony,"

Mitchell looked Anderson in the eye, "so help me God."

"so help me God."

Mitchell began typing.

Also personally appeared before me, H. G. Anderson, a reputable Citizen and well known to me says on oath that he is the same H. G. Anderson, mentioned in the above affidavit by D. F. Smith, as having went with the Deputy Sheriff F. E. Brooks, to make an examination of the child in the possession of W. C. Walters, and that they had the necessary warrant to arrest and detain the said W. C. Walters, in case the child was found to fill the description of the child mentioned in T. L. Loeb, wire to D. F. Smith, of December, 30, a copy of which is hereto attached, and that he and F. E. Brooks, deputy Sheriff made a careful examination of the child which the said W. C. Walters, had with him, and while the description tallied with that of the Dunbar child (Bobbie) in many ways, especially as to age, complexion, color of eyes and hair, they made a special and close examination of his left foot, and were unable to find any bad scar, as mentioned in T L Loeb wire to D F Smith or any semblance of a scar near his big toe, or anywhere else on his foot, and therefore reached the conclusion that this child was not Bobbie Dunbar, and did not arrest or detain the said W. C. Walters, and let him go on his way.

Affiant further states that he made this investigation with a view of securing a $6,000.00 reward for Bobbie Dunbar, which he understood was offered by C. P. Dunbar and the citizens of Opelousas, La., for his capture or return to C. P. Dunbar.

Sworn to and subscribed by each D. F. Smith, and H. G. Anderson, whose names appear above, this the 6 day of April, 1914.

Mitchell unrolled the paper from the typewriter and slid it toward Smith who signed in the space provided followed by Anderson. "We are trying to make this right."

Mitchell stamped the document with his official seal and sent the affidavit and telegrams to Tom and Hollis.

William Cantwell Walters' Defense File© #312

The men had searched in earnest for the scar that could reunite a family and make them rich men in the process, but it simply wasn't there. The Dunbars answered these seemingly damaging statements with ease. They claimed that Anderson and Smith had examined another child, one that Cantwell had before he kidnapped Bobby. The

Dunbars, along with their doctors, swore that the child in their possession had the telltale scar.

More evidence began to come in to Columbia. The following affidavit from Maggie Burks, along with the attached check it referenced,
placed Cantwell and Bruce in Pearl River County while Bobby played
at home in Opelousas.

Picayune, Miss.April 11 1914
State Of Mississippi
County of Pearl River

Personally appeared before the undersigned Justice of the Peace of said
County and State the within named Maggie Burks being duly sworn
on oath that William C. Walters and the child Bruce Anderson were at
S. L. Jarrells place in Pearl River County on Aug 17 1912 and that
the enclosed check was issued by Maggie Burks to Mrs. S. L Jarrell on
Aug 17 1912 in presence of W. C Walters and Mrs. S. L. Jarrell.

Witness my hand and Official Seal.
S. J. Moody Justice of the peace
William Cantwell Walters' Defense File© #316 & 317
(See p. 306)

The *Item* had several reporters in Opelousas to cover the trial. One
of these, Sam Blair, quoted a statement for the paper from the prosecution.

The Death Penalty will be Demanded

The coming of Saturday morning in this quiet little city brought with
it a touch of grimness. For after a conference among the three attorneys
who will combine in the prosecution of W. C. Walters on a charge of
kidnapping Robert Dunbar from his home here, the announcement
was made that when the trial is called Monday morning, every juror
selected must promise to find a death verdict, if it be determined that
the tinker-suspect actually is guilty.
The Item-April 11, 1914

The following article, publically ridiculed for Cantwell's dramatic flair, was sent in by Mignon Hall, another *Item* reporter, who visited Cantwell on Saturday before the trial began.

Vision of Death Comes to the Tinker, Walters On Eve of His Trial

Dream of a Dark Stream That Swept Him Out With It

"I AM PREPARED," HE TELLS REPORTER

By Mignon Hall

OPELOUSAS, La., April 11, 1914. A vision of death has come to W. C. Walters.

On the eve of the trial that may mean his hanging for the alleged kidnapping of little Bobbie Dunbar, it visited him as he lay on his prison cot.

Weird, strange, it was the vision of a dark stream, roaring water that swept him out with it, home and the sound of his mother's voice calling him through the night.

Till day Walters did not sleep. He spent the hours in prayer, pacing up and down the length of his narrow corridor and looking on the white stars from his window.

This vision has resigned him to whatever fate the jury may decide for him in his impending trial. He told me this Saturday as I sat with him and he played the rude harp fashioned with his own hands and his sole companion in the jail.

"I am now prepared for death if my dream meant that. Before my God, I am an innocent man, and I can look the world in the face and say so, but the innocent have often paid the penalty for the guilty. While I cannot believe God will forsake me in my tribulation, if it is His plan that I die on the gallows, I am ready to bow by head like my Saviour and say: 'Thy will be done, O Lord.'"

At that Walters raised his hand toward Heaven with a cry. "But hear what I say and remember what I tell you: If I am hanged, my blood will be upon the souls of those who caused my death. They will suffer in time to come, and they will be cursed if not now and suffer hard. God does not let a wrong go unpunished."

Then he told of his dream.

"It seemed that I was riding in a large canoe. When I started out the way looked clear in front and everything seemed bright. Only something in my mind seemed to trouble me so that I could not rest. Then the sky began to get gray. I heard the wind rising, and suddenly big waves began to come. I couldn't manage the boat any longer. I was caught in the swirl of the waters. Then I saw a vision of my old home back there in North Carolina, and I seemed to float away with the dream while the water was sucking me down—down. Something seemed to be pulling me, then far away I heard mother calling me, and I answered her back: 'Yes, mother, I'm coming,' just like I used to when I was a little boy. And then the whole sea seemed to rise up and swallow me. That was the end of the dream."

Walters stood stiff and silent for a moment. Then he went to the window of his cell, flung open its little doors of glass and let the sunset of the April evening fall upon his bended head."

The Item–April 12, 1914

On Easter Sunday Julia arrived in Opelousas, accompanied by Walter Murray and Marion Stephens from Cantwell's hometown in North Carolina. They had been joined en route by David Bledsoe.

Tom and Hollis met them there and managed to get everyone registered in rented rooms, no small feat with the town nearly bursting at the seams. The rest of their tiny army consisted of Mr. and Mrs. Bilbo, Mr. and Mrs. Miley, Homer Moody, Levy Holleman, Reverend J. Q. Sones, B. J. Sones Sr., J. S. Thigpen, Mr. and Mrs. L. A. Thigpen, W. C. Bass, Ben Allsbrook, George Smith, W. W. Lott, Mr. and Mrs. Allen Goldman, John F. Norris, G.M. Donald and Reverend Holcomb. Two of their subpoenaed witnesses, a reluctant J. L. Linder and Alex Edwards, arrived later.

Cantwell prayed fervently and begged the crowd to join him. The cold-hearted saw it as an act of pure publicity. In the Dunbar household, Bruce sensed the mounting tension as Cantwell was proclaimed "as-good-as-dead."

Miss Hall recorded the meeting between Cantwell and Julia, which reflected none of the reported animosity between them.

Hug and Kiss Seal Greeting of Walters and Julia Anderson

By Mignon Hall

OPELOUSAS, La., April 14. For the first time since W. C. Walters took her child, Bruce Anderson, away from her at Barnesville, N. C., Julia Anderson late Monday afternoon met face to face with Walters.

It was up in the Opelousas courtroom, where the attorneys were holding a conference with the defense witnesses.

Julia entered with her attorneys. Walters did not see her at first, as he was walking about with a baby in his arms, the child of Mr. and Mrs. Goleman, of Poplarville. Neither did she see him.

Then suddenly he called out gladly: "Hey there." She turned to look and Walters was waving his free arm and making a rush toward her.

"Hey there, yourself," she said.

A hug and a kiss sealed the greeting.

Then Julia Anderson told the story in her own words.

"Poor Walters grabbed my hands and broke down, and said, 'God bless you, Julia,' and I almost cried. Then our attorneys let me talk to him for a little while. He seemed grateful that I had come to help him in the fight for his life. I told him I would stand by him and my child to the last. Then he told me all about the little things that Bruce had said and done while they were together: how he had often spoken of me and how terrible it was they had taken him away from him, when they had no right to.

"He told me little Bruce had asked for me only a day or two before they took him. He had said, 'Where is my mamma?' and Walters had asked: 'Who is your mamma, Bruce?' and the child had replied, 'Julia,' then added: 'And O, don't you wish that she was here with us now? We're rich. Why we've got oranges and apples and candy and peanuts and other things, and wouldn't she like them, though?'"

Julia Anderson said she intended to visit Walters in the jail again shortly. There was nothing particularly to discuss. They would probably talk mostly of old times and the child.

The Item

Mignon Hall interviewed Lessie next in which she is quoted in the Item: "I do not wish Walters hanged." The statement was immediately denounced by Percy and Lewis as being purposely misconstrued. An enraged committee of the town's leading citizens went to the paper's headquarters and warned Mr. Blair to refrain from publishing anything that might sway the jury one way or another. It was the beginning of the mighty paper's downfall.

Beginning on day one of the trial, the Dunbars' allies overran the courtroom before dawn attempting to convince the outside world, and possibly themselves, that the boy was Bobby.

Cantwell's brother Bunt, Bruce's father, arrived by train on Monday to offer his assistance but collapsed shortly afterward and said he felt drugged—a seemingly common occurrence in the area. He had been given several hypodermic injections by a doctor, but the newspapers claimed he was merely drunk. Bunt spooked and left town shortly afterward when it was intimated that he might be charged as an accessory, or as it was hinted, worse.

Brother of Walters Leaves Mysteriously as He Had Arrived

OPELOUSAS, La., April 15. The mystery that has evolved about D. B. Walters, brother of the accused man, grew Wednesday morning, when both the prisoner and his attorneys said that they did not know where the brother had gone.

D. B. Walters reached Opelousas unannounced Monday night. For some reason not yet made completely clear he was given lodging in the parish jail.

That the lodging was not a process of showing courtesy to a brother of a prisoner Sheriff Swords was emphatic in asserting.

"Our jail is not turned over as a lodging house for visitors," he said.

But that is as far as the sheriff would comment.

He admitted that the brother left the jail Tuesday.

"He probably has left town," was the explanation of Dale and Rawls, the prisoner's attorneys.

"He just stayed at the jail to visit with his brother. He is not to be a witness."

Walters was asked for some complete explanation of the brother's visit here. The prisoner drew his brows together in mock seriousness and proclaimed in a hoarse whisper:

"HE'S BEEN KIDNAPPED."

The Item

By Tuesday evening, under the watchful eyes of an intimidating group of men in the corner of the room, eight members of the jury had been chosen. They were George Lang, bookkeeper, Eunice; A. P. Collins, farmer, near Opelousas; Gaston Horaist, oil mill manager, Sunset; Faustin Soileau, farmer, Grand Prairie; Robert McClelland, farmer, near Opelousas; E. Fisher, city contractor, Opelousas; George K. Caillouet, merchant, Port Barre; and Frank Oliver, farmer and merchant, Frozard. On Wednesday morning, with the menacing group observing the process, the four remaining members were selected. They were Hyppolite Miller, merchant, Sunset; Walter Sibille, farmer, Sunset; Antoine Lamaury, manager Farmer's Union warehouse, Sunset; and J. B. Sibille, farmer, Sunset.

Judge Pavy looked over the group of men filling the jury box. "You men must not speak among yourselves for the duration of the trial, only to the bailiffs who will be with you at all times. You must not seek outside information or read the newspaper. Violation of these rules will result in your termination."

Percy opened the trial on Wednesday morning, the 15th retelling how his family had left for camp on August 22, 1912. "The camp is about 18 miles WNW of Opelousas. We have a cluster of small camp houses on a high bank about a half mile from the railway. Nobody lives anywhere permanently along that twenty-five mile stretch of line except one family of Negroes." He continued, "I got a message that next morning that I was needed in Melville for business, so I left camp around 9 or 10 in the morning. It was about 1:30 when Sebe found me and I received the call to return to the lake."

The courtroom, with seating for three hundred people, was overrun with over one thousand people at a time, the majority of them women from the area. They arrived before the doors were opened, lining up, lunch in hand, laying claim to every square inch of space to sit or stand on. Julia found herself relegated to the back row one day when none of the women up front would make a space for her.

People spilled beyond the bar, surrounding the bench, lawyers' tables, jury, and witness chair. The top of the small toilet cubicle was a prime location, as were the airy windowsills, as the surge of anxious flesh molded itself to the room.

Percy continued his opening remarks. "The first place I searched, naturally, was all along the lake bank, but we found no sign of him."

"Mr. Dunbar," said Tom, "I have heard that you found Bobby's hat in the water near the trestle."

Percy narrowed his eyes at the thorn-in-his-side attorney. Managing to keep his voice steady and strong, he turned to the jury, "Bobby's hat was never found."

"I have heard that Bobby's hat was not only found, it was found near a fresh alligator slide. Mr. Dunbar, how far is it from where the dog tracked the end of Bobby's path on the trestle to that slide?"

"A good forty feet, but the dog we used that day was not dependable and there was no evidence of Bobby having ever been in the water. We had two trainloads of people combing every inch of that swamp. We were positive early on that he had been stolen."

"Mr. Dunbar, what then was your purpose of dragging and then draining that lake if you were sure Bobby was not there? Didn't you dynamite the lake and gut larger alligators to check the contents of their stomachs?"

"Only to satisfy my wife's doubt about the child's fate."

The defense continued, "Mr. Dunbar, how did you know that the tracks leading to the railroad were Bobby's?"

"Less told me she pulled Bobby's shoes off just before he left to watch Paul Mizzie and when we looked at the footprints she recognized them."

"And how, sir, did she do that?"

"Bobby had a scar on the bottom of his left big toe and into his arch and it was present in the muddy imprint. It has since shrunk a great deal, as well as being worn away by going barefoot."

Percy gave his version of the events, including Hub's communications with Lott and Day and their subsequently sending photographs of the child to Opelousas. "I had been sent pictures of many different boys, but when I saw that picture I felt as though I had found my son. He was a dead ringer for Bobby."

The Defense countered, "And how long was it after you received this photo before you left to find the boy in the picture?"

"Two weeks," Percy grumbled. "Your Sheriff Hathorn had let the suspicious pair wander freely around the county for weeks so I wasn't sure where to look."

When Percy was asked about the boy's unexpected reaction when he first saw him in Foxworth, he said, "Terror! Pure damn terror! Walters almost ruined my boy!"

"Mr. Dunbar, why did you take so long in examining the child?"

"A few of his features had changed slightly over the eight months Walters had him. Bobby's adenoids were swollen, broadening the area across his nose and his eyes had acquired a squint from traveling in the bald-faced sun on the open road. I wanted to check other marks of identification, and I found them all intact."

"Mr. Dunbar," asked Tom, quizzically, "If you had just found your long-lost son, why," he paused, "why did you leave your child at the Wallace's home? You and your wife and other family members enjoyed one of the finest homes in this area and yet you drove away and left your long-lost child in a meager cabin."

"I purposely told my wife not to identify him that night to prevent Walters' lynching." Percy relaxed back into his chair and crossed his legs. "I am solely responsible for saving Walter's scrawny neck that night, besides Mr. and Mrs. Wallace were perfectly capable of caring for the child overnight."

Tom pressed the man harder, asking him about Loeb's description of the badly scarred toe, the major point brought out for the purpose of identification. "The child you took from Walters, the child in your possession has no such scar. I've seen his feet myself."

A noticeable clenching of Percy's jaw gave the only clue as to his inner turmoil.

"Mr. Dale, unless you have forgotten, my wife was not herself when she first made up the description. She simply placed too much emphasis on the scar in her initial account. Bobby has many other identifying marks we could have listed and found." Lessie pressed an embroidered handkerchief to her quivering lips, stifling an occasional sob.

"Yet for eight months," prodded Tom, "eight long months, no one bothered to alter the incorrect report." He turned his back on Percy, whose eyes were blazing fire. "No further questions, Your Honor."

Wallace Dunbar was sworn in next, describing Bobby's attempt to go with his father when he left camp. His son had gone along with Bobby and Alonzo to watch Paul Mizzie shooting gar. He told of finding Bobby's tracks along the railroad and the dog tracking Bobby's scent to the middle of the trestle.

"We searched this entire country for miles and miles and found no other tracks anywhere so we knew he had been grabbed on the bridge."

"Mr. Dunbar, if a person were to try and make it through the swamp to a road, off of the train tracks, how far would he have to travel?"

"It's at least six miles to a highway in one direction, and seven or more miles in the other. Part of the journey is overland portage and part by boat, but you'd have to know the waterway."

"So do you believe Mr. Walters was capable of going through a virtually impenetrable swamp," considered the attorney, "half-crippled, while towing a child and a boat and leave no trace?" He paused. "No further questions."

John Oge, the prominent attorney/politician of St. Landry Parish, took the stand next, describing the steep muddy bank on which the camp sat. Tom asked him if there were any other footprints on the ground walking beside Bobby's, to which he answered no.

"Mr. Oge, how long after the child disappeared did the next train come by?"

"Several hours."

When asked how well he knew Bobby before he disappeared, he answered, "Very well. The Dunbars and I are close friends and I saw him often. I am as positive as it is possible that the boy now in the Dunbar home is Bobby."

Mr. Richard, president of the local levee board, was called next. His testimony largely centered on his knowledge of the section of county around Swayze Lake.

"Despite the hardships in searching the area, we made a thorough search of the woods for miles in each direction and found no trace of the child anywhere but in a circuitous pattern near the train tracks. Bobby's footprints in the mud were well defined by the scar."

Mizzie testified that he was last one to see Bobby next to one of the shacks. "He was trying to crawl down the bank; he wanted to get into one of the skiffs with two older boys. I shooed him away and the next time I looked I saw him heading back toward the cabins.

"Bobby noticed that I had changed horses while he was gone. I have a dark horse now and he immediately asked about my old white horse." Mizzie's culpability in scolding and embarrassing Bobby, like Percy's, had faded away with the finding of this child.

Dr. Lawrence Daly, who was present on the day of the disappearance, mainly corroborated the earlier testimony. "Mrs. Dunbar said she could identify Bobby's track if she could see it and she did; it was very distinct." He ended his testimony by stating that he would swear the child was Bobby.

Dr. Anderson described his two examinations of the boy, first at the Bilbos' where, he stated, there was no scar found on the child's foot. "I was also at the identification at Foxworth. I looked for the scar and was still unable to find it. When Lessie arrived at the home, she looked at his feet almost immediately and became hysterical when she couldn't find the scar."

Hollis asked, "Is it not a fact that before his arrest, Walters offered to take Bruce to the Dunbars for an examination?"

"Yes, I have heard that." The courtroom fell into chaos with Pavy hammering the desk with his gavel.

By the time Cantwell took the stand the crowd of anxious spectators had pressed in behind the witness's chair and Pavy's massive desk, totally filling the space.

Dubuisson asked Cantwell what he knew about the night the Dunbars came to Foxworth to see the child.

"Mr. Dunbar accused me of having kidnapped his son. I tried to explain mine and Bruce's relationship but he ignored me and challenged every word I said." Then Cantwell addressed Percy directly, but the younger man kept his face turned downward. "You treated me like dirt, Mr. Dunbar." He let the words hang in the air. "I may not possess riches equal to what you have earned on earth, but thanks be to God, I am a rich man. I'm rich with the truth."

The courtroom had to be silenced once again. Cantwell continued, "They questioned me at the jail while Mr. Dunbar went to pick up his wife and bring her to see Bruce for herself." He paused, looking as baffled today as he did in April last year. "I couldn't wait for her to arrive and set matters straight once and for all."

He continued, "Sheriff Hathorn returned to the jail around...three a. m. and told me that Mr. and Mrs. Dunbar wanted to see the child again in the day time. I'll be honest, I am not the fainting type, but my legs fell out from under me after hearing this."

Bruce entered the courtroom carried aloft by Veazie, to be shown to the witness and jury. Cantwell eagerly searched the boy's face, hoping for recognition. "That is Bruce Anderson," he called out. "Bruce!" But when their eyes met, Bruce asked to be taken away. He had been told one year's worth of horror stories about Cantwell, plus he could only assimilate one life and for the last year, it had been Bobby's.

The titillation of seeing the famed child was followed by a first-hand dramatization of Sheriff Charlie Day's one-on-one dealings with Cantwell and Bruce around Columbia.

"I met Walters on the night of April 6. I knew right away something was amiss. Here was this foot-loose, half-crippled gentleman driving around like he owned the place, with a bright, well-mannered four-year-old. I arrested the old man because he looked like any other vagrant."

Looking toward Cantwell he stated, "The man was something of a smart-talker. Tried to confuse me as to whom the child belonged." A smirk played across the lawman's face, "He ended up saying that the boy belonged to a woman in North Carolina named Julia Anderson.

"The kid was real cute, friendly like," he said with a wide toothy grin, "and he kept me entertained. I wanted to get a picture of him to send to the Dunbars, and Mr. Walters conveniently had on his person a letter—written and sealed—to be sent to his parents. Well, there were actually two letters and two photos, one letter and photo for his parents and one letter with a photo for Julia. I took possession of one of the photos to send to Opelousas. **(See p. 58 States article "Saw Letter Opened"—The letter referenced was Cantwell's response to Julia's March 1913 letter on p. 276)**

"Right then and there..." with astonishment spreading over Day's face, "Walters offered to let me take the child to Opelousas. 'If it aint the Dunbar child,' he said, nonchalantly, 'bring it back.' Stanley Hathorn instructed me to release the man and in turn I mailed the photo to Percy. I guess you could say I cracked the case."

Cantwell had re-glued the envelope Day spoke about and mailed the letters to his parents' house.

John Fortenberry of Hub, who had traveled to New Orleans with Percy to pick up Lessie, and was also a witness at the Foxworth examination, testified. "I heard Mr. Dunbar telling his wife not to recognize the child that night." His other role in the drama was not quite so striking: he had helped circulate a petition in Columbia calling for Cantwell's extradition.

Dr. Hawkins of Palmetto, Louisiana, claimed to have seen the child's track. He also helped John Fortenberry circulate the petition calling for Cantwell's extradition.

The three McComb City witnesses, Joe Johnson, B. L. Morgan, and W. D. Holmes, appeared in a row, relishing their moments in the spotlight, although their testimonies had evolved from the time they gave their affidavits in April 1913, their appearances in the Columbia courtroom in May 1913, and now.

W. A. Stogner, living between Columbia and McComb, pointed toward Cantwell. "That's him alright! I would know him anywhere. That is the man who told me he was in the neighborhood of Opelousas around the time Bobby disappeared."

Cantwell listened numbly to the detailed accounts of a stranger's life, an alter ego whom he'd never met. Four times a day as he was taken to and from his cell, he limped through the large, mainly unsympathetic gathering, courteously tipping his hat to the ladies. The Dunbars' supporters were estimated to outnumber Cantwell's approximately thirty to one, and many of them were armed. Hollis carried a pistol in his coat pocket after hearing that, "Cantwell wouldn't leave the courtroom alive if he was acquitted."

Percy's younger sister, Miss Katie Dunbar, told of Bobby's recognition of her on the second day, mentioning several household objects he remembered in detail.

Lessie's sisters, Douce and Lorena Whitley and Mrs. Jack Dupree, testified in a row repeating almost the exact same testimony. "I knew Bobby then and I recognize him now." They added exacting details that the child "remembered."

Family friends, cousins, aunts, and uncles followed suit, some adding specific words or actions only Bobby would know, down to the lending of a pair of socks.

Lessie's cousin, Miss Christine Zernott, surprised the court when she said she didn't recognize the child brought to New Orleans.

Mrs. Frank Shute, wife of the Dunbar's physician, also caused a stir when she testified next saying, "I knew Bobby; I knew his marks and character. Every day I am more confused."

Opelousas Mayor T. L. Loeb did his duty swearing to the exchanging of telegrams in December 1912. William Mallet, who had testified during the Habeas corpus hearing, swore on oath that he knew Cantwell and had seen him near Alexandria on July 1912 in the wagon with the painted curtain, W. C. Walters—Stovemender. The courtroom erupted *en masse*, clapping, cheering, and embracing.

The prosecution called a Mrs. Hodges who swore that she saw him in Rapides Parish on July 22, 1912.

A. B. Dantin, the boilermaker in Alexandria claimed, "On August 6, 1912, I saw Walters in my shop. His wagon was out front with W. C. Walters—Stovemender written on the curtain."

William Cantwell Walters' Defense File© #320

JULIA ANDERSON LONGS TO LOOK UPON 'BOBBIE' IN COURT

"Two Mothers" Do Not Notice Each Other As They Watch Trial

Opelousas, La., April 16. With every day as the trial continues stronger grows the proof that the battle now being waged is a woman's conflict. A struggle between two mothers.

By the time that the testimony of Mr. Oge had been well begun Thursday morning several hundred women—most of them mothers—had come into the court room and been seated within the attorney's enclosure. Other women came, and these stood patiently during the entire morning and heard the reading of every word of testimony.

Within two hands' reach of each other and on the same row of seats were the two mothers, Mrs. C. P. Dunbar and Julia Anderson. The two women sat within close watch of the jury. They sent flashes of appeal at the 12 men who by now had become sufficiently used to their position as to display the usual juror's stoicism.

But not a glance passed between the two women. Both stared at the jury box or the witness stand and avoided the eyes of each other.

Here is a strange contrast in the appearance of the two mothers. Mrs. Dunbar is slender and of features that lend themselves readily to animation. Undeniable, she is pretty. Julia Anderson is heavy in build to the approach of fatness. Her expression seldom changes. The eyes of both women are blue. They make the one mark of resemblance.

In the court Thursday morning Mrs. Dunbar was dressed in a pretty gown of a gray lilac texture. A little black hat trimmed with flowers of blue perched upon her dark brown hair.

Julia Anderson, the other mother, wore a heavy suit of brown; it was a tailored suit and not expensive. Her hat was dark. A veil cast a lattice work of thread across her face.

Always during the morning Julia Anderson cast cautious glances about the courtroom. She was looking—looking—waiting; the boy had not appeared.

Not since she underwent the identity test in New Orleans has this "other mother" seen the child she calls her own. She came to court Thursday morning with the avowed intention of seeing the child.

"They can't keep me from looking at him, at any rate," she cried just before she entered the courthouse door.

The Item

But they did keep her from looking at him until *much* later. Julia's presence was so inflammatory she was strongly advised by the Court and her attorneys to remain in her hotel room, for Lessie would soon take the stand. Pavy already sensed the crowd becoming unmanageable. Julia reluctantly agreed, but she shared her displeasure with the hovering journalists.

Mrs. M. E. Sloan of New Roads, Louisiana, which is just above Baton Rouge, claimed to have boarded Cantwell in her home in January 1912. She said he was traveling in a canvas-covered wagon with three fine horses, and that he had for companions a sickly pale-faced child around six years of age and another man whose name she did not remember. She pointed an accusing finger at Cantwell. "That is the man!"

The courtroom erupted again with clapping and cheering, taking longer each time to come to order.

J. L. Linder and his traveling companion, Alex Edwards, arrived in town just as the Defense had called for a continuance. Linder reluctantly took the stand and refuted Mrs. Sloan's testimony. He claimed to be a traveling stove-mender and salesman from Alexandria who had also been hounded for months after Bobby disappeared. That he was supposed to have been a near double of Cantwell could explain the sighting of the organ-mender all over Louisiana, but Mrs. Sloan asserted that her boarder was Cantwell, not Linder. She said she recognized him from his pictures in the paper. The Defense had hoped to show how easily mistaken witnesses could be in their identification.

Linder griped, "We were in New Roads at Mrs. Sloan's in November 1911 and in Opelousas around Thanksgiving last year and returned home by Christmas. I was in Forest Hill, just below Alexandria in January 1912." Linder offered the court no extra information; and acknowledging the hard feelings against him after his testimony, he wanted to get out of town safely for Opelousas was armed to the teeth. Hoping to secure that goal, Linder let it be known that he was considering a suit against the Defense for damages in causing his unwanted notoriety.

Mrs. McManus, the widow who ran a boarding house in Pineville, Louisiana, on the outskirts of Alexandria, had stated in the *Habeas Corpus* hearing, "I've known Mr. Walters since 1910 when he worked in our town and first boarded with me. He was there again in the fall of 1911 and when he left there he was going down toward Lake Charles in a wagon stove-fixing and selling his harps."

Today she testified, "Walters was in Pineville in 1909."

Cantwell swore that he had never been in that part of Louisiana. "They are lying about me!" Whether these men and woman were seeking publicity or had been rewarded in some way for their fabricated testimonies is a matter for speculation.

Two witnesses, unknown by the Defense, were called next. Steve Bennett of Poplarville, Mississippi, took the stand saying that he saw two men with two ill-kept boys in September 1912 in a local restaurant. "The two men looked enough alike to have been brothers."

Directly after Bennett's testimony, Miss Kate Collins, a spinster of Poplarville, took the stand. She had been working in the restaurant mentioned. "I saw W. C. Walters and another man, possibly his brother, on the first or second Saturday in September. They had two young boys with them, one healthy and the other sickly." She theorized that Cantwell had Bruce with him at that time and that his brother had possession of Bobby Dunbar and that the men had swapped the children that day to conceal the kidnapping. Her testimony was particularly damning.

Thankfully, Miss Collins' testimony was included in the newspaper's coverage of the trial. One man in particular read the woman's account and realized that he and his son were the individuals she had described as meeting with Cantwell. His information would not be received until the conclusion of the trial.

The Defense was hit with another bizarre theory when Miss Loveless, the nurse from McNeill, Mississippi, testified that a non-limping man calling himself W. C. Walters had a sickly, web-toed child he called Bruce with him on August 18, 1912. "I bathed that child." Two months later, after Bobby's disappearance, a limping man calling himself W. C. Walters returned with a healthy child named Bruce that had no webbed toes. She described the two boys as looking alike but being of different temperaments.

Mrs. Nix of Port Barre, Louisiana, sporting a voluminous feathered hat, took the stand next. She stated that Cantwell came to her home on the morning of August 23, 1912, the day Bobby disappeared and had tried to coax her child away. "That man asked me if I didn't want to go play," her son had reported to his reproving mother.

"I invited the man in," she stated, "and he volunteered to fix my stove in exchange for a meal." She testified that he brought up the subject of webbed toes. He left after asking about the railroads and the directions to Swayze Lake.

Cantwell peered beseechingly at each witness during their testimony, usually when they were pointing him out as the kidnapper. "How can these ordinary people be so black-hearted?" he wondered as he ran his eyes over the jurymen for the hundredth time. Bruce was brought into court several more times in the protective arms of Lewis or Veazie. On one occasion the boy wiggled free and was allowed to wander about the room. He caught sight of Cantwell and this time he spent several minutes studying him before his attention was diverted. It was too late for memories now, for he had long since accepted Lessie and Percy as his parents.

The room quieted as Mr. Ansley, the bridge carpenter, was sworn in. He acknowledged Cantwell as being the man he saw three times around Swayze Lake on August 24, 25, and 26. "Walters asked about the reward for the boy."

Preston King, Percy's uncle who was searching for Bobby at Swayze Lake the day after the disappearance, supported Ansley's testimony. He claimed to have met the limping Cantwell on the tracks and they had discussed the reward money. "There is the man I met that day," he stated, pointing to Cantwell. The spectators again burst forth with cheering and catcalls and Pavy threatened to clear the courtroom.

Lessie's arrival in court caused a grand stirring in the room as she was sworn in and settled with family and friends physically surrounding her chair. It was deathly silent as she began reliving the horror of August 23, 1912. Tears began to flow almost immediately adding vulnerability to her impeccable façade. Percy placed a supporting arm across her shoulders as she choked back sobs. "I had to leave my baby… all alone…in the dark…afraid. I thought I could hear him calling me." Lessie's mother grabbed her daughter's hand bravely as the young woman composed herself. The testimony moved toward the identification in Foxworth.

"I knew it was Bobby the instant I saw him," she declared, a little too eagerly. "My husband told me not to identify him just yet for he believed Walters was the head of a gang of kidnappers and he wanted to try and catch all of them all unaware." She wept openly again when she told of how terrified Bobby was when he first came home, "of everyone and everything".

When the Defense got around to asking the delicate woman about the "big toe on left foot badly scarred from burn" used in the Dunbars' description of Bobby, she basically said that it was Percy who had handled all of that and in error had placed too much emphasis on it. "I was too ill at the time to catch the mistake."

Lessie's mother and Percy's mother and father, Bobby's grandparents, each identified the child as Bobby, telling specific incidents that only Bobby would have known about.

Mrs. Bercier, the wife of one of Opelousas' leading physicians and citizens and good friend of the Dunbars, identified Bobby next.

Dr. F. C. Shute, the family's physician, rounded out the State's witnesses. "I have known Mr. Dunbar for 8 or 10 years and I have known Mrs. Dunbar for 5 years. They are not only patients, we socialize together and I recognized Bobby on his return. I examined every inch of him to be sure."

Concerning the scar he said, "It took me months to get healthy skin to cover the wound. I would have to say the resulting scar on the toe and below the ankle would be permanent."

William Cantwell Walters' Defense File #320

That night *Item* reporter Sam Blair noticed a difference in Cantwell as he made his nightly walk back to his jail cell.

A week ago when I came to Opelousas, before the beginning of the trial, Walters had met me with a smile. He had played for me music on the crude harp he had made in the jail. He had been gay and had told me the pet story that he prizes over all his stock of anecdotes.

On Monday, the opening day of the trial, the accused man had rubbed his hands together with enthusiasm and had fairly gurgled out the information:

"I am happy and I am certain of my acquittal. They would not think of hanging an innocent man."

Tuesday I again met Walters and he gripped my hand in a bubbling over of pleasure.

"I have been watching them while they selected the jury," he whispered, "and, say, I didn't know that I had so many friends. Isn't it lovely that people are so honest?"

On Wednesday, Walters saw the jury completed. He studied closely the face of every man. Then, when I stopped him in the evening, and asked him how he judged the situation, he beamed and confided happily that, "They look like praying men. I am safe in their hands."

Grows Bent in Single Day

But Thursday night, with the adjournment of the court, after the overwhelming evidence of the state had been entered; after Mrs. C. P. Dunbar, mother of Bobbie, had taken the witness stand and had brought tears of sympathy to the eyes of half a thousand women and men who heard her testimony; after half a dozen men had testified that Walters, four months before his arrest at Hub, Miss., had shown them at McComb City, Miss., identification cards of the missing Bobbie Dunbar and had informed them that the child he had with him was the Bobbie for which a reward of $6,000 had been offered; after other witnesses had sworn during the session at night that Walters actually had been seen within a short distance of the place of the disappearance of the child, and that within a few days of the time when Bobbie dropped from sight—after these things had been brought out in the course of a single day—Walters grew white and bent, and no longer paraded as he marched the pathway from the court house to his prison cell.

His head was sunken on his breast and the buoyancy was gone from his step. He looked down at the narrow path across the little stretch of grass. Perhaps he was wondering how many feet had helped to beat down that path just as his were doing, and later had trod to that most terrible of all things—the gallows.

"Thing look bad," he said. "They do—look—very bad. I—"

The sentence was broken off. Walters moved, slowly onwards a few steps farther. Once more he seemed to speak but the words did not come.

The door to the jail was reached. The prisoner and his custodian stopped upon the step. Silhouetted there against the lighted opening, Walters' form trembled; his fingers moved.

"I am wondering," he said, "what I shall do when it comes my turn to take the witness stand. I—I will not cry, I guess. I know that I won't

be able to stand the strain much longer. I shall cry as Mrs. Dunbar cried. I am almost ready now to break down."

The keeper of the jail stood back in the half light of the interior. Thoughtfully he jingled two keys. Dr. Stubbs edged the prisoner through the doorway. Then there came a final pause. Walters touched the arm of the deputy who had his custody.

"Doctor," he faltered out, "won't you put a light globe in my sleeping room? You have been promising me that. I can't do any sleeping. Sleep is impossible now. I could read all night, if I only had a light."

Doctor Stubbs did not answer. He very gently moved the prisoner through the doorway. Then the door was closed."

The Item-April 17, 1914

All throughout the day on Friday, Julia and Mrs. Bilbo remarked that they were feeling sickly, an all-too-regular occurrence for defense witnesses visiting Opelousas.

On Saturday afternoon, Tom, Hollis, and Ed Dubuisson called the first of their witnesses and the truth finally began to be heard in Opelousas. "We will produce documentary evidence that Mr. Walters was not in the places claimed by the prosecution's witnesses or at the times testified to."

First on the stand Deputy Sheriff Lott said, "I saw the man and boy twice. The first time was in February 1913, and then on April 8, 1913, I stopped him for a thorough questioning. I wanted to see the child's feet. Walters threw his arms up in the air at me and fairly yelled, 'Take him to Opelousas and if he turns out to be Bobby, Mr. Dunbar can keep him!'" Lott shrugged his shoulders. "At that point I was fairly confident that the old man's story would pan-out."

Lott paused, reliving for the Jury another moment of clarity. "At Foxworth, Percy said the child's eyes were not Bobby's."

The ruggedly handsome Sheriff Hathorn came next. Looking out from under his heavy eyebrows and absently tugging on his mustache in thought, he described the attempted Foxworth identification. "I witnessed this kid fighting them off as if they were the Devil himself." He told of Mrs. Dunbar's flight from the house and of Mr. Dunbar's announcement that they would wait until daylight to see the boy awake before they made their declaration. "The crowds had been there all day and did not appreciate being kept waiting."

"I have seen the two photographs being shown by Day, the picture of the younger Bobby and of this child now living with the Dunbars. He says they are twin likenesses, but I must disagree. Place the child and Julia side-by-side and there will be the likeness."

Otto Fortenberry, jailor at Columbia, was also at the Foxworth identification, describing the scene in a manner similar to Hathorn's. As an added kindness he spoke fondly of his former prisoner's upstanding character.

Cantwell said a quick prayer before taking a seat in the witness's chair, a seat he would relinquish seven torturous hours later. When asked whom the child in question belonged to he answered, "The boy is mine—rather he's Julia's boy."

Cantwell began in a trembling voice to detail his past life, beginning with the getting of the child from Julia Anderson. "Julia and I were never really close until after Bruce and I had become good friends. One night she and I together cared for a sick neighbor who eventually passed away and she proved to be an angel in caring for the old man. We saw the true nature of each other after that night.

"I planned to educate the boy and leave my portion of the land in North Carolina to him."

He continued, covering his and Bruce's trip in detail from North Carolina to Georgia. The retelling of his visit to his sister's and then David Bledsoe's kept him constantly wiping his teary eyes with his handkerchief. He detailed his operation in Mobile and on into Mississippi to the Bilbos' in July. He spoke without a script or page of reference, holding the dates and events like a calendar in his head. When the Prosecution asked him about his absolute remembrances, he stated, "Ask God, it is He who gave me this ability."

Hollis spoke confidently, "We have shown every record verifying his wanderings with Bruce up until Aug. 27, 1912." Then they covered his whereabouts for the remainder of August; his stint in Charity Hospital from September 10 until October 12, when the Bilbos kept Bruce and Archie came to see the child; and on into December when Dr. Anderson and Mr. Smith came to the Bilbos' to examine Bruce.

Garland pressed Cantwell, "Is it possible that while you were in the hospital the boys were swapped?"

"Absolutely not!"

Garland changed directions, pushing Cantwell to admit to more severe punishments than the regular spankings children receive every day.

"I whipped him sometimes, I had to. But I *never* left any marks on his body. Nobody could say that I beat the boy."

(The stories about Bobby's abuse have remained one of the most controversial points of the Dunbar saga. It is one prevailing motive that would help to justify the Dunbars' actions in taking Bruce away, but Lessie herself said that she "knew Cantwell wasn't cruel to her child." Percy claimed to have seen whip marks on Bruce, but he also claimed to have seen the other 25 one-of-a-kind marks of identification specific to Bobby. He swore to have seen a scar that was not there. A boy that was not there. He created the remembrances of Bobby for Bruce, adding dozens of exhaustive fabrications.

This author chooses to trust the words that came from Cantwell's lips.)

"I've never been to Opelousas in my life."

"I never ate with my brother in Miss Collins restaurant and certainly never swapped a child there."

"I have never met any of the McComb City witnesses before. Never been in that town."

"I was not in Forrest Hill, Louisiana, in July 1912. Bruce and I were around Purvis, Mississippi, at that time."

Jurors frequently interrupted him, questioning some point of contention.

"I've never had a horse and tented wagon anywhere, not even at Mr. Mallet's. I own a surrey."

"I have never met Mrs. Nix. She must be crazy."

"I only remember Miss Loveless for her peculiar conduct."

"I have never been to New Roads."

"I had done some work for Mr. Stogner on credit, and when I came to collect, his family asked to adopt Bruce. They were very put out when I refused. I did tell them that I had been detained several times for being suspected of having the Dunbar boy."

"If I die today and go to heaven, I will answer the same before God. This boy is Bruce Anderson, whom I love dearly. He is not Bobby Dunbar."

* * *

After Cantwell's testimony, Harold Fox and *Item* reporter Lee Hawes, the self-appointed investigative agents from Louisiana had spun together their own detailed theory of two lookalike tinkers, two lookalike boys, same names, same occupations, same rigs, traveling cross-country from opposite points with an elaborate scheme to swap the children in a hidden shack near the Bilbo's home. Hawes wrote, "We know that Walters and the boy crossed near Baton Rouge to the east bank of the Mississippi and it is reasonable to presume that what the state supposes was actually what was done."

Fox and Hawes published the report and included a sketch of the area, attempting to bear out their peculiar story and even added an accessory, a Negro woman named Rickets. In their months of speculation they had missed one main point: the people who knew Cantwell and Bruce would certainly be capable of telling the difference if someone else showed up in their place claiming to be them.

The Item – April 19, 1914

Halfway through the trial, the *Item* described Julia's condition.

Half Delirious, Julia Anderson Pleads She May Get Her Boy Bruce

BY MIGNON HALL

OPELOUSAS, La., April 20. Sick and for a time demented and following a sleepless night and two days, in which but the barest nourishment has passed her lips, Julia Anderson, mother of Bruce, Monday morning is praying but one prayer; asking but one boon of God.

Knowing that Mrs. Dunbar on the witness stand swayed the great throng with her when, in tears, she told her little story of Bobbie's disappearance last week and won the hearts of those who heard her.

Julia Anderson is asking God to give her the strength to win the jury to her cause, beyond and past the testimony of that other woman.

She became excited when she began to speak of it.

"It's the right that's got to prevail," she declared starting up from her pillow in a half delirious condition.

"And the right is that's my child. No merciful God would let them take him from me like that. I've got to make them people see. I've got to make them know that if they take him it will be a sin before the Almighty."

"I'm going to say what I've got to say, for I've got a lot to tell. And then if they beat me down—if they beat me down as its rightful mother—well—"

She could not finish for a little stifling sob choked her.

The doctor has been called to see the sick woman twice during her illness and has advised quiet. Very few people—and these only closest acquaintances she has made since her arrival here, have been admitted to her room.

Saturday she created a sensation in the hotel when for a time she became demented and screamed frantically; "Bruce, Bruce."

When the maid ran to her room she found her laying about the floor and wringing her hands. Her trouble is the result of an illness in North Carolina just before she left for Opelousas aggravated by a heart weakness and the nervous strain under which she has been laboring since the trial began.

The Item

* * *

William Murray, Julia and Cantwell's mailman friend from Barnesville, North Carolina, took the stand, giving the account of Tom Dale's letters to Mr. and Mrs. Walters and Julia. He shook his head dejectedly when he told of the earlier request from the *States* for information which he had sent them, one day before Tom's request.

At this juncture, Bruce was brought into the courtroom and placed in front of Murray. The man looked him over, turning his face side to side, rubbing his head and hands. "This is Bruce Anderson, the son of Julia Anderson. I know him well."

Cantwell's nephew, F. M. Stephens, took the stand. He recognized Bruce and corroborated his uncle's testimony.

Mr. Oge testified next that there had been a deformity in Bobby's tracks and how Lessie had recognized them by that deformity. "I saw no other tracks near the child's. He was walking by himself."

Much had been made over Bruce's being barefoot when taken from Cantwell, as if he owned no shoes, so Tom asked Oge why the child was barefoot in the swamp.

"We had him wear shoes, but he must have pulled them off."

He told about the thick wooded area around the lake where the searcher's clothing was literally ripped off their bodies. "We never found any children's tracks in these woods." He continued telling about how the child had changed as it grew older. He offered no explanation as to how Bobby was left alone in such a dangerous place. He also offered no answer when asked why Cantwell would have been on the railroad tracks in the middle of a swamp in the first place.

Dr. Anderson pointed out how easily mistaken one can be in an identification, pointing out the wagon curtains with W. C. Walters—Stovemender painted on the side.

Sheriff Day reiterated the taking the photo of Bruce out of the letter addressed to Julia Anderson and of Cantwell's suggestion for him to bring the child to Opelousas.

D. L. Bledsoe, Cantwell's lifelong friend and mentor, vouched for the accused man and child. "This is the child that was at my house in Georgia during the Spring of 1912."

Levy Holloman confirmed that Cantwell and Bruce were at his house on August14 and 15. Cantwell had bathed Bruce at his home and Holloman testified that the two smaller toes on his left foot were slightly webbed.

Mr. Donald took the stand next. "My name is G. M. Donald and I am the shipping agent at McNeil, Mississippi. On Tuesday August 20, 1912, W. C. Walters received a package addressed to him there and signed his name on the receipt in my presence. Dale and Rawls have that receipt here with them."

Emille Thigpen from near Poplarville testified that he saw W. C. Walters, "the first time was the last week in July or 1st week in August 1912. I then saw him again on August 24, 1912. Walters made a talk from the pulpit at Whitesand Church about the organ. I can remember no particular marks or features on the boy except a cow-lick."

J. S. Thigpen of Poplarville took the stand next. "I saw W. C. Walters and Bruce on August 23 at my home and they stayed all night. I also saw Walters at church on Sunday. Our singing school was to start on August 26."

Rev. G. W. Holcomb, W. C. Bass, Ben Alsobrook, and George Amacker each took the stand giving the same testimony as in the Habeas Corpus hearing, proffering alibis for the pair.

Dee Morgan, the brother of D. L. Morgan—one of the McComb City witnesses, was called to the stand. He stated that D. L. had only testified to coming across Cantwell and Bruce as a lark. He stated that his brother was a drunk and couldn't always be believed. Dee stated that the man they met in McComb was redheaded with a red complexion.

Julia's and Mrs. Bilbo's condition worsened dramatically. Dr. Saizan, one of the men in charge of Julia's examination of Bruce in Opelousas, confined her to her bed and performed a surgical procedure on her in the Lacombe hotel. On Wednesday, April 22, Julia was sworn in as a witness while lying on a cot in the parlor of the hotel. The attorneys were present, as well as the judge, jury, stenographer, and a few reporters. When Bruce was called into the room, Julia held out her arms and called to him. He went to her and she wrapped her arms around the little boy and kissed him. To the horrification of the Prosecution attorneys, he kissed her back. Lewis pulled the boy away from her and took him out of the room.

Julia was questioned again on the most private details of her life. "The first time I saw Bruce here I wasn't treated fair. I was a helpless stranger with everybody against me. They put me in a dark room with several other children and I knew Bruce wasn't there. Later, when they brought him in with the other children I recognized him right away, but Mrs. Dunbar grabbed him and said he was hers.

"I saw him the next day and I knew in an instant he was my own flesh and blood." Julia told about being threatened at the Opelousas inspection of her child but would give no names. They were very likely sitting in the room. She did say that she would accuse Percy Dunbar of kidnapping.

The Prosecution asked her about the left foot of her son. "It is just like mine," she answered, removing her left foot from the covers. Bruce was brought to her bedside and his left foot was compared to Julia's. The two smallest toes on his foot were webbed, the same exact two toes with webbing as Julia's foot. She was barely able to sit up and get one quick hug before he was removed—from the room and from her life. She had not been allowed more than a few moments with Bruce and each had been carefully scripted.

Back in the courtroom, Mrs. Myley took the oath next and was questioned about the dates the boy was in her home. When Bruce was brought in, he climbed up beside her and they shook hands. As they progressed to asking if she had washed the boy and seen the webbed toes, Lewis leapt to his feet. "I want to cross-examine the witness before the shoes are removed." He asked which foot the defect was on, but she could not remember. When the shoes did come off, Mrs. Miley pointed out the webbing for the judge and jury. Tom described the examination of Julia's foot, with the exact matching webbing, to the courtroom.

Passing through the spontaneous press conference on his way out, Bruce paused timidly, waiting for silence. Turning to Lessie he said,

"You are my dood Mama. The old man told me you were dead and thrown in a creek." A moment later he dropped his eyes and said, "Bruce went to the graveyard."

Mr. Cowart from Hub, Mississippi, took the stand repeating the whispered message he said the child told him last April. "Bruce is my new name, but I've got an old name…it is Bobby. And I've got another papa who is a good papa and a good mama who is away off."

"He is lying!" shouted Cantwell.

Allen Goleman was brought into the courtroom, where a substitute child was placed on the stand. He was asked if it was the child he knew as Bruce Anderson. He answered, "No it doesn't look like him." When Bruce was brought in he said, "That is the fellow I know as Bruce."

The Defense called Mr. Stetly, one of the searchers at Swayze Lake. He said he had met a tramp on the railroad track, not Walters.

Mr. Robertson, a civil engineer, had mapped out the swamp in question and said that only if a person knew the landscape well enough, could he make it cross-country. He had found bare-footed tracks there, but they were too large to be Bobby's.

Two other searchers, Mr. White and Mr. Eastham, told about the perfect impression the scar made in Bobby's tracks.

The Defense dropped a bombshell when it introduced five witnesses from Opelousas: Mrs. R. Mornhinveg; Mrs. W. B. Roberts; J. P. Barnett; Miss Fannie Bowden, the Dunbars' neighbor; and Mr. M. Pulford, who had each known Bobby for years before he disappeared. They had failed to see any resemblance between him and the child brought back by the Dunbars.

Dr. Saizan, who had been at the first Opelousas identification, contradicted Dr. Shute, the Dunbars' doctor, on some of the child's identifying characteristics.

At this point in the trial, just as it was her time to testify, Matilda Bilbo's blood-pressure suddenly reached a critically high level. Against her protests, Jeptha Bilbo carried her to New Orleans for treatment and then home.

The Defense called Dr. Haas, the chairman of the committee that arranged the identity test in Opelousas. He admitted that the slight mark on that child's foot was probably not the result of the burn the Dunbars had described. Haas continued, "Julia Anderson pointed to the child in question and said, 'I believe deep down in my heart it is my child.'" The good doctor continued, revealing that John Lewis had lied about when he joined Julia on her first trip to Opelousas. Lewis had always claimed to have joined Julia closer to Opelousas in New Iberia, Louisiana, when in fact he had gotten on the train with her much earlier, just outside of New Orleans.

The first witnesses the Prosecution brought forth in rebuttal were Mr. H. L. Waxter and then Joe Johnson from McComb City who refuted the earlier testimony of Dee Morgan. Johnson claimed Dee Morgan had a bad character.

Mr. Budden, who was working with Mr. Ansley on repairing the railroad bridge at Swayze Lake, looked at Cantwell. "The man we saw greatly resembles Mr. Walters in every way." When Dubuisson cross-examined Mr. Budden he asked if, "he would be willing to have this man sent to the gallows on his identification?"

Budden answered, "I can't be positive that this is the same man."

Ogee Hargroter, who was with Ansley, stated that Cantwell was the man they had seen on the tracks.

Dr. Charles F. Boagni, a member of the men's committee who had arranged Julia's identity test in Opelousas, said that he had selected the children for the event and that Julia had claimed Alonzo as her son. When Julia saw this in print after the Opelousas test, she had sworn to her attorneys that the incident never occurred.

Responding to Dr. Haas's previous claims, and in a highly defensive tone, Mrs. Lewis testified that, "Julia Anderson was afforded every hospitality in our home, and she claimed that the child taken from Walters was not hers."

Mr. Williams of Lumberton, Mississippi, swore that he had seen a man who resembled Walters at the McComb depot during the time Cantwell was supposedly traveling from Columbia to Poplarville.

Miss Lass and Mr. Piggford of Opelousas testified that when Julia came for the identity test in Opelousas she said that the Walters' family told her that she must identity the child or she had better not come back to North Carolina. Julia had denied this story as well when it was published in the paper shortly after the identity test.

Reverend E. C. Bennett, a Methodist preacher from Longville, Louisiana, caused a major skirmish when he swore, "I saw two men, W. C. Walters and his brother D. B. Walters, in Longville about first of June 1912, traveling in a wagon with 'W. C. Walters—Stove Repairer' written on the side. The two men said they had come over from Mississippi.

I talked to them several times." Garland asked if Bennett could identify this prisoner as the man he saw at that time, and he answered, "Yes, Sir."

Dubuisson asked him if either of the men had a limp, to which Bennett answered, "One man limped, the taller one."

"Was the prisoner the man who limped?" To which Bennett answered, "I do not think it was." Judge Pavy pounded on his gavel for a full minute until the room finally settled.

Dubuisson continued, "Are you willing to be positive enough about the identification of this man if his life or death hung upon it?"

Garland again yelled, "Objection!"

"Sustained."

Mr. Winberry, a minister of DeRidder, Louisiana, took the stand and stated, "I saw this man, who said his name was Walters, in my town in June 1912."

Mr. Scarborough, also of DeRidder, corroborated Bennett's testimony in detail.

Judge O. L. Mayson of Merryville, Louisiana, swore to having seen Walters drive through his town in June, 1912, with "Stovemender" written on his wagon.

Bennett, Winberry, Scarborough, and Mayson had met Linder and his traveling companion, stove-menders by trade, but they insisted that the man they met was Cantwell.

The Item & William Cantwell Walters' Defense File© #320

Halfway through the trial Dr. C. C. Bass of Tulane University in New Orleans wrote to Tom and Hollis.

4/20/14
Hons Dale & Rawls, Opelousas, La.

Gentlemen;

I have noticed with considerable interest and appreciation your excellent work in protecting the poor old tinker Walters from being robbed of his liberty if not his life by fanatics a father and mother whose conscience permits them to conjure up the fancy that some other child is their own, numerous witnesses who can draw upon their imagination to the extent of testifying to things that they know full well are not true and finally the general public who have allowed sentiment to lead them to come to conclusions which are not warranted by the facts. As a scientist accustomed to weighing all the evidence and without prejudice I have known all the time that the child now under controversy was Bruce Anderson. The case has been the more interesting to me because I had never before realized that it would be possible to so long and so thoroughly jeopardize the life of a perfectly innocent man. I now have a greater regard, appreciation, and respect for the legal profession than I have ever had before.

I have noticed newspaper statements to the effect that you would give up the child if you could free Walters and the suggestion that he might be left with the Dunbars. Also that you sympathize with them etc. I must say that I think this is a very incorrect view and that you would fail to serve the public and the world best unless you prove beyond doubt the identity of the child. As for the Dunbars, they are not entitled to sympathy or quarter. If they are mentally unbalanced sufficiently to allow them to make the effort they have to destroy an innocent man they are a source of danger to others and should be restrained as we do others who try to destroy life or property. The child should be restored to W. C. Walters from whom he was kidnapped and it is the duty of the Mississippi officers who permitted the kidnapping knowingly to return him. Wishing you success and again assuring you of my esteem.

I am Yours very truly
C. C. Bass M. D.

William Cantwell Walters Defense File© #325

They also received some much needed encouragement from Sheriff Hathorn.

Thomas S. Dale & H. C. RawlsApril 23d /1914
Opelousas, La.

Dear Friends:—

You are making yourselves immortal. The defense for W. C. can't be equaled—a golden chain without a missing link. There is no jury in the world who can convict a man with such a world of evidence in his favor. Conscienceless indeed must be the man or set of men who will sweep aside such testimony as has been produced for Walters without quaking and trembling for their future. God only knows what their verdict will be but if in there throbs the warm hearts of honest men and not the blood of snakes and "Cagen wretches" they will restore liberty to the old man. My hopes are: You will save his neck. I believe You'l do it. I know you must be tired and almost worn to a frazzle but fight on & on. I have agreed to pack you both on my shoulders through town—that some people may appreciate Real heroism.

S. J. Hathorn
William Cantwell Walters' Defense File© #331

On Friday, the 24th day of April, the trial drew to an end with closing arguments. Blair captured a scene from that day on paper, an indelible moment that forever pricked the souls of the jurors.

Walters Makes His Appeal to the Jury with Harp and Song

BY SAM BLAIR

OPELOUSAS, LA., April 25. The strongest appeal yet given by W. C. Walters to the jury that is about to weigh him in scales of life and death was presented by the prisoner Friday noon. It was not an appeal of words nor of gesture. It was the most poignant appeal in the world, for it was an appeal of music.

Friday morning the jury was removed from the courtroom and held on the courthouse square until half an hour after noon, while attorneys angled over the technical legal question of evidence admissibility. At noon the prisoner was taken back to his cell. For half an hour the jury and its guard lolled on the grass, almost directly beneath the cell window of the tinker. And Walters looked out and recognized them all and proceeded to play for them and sing a little.

The jurors were half dozing, half playing under the tree—broken rays of the late morning sun, when suddenly from above came the gentle vibration of harp strings. The twelve men sat up and listened. There came with the harp strains a man's voice singing:

"Though like a wanderer, the sun gone down,
Darkness be over me—my rest a stone.
Still all my song shall be.
Nearer, my God, to Thee,
Nearer, my God, to thee—nearer to Thee."

Two jurors had been playing mumbley-peg with a pocket knife.
One of them closed the blades. Both ceased their game.

Another verse of the old, old song was strummed out and sung. The
jurors looked at each other, but none of them smiled.

Then there came another song. The voice of the singer was not of
delicate pitch, nor is Walters a great musician, but some way the tone of
the man seemed softened. It seemed to mingle with the listless shadows
of the trees and the drone of the life on the almost deserted square.

The twelve men who listened were very sober as the singer came to
the words:

"A charm from the skies seems to hallow us there,
Which sought through the world is not met with elsewhere.
Home, home, sweet, sweet home;
Be it ever so humble, there's no place like home."

The harp strings grew faint at the ending, but they did not cease to
vibrate, for they grew again into crescendo, and the prisoner raised his
voice in song:

"Jesus, lover of my soul, let me to Thy bosom fly,
While the nearer waters roll and the tempest still is high.
Guide me, O, Jehovah, guide me."

The song was left unfinished. A new inspiration came, and Walters
threw all his soul into the making of his last song appeal.

"Some Day the Silver Cord Will Break," was what he sang. The
words still were floating downwards as the jurors rose at the solicita-
tion of their guards and proceeded slowly to their hotel.

W. C. Walters had argued his case.

The Item

Tom and Hollis were exhausted. The two attorneys, with Dubuisson's expert guidance through the unfamiliar territory of the Napoleonic Code (Louisiana's legal system based on French and Spanish codes instead of English common law) had done everything humanly possible. There was nothing left to do but encourage one another and pray.

On Monday afternoon, April 27, the *Item* published another article from Blair detailing the events of the day.

POSSIBLE VIOLENCE CAUSES THE COURT TO PROTECT TINKER

Final Argument of District Attorney Garland and Judge Pavy's Charge to the Jury Marks Monday Morning Session.

JURY DISAGREED AT THE NOON HOUR; ASKS TO BE SENT OUT FOR DINNER

Prisoner Appears to Be Calm During the Deliberations, but Refuses to Discuss With the Dunbar Relatives His Visits to Louisiana—"Bobbie" and Mother Are Absent During Final Argument and Charge

BY SAM BLAIR

With the jury that holds the fate of W. C. Walters, charged with kidnapping, retired for more than three hours, as this edition goes to press, one of the most remarkable situations ever developed in criminal court procedure ensues as a result of the fury of sentiment that has outgrown from the progress of the case.

Walters, the defendant, will not be in the courtroom when the verdict of the jury is rendered. He will be lodged in the parish jail and behind locked doors and under a special guard of deputy sheriffs will receive the verdict by special messenger.

The order responsible for this unusual and astonishing situation was issued immediately after the jury's return from lunch by Judge Pavy. Information, unverified but persistent, reached the judge to the effect that fifteen men were in the courtroom bearing concealed weapons.

Information was also circulated of purport that these fifteen men had taken pledge that the prisoner never should leave the courtroom alive in the event of a mistrial or a verdict of acquittal.

That the feeling in Opelousas has reached the breaking point has been evidenced by a half dozen official actions taken by the court and peace officials. Governor Hall has asked the sheriff of St. Landry parish if he needs the aid of the state militia. The sheriff, while refusing aid from the outside has taken the precaution of adding to his staff of deputies. Judge Pavy's order excluding Walters from the courtroom when the verdict is given is taken as the last word in the proof that a situation of vast danger has been approached.

Opelousas has taken on the aspect of potential explosive. Tenseness and atmosphere hang over this quiet town.

Mingling with the breezes that sweep through the trees that stand about St. Landry parish court house there comes a current that carries whisperings of foreboding.

Men are congregated in little knots of grimness. There are few faces that smile. Walters huddles in a far corner of his cell.

And the jury still deliberates and the men of Opelousas still are waiting.

The jury left the box at 11:07 o'clock. The court room burst at once into a buzz of excitement.

Few left their seats. Judge Pavy hammered once more for order.

Walters remained in his seat until the noon adjournment. Slowly he seemed to limpen. He fumbled with pictures and documents used as evidence that rested on the table before him.

Following the opening of the court and the closing section of the district attorney's speech, Judge Pavy read his charge to the jury and the 12 men were led from the court room proper into the little conference room at the rear of the judge's bench, the room where so often earlier had the attorneys and witnesses and the prisoner himself retired for conference and for a moment of rest.

While the jury was out, the court room took on the aspect of a great mass of explosives, already fused and lacking only seconds before the crashing noise and flame and smoke should tremble the verdict.

The spectators buzzed and swayed, a great wedged throng of feeling. Special deputy sheriffs edged their way to the street.

Judge Pavy sat warily on the bench and gripped his gavel in readiness to hammer it down in the interests of justice and against any rising of popular sentiment.

The prisoner was no longer tense. He was alternately hopeful and limp.

THERE MUST BE JUSTICE

"There must be justice," he said during these moments of waiting.
"There must be justice for there is a God."

 C. P. Dunbar, father of Bobbie, waited outside the court room.

 He was not limp. Neither did he pray.

 C. P. Dunbar was grim. The bare suggestion of a smile crossed his
lips. That was all. His lips spoke little.

 He was sure he knew. He was satisfied already.

The Item

By five o'clock the jury had reached a decision. In spite of the previous announcement, Cantwell was escorted into the courtroom. Pavy
felt that Cantwell would be safe enough there with the coming verdict,
but he gave out a stern warning before he would begin. Not one breath
could be heard when the foreman handed Pavy the verdict: "Guilty
without Capital Punishment," he boomed, and the room went wild. It
was a compromise to placate the Dunbars, while keeping Cantwell's
blood off of their hands.

Julia, therefore, remained in an endless legal purgatory, no closer to
regaining her son than she was one year ago. Sick in body and spirit, she
said a weak goodbye to Cantwell and was taken to Charity Hospital in
New Orleans for treatment. The remainder of the Defense witnesses
headed for home. Tom and Hollis said their goodbyes for now and
returned to Columbia to work on Cantwell's motion for a new trial.

But they weren't forgotten.

Opelousas, La.
Messrs. Dale and Rawls—Columbia, Miss

Gentlemen -

It is with every kind thought and my very best wishes that I send you
this box of flowers. Words are inadequate to express my appreciation
for the noble fight you made here in the camp of the enemy for your poor
old client.

 I—am sorry that I was unable to present the flowers in person for I
too feel that this poor old man is innocent, and I, do pray that God will

guide the men that hold his fate in their hands. I—did not know you were gone until I reached the hotel this eve.

With very best wishes for your future success

I—am very Respt.
Mrs. J. E. Redditt.

William Cantwell Walters' Defense File© #334

New Orleans La April 28—1914
Messrs Dale and Rawls

Gentlemen

Congratulations for the masterly way, You fought for Justice; My Life touches a large circle, and, these congratulations, express the opinion, of many in this circle.

Sincerely Yours
A Louisiana Lady—Wishing You success, in ultimate vindication

William Cantwell Walters' Defense File© #335

On the evening of the verdict, Sam Blair visited Cantwell for the last time, recording the solemn occasion for the paper.

"Of course, I still have lots of hope. A man who prays always has hope. But if things should turn out differently and—and the jury should have its wish and I should die in prison, I want to be brought right back where they took my life and I want to be buried here as a lasting token to the men and women here of what a fearful thing is justice that was wrong."

Then he recited again what he had written for The Item during the morning, just after the jury had retired to begin its deliberations.

"The epitaph I wish on my tombstone," he said, "is this:

"Here lies the body of William Cantwell Walters, foster father of Bruce Anderson, kidnapped by the Dunbars."

He tiptoed to the window of his cell and listened to the wild night noises that came up from the base of the prison walls. Men, many of them intoxicated, were passing about the jail. Hoots and calls came often but they were made of noise alone and Walters well knew that the real danger of violence to himself had been successfully tided over.

"It's funny how happy they are down there," he said. "Just because a poor old man has been consigned to a prison for the rest of his life, they have become so happy. And some of them must know that I am innocent too. But maybe they haven't stopped to think. So perhaps they can't be blamed so much."

But I suggested that I had come for some direct message to the people of Louisiana, some word at the ending of the famous trial to the men and women of the commonwealth that had convicted him.

And it was just a word that Walters gave me. He wrote it out in the darkness on a scrap of paper torn from some uncertain package. We said goodbye.

The jailer yawned as he let me out into the night. The crowds about the jail had moved on to the edge of the sidewalk and were breaking into lines moving away. Voices all about rose and fell in strains of harshness and of discord. From up above through the grating of the prisoner's cell there came the faint suggestion of harp strings still a-vibrant.

I peered at the scrap of paper, written in the scraggly, cramped hand of the tinker-preacher. It was Walters' last message to the world.

It was a single word.

"Mizpah."

The Item-April 28, 1914

Chapter Thirteen
Down the Watkins Railroad

Cantwell's small team of lawyers and his many friends dusted themselves off and began once more trying to force the issue of the man's innocence. D. F. Smith, aggrieved with himself for contributing to the conflict, searched throughout Pearl River County until he found the man and his son who ate lunch with Cantwell and Bruce in Kate Collins' restaurant.

Carriere, Miss. May, 4th. 1914
Messrs. Dale & Rawls,
Columbia, Miss.

Dear Sirs:

In the interest of justice I write to state that William Winingham, living near Millard, Miss. this County (Pearl River) is the man who eat dinner at Miss Kate Collins, restaurant in Poplarville at the same W. C. Walters, was there with Bruce Anderson, and in this connection will state that Mr William Winingham, had his little child there with him on that day, and he is the same man that was there who no doubt Miss Collins, swore looked like Walters, brother and claiming that the children was swapped there at that time.

If necessary I will get Mr Winingham's, affidavit to this effect, if you think that it will help you in securing a new trial for Walters.

William Winingham, is an old citizen of this County and is well known in the neighborhood in which he lives, and the fact is I have known him personally for the past 20 years, and I think that his evidence will be valuable in Walters' defense especially to counteract Miss Collins' testimony, and another thing is that he has no interest in Walters' case except to just tell the truth.

It seems that the prosecution would have the public believe that the people of Pearl River County would do almost anything to get Walters out of his trouble, even to the extent of swearing falsely, but this is not true, and speaking for myself I will state that I at one time done all I could to show that the child Walters had was Dunbars' child, but I have been convinced against my will, and I believe that any honest man who will take the trouble to investigate as I have, and talk to the honest citizens of Pearl River County, who have no interest in this case except to tell the plain unvarnished truth, they will become convinced as I am, that this child in question is not Bobbie Dunbar, but Bruce Anderson.

Anything that I can do for you down here at any time let me know and I will gladly do it, because I am for fair play and Justice even if it was a dog being tried for his life, and I believe that I owe that much to Walters, and I am willing to give him that service free, with no hope of reward here on earth, but I feel that there is a day coming when at judgment before the bar of God that Walters, will get justice, and also the people who unearth the truth in his case will also get a reward greater than any that could be given them here on earth, and I am afraid that the people who are persecuting and swearing falsely against Walters, will open their eyes at judgment in the lake that burns with fire and brimstone.

When I can do anything for you command me.

Yours Truly,
D F Smith

William Cantwell Walters' Defense File© #344

When Julia was released from Charity Hospital, Tom and Hollis sent for the ailing woman to come to Columbia. In each of their minds they had to know that Bruce would remain Bobby Dunbar—was already Bobby Dunbar. He would carry and maintain that veneer for the rest of his life. Julia refused to accept that reality. "I'll never give up on my Bruce till my dying day," she wept.

Mrs. Bilbo and Mrs. Miley came to Columbia, and like Ruth clinging to Naomi, the three of them left together for Pearl River County where she was taken under their protective wings.

Cantwell's fate, however, was still within the lawyer's reach.

Ten days after the verdict and from many miles apart, Tom Dale, Hollis Rawls, and E. B. Dubuisson prepared and filed a motion for a new trial on the following grounds: *The following is quoted except for two comments in parenthesis*

"*First, because the verdict of the jury rendered herein in is contrary to the law and the evidence.*

Second, because the trial of this cause was not conducted so as to keep the jury together, free from contact with the outside world, and free from outside pressure and influence in behalf of the prosecution. From Monday, April 13, 1914, when the empaneling of the jury was begun, until the verdict was returned on Monday, the 27th, the jury was lodged at the Lacombe Hotel. Each juror occupied a separate room, but some of the rooms connected with each other by doors and some did not. That meant some jury members had been communicating with each other out sight and hearing of the bailiffs or deputy sheriffs, or other jury members.

That in passing to and from the jury box on entering and leaving Court, in going to and from the Court House to and from the Lacombe Hotel and in going to and from their rooms in said hotel, the jury passed through and came in contact with enormous crowds hostile to mover (Cantwell), whose adverse comments the jury could and did hear.

That at the Lacombe Hotel the acoustics are such that persons occupying such rooms as said jurors occupied, even when the doors are closed, can hear almost perfectly conversations carried on in ordinary conversational tones in the adjoining rooms and corridors and in the rooms immediately above or below those occupied; that at the hotel and all over the city the prosecution against Walters was the principal and sole topic for discussion. Jurors could hear outsiders, and outsiders could hear jurors.

That during the many recesses of the Court the jury was allowed to occupy the public music stand and benches on the public square on which the Court house is situated, where many people congregated, and where the jury could and did hear many comments adverse to mover.

That from the time when the trial began on Monday, April 13th, 1914, every available seat reserved for the public in the Court room was occupied; that the crowd increased from day to day, filling the aisles and the space within the railings reserved for the use of the Court, its officers, employees and others having business in said reserved space, and filling every other space in the Court room including the space against the rear, side and front walls of the room, and many of the crowd even sitting and standing on the window sills, standing on the seats and backs of the benches, and climbing up and sitting or standing upon the toilet room partition in the rear; that the crowds in the halls and anteroom and at the head of the stairs leading into the Court room were so dense and uncontrolled that the attorneys or witnesses having occasion to enter or leave Court during the sessions had to fight their way through; that this disorder continued to grow worse until finally, on Friday, the 17th day of April, the space within the railing reserved for the Court, its officers, the jury, and the Judge's bench was so crowded with spectators packed with a surging mass of humanity like sardines in a box; that so intolerable did these conditions become, that the presiding Judge adjourned Court from the noon recess of said day until the next morning, in order to make other and different arrangements from those which had up to that time prevailed for preserving order and decorum in the Court room;

That the crowd which packed the Court room and approaches as aforesaid was hostile to mover, and several times broke into applause when points adverse to mover were made by witnesses or counsel for the State;

And that mover was tried in surroundings so hostile that a mighty cheer went up from the crowd assembled outside the Court house when the verdict was made known to them.

Now mover avers that a trial conducted under such circumstances and amidst such surroundings was not the "speedy public trial by an impartial jury" guaranteed by the Constitution and laws of this State, and the verdict of the jury herein should be quashed and set aside and a new trial granted.

Third, because since the verdict of the jury was rendered herein mover has discovered the following new not cumulative but independent evidence to rebut testimony offered by the State on the trial, to wit:

(a) (The attorneys detailed Julia's examination of Bruce in Opelousas.) It was shown by evidence introduced by the State, that Julia Anderson was in a super-nervous and excited condition during the ordeal of the test, but although the cause of her excitement and nervousness was known to the Court, the District Attorney and his associate coun-

sel, all of whom were present at said test, it was not known to mover or his counsel until after the verdict, that cause was not placed before the jury by counsel for the State;

That that cause resulted from E. P. Veazie, when informed that Julia Anderson had failed to identify either of the children as her boy, in the presence and hearing of Julia Anderson in the exuberance of his enthusiasm clapped his hands in a cheering manner, and exclaimed in a loud and exultant tone of voice: 'She has failed to recognize him!' That said hand-clapping and exclamation of said Veazie were well calculated not only to make poor Julia nervous and excited, but also to cause her to hesitate to claim "Bruce-Bobbie" as her own against the adverse claim of Mrs. Dunbar among her friends and adherents. Neither mover nor his counsel knew of said hand-clapping and exclamation of said Veazie as aforesaid until after verdict; that mover can prove by said A. Leon Dupre and no doubt by the other gentlemen who were present, that said occurrences did take place, and that Julia Anderson was visibly and seriously affected by them; that said evidence would have been material to mover's defense and would have gone a long way to explain and modify the alleged failure of Julia Anderson to recognize "Bruce-Bobby" as her child, and especially in view of the fact that she claimed "Bruce-Bobby" as her own, under less trying circumstances, on the next day; and mover is entitled to a new trial in order that he may lay said evidence, along with his other evidence, before a jury.

(b) The State, in making out its case, produced as a witness one Miss Kate Collins, of Poplarville, Mississippi, who swore that on either the first or second Saturday of September, 1912, mover took dinner in said restaurant; that mover had with him a child who looked like "Bruce-Bobby"; that there was another man with mover who looked like mover and appeared to be a twin brother of mover, and that this other man had another child who looked like "Bruce-Bobby"; that the child with mover was a healthy, fine specimen of a boy, but the child with the other man then in the restaurant was delicate and sickly looking, and that the child with mover seemed to be under the perfect control of mover, while the other boy seemed unruly and not to obey the man who had him in charge.

The State offered this evidence in support of its theory that Bruce was exchanged for Bobby at that time, and argued that the other man whom Miss Collins claimed to have seen in the restaurant was a brother, partner or accomplice of mover, there to aid and abet in the alleged exchange.

Mover admitted having entered a restaurant in the town of Poplarville with the child Bruce Anderson, but mover denied that he was in said restaurant or neighborhood for the purpose of the alleged exchange, or that he came there in company with a brother, partner or accomplice, leading another child.

Now since the verdict herein was rendered mover has discovered that one William Willingham, living near Millard, Mississippi, happened to be a patron of said restaurant at the same time that mover was there with Bruce Anderson, and that said Willingham had with him his little boy, who somewhat resembled Bruce; that said Willingham is willing to come to Louisiana to testify should a new trial be granted, and his testimony would thoroughly and completely explain and render innocuous the testimony of Miss Collins, which was greatly damaging to mover's case, and that a new trial should be granted in order that mover may avail himself of the testimony of said William Willingham.

(c) The State introduced in rebuttal the testimony of Mrs. M. E. Sloan, of New Roads, La., who declared that in January, 1912, seven months before Bobbie Dunbar disappeared, she saw mover at New Roads, Louisiana; that mover stayed at her house from a Thursday evening to Monday morning in said month; that he, mover, was traveling in a canvas-covered wagon with three fine horses; that he had for companions a sickly and pale-faced child six or seven years old, also a man whose name the witness did not remember exactly, but which was something like Whitney, Whitlow or Whitlock.

Now mover has just been informed by E. B. Dubuisson, Esq., that he learned after the verdict, from Louis Goldman, Esq., a prominent attorney of Biloxi, Mississippi, who was then, like Dubuisson, attending the Louisiana-Mississippi Bar Convention held at Gulfport, Mississippi, on April 30ᵗʰ and May 1ˢᵗ, 1914, that he had positive information that one Mr. Davis, then at Biloxi, accompanied by his wife had occupied rooms at Mrs. Sloan's at New Roads, Louisiana, from January 1ˢᵗ to March 19ᵗʰ, 1912, and that at no time during said period was mover at said place with a child, nor was any other person there accompanied by a child at the time testified to by Mrs. Sloan; that Davis and his wife furthermore were at New Roads, La., a month or two prior to the time testified to by Mrs. Sloan, in November, 1911, and there met one stove-mender J. L. Linder, of Alexandria, La., who was there with a canvas-covered wagon and three horses, and accompanied by a child and by a man named Tutstone Woodville, substantially as described by Mrs. Sloan; that said attorney, Louis Goldman, Esq., had agreed to obtain an affidavit as to these facts and to forward same to mover's attorney at Opelousas, but was unable to do so before now owing to the absence of Davis from Biloxi; that said attorney telegraphed to mover's attorney on May 7th that Davis had just returned and made affidavit to the facts above stated, which affidavit had then been forwarded to mover's attorney and is now momentarily expected by him.

Mover avers that the testimony of Davis will entirely refute the testimony of Mrs. Sloan and can be supported by the other parties named in his affidavit, and that mover should be granted a new trial in order to enable him to place said testimony before a jury.

Fourth, because the Court erred to mover's prejudice in certain rulings made during the trial and in charging the jury as shown by bills of exception reserved by mover to such rulings and to such charge on file herein.

W H E R E F O R E, the promises and annexed affidavit considered, mover prays that a new trial may be granted to him herein, and for general relief.

By his attorneys,
Dale, Rawls, and E. B. Dubuisson"
William Cantwell Walters' Defense File© #350

The hearing on this motion was set for May 18, Cantwell's sentencing date.

On May 15th, 1914, William Winningham offered his sworn statement.

Personally appeared before me, J. P. Mitchell, a Justice of the Peace, and Exofficia Notary Public in and for said County and State, William Winningham, well known to me and a citizen of Pearl River County, who being duly sworn says on oath that he remembers taking dinner in a restaurant on main or front street near the Barber Shop in the fall of 1912, and that he had with him on that occasion his little five year-old son named Johnny and that one W. C. Walters, and a small child which he called Bruce, took dinner at the same Restaurant at the same time only at separate tables. He remembers being in conversation with the said Walters, and he also remembers that there were two ladies in this Restaurant, one in the cooking department and the other one waiting on the tables.

Affiant states that he is personally acquainted with W. C. Walters, and the little child that he had with him on that occasion having met them several times in the Sones settlement and at Sones Chapel Church previously to the meeting in the Restaurant at Poplarville. He remembers that his child and the one that Walters had with him were about the same age, the only difference was that his child was not as stout, and did not look as healthy as the one that Walters had with him, and that his child was more of a sallow complexion, and his hair just a little darker than the child's hair which Walters had with him.

Affiant further states that he and his child are well known in the neighborhood west of Millard, Miss. where he has resided almost continually since living in the County, he refers any person making enquiry as to his character and reputation to Mr. N. Batson, who is an ex-Sheriff, ex-Chancery and Circuit Clerk, and ex-Treasure of Pearl River County, now residing at Millard, Miss.

Affiant further says on oath that his meeting with W. C. Walters in the restaurant at Poplarville was entirely by accident and that they simply conversed while there and went their respective ways.

Affiant states that he had never heard anything about having been accused of being W. C. Walters' brother until after or during the trial of W. C. Walters when he read the report of Miss Collin's testimony in the daily papers.

Affiant further states that this affidavit is made free and voluntarily on his part, and that he is not interested in the conviction or acquittal of W. C. Walters, except to tell the truth that justice may be done.

William Cantwell Walters' Defense File© #366

Dubuisson received an affidavit from Mr. R. B. Davis stating that the two stove-menders mentioned during the trial were named Linder and Tutstone. Mr. Davis and his wife had roomed at Mrs. Sloan's boarding house in 1912, at the same time as these men and the little boy that accompanied them. He stated that no one else with a child or in the profession of stove mending roomed there at that time. Dubuisson, working with his secretary, Alex Robertson, continued to investigate.

The three attorneys filed a motion in arrest of judgment stating, "Act No. 271 of the acts of the General Assembly of this State for the year 1910, approved July 7th, 1910, and entitled: 'An act to amend and re-enact Section 805 of the Revised Statutes of Louisiana; to define the crime of kidnapping and to prescribe a penalty therefore,' under which the said W. C. WALTERS, is being prosecuted herein, is unconstitutional, null and void."

William Cantwell Walters' Defense File© #352

Cantwell's attorneys also filed four bills of exception. The first bill stated that the child taken from Cantwell was Bruce Anderson, not Bobby Dunbar. They had proven that Cantwell was in Mississippi at the time Bobby disappeared and therefore could not have kidnapped him.

The second bill referred to the question that the Defense asked of Reverend Bennett attempting to probe his conscience when he was on the stand. "Reverend Bennett, suppose the fate of this defendant depended upon your positive identification of him as being the same man that you saw at Longview in May or June, 1912, and that if you identified him positively as the same man, he would be hanged, and if you could not identify him positively as the same man he would go free, would you still persist that the defendant was the same man that you saw at Longville." The prosecution objected, but no reason was given. The objection was sustained, also without any reason being given.

The third bill dealt with the written charge as prepared by the Court and submitted to them. They requested a change in the wording of the charge, stating that it was, "erroneous in law and calculated to mislead and confuse the jury."

The fourth bill stated, "An averment of the bill of indictment in this case is that the crime charged was not made known to an officer having authority to direct an investigation thereof, until the 22nd day of April, 1913. (Cantwell had been arrested on April 21 on the word of the Dunbars without any proper investigation or authorization.) This averment was necessary in order that the indictment might show on its face that the defendant was amenable to the law. This averment being material and necessary, it was incumbent upon the State to prove it to your satisfaction beyond a reasonable doubt." It continued with "if the evidence offered in that behalf be sufficient to raise a reasonable doubt the prisoner is entitled to the benefit of that doubt on this issue as well as on all other issues in the case."

William Cantwell Walters'
Defense File© #'s 353, 354, 355, & 356

On the morning of May 19, 1914, all of the Defense's motions and bills were over-ruled, and William Cantwell Walters was sentenced to life in prison for the kidnapping of Bobby Dunbar. Someone entered his locked cell that evening and gave him a vicious beating. His attorneys began working feverishly on their appeal to the Louisiana Supreme Court.

That same afternoon Dubuisson received a letter from his secretary, Alex Robertson, containing information from J. L. Linder—information that was withheld until the sentencing date, a fact Robertson made note of.

COPY of letter received from J. L. LINDER, dated Alexandria, La., May 14, 1914, postmarked Fayette, Miss., 4 P. M., May 18, 1914, received Opelousas, La., (not postmarked) at 4 P. M. on May 19, 1914, after sentence was passed on W. C. Walters.

Alexandria, La., May 14, 1914,

Mr. Alex robinson

Dear sir your letter was fowarded to me yes I am in hopes Walters will get a new trial I no at the trial in Opelousas thear whear some people swore lies on old Walters

Yes I was in new roads with a man By the name Jessie Tutchstone and all so my little Boy at the time he was 9 years old in the year of 1911 it was late in the fall or the first of winter

Now Mr. robinson here is man not known in this trial By the name of Jessie tutchstone he went By the name of J. W. King he lived in Alexandria the year of 1912 and fixed stoves all down the Watkins railroad and at Cravens saw mill, at Fulerton mill, Derider, Longville, Merryville he told me he was at a speaking in Merryville he was all over that mill country he was at Oakdale all so he is the same man was with me at new roads and we was at Mrs Sloan house this is true I think Jessie Tutchstone or J. W. King is the name he goes by lives at Teneha,

Texas he is eather thear or at Shreveport, La. Now Mr. Robinson all I am goin to do is to tell the truth and nothing But the truth I had fixed Rev. Benett stove and all so mr. J. W. King fixed his stove if mr. Walters gets a new trial i wish you would try and have Jessie Tutchstone nick name J. W. King sumonds to court as you asked me to tell you the truth i am telling it now Mr. Robinson please don't sumonds me any more for i don't want to see opelousas as long as I live all tho Walters ought to have a new trial and i am in hopes he will get it

I will close hoping you good luck and sucess.
i am working the north part of miss.

Yours truly,
J. L. Linder.

William Cantwell Walters' Defense File© #387

When Julia received the news about Cantwell's life sentence, she wrote to Tom.

may 21 1914
Poplarvile miss

mr thomas Dale

Deare friend I will write you a few Lines to Let you heare from me I Learn that mr walters could not get a new trial I want you to Let me no at once what we can do next don't you think that I can get a case against them fore my child it seams Like I cant stand it I heard that they Liked to beat walters to Death I don't know how true it is I want you to Let me heare from you at once I will close fore this time hope to heare from you real soon

your friend
Julia Anderson

William Cantwell Walters' Defense File© #390

Julia gradually settled into Pearl River County life and was introduced to a local man, Ollie Rawls, a cousin to Hollis. His strength upheld her as she despaired over her stolen son and Cantwell's miserable fate. They married shortly thereafter.

Tom, Hollis, and Dubuisson compiled a strong appeal in Cantwell's behalf, contesting the lack of separation of the jury and admitting the newly discovered evidence. The hearing was set for June 13.

D. L. Bledsoe did his best to garner support for the helpless gentleman.

Iron City Ga. May 23rd 1914.
Dale & Rauls
Columbia Miss.

Gentlemen,

The Citizens of Robinson C. NC. called a mass meeting on last Thursday 21st and Invited Mr Stephens & Murry whom you meet at Opelousas to meet with them & Inform them the way & maner Walters was treated at his trial. I have not as yet heard the results of the meeting But the Intention of the meeting was to raise money to carry the case to a finish. I am asked to write a full account of the trial for the Robisonian the county paper of Robison C. NC. as I saw it. At this time I have a fearful case of sore eyes & I am asking you to Please write it for me & foward it to me at once & I will sign it & foward it on. I am the biddie that has got the thing going in your behalf. I may make a 600 mile trip up there and make four speeches in behalf of W C. If I do we will raise a sufficient amount to work with. I have been arrousing a lot of Inthusiasum in that direction. So If you are not boged up in some court you be sure and do as I have requested. I have received three letters from Mr Dubuison since I left that hell of a whole called Opelousas, He thinks I will do him a lot of good. There is no use to try Walters in Louisana as that rotten Item as poisoned the minds of the citizens to the Extent that it is a matter of Impossiability for him to meet Justice in the minds of a rotten set of Devilish Catholics. Old governor Brewer ought to be put in W C. W place for the same time For Gods sake ride your State of a Judas and elect you a governor that has a back bone backed by comon sence. I am your friend to the end.

I am yours most cordially.
D. L. Bledsoe

William Cantwell Walters' Defense File© #392

The attorneys received an invitation from the Citizen's Group of Robeson, North Carolina, who guaranteed they could raise a significant amount of money if they would come there and speak on Cantwell's behalf. The group would reimburse their travel expenses. With the possibility of a new trial being granted by the Louisiana Supreme Court, the attorneys were desperate for financial help. Tom and Hollis had spent well over one thousand dollars out of their personal pockets already. If the fight were to begin anew, the attorneys were more than willing to go begging for monetary support.

William Cantwell Walters' Defense File© #'s 393 & 413

On May 27, 1914, Cantwell left Opelousas shackled and under guard. His transfer papers were for the Parish Prison in New Orleans to begin serving his life sentence. The prison didn't allow harps.

New orleans June the 6th 1914

Messers Dale & Rawls

Yours to Hand of June the 4th Just would Beg to say that I am Highly Pleased at the Result now in Progress of things Receaved the stamps with many thanks But am at A Loss to no what to Do or say I see it Begins to Put you in A Rather unfortunate Position My Case was taken By Mr Dale For A stipulated Fee which has Been Away over Drawn and I you well no Has used Every means to Entreate to Everybody I Could Reach And you Fail to Give me Mr Raines Full name and they Have not Corosponded with me at all And I should think that you Could Better Put the matter of Fineance Before them than I Could Even If I Knew who to write to I Could not tell who to write to And it Begins to Look like A Fruitless Fight there Has never Been one Point Gained that I Can see I think the officers of Miss are amendable to me For the Loss of My Little Boy and Every thing I Had I was Robed in what you might say in Broad open Day Light And It Looks to me Like An Injunction Could Be Filed Against the Courts of La And Bring up the Guiltie Parties to the Courts of miss I Have all the Evidince there to Prove that theres A Conspiracy I was Kidnaped me and my Little Boy Bruce you Should I think Know who is Implicated In the Kidnapping me And Bruce there is Charlie Day Dr Anderson Ed Lampton and Likely Mr Wallace And Material Accessors John

Fortenberry and Ed Lamptons son Besides many others I think the Best thing that the Peoepple there and In opelousas that are Implicated to Get togeather and Make up the muny And Pay me A Reasonable Damage And Give me my Boy Back And I Beleave you Could Do good there By Agitating this matter A Few Days Ago A man Came here to see me and wanted to no If thy would Give me my Boy Back and Claim Mistaken Identity what I would Do And I told him that I Could not say until I would Consult my Attornys He Claimed to Be An Item Reporter But I Beleave He was sent here By the Dunbar Faction I Beleave If this thing was Put Before them Right thy would come A Cross And it Looks to me Like it is time something should Be Done It Looks Like there should Be some Law to Protect A man with His Life and Propertie this is A stain that Columbia And the officials of Marion Co will nevr Get wiped out And the Farthr it Goes the Deeper it will Get and Opelousas is worse But I dont think the Good Peoepple EAther there or Here will stand Back much Longer And Let it Go

About the Fineancial Proposition you Can Put it Before these Peoepple there and in NC In the Mean time send me the Address of Any that Corisponds with you And I will see what I Can Do Since I Have Come Here I Have not Got Much Mail I Had wrote letters About 3 days Before I Came Hire And Have waited And wrote the Postmaster to Change my Mail But it Dont come I think the officials here are Vay Careful about you mail I am vay well Pleased with the manigement so far About My Physical Condition I will Have to Have the water Drawn soon A Friend of mine Here in NO is to Come to see me to Day and I will try to Get Him to Get A Doctor to work on me so I will Close with many Good wishes For your success and Health I Have been Looking For A Letter From S J H & O B F But it Dont Come

your obedient seirvant
W C Walters Parish Prison
Neworleans La

William Cantwell Walters' Defense File© #410

The publicity had always leaned heavily in the Dunbars' favor, but with the trial over, witnesses gone home, and Cantwell out of the way, the press turned the glare of the spotlight on them alone, amplifying every naked flaw and defect in their façade. The constant scrutiny quickly became tiresome, but they had bought in for a lifetime of it. Percy whined that *they* were now experiencing open malice in their own town. Lessie said it was a great sorrow to her that the publicity prevented *their* living quietly.

On June 29, 1914, Tom and Hollis received an optimistic telegram from A. J. McMullen. "The Louisiana Supreme Court has ruled that the law under which Cantwell was convicted is unconstitutional, with the verdict and sentence set aside."

Hollis quickly posted a letter to Cantwell.

Mr. W. C. Walters, July 1, 1914
C/O Parish Prison,
New Orleans, La.

Dear Friend Walters,

Mr. McMullen, of the Daily States, sent us a telegram Monday announcing the verdict of the Supreme Court, and we do not believe that you could have felt as good or any better over this victory than we did. We immediately wired Mr. McMullen to protect your every interest, and if they should release you Monday or Tuesday to put you on the first train for Columbia and draw on us for the expense. Our purpose being to get you out of Louisiana as early as possible. We know, however, that the judgment of the Supreme Court would have to be certified at Opelousas and then returned to New Orleans before you could be legally released.

We are today in receipt of the opinion of the court and our victory was a sweeping one. The court adopted for its opinion the brief filed by us, a copy of which the writer sent you some days since.

There is some talk that you have perhaps noticed in the papers about trying you under the old law of 1870. In Mississippi this mind of procedure would not go. A plea of former jeopardy would acquit you, and we are advised that this is true also in Louisiana.

We feel, therefore, that you need rest no uneasiness. The attorneys for the state are allowed by law fourteen days within which to file their suggestions of errors in the Supreme Court. They of course will do this and delay the matter just as long as they can.

The people of Robeson County, North Carolina, have arranged a big Mass-meeting on July 4th at Lumberton, North Carolina, and have wired for one or both of us to be present. We have accepted the invitation, and either Mr. Dale or the writer will leave tomorrow, Thursday, for North Carolina. If possible, we will come through New Orleans and will be out to see you and discuss the case more fully than we can do by letter. In the meantime, keep up your courage, quit your talkin especially to newspaper men, and take things easy, because it has broken our way at last. As we have always told you, we are with you until the end. Let us hear from you and expect us to see you the earliest moment we can get away from our term of court. With all good wishes and congratulations to you, we beg to remain as ever,

Your friend,
Hollis Rawls

William Cantwell Walters' Defense File© #430

Cantwell, sweating out his second summer behind bars, had finally received his first legal victory and that at the hands of the Louisiana Supreme Court. With his elation, his mouth was getting the better of him as he boasted that, "Louisiana will soon be opening wide its prison doors for me, but my victory will only be complete when Bruce is returned to me. I am expecting total recompense for my attorneys and the damage done to my character." One week later, he heard from the attorneys again.

Mr. W. C. Walters, July, 8, 1914
C/O Parish Prison,
New Orleans, La.

Friend Walters:

We returned yesterday from a trip to Lumberton, North Carolina, your old home, where on the 4th day of July, we addressed a gathering of the citizens of that county, estimated from four to five thousand people. To tell you the people entertained us royally and are deeply interested in your welfare would be expressing it mildly. Mr. Thomas L. Johnston, an attorney of that city entertained us and every one did everthing possible for our comfort.

The trip was a hard one but we had a very delightful time. They assured us that they are going to assist you financially and see that you get a fair and square deal. Mr. K. M. Barnes, Mr. Stevens, and Mr. Johnston have started a systematic canvas of the city for funds to aid you in your defense, and we are confident they will be able to accomplish something. The trip was an expensive one to us and they assure us that they will bear these expenses later on. We expect to receive a copy of the Robisonian in the next few days containing an account of the meeting and speaking, and when it comes we will send it to you. We met a number of your old friends and they say that they are going to help you all they can.

On reaching New Orleans Monday we met Mr. Lee Garland, District Attorney. He had come over to New Orleans for the purpose of filing a motion for a new trial in the Supreme Court.

Under the laws of Louisiana the side that loses on appeal has thirteen days within which to file a motion for a rehearing. They knew the court would adjourn Saturday night for its summer vacation until October 1st. They waited, therefore, as they had a right to do under the law until after the court had adjourned and then filed this motion. The motion can not possibly be heard until October. Under the law you are not subject to bail nor would a writ of Habeas Corpus get you out. There is nothing to do except to wait the reconvening of the Supreme Court. We regret this situation indeed, but they simply took advantage of their practice and proceeding, which is legal, but it is going to work a great hardship on you.

With the assistance they promised us from North Carolina, we are confident we will put your feet on the ground a free man. At any rate keep up your courage. Don't talk any more than you can help, and one member of the firm will be to see you just as soon as we can get to New Orleans again. We only had a few hours on our return and had to spend most of this in the Supreme Court looking after this motion for a new trial. With best wishes we beg to remain as ever,

Your friends,
Dale & Rawls

William Cantwell Walters' Defense File© #435

Cantwell, who had finally received a reason to be optimistic, found himself knocked to the ground once more by the callousness of Garland and the Dunbars. Their motion guaranteed them at least three more months without Cantwell's interference in their lives. If he were to expire over the summer due to the harshness of life in the State's prison, they wouldn't shed a tear.

M. A. Stephens of North Carolina printed an appeal to be circulated among the people of his area.

A PLEA FOR THE INNOCENT

Dear Friend and Brother:

In the interest, as I believe, of an innocent man, is this little leaflet sent out, and if it, perchance, finds its way to you, will you give it some consideration, and think of it as an opportunity to be a helper to the helpless? The author of this little leaflet has nothing at heart but to help the man that is in sore need. Therefore to any and all who are willing to help the innocent is this appeal made.

Mr. W. C. Walters, of Robeson County, N. C., falsely accused, as he has proven by as good men and women as there are in North Carolina, Georgia and Mississippi, is confined in prison in New Orleans, La., awaiting another trial in the courts of Louisiana -- no one to help him and no money with which to help himself. Mr. Walters has an aged widowed mother living near Barnesville in Robeson County, financially unable to give him any more assistance, and that mother loves that boy.

Many friends know or believe, at least, that Mr. Walters is falsely charged with the crime of kidnapping one Robert Dunbar of Opelousas, La., because he was found with a little boy in Mississippi -- little Bruce Anderson, who went with Mr. Walters from his mother's home near Barnesville in Robeson County, N. C. Little Bruce Anderson was taken from Mr. Walters and Mr. Walters put in prison to be tried for his life according to the laws of the State of Louisiana.

Therefore, in the name of right and Christian love for the innocent and suffering of one of our fellow beings, I make this appeal to the ministers and Christian people of Robeson and Columbus Counties, that each church and pastor take a special collection, let the amount be little or much, and forward the same to M. G. Williamson, Evergreen, N. C., to help Mr. Walters secure and keep his attorneys, who have stood so nobly by him during his first trial.

Dear Christian men and women, as a minister of truth and righ-
teousness, I appeal to you to help the man, and we shall all be glad some
day.

M. A. Stephens.
Evergreen, N.C.

William Cantwell Walters' Defense File© #489

The Louisiana Supreme Court reconvened in October and it fell to
Hollis to explain their latest predicament to his friend.

Mr. W. C. Walters, Oct. 22, 1914
Parish Prison,
New Orleans, La.

Friend Walters:

Your note of the 20th came duly to hand, and immediately following it
a telegram advising that the Supreme Court had granted a re-hearing
to the state in the matter of your appeal. We regret this exceedingly, but
feel that it will only delay the final out-come. We are to-day taking
the matter up with Mr Dubuisson at Opelousas and have asked him
to advise us what steps we should now take and when in his opinion
the case would be argued again before the Supreme Court. Just as soon
as we hear from him we will advise you. In the meantime you under-
stand that so far this does not mean a new trial of the case on its merits.
It only means that the Supreme Court will re-set the case before that
tribunal and we will have to again argue same orally. If they stand on
their former opinion you will go free. If they reverse this, in all likely-
hood you will be re-indicted in Opelousas and have to be tried again.
If the Supreme Court holds the present law unconstitutional, they will
attempt to try you under the old law of 1870. The maximum penalty
under that law is ten years imprisonment instead of a life sentence or
death as is the case under the law you were first tried upon.

Keep up your courage. Do not talk too much and make the very
best of it you can. We will stay with you to the end. It does look like,
however, that some of your friends or kin people would put up some
money. We have never received one dime from North Carolina. So far
they have failed to pay our expenses on our trip over there at their in-

vitation. We spent on that trip alone $250.00 and have never gotten a dime of that back. We cannot understand what is the matter with Mr. Barnes, Cashier of the bank at Lumberton or with your other friends. Why don't you write them? With regards, we beg to remain,

Sincerely yours,
Dale & Rawls

William Cantwell Walters' Defense File© #460

The news of the rehearing nearly crushed Cantwell. He had predicted his upcoming release for months. He had seen it unfold in his head one-hundred times and practiced his I-told-you-so speech. However, equally painful was the disillusionment of receiving nothing monetarily from his home state. He knew as well as anyone that the area had been poverty stricken for years, but he thought his fellow citizens would rise up together and sacrifice something for him. The two attorneys had given a commanding 4th of July performance touching on the trial's highpoints and Cantwell's needs, but the people in attendance had come for the free show.

Three and a half weeks later, Cantwell received word from Hollis.

Mr. W. C. Walters, Nov. 17, 1914.
c/o Parish Prison,
New Orleans, La.

Friend Walters,

While victory crowned our efforts on appeal in the Supreme Court, yet we were disappointed, for the reason that the Court reversed itself as to the constitutionality of the kidnapping law. This means now that you will have to stand trial again just as if the case had never been tried.

We are writing Mr. Dubuisson and perhaps when we hear from him can give you some definite idea as to when the case will be called for trial again. Now, Friend Walters, if you have ever called for help through letters, get busy. Mr. Dale and the writer will, of course, be with you at the trial.

While we are not able financially to pay our personal expenses, hotel bills, railroad fare etc., in connection with the trial, yet we will do this without murmur and donate our services to you free of charge, as we have in the past; but we are not able financially to carry a swarm of witnesses with us like we did before and pay a thousand and one other bills that we were called upon to pay personally at your last trial. Some help, therefore, must come from somewhere.

Your friends and kin people in North Carolina have quit writing us altogether and as yet they have not sent us one dime, even failing to pay our expenses to Lumberton, after inviting us to be present with them. Get in touch, therefore, with all these people; tell them the situation, as the issue means life or death to you.

You may expect to hear from us again just as soon as we learn something definite to advise. In the meantime, keep up your nerve and cut out your newspaper talk. With regards, we beg to remain,

Very truly yours,
DALE & RAWLS
William Cantwell Walters' Defense File© #471

At this absolute lowest point, Tom and Hollis received a letter from Dubuisson which they thought referenced the Defense's next possible move.

Messrs. Dale & Rawls, Nov. 22, 1914.

Gentlemen:

Like you, I have failed to receive a copy of the last decision of the Supreme Court in the Walters case. However, it is plain from the newspaper reports that the Court recalled its former decision holding the act unconstitutional, but remanding the case for a new trial. It will therefore have to be tried anew under the same law.

A change of venue under our law would do you no good. The law provides that when a change of venue is granted the trial shall take place in an adjoining parish of the same judicial district, or of another district adjoining in which there will first be a term of court. All things considered I believe you would have as much chance in a new trial at Opelousas as in one of the adjoining parishes. If you could obtain a change of venue to New Orleans, I believe your chances for an acquittal would be most excellent.

I don't think I shall be with you in the new trial, as I intend to ask the Judge to relieve me from any further duty as counsel appointed by the Court to assist the defense. I feel that I have done my full duty to the Court, and that I am entitled to relief.

Very truly yours,
E. B. Dubuisson.
William Cantwell Walters' Defense File© #475

Hollis fairly begged in his return message, "As we have before attempted to feebly express to you, your assistance has been invaluable and there is no one now that could give us the assistance in the second trial that you could render. If the officials of the Parish insist on another trial, we shall respectfully insist that you be with us if possible."
William Cantwell Walters' Defense File© #476

Dubuisson replied, "I beg to say that my decision not to participate in a new trial if I can obtain the Court's consent to be released is unalterable. However, I do not think that the case is going to be called up for trial again. I received an intimation from one of the Court officers a few days ago that if bond were applied for, it would probably be granted, and that the solvency of the bondsman tendered would not be too closely scrutinized."
William Cantwell Walters' Defense File© #477

Tom wrote to Garland two days later.

Hon. Lee Garland, December 9, 1914.
Opelousas, La. IN RE: WALTERS CASE.

Dear Mr. Garland,-

Some several days since we had a letter from Mr. Dubuisson who tells us that it is his intention not to be further connected with the Walters case, if the Court will release him; and in this same letter Mr. Dubuisson advised us that possibly we would be able to get bail for Walters.
We feel sure that the granting of the bail in this case would depend altogether on your disposition in the premises. Under our law this would not be a bailable case and we should not think it would be under

the laws of Louisiana, if application of bail should be strenuously con-
tested. We like, however, that the people of your Parish and your State
are of the opinion that Walters has been already sufficiently punished
for whatever connection he may have had with Bobbie Dunbar, if any
such he did have; and it may be that under these circumstances you
would not oppose an application on our part for bail.

Understand, Mr. Garland, that in writing you about this matter
and in this way, we do so in perfectly good faith and with no intent or
purpose whatever to ask of you anything except the honest, conscien-
tious performance of your duty.

It has in a way been intimated to us that the officials of St. Landry
Parish probably would not want another trial in this case on account
of the very heavy expense attached thereto; and if this be true, we feel
like the old man ought to be entitled to bail.

Kindly let us hear from you with reference to this matter, and oblige,

Very truly yours,
DALE & RAWLS
William Cantwell Walters' Defense File© #479

Garland never answered the letter. Or the next. Or the next. He
would not be rushed.

During the wait, Hollis answered an exasperated letter from Cantwell, sending him some long overdue news.

Mr. W. C. Walters, December 14, 1914.
Parish Prison,
New Orleans, La.

Friend Walters,

On account of illness the writer has been out of the office hence our
correspondence has necessarily been compelled to wait. This accounts for
your not having heard from us as promptly as you thought you should.

We feel that you should not grow impatient and we do not at all
appreciate the tone in which your last letter is written. It seems to the
writer that from the fight, the donations, and sacrifices that we have
made in your behalf, that these things would cause you to consider be-

fore you jumped to the conclusion that we are not trying to help you further.

As to the pictures of Bruce: We only have one of each now in our file and we cannot spare them even to you, for in the event of another trial we would need them in your defense. If we go to trial the second time, Mr. Dubuisson will not be with us.

We have some confidential information and if you know what is good for you now, you will not give this out to any one, and most certainly not to a newspaper man. It has been suggested to us, as coming from the attorneys for the State that no fight will be made upon our application for bail, nor will the solvency of your sureties be too closely investigated. In other words, the intimation is that the State and the Dunbars are sick of the fight and that if we can get anybody to go your bond, you will again be a free man, and never placed upon trial again for this crime.

We have taken the matter up direct with District Attorney Garland, and should hear from him during the course of this week. We will advise you just as soon as we do. We are with you to the end, and propose to give you in the future, as in the past, our very best legal services and ability.

Keep up your courage and whatever else you do, do not communicate the contents of this letter to anyone. With regards, we beg to remain,

Sincerely your friends,
DALE & RAWLS.

William Cantwell Walters' Defense File© #481

On December 31, Hollis wrote to Dubuisson. "Immediately before the holidays we addressed a letter to District Attorney Garland, making inquiry as to our probable chances of procuring bail for Walters, and to date we have had no reply from him. We are writing him again along this line, and if it would not be requesting too much at your hand it would surely be a favor to us and to Walters if you would suggest to Mr. Garland the propriety of replying to our communications."

William Cantwell Walters' Defense File© #483

Hollis also wrote to Cantwell explaining the delay. "Make the best you can of a bad situation."

William Cantwell Walters' Defense File© #484

On January 20, 1915, Tom traveled to New Orleans for the purpose of intercepting Garland. The next day he wrote to Pavy.

Jan. 21, 1915

Dear Sir:

The writer had a talk with Hon. Lee Garland on yesterday in New Orleans, and it is by agreement with him and his consent that we are making this application for bail, and Mr. Garland tells us that he will readily and willingly consent for your order to this effect to be given. He will further consent for the order to provide that the sureties be furnished from states other than that of Louisiana.

Now Judge, you, of course, realize that Walters is indeed a poor man, as is set up in the petition, and comes from a poor family, and it will have to be to his friends, other than his family, that we will have to look to for sureties on this bond, if such we can get at all, and we will thank you kindly, if in your judgment Walters is admitted to bail, that you will fix the amount of bond at such a reasonable small sum as we will be able to procure for him. It shall be our purpose to get his bond made either in this state or in the state of North Carolina, or both.

Mr. Garland tells us that on account of this case having been tried at such an enormous expense at its former trial, it will probably be some several months before he will undertake to call it for trial again, if at all. This however, was said to the writer confidentially.

If in your judgment and discretion Walters is entitled to bail we will appreciate your order for such, and will kindly ask that you send the order to us and we will arrange for one of us to go to New Orleans and procure his release after the bond has been made and approved by the proper official of your parish. Kindly let us hear from you at your earliest convenience, and with kind personal regards we beg to remain,

Yours very truly,
Dale & Rawls

William Cantwell Walters' Defense File© #492

Tom's application began with the usual obeisance and the basic facts of the charge: Cantwell being tried, convicted, and sentenced; was aggrieved and appealed the decision; judgment and sentence set aside; now asking for a low bond.

"Long, continued and further confinement in jail will endanger Petitioner's life and health.

"He is a poor man, having already spent his all in undertaking to make his defense to the crime charged against him.

"He has no friends or relatives residing in the State of Louisiana who would sign an appearance bond for him, but will be in a position to furnish bail in a reasonable sum with sureties from other states.

"And as in duty bound Petitioner will ever pray."

William Cantwell Walters' Defense File© #493

Cantwell's release likely hinged on one condition, one decision between Tom Dale and Lee Garland made on a frozen sidewalk in New Orleans. That there would never be any attempt to remove the child from the Dunbars.

Hollis appealed to their friend John Blank for help.

New Orleans, La. Feb. 8, 1915

Dear Sir & Friend:-

For your many past kindnesses to our firm and the courtesies shown us while in the City a pleasant memory will always linger. We are fixing once again herein, however, to ask an additional favor. You have perhaps noticed from the public press an agreement with our firm and the District Attorney and Attorney General relative to bond in the Walters case. Since that time we have prepared and filed our petition before Judge Pavy, and he has now granted bail in the sum of FIVE HUNDRED DOLLARS, and we are advised privately by Mr. Dubisson and the District Attorney at Opelousas that the case will never be called for trial; that the giving of the bond is more or less a matter of red tape and will never amount to anything; that they are thoroughly sick of the Walters case and never expect to put him on trial again. The order for bail, however, provides that the sureties must be residents of Louisiana, and it is in this connection that we desire your assistance. Either Mr. Dale or the writer will be in New Orleans towards the last of this week for the purpose of attempting to make this bond. Having a limited acquaintance in the City, we deemed it best to put this situa-

tion up to you for advice. The bond will never amount to anything, and we are advised that the solvency of our sureties will never be inquired into, and we are confident that with your assistance we could procure the necessary names to secure the old man's release.

Sincerely yours,
Dale & Rawls

William Cantwell Walters' Defense File© #498

On February 17, 1915, after spending 725 days in jail, William Cantwell Walters was finally released. His feeble body lay curled on his side on a stretcher heading directly to Charity Hospital in New Orleans for treatment on his knee and other ailments resulting from his incarceration. As soon as his doctor would release him, he exited the state of Louisiana heading to Poplarville. Hollis caught up with the gentleman there.

Mr. W. C. Walters, March 1st, 1915
Poplarville, Miss.

Dear Friend Walters:

We hope that you are enjoying your freedom to the fullest possible extent. One or more picture concerns have been in communication with us relative to having you appear as an attraction at their theaters, and we have also had this matter up with Mr. Harry Sellers, your friend and ours. We had thought that you intended staying a while in the hospital in the City, but glad to know that you are able to navigate without it. Mr. Sellers advises us that he is negotiating a contract for you that is a good one and suggests that neither you nor any one for you sign any kind of contract with any concern until he can see you. We have known Mr. Sellers for quite a while and he is a thorough honest and reliable gentleman, and we are sure that neither you nor us will make any mistake in entrusting him with this matter. Kindly let us hear from you by return mail telling us where you are and what you intend doing in the immediate future. It seems to us that as soon as you can it would be a splendid chance to make some money for you to exhibit yourself under contract with a reliable company, but there are so many crooked concerns that you want to be very careful as to whom you sign with, or you will get beat out of everything. Awaiting your reply and with regards and best wishes for your continued success and happiness, we beg to remain, as ever,

Your friends,
Dale & Rawls

William Cantwell Walters' Defense File© #499

In a shaky hand, Cantwell replied once more to the men who had staunchly stood by his side.

Mess Dale & RawlsCarriere/ Mch the 6th 1915

Columbia Miss

I Receaved your Highly Appreciated Letter yesterday At Poplarville Did not Have time to write yesterday Am now waiting to Get Mr Sellers on the Phone If Get Him I will Let you know in this Letter what my Next Move will Be

4 Pm I Got Mr Sellers on the Phone this Am and He told Mr T S Dale was in the City and would Call me Again of Seeing him And I Have waited till now And no News And Dont Look for Any Hearing this Pm I Cant tell what to Do I am Here with no money to Get Any where And no way to Get any I Spent Last Knight with Bro Holcomb I will Likely Be Here monday morning

Respectfuly yours
W C Walters

Sorry I Could not Get to Columbia

William Cantwell Walters' Defense File© #500

Tom assured the ailing and destitute gentleman that they were still committed to his safety and wellbeing.

Mr. W. C. Walters,March 9, 1915
Carriere, Miss.

Dear Friend Walters:

We are in receipt of your letter and note what you have to say with reference to being with Bro. Holcomb and have no money to come to Columbia on. If you will get Bro. Holcomb to let you have money enough to come up here with we will return it to him, and this letter shall be your authority for calling upon him for a sufficient amount of money to pay your expenses from Carriere to Columbia.

Few days since the writer was in New Orleans and saw Mr. Sellers. Mr. Sellers, however, has not as yet succeeded in landing anything worth while. While there the writer had a long talk with Mr. Streetly, whom you met while in the City, and Mr. Streetly is still very anxious to sign up with you for a show in New Orleans of several days duration, and then a general trip over the south. We think this about the best opening now for you, and if you will come here to us upon receipt of this letter we will put you in touch with Mr. Streetly, or if you had rather go direct to New Orleans advise us over phone and we will get in touch with Mr. Streetly and arrange with him to take charge of you. So when you get this letter, if you want to go back to New Orleans to see Mr. Streetly, get Mr. Holcomb to let you have money enough to get to New Orleans and he draw on us for this amount. Phone us so we can get in touch with Mr. Streetly and have him meet you. At the same time we will let Mr. Sellers know what we are doing so that he will understand our position in the matter. Streetly says that he can make it profitable to you for some time in New Orleans, and then after working the City he will go on a tour with you, and he thinks both you and him will be able to make good money out of this scheme. To say the least of it you are not making anything at Carriere. Let us hear from you right away. With regards, we are,

Yours very truly,
Dale & Rawls

William Cantwell Walters' Defense File© #502

Chapter Fourteen
The Newspapers

SKETCHED IN OPELOUSAS DURING THE EXCITEMENT
The States-May 4, 1913

LATEST PICTURE OF DUNBAR MOTHER, CHILD, RELATIVES AND ATTORNEYS WHO REPRESENT THEM IN THE NOTED CASE

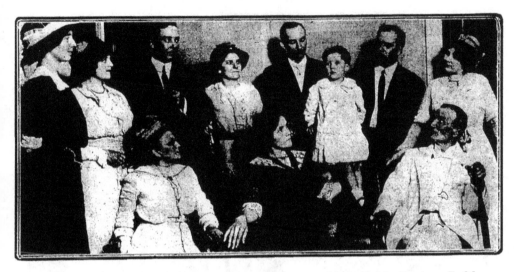

Left to right, standing - Mrs. Christine Zernott, Mrs. F. M. Dunbar, F. M. Dunbar, Mrs. John W. Lewis, Archie Dunbar, S. H. Fox, Mrs. S. H. Fox. Seated - Mrs. W. B. Dunbar, Mrs. C. P. Dunbar, "Bobby" and B. F. Sherrouse. Especially posed for *The Item*-June 9, 1913

Julia Anderson
The Times-Democrat, May 1, 1913

HERO, "VILLIAN," AND OTHER CHARACTERS IN TWO STATES DRAMA

PICTURED PRINCIPALS

The judge, the principals, some of the attorneys and witnesses of the nation famous Dunbar Walters case are here pictured.

Few cases in the South have attracted so much attention in the public mind and press as the identity of the five year-old blue eyed boy, the pivot around whom the legal machinery of two states have revolved for the past two months. Saturday's decision by John M. Parker that the child is the son of the Dunbars, is the first decisive step that has been taken.

The Item-June 8, 1913

Which Is the Mother of This Boy

If it is humanly possible to tell you, you will get the answer in The Item.

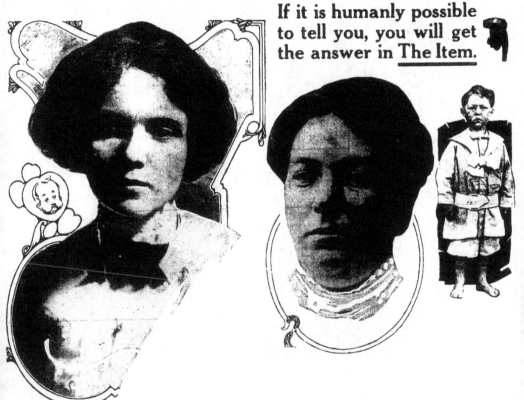

Left: Mrs. C. P. Dunbar who claims she is the mother of the boy and challenges the world to dispute the testimony of her own mother love.

Middle: Julia Anderson claims the child as her boy Bruce Anderson, whom she let go walking with C. W. Walters about three years ago, and whom she has never seen since, unless "Little Bobby" Dunbar is Bruce Anderson after all.

Right: For the courts to decide. This is either little Bobbie Dunbar or Bruce Anderson. Two states are wild with excitement over the trial in which a man's life hangs on the verdict.

The Item-April 9, 1914

Is this Bobbie Dunbar or Bruce Anderson? Upon the identity of this child hangs the life of one man and the happiness of all concerned. The question must be decided, causing someone to suffer.

The Item-April 11, 1914

On his thousand-string hand-made harp, W. C. Walters plays for the crowds that daily gather in the jail yard under his cell window at Opelousas. It gives good music and helps to drive dull care and troubles out the steel-barred windows, says the accused tinker. This is the first photograph of the harp, and shows Walters playing to a crowd under his window at the jail. Walters posed at the harp especially for The Daily States.

The Daily States-
April 12, 1914

"This is my best photo," says W. C. Walters. He posed especially at the jail yard for The Daily States and took a lot of pains to "dress up." Evidently life in jail isn't so bad; at least, it hasn't caused Walters to become pale or thin. He eats well, plays his harp, and is confident.

The Daily States-April 13, 1914

W. C. Walters Addressing Crowd From Jail

The Item-April 13, 1914

Left to right: E. B. Dubuisson, Thomas S. Dale, and Hollis C. Rawls

Justice Weighs Pleas in Fight of Mothers

The Item-April 12 & 14, 1914

This picture shows Mr. and Mrs. Dunbar. In the mother's arms is her second child, Alonzo. They claim that the child held in the father's arms is their kidnapped child, Bobbie. Walters says he is Bruce Anderson.

The Item-April 12, 1914

Can These Eyes Solve Walters-Dunbar Case?

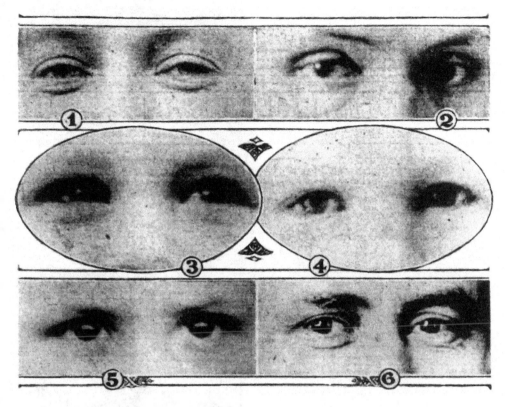

Here is an opportunity for a remarkable study in eyes, and one that may solve for your own complete satisfaction the question whether the boy who is the central figure in the trial of W. C. Walters is Bobbie Dunbar or Bruce Anderson.

At the top, on the left, are shown Julia Anderson's eyes. On the right are those of Mrs. C. P. Dunbar. Which is the mother?

In the center, on the left, is the picture of the real Bobbie Dunbar, taken before he left his home. On the right of the center panel those of the boy whom all claim.

Below, on the left, are the eyes of Alonzo Dunbar, the younger son. Next to his are those of C. P. Dunbar.

The Item-April 15, 1914

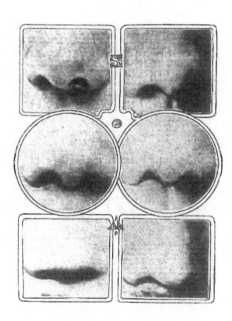

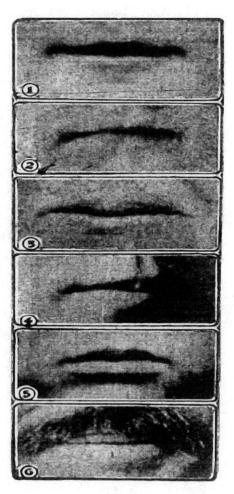

Can You Pick the Boy By His Nose?   Their Mouths

At the top, on left, are shown Julia Anderson's nose. On the right that of Mrs. C. P. Dunbar. Which is the mother? In the center, on the left, is the picture of the nose of the real Bobbie Dunbar, taken before he left his home. On the right of the center panel that of the boy whom all claim. Below, on the left, is the nose of Alonzo Dunbar, the younger son. Next to his is that of C. P. Dunbar.

From top to bottom they are the real Bobbie Dunbar, the boy whom both factions claim, Julia Anderson, Mrs. Dunbar, Alonzo Dunbar and C. P. Dunbar. Decide the relationship for yourself.

The Item-April 16 & 17, 1914

Compare the Full Faces Now

From left to right: Julia Anderson, Bobbie Before Disappearance, the Present Bobbie, Mrs. Dunbar, Alonzo and Mr. Dunbar

The Item-April 19, 1914

"Trist" has here portrayed Walters as he appeared on the witness stand at Opelousas Saturday, a scene in the courtroom when Julia Anderson's letter was offered and "Bobbie" leaning over Attorney John W. Lewis' shoulder and smiling while his foot was being shown the jury.

The Item-April 20, 1914

Mr. and Mrs. C. P. Dunbar and Alonzo Dunbar and the boy claimed by the Dunbars as their kidnapped son, Bobbie. These new photos posed for The Daily States, are declared excellent. Mr. and Mrs. Dunbar are at the top and, left to right in lower panel, are Alonzo and "Bobbie."

The Daily States-April 15 & 21, 1914

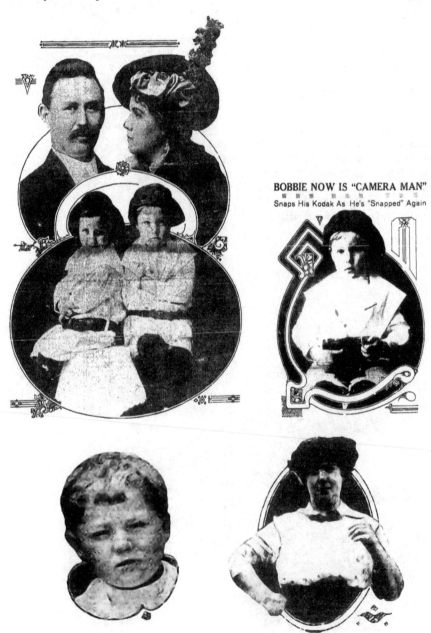

"Bobbie" and Julia-*The Item*-April 15 & 21, 1914

Here are some of the witnesses who passed through New Orleans on Monday on their way to Opelousas to testify on behalf of the tinker in the famous Walters-Dunbar case. From left to right they are Mr. and Mrs. J. A. Goldman and baby, of Poplarville, Miss.; George Bayless, of Columbia; Charles Day, of Hoke's Bluff, and W. C. Bass, of Poplarville.

The Item-April 13, 1914

Principal Witnesses for State in Dunbar-Walters Case and Their Testimony as Seen by 'Trist'

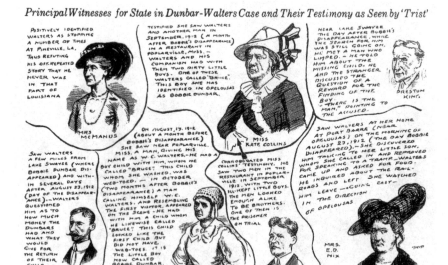

Positively identified Walters as stopping a number of times at Pineville, LA., thus refuting his oft-repeated story that he never was in that part of Louisiana. Mrs Mc-Manus

Testified she saw Walters and another man in September, 1912 (a month after Bobbie's disappearance) in a restaurant in Poplarville, Miss. Walters and his companion had with them two dirty little boys. One of these Walters called "Bruce." This boy she has identified in Opelousas as Bobbie Dunbar. Miss Kate Collins

Near Lake Swayze the day after Bobbie's disappearance, while the search for him was still going on, he met a man who limped. He told him about the missing child. He and the stranger discussed the question of a reward for the finding of the boy. "There is the man," pointing to the accused. Preston King

Saw Walters at her home at Port Barre (near Opelousas) on the morning of August 23, 1912 (the day Bobbie disappeared). She discovered him talking to her little son, whom she called in and reproved for speaking to a tramp. Walters came up and asked for food. He inquired about the railroads and left. She watched him leave -- going east -- in the direction of Opelousas. Mrs. E. D. Nix

Corroborated Miss Collins' testimony. He saw two men in the restaurant in Poplarville in September 1912, with two ill-kept little boys. The men looked enough alike to be brothers. One of them is the prisoner on trial. Stephen Bennett

On August 19, 1912 (about a month before Bobbie's disappearance) she saw near Poplarville, Miss., a man, giving his name as W. C. Walters. He had a boy child with him, whom he called "Bruce." This child whom she washed, was web-toed. In October (two months after Bobbie's disappearance) a man calling himself W. C. Walters, and resembling the first visitor, appeared on the scene. He had with him a child whom he likewise called "Bruce." This child looked like the first child but did not have web-toes. It is the little boy now called Bobbie Dunbar. And the accused is the man who had him in charge. Miss Loveless

Saw Walters a few miles from Lake Swayze (where Bobbie Dunbar disappeared) and within several days after August 23, 1912 (day of the disappearance). Walters questioned him as to how much money the Dunbars had and what they would give for the return of their child. Frank Ansley   *The Item*-April 18, 1914

Walters Witnesses as Seen by Trist

LEVI HOLLIMAN

W. H. MURRAY

F.M. STEVENS

J.J. SCARBOROUGH

PASTOR HOLCOMB

The Item-April 25, 1914

Barnesvill, N.C.

March/1913

Mr Wil Walters

Deare sur I will ansure yours at hand to day glad to heare from you and Bruce

glad to no you were getting a Long so well

I am not my self

I am in Lots of truble

frank came home from georgia and started to cutting up and I Left an I moved Wensday and my baby died thursday and Burrid to day and I have got no body now but my self and in Lots of truble and not a bit of money and I dont know what I will do no one to care fore me nor to help me

I want you to send me yours an Bruce Pictur so I can see it one more time

I have rote you some times and sent you Bruces age twice he was fore years old the 18th of december

Burneice I gave to Chadborn and I havent no one well I will close rite to me as often as you can and send me your and Bruce Pictur and tell him I Love him still tell him to all ways Love his mama well I will close rite soon to youre friend

Julia Anderson

The Item-April 21, 1914

Chapter Fifteen
The File

Top: Bobby Dunbar WCWDF #2
Bottom: Bruce Anderson WCWDF #4

Smith and Loeb's telegrams WCWDF #'s 310 & 311

Percy Dunbar's receipt—courtesy of Jarvis Lowe and
the Marion County Historical Society

Day driving Bruce to the Lampton Home WCWDF #3

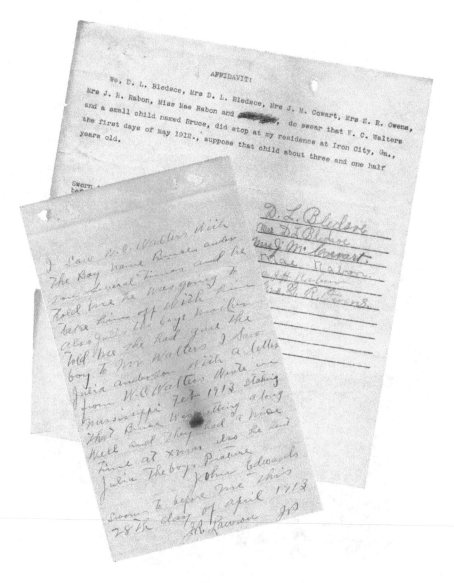

Affidavits from Georgia and North Carolina

WCWDF #'s 17 & 18

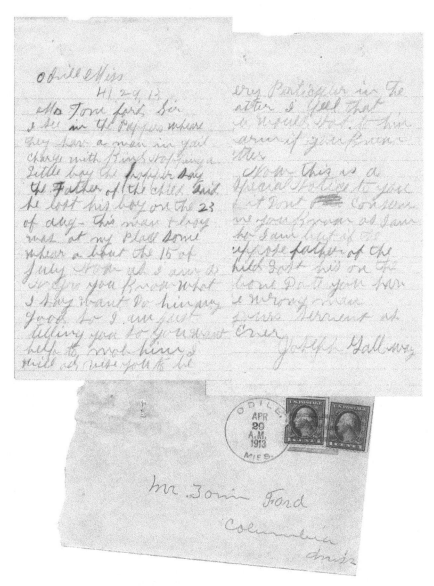

Joseph Galloway's letter WCWDF #31

Executive Department
Jackson, Miss.

EARL BREWER   W. J. BUCK
GOVERNOR   PRIVATE SECRETARY

April 29, 1913.

Dale & Rawls,
        Columbia, Mississippi.

Gentlemen:-

        I am in receipt of your letter of the 28th
in regard to the kidnapping case, and note what you
say.   This matter has certainly had me up in the air.
The people at Opolusas strongly insist that the child
is the Dunbar child, and they have written, wired and
phone me that the child was recognized by his playmates and the citizens there immediately on his return.   I am also in receipt of letters from Georgia
stating that Walters left North Carolina in 1912 with
a child corresponding in age to this one, and insisting that the child taken by the Dunbars is not their
child.

        I am anxious to have all the proof of this
matter presented as soon as possible, because the
requisition should be either turned down outright, or
honored.   If you could get your proof together and
fix some day for a habeas corpus hearing, giving the
Louisiana people an opportunity to bring such evidence
as they may have, the matter could be disposed of in
that way by a Chancellor, and I would not be put to
the necessity of acting as Judge and jury, and pass
on evidence.   What do you think of this?

        In no event do I wish Walters turned aloose
without my knowing it, because I have assured the
Louisiana authorities that he would be held until the
matter was sifted to the very bottom.

        Yours truly,

        Earl Brewer
                GOVERNOR.

B:B.

Governor Brewer's letter-WCWDF #32

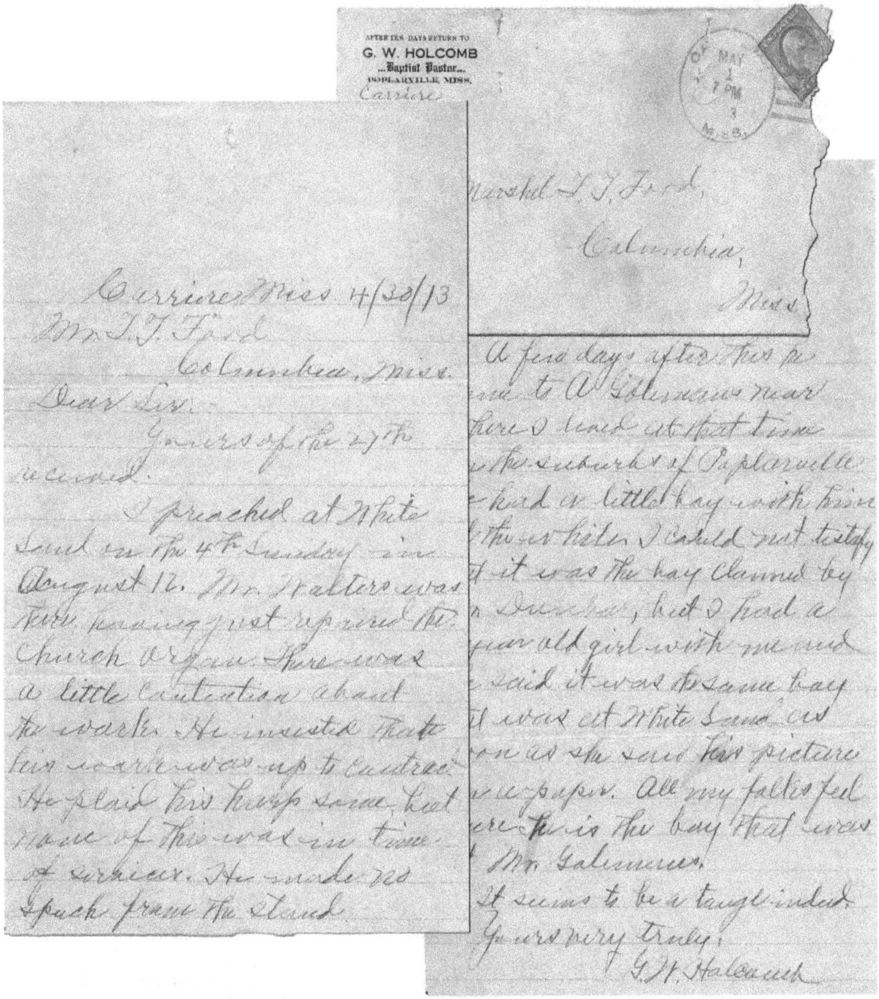
AFTER TEN DAYS RETURN TO
G. W. HOLCOMB
...Baptist Pastor...
POPLARVILLE, MISS.
Carriere

MAY 1 7 PM 3 MISS.

Marshal T. T. Ford,
Columbia,
Miss.

Carriere Miss 4/30/13
Mr T. T. Ford
Columbia, Miss.
Dear Sir.
Yours of the 27th received.
I preached at White Sand on the 4th Sunday in August 12. Mr. Walters was there having just repaired the Church Organ. There was a little contention about the work. He insisted that his work was up to contract. He plaid his harp some, but none of this was in time of service. He made no speech from the stand.

A few days after this he came to A. Gilmore's near where I lived at that time in the suburbs of Poplarville he had a little harp with him this was his. I could not testify that it was the harp claimed by Mr. Dunbar, but I had a year old girl with me and she said it was the same harp that was at White Sand as soon as she saw his picture in the paper. All my folks feel sure this is the harp that was at Mr. Gilmore's.
It seems to be a tangl indeed.
Yours very truly.
G. W. Holcomb

"...a tangl indeed." by Pastor Holcomb - WCWDF #34

Top: Bruce being posed as Bobby with Lucille DeVerges in New Orleans
Bottom: Souvenir postcard with Bruce

WCWDF #'s 5 & 6

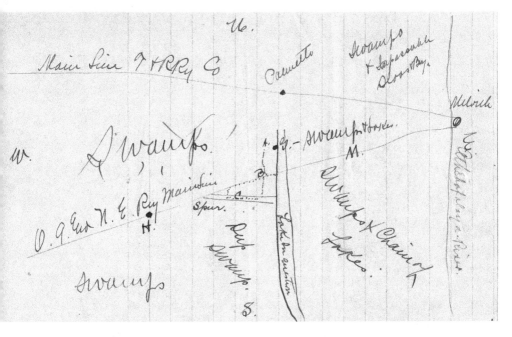

Above: Map from Dr. Strange
Below: The same map with the locations labeled by the author

WCWDF #42

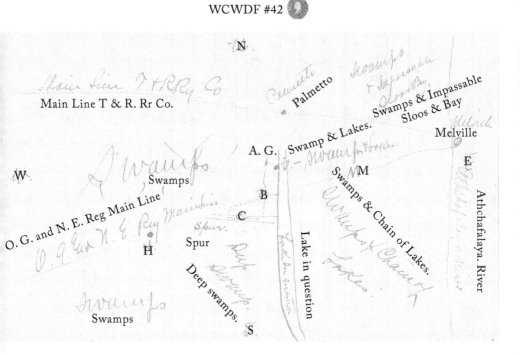

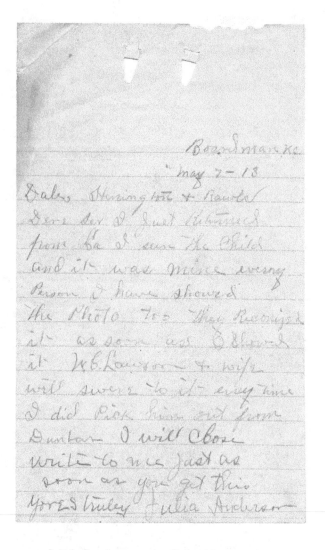

Julia's first letter to the Columbia attorneys

WCWDF #55

State of Mississippi.   WCWDF #72

Pearl River County.

This day personally appeared before the undersigned official in and for said County and State G M Donald of said County and State, who being by me first duly sworn on his oath says:-Our records shows that a package from Chicago was delivered to a man who signed W C Walters on August 20th 1912 and on same date a package was forwarded to W H Meeks New August Miss by WCW This man had a Little Child with him when here on 8/20/12

Witness my signature this the 15 day of May, A. D. 1913.

G. M. Donald Affiant.

Sworn to and subscribed before me this the ____ day of May, A. D. 1913.

(Seal) A McGill

McNEILL, MISS Official. Notary Public

Sones' affidavit-WCWDF #78

State of Mississippi
Pearl River County.

This day pearsonally appeared before me the undersigned authority in and for said county and State. Ben J. Sones, Sr, who being by me first duly sworn says on oath that to the best of his knowledge and belief W. C. Walters the alledged Kidnapper came to my home on the evening of the 21st day of August 1912, and remained at my home until the morning of the 23rd day of August 1912, and he had with him at that time a little boy he called Bruce.

Witness my signature this the 17th day of May 1913
B J. Sones, Sr

Sworn to and subscribed before this the 17th day of May A. D. 1913.

J. A. Mitchell
Justice of the Peace

State of Mississippi,

Pearl River County.

This Day personally appeared before the undersigned official in and for said County and State ---J. S. Thigpen of said County and State, who being by me first duly sworn on his oath says:-

W. C. Walters the alleged kidnapper now in jail at Columbia, Miss., came to my place on the 23 rd. day of August, 1912 and spent the night with me. The next day August 24th. worked some on my sewing machine and left the same day.

Witness my signature this the 15th Day of May, a A. D. 1913.

J. S. Thigpen
Affiant.

Sworn to and subscribed to before me this 15th day of May, A. D. 1913.

D L Archer
(Seal.)   Official.

J. S. Thigpen's affidavit by D. L. Archer

WCWDF #74

State of Mississippi
Pearl River County.

WCWDF #76

This day personally appeared before me the undersigned authority in and for said County and State the within named Mrs. L. A. Thigpen who being by me first duly sworn says on oath:-

That W. C. Walters the alledged Kidnapper who is now in Jail at Columbia Miss. came to my home on August the 24th 1912. and left on August the 25th.1912. and he had with him at that time a little boy he called Bruce.

Witness my signature. the 16th. day of May 1913.

Mrs. L. A. (her + mark) Thigpen

Sworn to and subscribed before me this the 16th day of May A. D. 1913.

J. A. Mitchell.
Justice of the Peace.

STATE OF NORTH CAROLINA

COLUMBUS COUNTY.

Julia Anderson, being duly sworn, deposeth and says:

1-   That she is a resident of North Carolina and has always
during her life remained, and held North Carolina as her home:

2--   That she is the mother of one Bruce Anderson, a child
five years old, and the said Bruce Anderson is now, or was
30 days ago, in the possession of _____ Dunbar:

3--   That the said child held now in the possession
of the said _____ Dunbar is her child, Bruce Anderson:

4--   That during the year 1912 she gave the body of her
son, Bruce Anderson to one W.C.Walters, a native of North
Carolina, with the understanding that Walters was to take
said child and return same to her upon her request. She further says that she has seen the child held by the Dunbars
and that the child held by the Dunbars is the child she gave
Walters in the presence of _____ Stone, and this was
the last time she had seen Bruce Anderson until she saw him
in possession of Dunbar.

This 30th day of *May*, 1913.

Julia Anderson

Sworn to and subscribed
before me this 30th day of *May*, 1913.

E. K. Brown
Justice of the Peace
Columbus County
N. C.

STATE OF NORTH CAROLINA

County of *Columbus*

I, *L. A. Stanley* Clerk of the Superior Court of the aforesaid County and
State, do hereby certify that *E. K. Brown* was at the time of signing the foregoing (or
Justice of the Peace
annexed) certificate a duly commissioned and qualified Notary Public in and for the County of
Columbus, State of North Carolina, and as such full faith and credit is due to his official
acts; and further that his signature thereto is in his own proper handwriting.

In testimony whereof I hereunto set my hand and seal of office, this *30*

day of *May* 1913.

L. A. Stanley
Clerk of the Superior Court.

Julia's affidavit WCWDF #104

New Orleans, May, 28, 1913.

Messrs Dale & Rawl , Attorneys,

Columbia, Miss,

Gentlemen-

Yours of the MR 24, to hand, contents noted,
In answer to your request of me to procure certificate
or affidavid from Lou Rose, He refused to let me have certificate
stating thathe had no time to spend in courts on this matter
and it was of no interst to him to give certificate or make *affidavid*
He seems to favor the Dunbars. But I will swear thathe told me
just what I have written to you, I think I can find the daily paper
that quoted the proposition in question between Rose and theDunbars.

Yours truly, *John Blank*

Theater Manager Says Dunbar Asked $1,000

Incensed because The States in an exclusive store Monday quoted Attorney Dale, of Columbia, Miss, as saying that the manager of the New Orleans Hippodrome "confirmed the report that Mr. Dunbar had been trying to obtain a contract to show Robert, the father of the kidnaped boy issued a statement to the public Wednesday in which he branded this statement as a vile and conscious falsehood.

The following is a signed statement from Lew Rose, manager of the Hippodrome, sent to The States Thursday.

Regarding the controversy in relation to the Dunbar child and the Hippodrome management, allow me to say this:

The day I heard the child was found in Columbia, Miss, I wired via Western Union, a proposition

I proposed to Mr. C. P. Dunbar to give him 50 per cent of all over a certain amount and agreed to guarantee him $200.

He asked me to put that in writing, which I did, and he said he would take same home and consult his wife. This ended my dealings with Mr. C. P. Dunbar.

Very truly yours,

LEW ROSE,
Manager Hippodrome.

Mr. Dunbar, in his public statement, also took occasion to brand as untrue a report by a States correspondent saying "It is known also that the manager of the New Orleans Orpheum has been approached."

With regard to this Walter Katt-man, press agent for the Orpheum said Thursday:

"Hamlin and Benz of the Item staff approached me some time ago and said they had the exclusive state-ments to the Dunbar boy and that they wanted to arrange for an Orpheum contract. I told them it was useless for them to try any further as the Orpheum would not stake 'freak' acts."

States June 6/1913

Top: John Blank's letter to Dale and Rawls
Bottom: States article

WCWDF #'s 101 & 328

THE KIDNAPPING OF

Robert Dunbar

22 SCENES

Showing W. C. Walters, the villianous looking man alleged to have kidnapped little
Robert Dunbar. Columbia, Miss., where
the grief-stricken mother, with her husband, found their little son, Robert. The
Dunbars on their arrival at New Orleans.

JULIA ANDERSON

The woman from North Carolina, who claims
that little Robert Dunbar is her long lost son.
The reception given the Dunbars on their arrival
in their home town, Opelousas, and several other
touching scenes around the Dunbar home after
the reuniting of their little son.

PICTO THEATRE

Thursday, June 12

Three reels of our usual high-class motion pictures in addition.

HEARTS OF THE FIRST EMPIRE 2 Reel Special

A love story in the gorgeous costumes of Napo-
leon I time. The Vitagraph's best players produce these reels.

THE COUNT'S WILL

American Pathe play. Why do they make so
many heroes counts and why are so many stories
set in high society life?

Don't forget our coupon books---$1.50 worth for $1.00---15 tickets

Call at the ticket office for them or ask for further information.

PICTO Theatre

That Popular Photo Play House

Admission Always the Same--5 and 10c

Leader Print, Brookhaven, Miss.

1913 Dodger-WCWDF #122

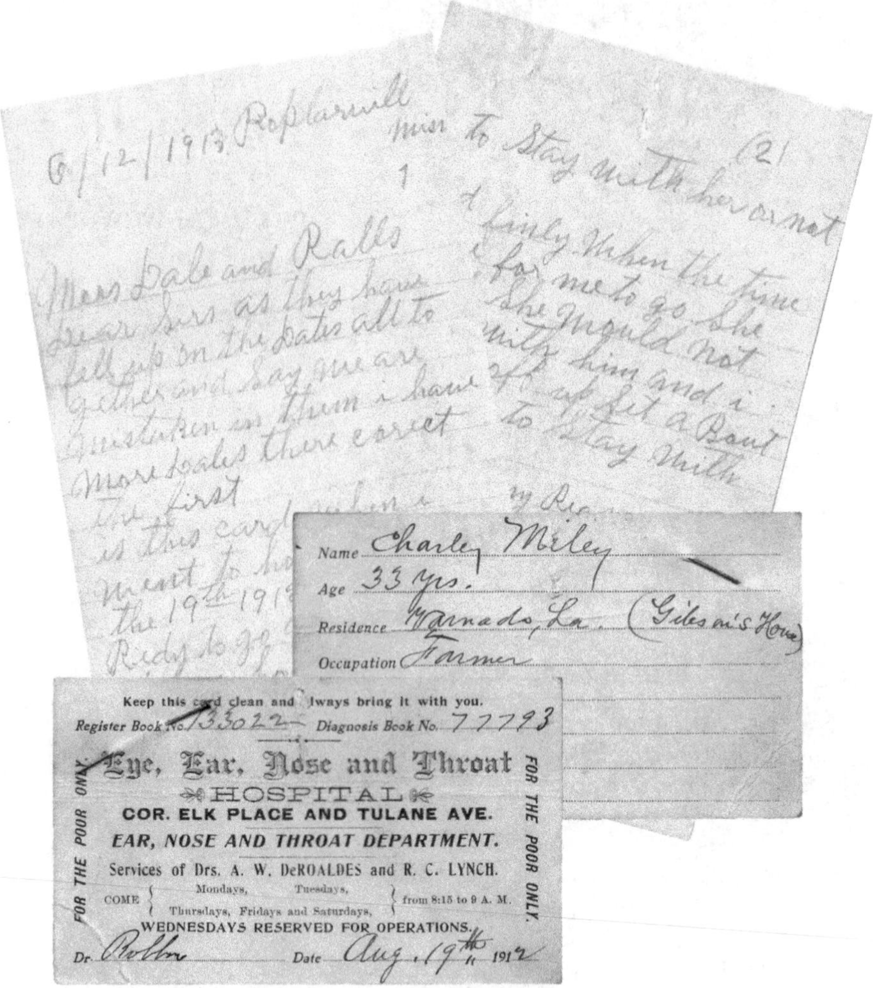

6/12/1913 Poplarville

1

Mess Dale and Ralls
Dear Sirs as they have
fell up on the dates all to
gether and say we are
mistaken in them i have
more dates there corect
The first
is this card when i
ment to ha...
the 19th 1913
Rady to go

miss to Stay with her or not (2)
finly When the time
for me to go She
She would not
with him and i
up set a Bout
to Stay with

Name Charley Miley
Age 33 yrs.
Residence Warnado, La. (Gileson's Hou...)
Occupation Farmer

Keep this card clean and always bring it with you.
Register Book No. 133022 Diagnosis Book No. 77793

Eye, Ear, Nose and Throat
HOSPITAL
COR. ELK PLACE AND TULANE AVE.
EAR, NOSE AND THROAT DEPARTMENT.
Services of Drs. A. W. DeROALDES and R. C. LYNCH.
COME { Mondays, Tuesdays, Thursdays, Fridays and Saturdays, } from 8:15 to 9 A. M.
WEDNESDAYS RESERVED FOR OPERATIONS.
Dr. Robb Date Aug. 19th 1912
FOR THE POOR ONLY. FOR THE POOR ONLY.

Charley Miley's letter and appointment card

WCWDF #'s 125 & 126

STATE OF MISSISSIPPI,

PEARL RIVER COUNTY.

    This day personally appeared before the
undersigned authority in and for said County and State
Mr. and Mrs. Allen Goldman, who being by me first duly
sworn on their oaths say that on the 4th day of July, 1912,
~~four~~ of their nieces who reside in *West Butler*
Alabama, came to their home in Poplarville, Pearl River
County, Mississippi, to pay them a visit, ~~and that these
nieces used for transportation from Alabama what is known as
a thirty day limit return trip ticket,~~ that these nieces spent
four weeks at the home of affiants on this visit and
returned to their home in *West Butler*
Alabama, on or before the 4th day of August, 1912, ~~using the
unused coupon of the thirty day limit return trip tickets that
they had purchased for their transportation.~~ They they were
accompanied to their home in *West Butler*
Alabama, by _____1_____ ~~children~~ of affinats for a return
visit.
    That while the said ~~four~~ nieces of affiant were
with them they paid a visit to the home of Mr. & Mrs.
Jeptha Bilbo at Bilbo, Mississippi, on the 21st day of
July, 1912, and there was at that time staying at the home of
Jeptha Bilbo W. C. Walters, the alleged kidnapper now
confined in jail at Columbia, Mississippi, and he had with
him a boy child that he called Bruce. That both of said affiants
saw said child on this visit and have seen him many times
since. That the last time they saw said child was on
Saturday afternoon, the 7th day of June, 1913, in the
Monteleon Hotel in New Orleans, La, said child being in
possession of Mr. & Mrs. C.P. Dunbar of Opelusas, La., and
that they know that this was the same child that they saw
with W.C.Walters on the 21st day of July, 1912, at the
home of Jeptha Bilbo in Pearl River County, Miss.
    Affiants say further under oath that on the ____ day
of August, 1912, said W. C. Walters accompanied by said
child came to their home in Pearl River County, Mississippi,
and spent some time at the home of affinats, and that the said
W. C. Walters and with him at that time the same child that
affiants saw and inspected in New Orleans, La. on the 7th
day of June, 1913.

    Witness our signatures, this the 13th day of June,
A. D. 1913.

Sarah Goleman

J. Allen Goleman

    Sworn to and subscribed before me, this the 13th
day of June, A. D. 1913.

W. A. Rouse
OFFICIAL
Chancery clerk

Goleman's affidavit-WCWDF #139

case.

The following is the opening statement of the Governor as he dictated it to his secretary, W. J. Buck: "I have been of the opinion all the while that a mistake had been made and I am now thoroughly convinced that the child now in the possession of the Dunbars is Bruce Anderson and that W. C. Walters is innocent." The above statement was objected to by Mr. Coutierie, legal adviser of Governor Brewer, and it was then withheld by the governor and the following was dictated and later give to the public:

"In passing upon this application for requisition I have done so with great care and caution in view of the fact that this case where a man is to be taken out of the jurisdiction of this State and removed far from his witnesses and to be delivered for trial in a State where they have no jurisdiction of his witnesses and where their attendance to testify for him cannot be compelled. I therefore refused to grant this requisition hastily until I could give the Louisiana authorities ample time to consider the question well, and as a practical man, knowing the popular excitement that attends such matters all over the country, and as there was some time to elaspe before court would convene where he was to be tried, I could see no harm that could come to anyone by a reasonable delay.

"There is a sharp conflict in the facts. Many good, reputable, disenterested witnesses in this state willing to swear positively that this man was in Mississippi, and that this child is Bruce Anderson and not Robert Dunbar. But this is a question of fact that I think should be decided by the court of Louisiana, and the courts of that state, it may be presumed, will give the man a fair and impartial trial.

"I have sufficiently delayed this matter to give time for the passions of the people to subside and for all parties, to be heard and believe that this question is one that should be decided by the courts and not by me, and I therefore grant the requisition.

"All the questions of his guilt or innocence are matters of fact for the court or jury to decide, and which I do not undertake to decide. For instance, it is contended by his counsel that he was not in the state of Louisiana at the time of the commission of the offense. This question I do not decide, but simply hold that all questions involved in it as to his guilt, or innocence are questions for the court and not for the governor."

The hearing was held at the governor's mansion beginning at 8:30 Tuesday night and continuing until 11 o'clock.

MISSISSIPPI

EXECUTIVE DEPARTMENT
JACKSON

EARL BREWER
GOVERNOR

W. J. BUCK
SECRETARY

June 26, 1913.

Dale & Rawls,

Columbia, Mississippi.

[Men]:-

I am in receipt of your letter requesting that [ ] you a copy of the opinion rendered when I granted [requi]sition for Walters, and I do this under my [ ]e. I do not see how it could have any bearing [ ]plication, but that is a matter for you gentle[men to d]etermine among yourselves.

I am glad to know that the people as a rule [ ] my course in the penitentiary matter.

Yours truly,

Earl Brewer
GOVERNOR.

[T]his was published in your county paper and it [ ] gave it out. You can use that and this letter [ ]used as the certificate

Governor Brewer's requisition statement-WCWDF #185

This photograph was taken on the way to the habeas corpus hearing in Poplarville in July 1913. After being locked away for ten weeks, Cantwell was finally getting the chance to stand up and present himself for judgment. His simple, stoic image is in sharp contrast to the "villainous looking, unkempt tramp," described by the Louisiana papers. His gaze is direct and unafraid, his expression calm, yet determined.

William Cantwell Walters-WCWDF #205

Photo 1913

Cantwell sent the previous picture, along with the following newspaper photo of Roderick, and a letter, to Dale and Rawls.

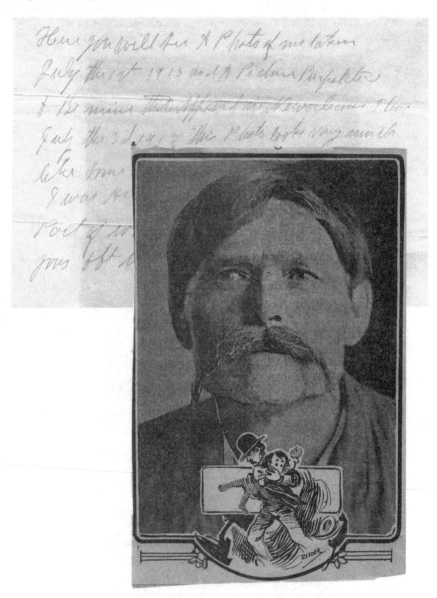

Roderick-WCWDF #'s 204 & 206

Here you will see A Photo of me taken July the 1st 1913 and A Picture Purported to Be mine that Appeard in New orleanes Item July the 3d 1913 this Photo looks vary much like some I had taken A Few Days Before I was Arrested By this you can see Part of what they are Doing to me

Yous Oft   W C Walters   Columbia Miss

Kleinpeter's letter to Dale and Rawls-WCWDF #207

Get a picture from the "Item" and one from the States - of this morning.

The State's picture I find is a correct picture of "Walters" that of the "Item" is that of "Roderick".

The prosecution will attempt to prove by two or more witnesses that the picture shows the man who admitted the boy is the Dunbar boy _____

T. K. (signed)

I knew "Roderick" _ &C. _

New Orleans, La., July 31th.1913.

Messrs Dale & Rawls,Attorneys,

Columbia, Mississippi:

Gentleman:--
        Enclose find a copy of letter taken from the New Orleans,
Item said letter writen in figures ~~and~~ and subsituted by letters
which I presume you will be able to read as I have.   The key of this
letter is as follow. #1 represents A #2 - B   #3--C   &c.
                                                      for
        This may be of some benifet to you and ~~on~~ that reason I am
sending it to you.   This letter has been published twice in succession in the daily Item.

                                    ~~yours~~ truly,

                                         J. B.

                                    Opelousas, La., July 26th.

Wellwisher,

        Dear Sir:--
I will be in New Orleans, on Aug. 6th. and 7th. at the Cosmopolitan
Hotel and would be glad to meet you if possible. What passes between
us will be strictly confidential for my only object in going ~~further~~
further into this matter is to show a lot of people what fools they are
if you can meet me write me here as soon as you see this.

        Yours Truly,

            C. P. Dunbar

John Blank's letter-WCWDF #221

Anonymous threatening letter-WCWDF #223

NORTH CAROLINA,

Robeson County.

     Personally appeared before me, the undersigned Notary Public,
in and for the State and County aforesaid, George Anderson and
wife, ⟨Beddie⟩ _ _ Anderson, who, after being duly sworn
says: They are the parents of Julia Anderson; that when Julia
was about _17_ years old she married Elisha Floyd of Columbus
county, North Carolina: That she and the said Elisha Floyd lived
together about five months and separated; that there was born
to the said Julia Anderson Floyd after said separation a boy
child ; that said child is now about five years old; that the
name of said child is Bruce.

G W Anderson

Beddie x Anderson

Sworn to and subscribed before me August 25, 1913.

W H Kinlaw
     Notary Public.

My commission expires March 27, 1914.

STATE OF NORTH CAROLINA,   In the Superior Court.
   Robeson County.

I, __*B. Skipper*__ Clerk of the Superior Court in and for
the County and State aforesaid, do hereby certify that __*W H Kinlaw*__
whose genuine signature appears to the foregoing certificate, is now and was at the time of signing
the same, an acting __*Notary Public*__ in and for Robeson County,
and duly qualified according to law, and that full faith and credit is due to all his official acts as such.

   Witness my hand and seal of said Court, this __25th__ day of __August__ 1913.

_____
          Clerk Superior Court.

George and Beddie Anderson's affidavit-WCWDF #242

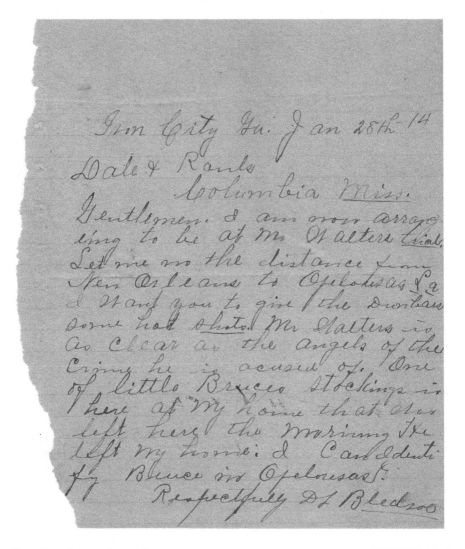

Iron City Ga.   Jan 28th -14   WCWDF #269
Dale & Rawls
Columbia Miss.

Gentlemen, I am now arrangeing to be at Mr Walters trial. Let me no the distance from New Orleans to Opelousa La. I want you to give the Dunbars some hot shots. Mr Walters is as clear as the angels of the crime he is acused of. One of little Bruces stockings is here at my home that was left here the morning He left my home; I can Identify Bruce in Opelousas.

Respectfuly DL Bledsoe

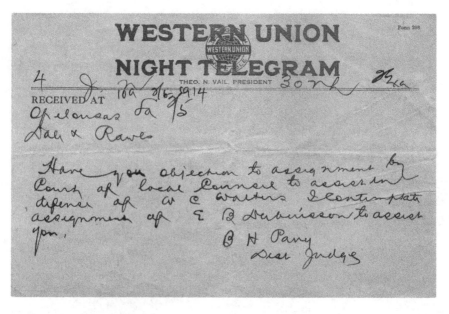

4   J. N 109 2/6 1914   30 nh 2xa

Opelousas La 2/5
Dale & Rawls

Have you objection to assignment by Court of local Counsel to assist in defense of W
C Walters I contemplate assignment of E B Dubuisson to assist you.

B H Pavy
Dist Judge

WCWDF #281

Smith and Anderson's affidavit-WCWDF #312

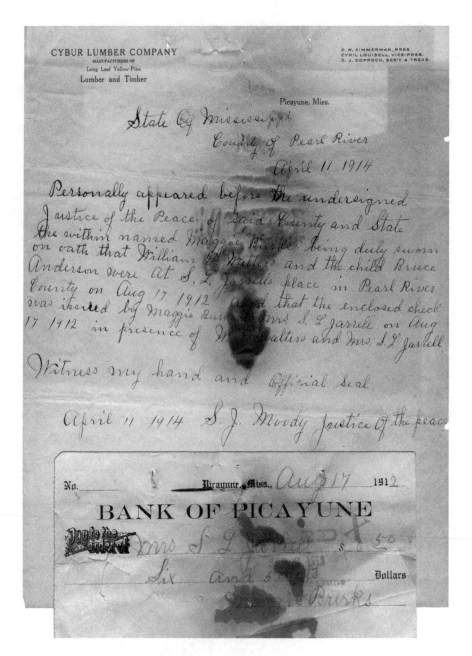

Maggie Burks affidavit and check

WCWDF #'s 316 & 317

State of Mississippi,
Pearl River County.
    Before me came J. J. Scarborough who upon oath says that
during the year 1912 he was postmaster at Poplarville, County and State
aforesaid, and that on August the 7th of said year W. C. Walters came
into the post office and made out application for money order of whihh
the attached is a true copy. He had a small boy with him who remained
in buggy or one horse hack during the transaction. Part of the month
of October 1912 said Walters stayed with a Mr. Coleman who at that
time lived a little over a quarter of a mile North of my place. I
would not be able to identify the child as I never thought of
beingsalled upon in the case. About two to four weeks prior to
Walters' arrest, I again saw him drive through the main thorough-
fare of Poplarville with a small boy, but I could not say whether
it was the same child or not.

    Sworn to before me a Notary Public in and for said County
and State aforesaid this the 17th day of Aprilp 1914.

Scarborough's affidavit- Smith's affidavit-Cantwell's money order application

WCWDF #322

- 2 -

My only aim and interest in writing to you,
gentlemen, is to encourage you to fight on, as you are gaining ground all the time, and victory will perch on your banner
in the end, and Walters will never hand if the evidence
that you all are producing will be taken into consideration
by the trial jury, which I think it will.

Hoping that justice will be done to all, and
especially to the accused, I am

Very respectfully yours,

Rev. Marion B. Monroe.

Traveling Evangelist
3324 Camp St., N. O. La.

P. S.   I do not believe Walters guilty, but that a grave
mistake has been made by the identity and prosecution, and
that in the end he will prove to be innocent.

"FINEST ALL-YEAR HOTEL IN THE SOUTH"   "NEW YORK'S IDEAL SUBURBAN HOTEL"

ALFRED S. AMER, General Manager
W. J. QUINN, Jr. Assistant Manager

N.Y. Headquarters & Booking Office
The Vanderbilt Hotel,
Park Avenue at 34th Street,
NEW YORK

The St. Charles
NEW ORLEANS, LA.
Alfred S. Amer & Co., Ltd. Proprietors

New Orleans, La.
April 21, 1914.

The Edgewood
GREENWICH, CONN.
The Alfred S. Amer Co. Owners & Proprietors

Hon. Messrs. Dale & Rawls,
Defence Attorneys,

For W. C. Walters, now on trial at Opelousas,
La. for his life for the alleged kidnapping of the supposed
child of Mr. & Mrs. Dunbar, now in custody of C. P. Dunbar, of
Opelousas.

My dear Sirs:-

I wish to say by writing you two gentlemen not
to be at all dismayed or discouraged, as all law-abiding, good
citizens who wish to see justice and fair play, can't help but
congratulate you for the noble stand you are taking in trying
to save the life of an innocent man who is being so greatly
persecuted, and am sure that victory will be yours in the end,
and if the twelve men who are now sitting on his case were impartial and just in their findings, they can't help but do any
thing else according to the oath which they have taken in the
sight of God and man but to give Walters the benefit of a reasonable doubt, and acquit him, for I have watched this case
from the very beginning and am carefully studying all testimony
that is being given for and against him.

I visited Opelousas on the 29th of June last;
shook hands with the boy on the fire truck in the courthouse
square; gave him a nickle, and right afterwards went to the hotel and made myself known to Mrs. Dunbar, and if I am any judge
at all of human nature, I don't think that the boy that I saw
on the truck looks like Mrs. Dunbar, and I firmly believe that
the good woman has made a mistake in identifying him as her son,
Bobbie; but, on the other hand, you will see a fac-simile
resemblance in the features of the boy to those of Julia Anderson.

I also attended the habeas corpus trial of
Walters, of Poplarville, Miss. last July 2nd, and I must say
that I never listened to a clearer alabia than the one that
was offered by you all in behalf of Walters by so many reputable Mississippi citizens and was more than astonished the next
day when I heard that Hon. Judge Weatherby had ruled against him.

Encouraging letter from New Orleans-WCWDF #329

Encouraging letter from Columbia-WCWDF #331

Thomas S Dale & H C Rawls   April 23d /1914

Opelousas La

Dear Friends: -

You are making Your selves immortal. The defense for W. C. cant be equaled - a golden chain without a missing link There is no Jury in the world who can convict a man with such a world of evidence in his favor. Conscienceless indeed must be the man or set of men who will sweep aside such testimony as has been produced for Walters without quaking and trembling for their future. God only knows what their verdict will be but if in there throbs the warm hearts of honest men and not the blood of snakes and "Cagen wretches" they will restore liberty to the old man. My hopes are: You will save his neck. I believe You'l do it I know you must be tired and almost worn to a frazzle but fight on & on. I have agreed to pack you both on my shoulders through town - that some people may appreciate Real heroism

S. J. Hathorn

Iron City Ga. May 23rd 1914.
Dale & Rawls
Columbia Miss.
Gentlemen, The Citizens of Robinson C. N.C.
Called a mass meeting on last Thursday 21st and
invited Mr Stephens & myrry self down you met
at Opelousas. to meet with them & inform
them the day & manner Walters was treated
at his trial. I have not as yet heard the
result of the meeting But the intention
of the meeting is to raise money to carry
the case to a finish. I am asked to with
a full account of the trial for the Robisonian the County paper of Robinson C. N.C. as I
saw it. At this time I have a fearful
case of sore eyes. & I am asking you to
Please write it for me & forward it to me
at once & I will sign it & forward it on.
I am the biddie that has got the thing
going in your behalf. I may make a 100
Mile trip up there and make four
Speeches in behalf of N.C. If I do he will

[right page]
t amount to
arrousing a
hat election. So if
some court you be
requested. I have
Mr Dubuison. Since
called Opelousas: there
a lot of good.
is no use to try Walters in Lousaina as that
rotten item as poisened the minds of the
Citizens to the Extent that it is a matter
of Impossiability for him to MEET Justice
in the minds of d rotten set of dirtish
Catholicss. Old governor Bruner ought to
be put in W.C.W Place. for the same time
For Gods sake ride your State of a Judas.
and elect you a Governor that has a back
bone backed by Common sence. I am your
friend to the end.
                    I am yours most Cordially:
                            D.L. Bledsoe.

Letter from Cantwell's friend David Bledsoe-WCWDF #392

WCWDF #400

Messres Dale & Rawls   NEworleans La June the 3d 1914

Dear sirs

I see From the Press Reports that my Case Has been Filed in the Supreme Court   Mr
Dubison said He would try to Get the Case set up And Get A Hearing Before it Ad-
Jorned   If the Supime Court Fails to Release me or Grant me A New trial I want it
Appealed to the United States Supime Court   I Have wrote Mr Dubison to this Affect
I Have Failed to Receave the stationary Promised   I Dont Get much mail now   I Have
been Depending on my Mail Being Changed   there must Be something Careless at
Opelousas   I am not Feeling well at all   I need some attention that I Guess I will Fail
to Get Here   I Had Rather Be operated on By A Private Physition   I am Looking For
A Friend to Day   will see what he will Do   Write soon or come

W C Walters

D. F. SMITH
DEALER IN
GENERAL MERCHANDISE AND BUYER OF
COTTON AND PRODUCE

CARRIERE, MISS.

June, 7th. 1914

Mr J.C.Barnes,
Lumberton, N.C.

Dear Sir:-
    I notice in todays New Orleans Daily States, that the people of your State are making preparation to assist W.C.Walters, in getting a new trial on the charge of kidnaping C.P.Dunbars, child at Opelousas, La. August 23rd. 1912, and I am writing this to say that I think he needs help and I believe that it is the duty of all honest people who want to see justice done to help him to fight this charge.
    I am enclosing a clipping from the paper mentioned above which will speak for itself, and while I have contibuted $25.00 to help him I am still willing to do more, as I am convinced beyond every reasonable doubt that he is not guilty, and I am willing to work at night to make money to defray the expense of his defense, and I feel that it your duty as citizens of his native State and home to do what you can to help him.
    Messrs Dale & Rawls, have stood by him nobly and are still fighting for him, spending their own money doing it because they know he is not guilty, and I believe that the honest people both far and near should & will help them in a finantial way if they could only know what I know about the charge they have against him.
    Walters did not get a fair trial at Opelousas, or he would have come clear, however there were many lies sworn against him which has since come to light and have been shown to be faulse, and the only strong evidence against him is that Dunbar and his wife say that the child taken from Walters, is theirs, but with all the other facts in the case I am fully convinced that they are just simply lying and have some motive not yet revealed in doing so.
    I live in Pearl River County, Mississippi, right where Walters was at the time that Dunbars, child was lost, and I know at least 25 good honest citizens living in this County, whom I have talked with and who say positively that they saw Walters, and this same child here in this County prior to the date the Dunbar child was lost, and besides he was well known by most of these people who positively identify this child as the same child Walters, had when he first come to this County and another thing Walters, has never acted like a guilty man for the reason that he had all oportunity skip after he was accused of this crime and did not do it, and has told a straight tale about where he got this boy and where he has been, and who he has stopped with since leaving North Carolina, and all that he has ever said about it has proven to be true.
    I hope that your people will get busy and do what you can for this old man, and what ever assistance you can give him will be appreciated by him and his Attorneys, and all honest people who know the truth of this afair, and we have to do is to bring the truth out so that the public can see it as it is, and I believe that public sentiment will fource them to abandon the charge against him.
                    Very respectfully,

D H Smith

Copy of letters for your information

Copy of Smith's letter for Dale and Rawls-WCWDF #412

William Cantwell Walters' last letter in the file

WCWDF #500

CAROLINIANS HOLD A MASS MEETING FOR WALTERS

People of Convicted Kidnaper's Native State Invite Lawyers to Come There.

While Mr. and Mrs. C. P. Dunbar are rejoicing over the recovery of the little boy they claim to be their kidnaped son, and while the people of Louisiana are congratulating them upon their victory in establishing their right to the custody of little "Bobbie," the people of North Carolina are voicing their indignation at what they term a miscarriage of justice, according to a letter received by W. C. Walters Saturday morning from his attorneys, Messrs. Dale and Rawls.

The Mississippi attorneys, who stood steadfast by Walters throughout his trouble, and who bent every energy to establish his innocence at Opelousas of the charge of kidnaping Bobbie Dunbar, have accepted an invitation to address a mass meeting at Lumberton, N. C., some time before June 15.

That the people of Walters' native State still believe in his innocence and that they are proving this in a substantial way, is evident from the tenor of a letter received by Messrs. Dale and Rawls, an excerpt of which was embodied in a letter addressed to Walters by his attorneys.

Carolinas Hold A Mass Meeting.

The information comes from J. C. Barnes, cashier of the bank at Lumberton, N. C., and said to be among the most substantial and influential citizens of that section. Lumberton is the seat of Robertson county, N. C., and is eighteen miles from aBrnesville — Walters' native town.

The letter to Messrs. Dale & Rawls states that the people of Lumberton held a mass meeting recently to voice their protests against the conviction of Walters. They want to know more of the case, and ask that the Walters' attorneys give them data, concluding by requesting either one or both to go to Lumberton to addres another mass meeting to be held

shortly. The people of Walters' State, according to the letter, are prepared to lend financial assistance in securing for Walters a second trial, and in establishing his innocence, in which they religiously believe. Walters showed his pleasure upon reading the contents of the letter.

Walters Still Sure He Will Be Freed.

Walters is as sanguine of success in eventually gaining his freedom and being exonerated of the charge of kidnaping as he ever was.

"What would you do in the event the Dunbars would give you the child and enter a plea of mistaken identity?" Walters was asked by a States reporter Saturday morning.

"I would not be at all satisfied. I want more than the boy and my freedom. I will prove my innocence yet, and the people of Louisiana — at least those who had anything to do with my prosecution — will yet hang their heads in shame.

"If they give me back my boy and restore me to citizenship and in addition give me $20,000 I will be satisfied. Not before. I have suffered great humiliation and mortification, and I believe $20,000 is little enough, since I have been made a pauper and have no place on earth to go after I get out of jail."

Chapter Sixteen

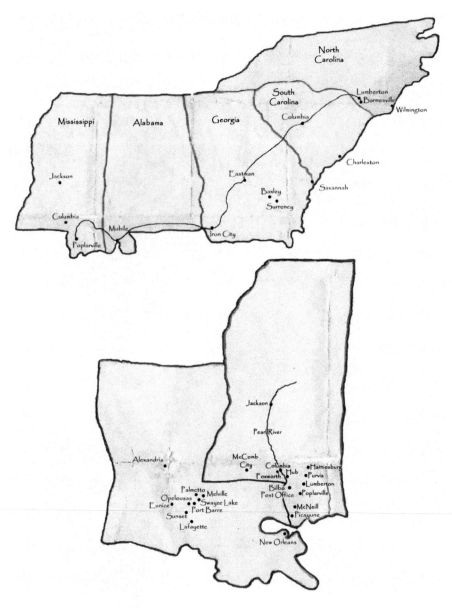

Top: Cantwell and Bruce's route from North Carolina to Mississippi
Bottom: Points of interest in Mississippi and Louisiana

H. J. Harvey's photo of Lessie and Bruce at *The Item* April 23, 1913

Photo courtesy of Sharon Bond

Julia

Bruce on the left, and Alonzo

Photo courtesy of Sharon Bond

"Bobby's" family from *The Morning Advocate* October 10, 1948

Jewel Rawls Tarver, Hollis E. Rawls, Bob Dunbar Jr., and the author

The Columbian Progress August 10, 2002

Top: The Bilbo house
Bottom: Author's 1995 painting

Epilogue

Cantwell signed on with a stage show for a brief period of time, loquaciously sharing his story until he was detained for its salacious content. He was *encouraged* to move on. Impoverished from the two-year ordeal and in declining health, Cantwell found it much easier and safer to simply leave. The battered fifty-three-year-old man most likely headed to Florida or up into Georgia where he had siblings to help him start over. Michael Walters told me that Cantwell's young nieces remembered his returning to his childhood home a few years later via horse and buggy with pots and tools rattling out his arrival.

During the visit, he spoke of his maltreatment and the label of villain that followed his name. One relative claimed to have gotten a letter from him as late as the 1930's, but I have a hard time believing that he lived that long. The rumor has been circulated that he died from blood poisoning, but when and where he was buried remains a mystery. Did his gravestone carry the epitaph he wished? Whatever course the rest of his life took, he was never exonerated nor compensated and seems to have simply vanished.

Did Cantwell and Julia forever cling to their tattered shred of hope, or did they eventually accept that the truth was gone, completely and totally devoured just as the small boy who disappeared into Swayze Lake?

Julia and Ollie started their family when a son was born. "This one will be called Hollis," she stated, for she revered the self-possessed young attorney who'd always shown her dignity. I love picturing Julia rocking Hollis, smelling his hair, watching him sleep; and I hope the baby didn't prick her heart but healed it. These many years later, Julia's Hollis told me he thought Bruce knew what he was doing, pretending to be Bobby in order to gain a *better* life, but he never knew how hard Bruce fought to get away from that *better* life. Bruce likely experienced traumatic bonding with the Dunbars, and his earliest memories were lost and manipulated. He survived, crippled in spirit, but alive.

At some point during Bruce and Alonzo's childhood, Lessie left town for an extended period—without either boy. Whether she experienced a sudden, gut-wrenching realization that the child she had claimed wasn't Bobby or the gradual culmination of a thousand doubts, she fled. Or did she, too, know from the beginning? Lessie ended up relocating around the country and finally divorced Percy after he had a lengthy affair. (Percy had been arrested for attempting to kill this girlfriend's other lover.)

Opelousas incessantly buzzed about the boy who wasn't really a Dunbar, so Bruce and Alonzo were shipped off to the Dunbar grandparents' estate for privacy and then entered a military-style boarding school where Bruce struggled in his studies. Percy continued to swagger around Opelousas, rubbing elbows with those in power who had helped him *in his time of trouble,* which seemed to be a major portion of his life.

On the eve of John Parker's election to Governor in 1920, where Percy was the chairman of his St. Landry campaign, Percy and a group of men were supposedly hunting at Second Lake with Sebe Frilot, the guide who had seen Percy find Bobby's hat. Whether Sebe talked about the hat, criticized Parker's investigation, or revealed some other event isn't known, but Sebe was killed that night in the swamp, shot in the back by Percy.

Bruce spent much of his teenage years alone, having been emancipated by Percy. Alonzo, who shared his father's outgoing personality and swarthy good looks, would inherit Percy's holdings. Bruce, the once-golden boy, drifted in a no-man's land, and he was rumored to have been withdrawn, angry, distracted, and anxious.

Around eighteen or nineteen years of age, Bruce traveled to Pearl River County and introduced himself to two of his half-siblings, but the one-time meeting was awkward and very brief. They confided, "We were afraid his presence would hurt Mother, and she had been hurt enough for one lifetime."

My grandmother spoke of "Bobby Dunbar's" coming to see Hollis in Columbia; Tom Dale had died years earlier. Whatever transpired between the two of them remained private.

The young man eventually fell in love, married, and began his own family, often repeating the phrase, "I know who I am," to anyone who questioned him. Sadly, the following article from 1948 indicates otherwise and reveals just how brain-washed he was.

The Famous Case of Bobbie Dunbar

By Lillian Bourdier

What has become of the itinerant tinker, who was also a preacher, who was charged with kidnaping a 4-year-old boy, 36 years ago—an incident that stirred the entire nation—and who was found guilty of kidnaping in one court and subsequently freed in another?

Now grown to manhood, married, and living quietly in Opelousas, Robert "Bobby" Dunbar, the boy who was taken from the shore of Swayze Lake near Opelousas, would like to know the answer to that question. For Dunbar would like to see Walters again and perhaps delve deeper into the mystery which surrounded so much of the case and the trial and which helped make the case one of the most prominent kidnappings in the country up to the time of the Lindbergh case.

Celebrated Child

Dunbar was once the most celebrated child in the nation, but there is nothing about this quiet, unassuming man to remind his neighbors and friends of that—he has wiped out those eight months and the long years which followed when efforts were being made to bring his kidnaper to justice.

The Dunbars, his wife is the former Marjorie Byars of Eunice, live at 312 W. Park Ave., in Opelousas, with their three children, Bobby, Jr., 12 years old, John, 10 years, and the baby, Mary, 4 years old.

It was on Aug. 23, 1912, that it happened. Bobby was at Swayze Lake with his parents, Mr. and Mrs. Percy Dunbar (his father is now dead and his mother lives in California) and several friends on a fishing party. Bobby, as children often do, wandered away from the grownups. It was eight long months before he was found, disfigured, in the company of William C. Walters in Foxworth, Miss.

Recalls Fragments

Bobby clearly recalls being led away from the railway tracks by a man. He believes the man took him for companionship. His is the only story that actually ties in a second child—Dunbar related that after he had been with the man about two months another child was brought to the man by Julia Anderson. Bobby called him Bruce and said this

child died when he fell from the back of the wagon in which they trav-
eled while the man they were with mended stoves. Bobby said that he
was buried in a small town in Mississippi.

The Bobby Dunbar case was a famous one—probably the most talk-
ed of in America until the Lindbergh kidnapping. Aside from much
other publicity, Mrs. O. J. Cauvin of Abbeville wrote a song, "I Have
Found My Child at Last." But Bobby Dunbar and his family have
almost forgotten it. Mrs. Dunbar has no fear of a similar mishap for
their three children. They lead the regular, routine lives of healthy
youngsters.

"But, if Walters is still living, I would certainly like to see him," the
once-famous Dunbar says.

Morning Advocate Magazine-October 10, 1948

"He who began a good work in you will be able to complete it..."
Philippians 1:6

Afterword

In 2003, after reading *William Cantwell Walters' Defense File*, Margaret called to tell me that she was having serious doubts about her family's version of the story. It was a bitter admission, for she was as proud and protective of her research as I was of mine, though now she understood that a preponderance of her information was fabricated. Knowing that I was intent on sharing the file's information with the Anderson, Walters, and Rawls families, she convinced her father Bob, Jr., and a descendant of Alonzo Dunbar to both have DNA testing done.

When I got the results in a phone call from Margaret, I can't say I was surprised, just satisfied—her grandfather was *not* Bobby Dunbar. I should have tried to act more stunned by the announcement, but I and the people I had interviewed already knew the child was Bruce. Margaret asked me to keep the news to myself until she could reveal it at a later date, and I honored my word.

In 2004 when she and her father shared the news, there was a collective sigh of relief from the Anderson, Walters, and Rawls families as the Dunbars finally acknowledged the truth. Their stranglehold was broken, though Margaret let me know right away that the test did not prove that the child *was* Bruce Anderson. I couldn't believe what I was hearing. Cantwell had been exonerated, but Margaret insisted on keeping him under her grinding heel.

Revisiting my grandfather's case meant repeatedly delving into the callousness and duplicity that had ravaged so many innocent lives. Whenever animosity threatened to overtake me, however, I would imagine the hundreds of nights Cantwell sat alone in a dark cell, longing for the simple comfort of a candle; or I would picture Julia on her first trip to Opelousas, boldly looking forward, and then on the return trip, peering over her shoulder in fear and shame.

In 2008, Margaret appeared on PRI's *This American Life* covering "The Ghost of Bobby Dunbar." In the interview she took credit for organizing *William Cantwell Walters' Defense File* and went on to read, out of context, a portion of Cantwell's unsent letter from the file addressing the Dunbars. "I think you will Be sad A Long time But Hope not too bad."

Afterwards, when I went to visit Julia's children in Poplarville, they expressed extreme embarrassment in their mother's and their own portrayal on the program. Within a week after the show aired, Margaret and her father, Bob, Jr., each received a letter from me stating that *William Cantwell Walters' Defense File* was copyrighted material and that they did not have permission to use it. I notified the radio show as well; however, they rebroadcast the show a year later.

In the summer of 2012, Margaret and Tal McThenia released their book *A Case for Solomon* which they filled with unauthorized and incorrect material from *William Cantwell Walters' Defense File*. The hijacked material is marked in this book with a red oval stamp. The betrayal felt like walking into a wedding reception and discovering that an uninvited guest had sneaked in early and gobbled up the cake and was side-splitting proud of it, too. Just like Percy, Margaret lost something precious: her family's famous saga of Bobby Dunbar. Like Percy, she found a replacement in the file, simply taking the collection as her own. But to use it to once again weave doubts into the public's consciousness about an extraordinary man who loved a little boy and whom that boy loved back is disconcerting and dishonest. My prayer is that the readers of this book will come to know the true nature of this innocent man and of the steadfast lawyers who sought to defend him.

Acknowledgments

I am indebted to many individuals for their help in this venture: My grandfather and father for preserving this rich piece of history; Hollis Edgar Rawls and Jewel Rawls Tarver, Julia's children, for sharing her spirit with me; Dell Rawls Crisler, my aunt and Hollis C. Rawls' daughter, for letting me pick her brain; Michael Walters and the Walters family for their history and hospitality; Sharon Bond for research and encouragement; Margaret Dunbar Cutright; Charlotte Yarborough, Dr. David C. Berry, Ann Fortenberry, and especially Sandra Rushing for proofreading; Cass Barnes and the Marion County courthouse; Virginia Chain and the Marion County Museum; Tulane University; Jarvis Lowe; Sally Colbert Shaw; Elbert Hilliard; and Saradel Rawls Berry for assistance in cover artwork.

To my family, especially Jim, thanks and I love you!

Mizpah Names

Preface

Ben Rawls-Columbia, MS-attorney and banker-son of Hollis C. Rawls and father of Allison Rawls Bullock.

Hollis Clifton Rawls-Columbia, MS-Jr. attorney of Dale and Rawls.

Adele Rawls-Columbia, MS-wife of Hollis C. Rawls.

Charles Bruce Anderson-Barnesville, NC-four year-old boy in Cantwell Walters' custody.

Robert P. (Bobby) Dunbar-Opelousas, LA-four year-old boy who disappeared at Swayze Lake.

William Cantwell Walters (Ugly Papa)-Barnesville, NC-traveling repairman of musical instruments-foster father of Bruce Anderson.

Julia Anderson-Barnesville, NC-Bruce and Bernice's mother.

Clarence Percy Dunbar-Opelousas, LA-father of Bobby-business and real estate.

Lessie Whitley Dunbar-Opelousas, LA-from New Orleans-mother of Bobby.

Thomas Sebe Dale-Columbia, MS-Sr. attorney of Dale and Rawls.

Carol Rawls-aunt of Allison Rawls Bullock.

Margaret Dunbar Cutright-granddaughter of Bruce Anderson/Bobby Dunbar.

Robert Dunbar, Jr.-son of Bruce Anderson/Bobby Dunbar.

Hollis Edgar Rawls-Poplarville, MS-son of Julia Anderson Rawls-namesake of Hollis C. Rawls.

Jewel Rawls Tarver-Poplarville, MS-daughter of Julia Anderson Rawls.

Jeptha Bilbo-Bilbos' Post Office, Pearl River County, MS-ran post office and boarding house-Cantwell's alibi in 1912 and 1913-uncle of MS's Lieutenant Governor Theodore Bilbo.

MATILDA BILBO-Bilbos' Post Office, Pearl River County, MS-ran post office and boarding house-Cantwell's alibi in 1912 and 1913-wife of Jeptha.

MICHAEL WALTERS-Shannon, NC-Walters' family historian.

PRINCESS ANNE-NC site in Lumber River State Park near Cantwell's childhood home.

WILLIAM WALTERS-Barnesville, NC-Cantwell's grandfather.

CELIA WALTERS-Barnesville, NC-Cantwell's grandmother.

JOEL BULLOCK-author's husband's great, great, great grandfather.

HARMON THOMPSON-author's great, great, great, great grandfather.

DELL RAWLS CRISLER-daughter of Hollis Rawls and aunt of author.

HOWARD-Tilton Memorial Library of Tulane University-New Orleans, LA.

GENERAL HUERTA-President of Mexico 1913.

Prologue

MARJORIE BYARS DUNBAR-Opelousas, LA-married to Bruce Anderson/Bobby Dunbar.

MARY DUNBAR-Opelousas, LA-daughter of Bruce Anderson/Bobby Dunbar.

BOBBY DUNBAR, JR.-Opelousas, LA-son of Bruce Anderson/Bobby Dunbar.

JOHN DUNBAR-Opelousas, LA-son of Bruce Anderson/Bobby Dunbar.

LILLIAN BOURDIER-journalist for the Morning Advocate magazine.

MRS. O. J. CAUVIN-Abbeville, LA-song writer-"I Have Found My Child at Last."

Chapter One

J. PAUL MIZZIE-Opelousas, LA-butcher-shooting gar at Swayze Lake.

ALONZO DUNBAR-Opelousas, LA-two year-old brother of Bobby.

WALLACE DUNBAR-cousin of Percy at Swayze Lake-held Bobby back from following father.

PRESTON KING-Opelousas, LA-sheriff-Percy's uncle-at Swayze Lake camp-testified Cantwell was at Swayze Lake when Bobby disappeared.

MISS LORENA WHITLEY-Lessie's sister-at Swayze Lake.

MR. RICHARD-at Swayze Lake.

SEBE FRILOT-negro guide and caretaker at Swayze and Second Lakes.

DR. LAWRENCE DAILEY (DALY)-at Swayze Lake.

JOHN OGA (OGE)-St. Landry Parish, LA-attorney-planter-polititi-on-at Swayze Lake.

Chapter Two

MR. AND MRS. THOMAS LUMPKIN-Pearl River County, MS-hired Cantwell Dec. 19th through 24th of 1912-alibi for Aug. 21st of 1912.

GEORGE AMACKER- Pearl River County, MS-Cantwell's alibi for Aug. and Dec. of 1912.

DAVID BLEDSOE-Iron City, GA-professor-childhood friend and mentor of Cantwell-visited by Cantwell and Bruce in May of 1912.

J. A. MOODY-Poplarville, MS-sheriff-questioned Cantwell on Dec. 21st of 1912.

HOMER-Bilbos' grandson and playmate of Bruce.

RAMBLER-Bilbos' dog.

BERNICE ANDERSON-Barnesville, NC-Bruce's sister.

RODERICK DARREL OF DARREL OF THE BLESSED ISLES-by Irving Bacheller. (1903)

MR. BOYD-Pearl River County, MS-deputy-examined Bruce at Bilbo's on Dec. 26th of 1912.

D. F. SMITH-Carriere, MS-postmaster-telegram to Opelousas mayor-examined Bruce.

T. L. LOEB-Opelousas, LA-mayor-telegram to D. F. Smith.

F. E. BROOKS-Pearl River County, MS-sheriff-examined Bruce at Bilbo's on Dec. 29th of 1912.

H. G. ANDERSON-MS-physician-examined Bruce at Bilbo's on Dec. 29th of 1912.

Chapter Three

LADIES OF HUB-Hub, MS-telegram to Percy.

ARCHIE DUNBAR-Percy's brother-traveled to Bilbo's-examined Bruce.

M. A. COWART-Hub, MS-stock man-child's quote.

C. A. (CHARLIE) DAY-Marion County, MS-sheriff-took Bruce from Cantwell-receipt for child.

HAROLD AND OLA FOX-New Orleans, LA-Percy's first cousin and her husband-sheltered family at their Freret St. house.

JOHN FORTENBERRY-Marion County, MS-prosecution witness.

WALTER LOTT-Marion County, MS-deputy sheriff and constable.

OTT POOL-Marion County, MS- receipt for child.

J. D. (JEFF) WALLACE-Marion County, MS-Day's deputy-kept Bruce at his home-receipt for child.

MRS. WALLACE-kept Bruce and washed his feet.

STANLEY HATHORN-Marion County, MS-sheriff.

GEORGE BENZ-New Orleans, LA-Item representative-to Columbia with Dunbars.

WILLIAM LAMPTON-Columbia, MS-businessman-offered his house to the Dunbars.

L. C. WELLBOURNE-Marion County, MS-Chancery Court clerk-receipt for child.

JARVIS LOWE-donated receipt.

HENRY ESTORAGE-Opelousas, LA-Percy's partner-deputy clerk of District Court-clerk of Police Jury-former Mayor of Opelousas.

MARION SWORDS-St. Landry Parish, LA-sheriff-warrant for Cantwell from Estorage.

LUTHER HALL-Louisiana Governor-asks for extradition-appoints Estorage.

Chapter Four

SOPHIE WEBB RAWLS-Columbia, MS-Hollis C. Rawls' mother.

JAMES RAWLS-Columbia, MS-timber man-Hollis Rawls' father.

RUHAMA ATKINSON WEBB-Columbia, MS-Sophie's mother.

WALTER WEBB-Columbia, MS-merchant-married widow Ruhama-Sophie's father.
JAMES HOWARD RAWLS-Columbia, MS-James and Sophie's infant son.
TOM FORD-Columbia, MS-marshall.
JOBIE SWEENEY-at Foxworth identification-Bruce's statement.
WILLIAM HARRIS (HARRY) MOUNGER-Columbia, MS-attorney. (Father to Adele Mounger Rawls).
L. F. BROWN-Chadbourn, NC-Cantwell's cousin, knows Julia, and Bruce.
E. K. BROWN-Cerro Gordo, NC-Justice of Peace for Columbus County, NC-Cantwell's cousin, knows Julia, and Bruce.

Chapter Five

SARAH DALE-Columbia, MS-Tom Dale's sister-Dale and Rawls' secretary.
MR. SLADE-Purvis, MS-Cantwell's alibi July 12th of 1912.
MARK RAYBORN-Purvis, MS-Cantwell's alibi July 13th and 14th of 1912.
MR. DAVIS-Pinebur, MS-Cantwell's alibi July 15th of 1912.
MR. RAWLS-Pinebur, MS-Cantwell's alibi July 15th of 1912.
JOSEPH GALLOWAY-Odile, MS-Cantwell's alibi July 16th through 18th of 1912.
MR. HAM-Odile, MS-could not keep Cantwell and Bruce on July 16th of 1912.
WASH LOTT-Cantwell's alibi Aug. 19th of 1912.
BOB HARVEY-Cantwell's alibi Aug. 19th of 1912.
DAN HOLLEMAN-Pearl River County, MS-Cantwell's alibi Aug. 18th and 19th of 1912.
BILL STEWART-Cantwell's alibi July of 1912.
THE WHEATS-Bill Stewart lived at their home.
LEVY HOLLEMAN-Pearl River County, MS-Cantwell's alibi Aug. 18th through 20th of 1912.
CARLOS HOLLEMAN-Pearl River County, MS-Cantwell's alibi Aug. 18th of 1912.
ORVIS PENTON-Cantwell's alibi Aug. 18th of 1912.
MRS. JENKINS-Cantwell's alibi Aug. 18th of 1912.

Mrs. Loveless-McNeil, MS-nurse-Cantwell's alibi Aug. 18th of 1912-later said he returned with different child.

Mr. and Mrs. Loveless-Cantwell's alibi Aug. 18th of 1912.

Mr. and Mrs. Boone-Cantwell's alibi Aug. 18th of 1912.

Lost Smith-Cantwell's alibi Aug. 20th of 1912.

Slaydon Spears-McNeil, MS-merchant-purchased cattle from J. Q. Sones-Cantwell's alibi Aug. 20th and 21st of 1912.

Jeff Lott-Cantwell's alibi Aug. 21st of 1912.

Ben J. Sones, Sr.-Cantwell's alibi Aug. 21st through 23rd, Oct. and Dec. 24thof 1912.

J. Q. Sones-McNeill, MS-Missionary Baptist minister-Cantwell's alibi Aug. 21st of 1912.

Young Man (J. S.) Thigpen-Poplarville, MS-Cantwell's alibi Aug. 23rd and 24th of 1912.

George W. Amacker-lives near Whitesand Church-Cantwell's alibi Dec. 16th through 19th of 1912.

Old Man (L. A.) Thigpen-store owner-Cantwell's alibi Aug. 24th and 25th of 1912.

Holden's-Cantwell's alibi Aug. 24th of 1912.

G. W. Holcomb-Pearl River County, MS-minister-preached at Whitesand Church-Cantwell's alibi Aug. 25th of 1912.

Carl Bass- Poplarville, MS-timber cruiser-clerk Whitesand Church-log book for Cantwell's alibi Aug. 25th and 26th of 1912.

Mr. and Mrs. J. Allen Goleman-Poplarville, MS-Cantwell's alibi July 21st, Aug. 26th, and Oct. of 1912-Cantwell and Bruce stayed here for two weeks in Aug. and constructed harp.

Mr. and Mrs. James Pleasant (Alice) Walters-Barnesville, NC-Cantwell's parents.

J. M. Walters-Barnesville, NC-farmer-Cantwell's nephew.

Synthelia Walters Williamson-Evergreen, NC-Cantwell's older sister.

Albert Godchaux-New Orleans, LA-owner of Godchaux's department store.

Mrs. W. M. (the elder) Dunbar-Ola Dunbar Fox's mother.

John Glass-New Orleans, LA-advertising manager of Godchaux's.

Eugenie Deck-New Orleans, LA-clerk at Godchaux's

Wharton Mooney-New Orleans, LA-at Godchaux's.

WILLIAM WALTERS-Eunice, LA-trunk-photo in Item mistaken for Cantwell.

EARL BREWER-Jackson, MS-Governor.

DAN S. LEHON-investigator for Burn's Detective Agency.

W. J. BURNS-New Orleans, LA-detective-head of Burn's Detective Agency.

JOHN W. LEWIS-Opelousas, LA-attorney and friend of Dunbars-present at Opelousas identity test-prosecutor in the trial.

IRMA AND NATHAN ROOS-Opelousas, LA-Bobby's childhood friends.

F. C. SHUTE-Opelousas, LA-physician for Dunbars.

LEE HAWES-staff correspondent of the Times-Democrat at Bruce's examination in New Orleans.

Chapter Six

W. J. BUCK-Jackson, MS-Governor Brewer's private secretary.

WILLIAM H. MURRAY-Barnesville, NC-mailman.

(F. H.) FRANKLIN HUGO WALTERS-Cantwell's brother mentioned in Cantwell's April 8, 1913 letter to his parents.

VINITA-mentioned in Cantwell's April 8, 1913 letter to his parents.

JOE L. JOHNSON-McComb City, MS-employee of Illinois Central shop-affidavit stating Cantwell was there on Dec. 18th of 1912.

B. L. (D. L.) MORGAN-McComb City, MS-employee of Illinois Central shop-affidavit stating Cantwell was there on Dec. 18th of 1912.

W. D. HOLMES-McComb City, MS-employee of Illinois Central shop-affidavit stating Cantwell was there on Dec. 18th of 1912.

E. P. WILLIAMS-notary public.

GEORGE COOPER-Pearl River County, MS-Cantwell's alibi Dec. 15th of 1912.

JAMES TYNES-Pearl River County, MS-Cantwell's alibi Dec. 15th of 1912.

WARREN TYNES-Pearl River County, MS.

COTTON JOE STEWART-Pearl River County, MS-Cantwell's alibi Dec. 15th and 16th of 1912.

TOM STEWART-Pearl River County, MS-Cantwell's alibi Dec. 16th of 1912.

TOM AMACKER-Cantwell's alibi Aug. 25th and Dec. 17th of 1912.

MR. MITCHELL-Cantwell's alibi Dec. 17th of 1912.

JOHN EDWARDS-affidavit for Cantwell having Bruce.

J. R. LAWSON-Robeson County, NC-justice of peace.

IRADELL WALTERS WILLIAMSON-Dodge County, GA-Cantwell's older sister.

UGLY PAPA-Bruce's nickname for Cantwell.

Chapter Seven

ELISHA FLOYD-Columbus County, NC-married to seventeen year-old Julia for five months and separated-father of Julia's stillborn child.

JIM COWAN-shoe salesman-had an affair with twenty-four-year-old Julia-Julia falsely proclaimed him as Bruce's father to protect D. B. (Bunt) Walters, Cantwell's brother with whom she was in love.

D. B. (BUNT) WALTERS-Julia's elusive lover-secretly fathered Bruce Anderson-fathered Bernice, who was put up for adoption.

MILTON WILLIAMSON-Dodge County, GA-Cantwell's brother-in-law.

F. M. STEPHENS-Boardman, NC-postmaster-Cantwell's nephew.

JAMES E. EDMUNDS-New Orleans, LA-Item reporter-escorted Julia to New Orleans and Opelousas-present at Opelousas identity test.

E. P. VEAZIE-Opelousas, LA-attorney and friend of Dunbars-present at Opelousas identity test.

MRS. JOHN LEWIS-Opelousas, LA-Julia's Opelousas examination at her home-prosecution witness.

M. L. SWORDS-Opelousas, LA-sheriff.

CHARLES F. BOAGNI-Opelousas, LA-physician-present at Opelousas identity test.

J. A. HASS-Opelousas, LA-physician-present at Opelousas identity test.

J. P. SAIZAN-Opelousas, LA-physician-chairman of committee at Opelousas identity test.

A. **Leon Dupre**-Opelousas, LA-friend of Dunbars-present at Opelousas identity test.
B. **H. Pavy**-Opelousas, LA-judge of the Sixteenth Judicial District-presided over Cantwell's trial. (In 1935, his son-in-law, Dr. Carl Austin Weiss, Jr., shot and killed "Kingfish" Huey P. Long, for attempting to oust Pavy from power.)
R. **Lee Garland**-Opelousas, LA-district attorney-prosecuted Cantwell.
Wellwisher-anonymous letter writer from LA.
Edwin T. Bercier-Bobby's cousin.
Charles Chachere-Opelousas, LA-deputy sheriff.
Mrs. A. J. Bercier-Opelousas, LA-Edwin's mother.
A. **J. McMullen**-New Orleans, LA-States reporter-friend and contact of Dale and Rawls.
Mr. Ross-New Orleans, LA-States editor.
Douce Mornhingveg-Lessie's cousin-didn't believe boy was Bobby.
A. **J. Strange**-Opelousas, LA-physician-searched for Bobby at Swayze Lake.
Lamar Hennington-Columbia, MS-partner of Dale and Rawls.
Mr. and Mrs. W. G. Lawson-NC-friends of Julia-confirm photo is Bruce.

Chapter Eight

Uncle Sam-Bruce's original name for Cantwell.
Dr. Payne-New Orleans, LA-physician-treated Cantwell in Charity Hospital.
(Steven) McIntyre, (R. C.) Lawrence, and (James) Proctor-Lumberton, NC-attorneys-negotiated Cantwell land sale.
R. **R. Barnes**-Barnesville, NC-merchant-loaned Cantwell money against his land.
Allen Rawls-Poplarville, MS-bank cashier-cousin of Hollis-sent car to secretly carry witnesses to New Orleans.
E. **G. (Garland) Brown**-Whiteville, NC-attorney-Cantwell's cousin.
A Christian Woman-New Orleans, LA-letter to Dale and Rawls.

JOHN M. PARKER-New Orleans, LA-chairman New Orleans Board of Trade and Cotton Exchange-mediator of New Orleans identity test.

JOHN BLANK-New Orleans, LA-private investigator-working with Dale and Rawls.

LEW ROSE-New Orleans, LA-manager of Hippodrome theater.

SOL MYERS-New Orleans, LA-Rose's partner in the Hippodrome theater.

WALTER KATTMAN-New Orleans, LA-press agent for Orpheum theater.

HAMLIN-New Orleans, LA-Item staff.

NEIL AND MARTHA STONE-Robeson County, NC-employed Julia around the time she gave Bruce to Cantwell.

Chapter Nine

KATE COLLINS-Poplarville, MS-saw Cantwell and Bruce in restaurant-prosecution witness.

MR. FRANK-Louisiana movie man wanting contract to show Bruce.

T. R. (DOC) WILLOUGBY-Columbia, MS-attorney-associate of Dale and Rawls.

KATIE DUNBAR-Percy's sister-prosecution witness.

ABRAHAM E. OLIVEIRA-stenographer for the Dunbar Investigation.

MR. YATES-Columbia, MS-attorney-Governor Brewer's representative for the Dunbar Investigation-denied admittance to the investigation by Parker.

W. W. LOTT-Columbia, MS-Marion County deputy sheriff and constable.

HOMER MOODY-Poplarville, MS-farmer-Cantwell's alibi for July 19th of 1912.

CHARLES MYLEY-Poplarville, MS-Cantwell's alibi for July 21st of 1912.

JIM HOLDEN-examined Bruce in MS.

MRS. ELLA MYLEY-Poplarville, MS-Cantwell's alibi for July 21st, 28th, and Dec. 24th of 1912.

OZY BROOKS-Carriere, MS-deputy-examined Bruce at Bilbo's on Dec. 29th of 1912.

CHARLES RALPH-Pearl River County, MS-chancery clerk mentioned in the Dunbar Investigation-Cantwell's alibi for July 23rd, 1912.

EDNA MYLEY-Poplarville, MS-Bruce's six-year-old friend.

Chapter Ten

A. W. DEROALDES-New Orleans, LA-physician-listed on appointment card.

R. C. LYNCH-New Orleans, LA-physician-listed on appointment card.

DR. ROBBONE-New Orleans, LA-physician-listed on appointment card.

GIBSON's-Varnado, LA-Myley's former residence-listed on appointment card.

W. L. RUSHING-insurance salesman-wrote receipt-Cantwell's alibi Aug. 7th of 1912.

HIRRIAM E. NEWMAN-name on insurance receipt-Cantwell's alibi Aug. 7th of 1912.

J. J. SCARBOROUGH-Poplarville, MS-postmaster-receipt for Cantwell's money order on Aug. 7th of 1912.

MR. COUTIERIE-Jackson, MS-attorney-legal advisor to Governor Brewer.

A. E. WEATHERSBY-MS-judge of the Fifteenth Judicial District.

MR. A. KOENIG-Alexandria, LA-umbrella mender-prosecution witness.

A. A. HAMMOND-Heidelberg, MS-attorney.

G. M. DONALD-McNeill, MS-agent of Northeastern Railroad-Cantwell signed for package on Aug. 20th of 1912.

W. H. MEEKS-Cantwell sent this man a violin on Aug. 20th of 1912.

WASH LEE-conducted singing school at Whitesand Church on Aug. 26th of 1912.

OTTO (OTHO) STEWART-former clerk of Whitesand Church.

J. W. BLODGETT-Pearl River County, MS-timber owner.

J. J. AMACKER-Pearl River County, MS-Cantwell's alibi for Aug. 25th of 1912.

J. M. TYNES-Pearl River County, MS-Cantwell's alibi for first week in Aug. and on Aug. 25th of 1912.

BEN ALSOBROOKS-McNeill, MS-Cantwell's alibi for Aug. 22nd of 1912.

SAM JONES-hired by Alsobrooks to cut timber on Aug. 22nd of 1912.

JOE LUMPKIN-Cantwell's alibi for Aug. 23rd of 1912.

DR. HENDERSON-Mobile, AL-physician-treated Cantwell in May of 1912.

MR. MEEKS-New Augusta, MS-Cantwell's alibi for June of 1912.

JOHN YATES-New Augusta, MS-Cantwell's alibi for June of 1912.

MR. BLYTHE-Pearl River County, MS-shop owner-where Cantwell made frame for harp.

MR. McLENDON-Pineville, LA-Cantwell worked in his blacksmith shop in 1909.

MRS. L. McMANUS-Pineville, LA-restaurant owner-Cantwell ate lunch in restaurant in 1909.

WIDOW WAINWRIGHT-Pineville, LA-Cantwell ran her ferry in 1909.

WILLIAM MALLET-Forrest Hill, LA-deputy or constable-livery business.

MRS. L. A. THIGPEN-Cantwell's Aug. 24th and 25th of 1912 alibi.

J. A. McKINLEY-Columbia, MS-Marion County justice of peace-his docket held the charge against Cantwell on April 21st of 1913.

TOXIE HALL-Columbia, MS-Marion County district attorney-attempted to dismiss Cantwell's case on June 21st after Brewer honored the requisition on June 18th.

B. A. SYLVERSTEIN-Marion County prosecuting attorney-attempted to dismiss Cantwell's case on June 21st after Brewer honored the requisition on June 18th.

W. A. STOGNER-Tylertown, MS-quoted Cantwell as saying he was around Opelousas at time child was stolen.

A. B. DANTIN-Alexandria, LA-boilermaker-testified Cantwell was in Alexandria on Aug. 6th of 1912.

J. J. DUFFY-Alexandria, LA-shop foreman.

FRANK ANSLEY-Port Barre, LA-railroad bridge carpenter-testified Cantwell was near Swayze Lake on Aug. 24th of 1912-says only one family living between Port Barre and Melville.

THOMAS KLEINPETER-Lake Charles, LA-attorney assisting Dale and Rawls in Opelousas.

RODERICK-pictured in Item photograph labeled as W. C. Walters.

Chapter Eleven

A41084-Cantwell's assigned prisoner number.
MR. HERRING-Angie, LA-mentioned in Cantwell's letters.
MR. GRAHAM-Angie, LA.-mentioned in Cantwell's letters.
BUD WALL-mentioned in Cantwell's letters.
MR. BARNES-sawmill man-heard Dr. Anderson's quote.
E. B. SOUTHERLAND-Hub, MS-Percy's quote.
MR. REYNOLDS-Opelousas, LA-inspector for police department.
DAN SMITH-Carriere, MS-merchant.
WALTER MURRAY-NC-mailman.
JO MURRAY-Barnesville, NC-postmaster.
MC D. WALTERS-Barnesville, NC-farmer-Cantwell's brother.
SIDNEY LEE-Barnesville, NC-farmer.
QUIN BRETT-Barnesville, NC-farmer.
MARION STEPHENS-Boardman, NC-merchant.
MATHEWEL STEPHENS-Boardman, NC-preacher.
M. G. WILLIAMSON-Evergreen, NC-merchant-Cantwell's brother-in-law-married to Synthelia.
JETH WILLIAMSON-Evergreen, NC-Cantwell's nephew.
GENOVA WILLIAMSON-Evergreen, NC.
DOYLE BELL-Bayboro, NC-farmer.
JAMES BELL-Bayboro, NC-farmer.
J. R. GERRALD-Bayboro, NC-farmer.
ARNOLD BELL-Bayboro, NC-merchant.
SIMS ALLEN-Bayboro, NC-merchant.
ASBERY BELL-Bayboro, NC-merchant.
J. B. WALTERS-Baxley, GA-barber-Cantwell's brother.
HONCE WALTERS-Baxley, GA-barber.
J. I. POPE-Eastman, GA-ice and coal dealer.
M. M. WILLIAMSON-Eastman, GA-farmer-Cantwell's brother-in-law-married to Iradell.
JAMES POPE-Eastman, GA.
PROFESSOR ANDERSON-Iron City, GA-professor.

Sʏʟᴜs Fᴇʟʟᴏᴡs-Pinckard, AL.

L. Jᴏɴᴇs-Pinckard, AL.

Dᴀᴠᴇ Nɪᴄʜᴏʟs-Eastabuchie, MS.

D. L. Tʀᴀʏʟᴏʀ-Beaumont, MS.

Fʀᴀɴᴋ Bᴇᴀsʟʏ-New Augusta, MS.

Wɪʟʟɪᴀᴍ Rᴀʙᴏɴ (Rᴀʏʙᴏʀɴ)-Baxterville, MS.

Aʟᴇɴɢᴏ Rᴀʙᴏɴ (Rᴀʏʙᴏʀɴ)-Baxterville, MS.

Rᴜssᴇʟ Rᴀʏʙᴏɴ (Rᴀʏʙᴏʀɴ)-Baxterville, MS.

Mʀ. ᴀɴᴅ Mʀs. Pᴀʀᴋᴇʀ-Baxterville, MS.

Jᴏʜɴ Dᴀᴠɪs-Pinebur, MS.

Mʀs. Lᴇᴠʏ Hᴏʟʟᴏᴍᴏɴ-Cantwell's alibi for Aug. 18th of 1912.

Dᴏʟᴘʜ Sᴍɪᴛʜ-Bilbo Post Office, MS.

Gᴇᴏʀɢᴇ Sᴍɪᴛʜ-Bilbo Post Office, MS.

Jᴏʜɴ Dᴀᴠɪs-Hillsdale, MS.

Rᴇᴠ. Lᴏɴɴɪᴇ Lᴇᴇ-Lonnie Lee Post Office, McNeill, MS-preacher.

Isᴀɪᴀʜ Pᴇᴛᴇʀs-Percy's quote.

D. L. Cᴀʀʟᴛᴏɴ-Washington, D. C.-Acting Attorney General.

Rᴀᴅғᴏʀᴅ J. Wᴀʟᴛᴇʀs-Surrency, GA-Cantwell's brother.

Pᴀᴅɢᴇᴛᴛ ᴀɴᴅ Wᴀᴛsᴏɴ-Baxley, GA-attorneys hired by Cantwell's brothers.

Chapter Twelve

E. B. Dᴜʙᴜɪssᴏɴ-Opelousas, LA-attorney-Pavy appointed him to assist Dale and Rawls.

T. J. Wᴀʟᴛᴇʀs-Seminary, MS-dentist-contributed to Cantwell's defense.

V. B. Eᴀsᴛᴇʀʟɪɴɢ-Hattiesburg, MS-teacher.

J. P. Mɪᴛᴄʜᴇʟʟ-Pearl River County, MS-justice of peace and notary public.

J. H. Hᴏʀɴᴇ-Pearl River County, MS-manager of Western Union Telegraph Company.

Mᴀɢɢɪᴇ Bᴜʀᴋs-Picayune, MS-wrote check in Cantwell's presence on Aug. 17th of 1912.

Mʀ. ᴀɴᴅ Mʀs. S. L. Jᴀʀʀᴇʟʟ-Pearl River County, MS-recipient of Maggie Burks check.

S. J. Mᴏᴏᴅʏ-Picayune, MS-justice of peace

Sᴀᴍ Bʟᴀɪʀ-New Orleans, LA-reporter for Item.

Mɪɢɴᴏɴ Hᴀʟʟ-New Orleans, LA-reporter for Item.

J. L. Linder-Alexandria, LA-stove-mender-mistaken for Cantwell.

Alex Edwards-stove-mender.

George Lang-Eunice, LA-bookkeeper-jury member.

A. P. Collins-near Opelousas, LA-farmer-jury member.

Gaston Horaist-Sunset, LA-manager oil mill-jury member.

Faustin Soileau-Grand Prairie, LA-farmer-jury member.

Robert McClelland-near Opelousas, LA-farmer-jury member.

L. E. Fisher-Opelousas, LA-city contractor-jury member.

George Caillouet-Port Barre, LA-merchant-jury member.

Robert Frank Oliver-Frozard, LA-farmer and merchant-jury member.

Hyppolite Miller-Sunset, LA-merchant-jury member.

Walter Sibille-Sunset, LA-farmer-jury member.

Antoine (Arthur) Lamaury-Sunset, LA-manager Farmer's Union warehouse-jury member.

J. B. Sibille-Sunset, LA-farmer-jury member.

Dr. Hawkins-Palmetto, LA-prosecution witness.

Miss Douce Whitley-Lessie's sister-prosecution witness.

Miss Lorena Whitley-Lessie's sister-prosecution witness.

Mrs. Jack Dupree-Lessie's sister-prosecution witness.

Miss Christine Zernott-Lessie's cousin-prosecution witness.

Mrs. Frank Shute-Opelousas, LA-wife of Dr. Shute, the Dunbars' physician-prosecution witness.

William Mallett-prosecution witness.

Mrs. Hodges-prosecution witness.

Mrs. M. E. Sloan-New Roads, LA-prosecution witness.

Steve Bennett-Poplarville, MS-prosecution witness.

Kate Collins-Poplarville, MS-waitress-prosecution witness who claimed Bruce and Bobby were swapped in her place of employment.

Mrs. Nix-prosecution witness.

Mrs. Whitley-Lessie's mother-prosecution witness.

Mrs. Robert Dunbar-Percy's mother-prosecution witness.

Robert Dunbar-Percy's father-prosecution witness.

Mrs. Beicer-prosecution witness.

Dr. Stubbs-at Opelousas jail with Cantwell.

Otto Fortenberry-Columbia, MS-jailor-defense witness.

Rickets-prosecution claimed she was Cantwell's accessory in kidnapping Bobby.

Emille Thigpen-Poplarville, MS-saw Cantwell there the last of July or first of August of 1912.

Dee Morgan-defense witness.

Mr. Stetly-defense witness.

Mr. Robertson-civil engineer-defense witness.

Mr. White-at Swayze Lake-defense witness.

Mr. Eastham-defense witness.

Mrs. W. B. Roberts-Opelousas, LA-defense witness-recognized that the boy was not Bobby.

J. P. Barnett-Opelousas, LA-defense witness-recognized that the boy was not Bobby.

Miss Fannie Bowden-Opelousas, LA-Dunbar's neighbor-defense witness-recognized that the boy was not Bobby.

Mr. M. Pulford-Opelousas, LA-defense witness-recognized that the boy was not Bobby.

Mr. Waxter-McComb City, MS-prosecution witness-refuted the testimony of Dee Morgan.

Mr. Budden-prosecution witness working with Ansley on railroad bridge at Swayze Lake.

Ogee Hargroter-prosecution witness working with Ansley on railroad bridge at Swayze Lake.

Mr. Williams-Lumberton, MS-prosecution witness.

Miss Lass-prosecution witness.

Mr. Piggford-prosecution witness.

E. C. Bennett-Longville, LA-minister-prosecution witness.

Mr. Winberry-DeRidder, LA-minister-prosecution witness.

Mr. Scarborough-DeRidder, LA-prosecution witness.

O. L. Mason-Merryville,LA-judge-prosecution witness.

C. C. Bass-New Orleans, LA-physician-Tulane University.

Mrs. J. E. Redditt-Opelousas, LA-encouraged Tom and Hollis after trial.

A Louisiana Lady-New Orleans, LA-congratulations to the defense.

Chapter Thirteen

William Winningham-Millard, MS-in Kate Collins' restaurant with Cantwell and Bruce.

Louis Goldman-Biloxi, MS-attorney.

R. B. Davis-at Mrs. Sloan's in New Roads.

TUTSTONE WOODVILLE-accompanied J. L. Linder.

JOHNNY WINNINGHAM-Millard, MS-child in Kate Collins' restaurant with his father, Cantwell, and Bruce.

N. BATSON-Millard, MS-former sheriff, Chancery and Circuit Clerk, and treasurer of Pearl River County, MS.

ALEX ROBERTSON-Opelousas, LA-Dubuisson's secretary.

JESSIE TUTCHSTONE/TUTSTONE WOODVILLE/J. W. KING-Alexandria, LA, Teneha, TX, Shreveport, LA.

OLLIE RAWLS-Pearl River County, MS-cousin of Hollis-married Julia.

MR. RAINES-mentioned in Cantwell's June 6th of 1914 letter to Dale and Rawls.

ED LAMPTON-Columbia, MS-father of William Lampton.

S. J. H.-Stanley Hathorn.

O. B. F.-Otto Fortenberry.

THOMAS L. JOHNSTON-Lumberton, NC-attorney.

K. M. BARNES-Lumberton, NC-bank cashier.

HARRY SELLERS-New Orleans, LA-possibly signed up with Cantwell for a show.

MR. STREETLY-New Orleans, LA-possibly signed up with Cantwell for a show.

Chapter Fourteen

UNCLE HENRY-Opelousas, LA-in States sketch by Tisdale.

F. S. TISDALE-New Orleans, LA-States reporter and artist.

MRS. F. M. DUNBAR-Percy's sister-in-law.

F. M. DUNBAR-Percy's brother.

B. F. SHERROUSE-Ola Fox's uncle

V. MOREL-Item artist.

H. J. HARVEY PHOTO-picture in Item.

TRIST-Item artist.

MAXWELL-Opelousas, LA-photographer.

GEORGE BAYLISS-Columbia, MS-friend of Cantwell, Hollis, and Tom.

Chapter Fifteen

MRS. D. L. BLEDSOE-Iron City, GA-Cantwell's alibi for May of 1912.

MRS. J. M. COWART-Iron City, GA-Cantwell's alibi for May of 1912.

MAE RABON-Iron City, GA-Cantwell's alibi for May of 1912.

MRS. J. H. RABON-Iron City, GA-Cantwell's alibi for May of 1912.

MRS. S. R. OWENS-Iron City, GA-Cantwell's alibi for May of 1912.

LUCILLE DEVERGES-New Orleans, LA-child who played with Bruce.

A. McGILL-McNeill, MS-notary public.

D. L. ARCHER-Pearl River County, MS-official.

STONE-mentioned in Julia's affidavit.

L. W. STANLEY-Columbus County, NC-clerk of Superior Court.

LEADER PRINT-Brookhaven, MS-flyer.

H. K. ROUSE-Pearl River County, MS-clerk of Chancery Court.

REEDER-Item artist.

G. H. CRETIN-Opelousas, LA-proprietor of Lacombe Hotel.

GEORGE AND BEDDIE ANDERSON-Robeson County, NC-Julia's parents.

W. H. KINLAW-Robeson County, NC-notary public.

C. B. SKIPPER-Robeson County, NC-clerk of Superior Court.

THEO. N. VAIL-president of Western Union.

C. W. ZIMMERMAN-Picayune, MS-president Cybur Lumber Company.

CYRIL LOUISELL-Picayune, MS-vice-president Cybur Lumber Company.

C. J. COPPOCK-Picayune, MS-secretary and treasurer Cybur Lumber Company.

ALFRED S. AMER-general manager of The St. Charles Hotel in New Orleans.

W. J. QUINN, JR.-manager of The St. Charles Hotel in New Orleans.

MARION B. MONROE-New Orleans, LA-traveling evangelist.

J. C. BARNES-Lumberton, NC-cashier at bank.

Chapter Sixteen

SHARON BOND-Pearl River County, MS-teacher-historian on Bobby Dunbar story.

ALLISON BULLOCK-Columbia, MS-author-historian on Bobby Dunbar story.

Bibliography

Abbreviation *WCWDF*—William Cantwell Walters' Defense File © by Allison Rawls Bullock.

Mizpah page numbers are in parentheses at the end of each listing.

Alsobrook, Ben. Habeas Corpus transcript. *WCWDF* #200. (142)
  The Trial. Document. Trial notes. *WCWDF* #320. Articles. *The New Orleans Item* April 15-28, 1914. *The Times-Picayune* [New Orleans, LA] April 15-28, 1914. *The New Orleans Daily States* April 15-28, 1914. (197-225)
Amacker, G. W. Affidavit. *WCWDF* #80. (105)
  The Trial. Document. Trial notes. *WCWDF* #320. Articles. *The New Orleans Item* April 15-28, 1914. *The Times-Picayune* [New Orleans, LA] April 15-28, 1914. *The New Orleans Daily States* April 15-28, 1914. (197-225)
Amacker, J. J. Document. Habeas Corpus transcript. *WCWDF* #200. (142)
Anderson, Beddie. Julia's mother. Affidavit. *WCWDF* #242. (302)
Anderson, Charlie Bruce. Robeson County, NC. Son of Julia. Interviews. Hollis E. Rawls and Jewel Tarver Rawls. 2002 to 2008. (XVII) "The Famous Case of Bobby Dunbar." *The Morning Advocate* [Baton Rouge, LA.] October 10, 1948. (XXVII)
  Document. Quote. "No, my name is Bruce." Document. *WCWDF* #151. (32)
  Quote. "You are...mama." *The Daily States* April 22, 1913. (32)
  Document. Habeas Corpus transcript. *WCWDF* #200. (135-154)
  Quote. Article. Herman J. Seiferth and S. W. Ray. "Bobbie Dunbar Tells Of The Death Of Bruce: Tells Of Bruce's Death: Walters was inside." *The Times-Picayune* [New Orleans, LA] April 18, 1914. (156)
  (Bruce-Bobbie) The Trial. Document. Motion for a new trial. *WCWDF* #350. Articles. *The New Orleans Item* April 15-28, 1914.

The Times-Picayune [New Orleans, LA] April 15-28, 1914. *The New Orleans Daily States* April 15-28, 1914. (197-225)

Unknown. Photo. "Latest picture." *The New Orleans Item* June 9, 1913. (261)

Unknown. Photo. "Hero, 'Villian,' And Other Characters." *The New Orleans Item* June 8, 1913. (262)

Unknown. Photo. "Which is the mother of this boy?" *The New Orleans Item* April 9, 1914. (263)

Unknown. Photo. "Is this Bobbie Dunbar or Bruce Anderson?" *The New Orleans Item* April 11, 1914. (264)

Morel, V. Sketch. "Justice weighs pleas in fight of mothers." *The New Orleans Item* April 14, 1914. (267)

Harvey, H. J. Photo. "This Picture." *The New Orleans Item* April 12, 1914. (268)

Unknown. Photo. "Can these eyes solve Walters-Dunbar case?" *The New Orleans Item* April 15, 1914. (269)

Unknown. Photo. "Can you pick the boy by his nose?" *The New Orleans Item* April 16, 1914. (270)

Unknown. Photo. "Their mouths." *The New Orleans Item* April 17, 1914. (270)

Unknown. Photo. "Compare the full faces now." *The New Orleans Item* April 19, 1914. (271)

Trist. Sketch. "Trist has here portrayed Walters." *The New Orleans Item* April 20, 1914. (271)

Unknown. Photo. "Four of the stars in the Dunbar-Walters case: Mr. and Mrs. C. P. Dunbar." *The New Orleans Daily States* April 15, 1914. (272)

Maxwell. Photo. "Bobbie now is camera man." *The New Orleans Daily States* April 10, 1914. (272)

Unknown. Photo. "The boy called Bobbie." *The New Orleans Item* April 21, 1914. (272)

Unknown. Photo. *WCWDF #4.* (278)

Unknown. Photo. *WCWDF #3.* (279)

Unknown. Photo. *WCWDF #5.* (284)

Photo. Jacobs News Depot Company. Opelousas, LA. *WCWDF #6.* (284)

Harvey, H. J. Photo. *The New Orleans Item* April 23, 1913. (319)

Unknown. Photo. "Bruce and Alonzo." Courtesy of Sharon Bond. (320)

Unknown. Photo. "Bobby." *The Morning Advocate* [Baton Rouge, LA.] October 10, 1948. (321)

Anderson, George W. Julia's father. Affidavit. *WCWDF* #242. (302)

Anderson, H. G. Physician. Affidavit. Quote. "They made a special and close examination of his left foot." *WCWDF* #312. (15, 18, 32,189-191, 305)

The Trial. Document. Trial notes. *WCWDF* #320. Articles. *The New Orleans Item* April 15-28, 1914. *The Times-Picayune* [New Orleans, LA] April 15-28, 1914. *The New Orleans Daily States* April 15-28, 1914. (197-225)

Anderson, Julia. Robeson County, NC. Bruce's mother. Interviews. Hollis E. Rawls and Jewel Rawls Tarver. 2002 to 2008. (XVII)

Affidavit. *WCWDF* #104. (73, 74, 105,113, 291)

Letter. *WCWDF* #55. (95, 286)

Letter. *WCWDF* #116. (115)

Letter. *WCWDF* #208. (156)

Letter. *WCWDF* #235. (172)

Letter. *WCWDF* #246. (174)

Unknown. Article. Julia to Savannah. *The New Orleans Item* September 12, 1913. (175)

The Trial. Document. Trial notes. *WCWDF* #320. Document. Motion for new trial. *WCWDF* #350. Articles. *The New Orleans Item* April 15-28, 1914. *The Times-Picayune* [New Orleans, LA] April 15-28, 1914. *The New Orleans Daily States* April 15-28, 1914. (197-225)

Unknown. Article. "Julia Anderson Longs To Look Upon Bobbie In Court." *The New Orleans Item* April 16, 1914. (204)

Letter. *WCWDF* #390. (239)

Unknown. Photo. "Julia Anderson." *The Times-Democrat* [New Orleans, LA] May 1, 1913. (261)

Unknown. Photo. "Which is the mother of this boy?" *The New Orleans Item* April 9, 1914. (263)

Morel, V. Sketch. "Justice weighs pleas in fight of mothers." *The New Orleans Item* April 14, 1914. (267)

Unknown. Photo. "Can these eyes solve Walters-Dunbar case?" *The New Orleans Item* April 15, 1914. (269)

Unknown. Photo. "Can you pick the boy by his nose?" *The New Orleans Item* April 16, 1914. (270)

Unknown. Photo. "Their mouths." *The New Orleans Item* April 17, 1914. (270)

Unknown. Photo. "Compare the full faces now." *The New Orleans Item* April 19, 1914. (271)

Unknown. Photo. "Latest photographs." *The New Orleans Item* April 15, 1914. (173)

Letter. *The New Orleans Item* April 21, 1914. (276)

Unknown. Photo. Julia. Courtesy of Sharon Bond. (319)

Ansley, Frank. Carpenter. Port Barre, LA. Document. Habeas Corpus transcript. *WCWDF* #200. (151-154)

The Trial. Document. Trial notes. *WCWDF* #320. Articles. *The New Orleans Item* April 15-28, 1914. *The Times-Picayune* [New Orleans, LA] April 15-28, 1914. *The New Orleans Daily States* April 15-28, 1914. (197-225)

Trist. Sketch. "Principal Witnesses for State." *The New Orleans Item* April 18, 1914. (274)

Archer, D. L. Official. *WCWDF* #74. (289)

Barnes, K. M. Letter. *WCWDF* #393. (241)

Barnett, J. P. Opelousas, LA. The Trial. Articles. *The New Orleans Item* April 15-28, 1914. *The Times-Picayune* [New Orleans, LA] April 15-28, 1914. *The New Orleans Daily States* April 15-28, 1914. (197-225)

Bass, C. C. Physician. Letter. *WCWDF* #325. (219)

Bass, W. Carl. Affidavit. *WCWDF* #77. (105)

Habeas Corpus transcript. *WCWDF* #200. (140-141)

The Trial. Document. Trial notes. *WCWDF* #320. Articles. *The New Orleans Item* April 15-28, 1914. *The Times-Picayune* [New Orleans, LA] April 15-28, 1914. *The New Orleans Daily States* April 15-28, 1914. (197-225)

Unknown. Photo. "Here are some of the witnesses." *The New Orleans Item* April 13, 1914. (273)

Bayliss, George. Unknown. Photo. "Here are some of the witnesses." *The New Orleans Item* April 13, 1914. (273)

Bennett, E. C. Reverend. Longville, LA. The Trial. Document. Trial notes. *WCWDF* #320. Articles. *The New Orleans Item* April 15-28, 1914. *The Times-Picayune* [New Orleans, LA] April 15-28, 1914. *The New Orleans Daily States* April 15-28, 1914. (197-225)

Bennett, Steve. Poplarville, MS. The Trial. Document. Trial notes. *WCWDF* #320. Articles. *The New Orleans Item* April 15-28, 1914. *The Times-Picayune* [New Orleans, LA] April 15-28, 1914. *The New Orleans Daily States* April 15-28, 1914. (197-225)

Trist. Sketch. "Principal Witnesses for State." *The New Orleans Item*

April 18, 1914. (274)

Benz, George. Item reporter. "Item Reporter, With Dunbars." *The New Orleans Item* April 23, 1913. (22)

Article. "Harry Mounger." *The New Orleans Item* April 23, 1913. (34)

Article. "Big Deputy Sheriff: With a baby jackknife." *The New Orleans Item* April 23, 1913. (35)

Article. "Back To Carolina." *The New Orleans Item* May 3, 1913. (86)

Article. *The New Orleans Daily States* June 6, 1913. *WCWDF* #328. (292)

Bercier, Edwin T. Article. "Bobbie Fell In As Usual: There's no question." *The Times-Democrat* [New Orleans, Louisiana] May 2, 1913. (87)

Bercier, Mrs. Opelousas, LA. The Trial. Document. Trial notes. *WCWDF* #320. Articles. *The New Orleans Item* April 15-28, 1914. *The Times-Picayune* [New Orleans, LA] April 15-28, 1914. *The New Orleans Daily States* April 15-28, 1914. (197-225)

Bilbo, Jeptha. Bilbo, MS. Post office and boarding house. (XXI, 322) Document. The Dunbar Investigation. *WCWDF* #115. (118-120)

Document. Habeas Corpus transcript. *WCWDF* #200. (142-145) The Trial. Articles. *The New Orleans Item* April 15-28, 1914. *The Times-Picayune* [New Orleans, LA] April 15-28, 1914. *The New Orleans Daily States* April 15-28, 1914. (197-225) Unknown. Photo. "Hero, 'Villian,' And Other Characters." *The New Orleans Item* June 8, 1913. (262)

Bilbo, Matilda (Mrs. Jeptha). Bilbo, MS. Post office and boarding house. (XXI, 322) Quote. "Bruce was actually sitting in my lap." *The New Orleans Item* June 18, 1913. (31) Transcript. The Dunbar Investigation. *WCWDF* #115. (120-123) The Trial. Articles. *The New Orleans Item* April 15-28, 1914. *The Times-Picayune* [New Orleans, LA] April 15-28, 1914. *The New Orleans Daily States* April 15-28, 1914. (197-225) Unknown. Photo. "Hero, 'Villian,' And Other Characters." *The New Orleans Item* June 8, 1913. (262)

Blair, Sam. Item reporter. Article. "The Death Penalty will be Demanded." *The New Orleans Item* April 11, 1914. (192) Articles. *The New Orleans Item* April 15-28, 1914. (197-225) Article. "Walters Loses His Smile: First Held All Smiles: A week ago." *The New Orleans Item* April 17, 1914. (208)

Article. "Walters Makes His Appeal To The Jury." *The New Orleans Item* April 25, 1914. (221)

Article. "Possible Violence Causes The Court To Protect The Tinker." *The New Orleans Item* April 27, 1914. (223)

Article. "Recites His Epitaph: Of course, I still have lots of hope." *The New Orleans Item* April 28, 1914. (226)

Blank, John. Investigator. Letter. *WCWDF* #328. (43, 292)

Letter. *WCWDF* #101. (111, 292)

Letter. *WCWDF* #221. (158-160, 300)

Letter. *WCWDF* #216. (160)

Bledsoe, D. L. Iron City, GA. Unknown Article. "Walters, Divorcee, Once A Prominent Georgia Merchant." *The New Orleans Item* April 14, 1914. (13)

The Trial. Document. Trial notes. *WCWDF* #320. Articles. *The New Orleans Item* April 15-28, 1914. *The Times-Picayune* [New Orleans, LA] April 15-28, 1914. *The New Orleans Daily States* April 15-28, 1914. (197-225)

Letter. *WCWDF* #392. (240, 310)

Affidavit. *WCWDF* #17. (280)

Letter. *WCWDF* #269. (303)

Bledsoe, Mrs. D. L. Iron City, GA. Affidavit. *WCWDF* #17. (280)

Boagni, Charles F. Physician. The Trial. Document. Trial notes. *WCWDF* #320. Articles. *The New Orleans Item* April 15-28, 1914. *The Times-Picayune* [New Orleans, LA] April 15-28, 1914. *The New Orleans Daily States* April 15-28, 1914. (80, 197-225)

Bond, Sharon. Harvey, H. J. Photo. *The New Orleans Item* April 23, 1913. (319)

Unknown. Photo. Julia. (319)

Photo. "Bruce and Alonzo." (320)

Bourdier, Lillian. Article. "The famous case of Bobbie Dunbar." *The Morning Advocate* [Baton Rouge, LA] October 10, 1948. (XXVII, 325)

Bowden, Miss Fannie. The Trial. Document. Trial notes. *WCWDF* #320. Articles. *The New Orleans Item* April 15-28, 1914. *The Times-Picayune* [New Orleans, LA] April 15-28, 1914. *The New Orleans Daily States* April 15-28, 1914. (197-225)

Brewer, Earl. Governor of Mississippi. Letter. *WCWDF* #32. (64, 282)

Letter. *WCWDF* #94. (104, 109, 113)

"The Dunbar Investigation." *WCWDF* #115. (117, 118)

Letter. *WCWDF* #185. (130, 296)

Brown, E. Garland. Attorney. Quote. *WCWDF* #70. (104)

Quote. *WCWDF* #71. (104)

Letter. *WCWDF* #218. (135)

Brown, E. K. Justice of Peace. *WCWDF* #104. (105, 291)

Buck, W. J. Secretary to Mississippi's governor. Letter. *WCWDF* #14. (57)

Letter. *WCWDF* #185. (130, 296)

Budden, Mr. The Trial. Document. Trial notes. *WCWDF* #320. Articles. *The New Orleans Item* April 15-28, 1914. *The Times-Picayune* [New Orleans, LA] April 15-28, 1914. *The New Orleans Daily States* April 15-28, 1914. (197-225)

Bullock, Allison Rawls. Interview. Rachel Thompson Rowley. 2005. (XXIV)

Description of camping at Swayze Lake. *WCWDF* #320: Article. "Father Of Bobbie Is First Witness." S. W. Ray. *The Times Picayune* [New Orleans, LA] April 16, 1914: Letter. Dr. A. J. Strange. *WCWDF* #42. (1-8)

Map of Cantwell and Bruce's route. (318)

Photo. Bilbo House. 1994. (322)

Painting. Bilbo House. 1995. (322)

Bullock, Joel. Robeson County, NC. (XXIII)

Burks, Maggie. Affidavit. *WCWDF* #316. (306)

Document. *WCWDF* #317. (306)

Burns, W. J. Unknown. Article. "Burns Men Help Him." *The New Orleans Item* April 25, 1913. (48)

Carlton, D. L. Acting Attorney General. Washington, D. C. *WCWDF* #241. (163)

Collins, Kate. Poplarville, MS. The Trial. Document. Trial notes. *WCWDF* #320. Document. Motion for new trial. *WCWDF* #350. Articles. *The New Orleans Item* April 15-28, 1914. *The Times-Picayune* [New Orleans, LA] April 15-28, 1914. *The New Orleans Daily States* April 15-28, 1914. (197-225)

Trist. Sketch. "Principal Witnesses for State." *The New Orleans Item* April 18, 1914. (274)

Columbian Progress, The. Columbia, MS. Unknown. Photo. August 10, 2002. (321)

Cowart, M. A. Article. "Biggest Event In Bobbie's Life When He Meets

Grandpa." *The New Orleans Item* April 22, 1914. (18, 217)

Cowart, Mrs. J. M. Iron City, GA. Affidavit. *WCWDF #17*. (280)

Crisler, Adele Rawls (Dell). Interviews. 2002 to 2008. (XXIV)

Interview. "Hollis had spent much of his childhood." 2002 to 2008. (28)

Interview. "A ruptured appendix." 2002 to 2008. (33)

Interviews. "Bobby Dunbar's" visit to Hollis C. Rawls. 2002 to 2008. (324)

Cutright, Margaret Dunbar. Bruce's granddaughter. Interviews. 2002 to 2006. (XVIII-XXIV)

Interviews. Sebe Frilot. 2002 to 2006. (4)

Interviews. "Percy was rumored to have had many affairs." 2002 to 2006. (5, 10)

Interviews. Bruce and Alonzo's childhood. 2002. (324)

Broadcast. "The Ghost of Bobby Dunbar." *This American Life WBEZ Chicago, Public Radio International* March 14, 2008. (328)

Publication. "A Case for Solomon." *Free Press Simon & Schuster, Inc.* [New York] 2012. (328)

Dale and Rawls. Attorneys. Document. *WCWDF #350*. (115)

Document. Habeas Corpus application. *WCWDF #157*. (131)

Document. Habeas Corpus transcript. *WCWDF #200*. (135-154)

Appeal. *WCWDF #212*. (155)

The Trial. Trial notes. Document. *WCWDF #320*. Document. Motion for new trial. *WCWDF #350*. Articles. *The New Orleans Item* April 15-28, 1914. *The Times-Picayune* [New Orleans, LA] April 15-28, 1914. *The New Orleans Daily States* April 15-28, 1914. (197-225)

Document. *WCWDF #350*. (231)

Documents. Bills of Exception. *WCWDF #'s* 353, 354, 355, and 356. (237)

Appeal. *WCWDF #396*. (240)

Letter. *WCWDF #435*. (244)

Letter. *WCWDF #460*. (247)

Application for Bail. *WCWDF #493*. (253)

Letter. *WCWDF #499*. (255)

Dale, Tom S. Columbia, MS. Attorney. (XVIII)

Letter. *WCWDF #8*. (43)

Letter. *WCWDF #16*. (62)

Letter. *WCWDF #12*. (69)

Letter. *WCWDF #83*. (103)

Quote. Letter. *WCWDF* #102. (110)

"The Dunbar Investigation." *WCWDF* #115. (117-125)

Quote. *WCWDF* #216. (160)

Appeal. *WCWDF* #396. (240)

Letter. *WCWDF* #479. (250)

Letter. *WCWDF* #492. (253)

Application for Bail. *WCWDF* #493. (253)

Letter. *WCWDF* #502. (256)

Unknown. Photo. "Hero, 'Villian,' And Other Characters." *The New Orleans Item* June 8, 1913. (262)

Unknown. Photo. "Attorneys in the Walters-Dunbar case." *The New Orleans Item* April 12, 1914. (267)

Daly, Lawrence. Physician. The Trial. Document. Trial notes. *WCWDF* #320. Articles. *The New Orleans Item* April 15-28, 1914. *The Times-Picayune* [New Orleans, LA] April 15-28, 1914. *The New Orleans Daily States* April 15-28, 1914. (197-225)

Dantin, A. B. Boiler maker. Alexandria, LA. Habeas Corpus transcript. *WCWDF* #200. (151, 154)

The Trial. Document. Trial notes. *WCWDF* #320. Articles. *The New Orleans Item* April 15-28, 1914. *The Times-Picayune* [New Orleans, LA] April 15-28, 1914. *The New Orleans Daily States* April 15-28, 1914. (197-225)

Darrel, Roderick. *Darrel of the Blessed Isles* Irving Bacheller. 1903. http://www.gutenberg.org/ebooks/12102. (15)

Davis, R. B. Affidavit. *WCWDF* #357. (236)

Day, C. A. Charlie. Sheriff. Receipt. April 22, 1913. Courtesty of Jarvis Lowe and the Marion County Historical Society. [Columbia, MS]. (24, 279)

The Trial. Document. Trial notes. *WCWDF* #320. Articles. *The New Orleans Item* April 15-28, 1914. *The Times-Picayune* [New Orleans, LA] April 15-28, 1914. *The New Orleans Daily States* April 15-28, 1914. (197-225)

Unknown. Photo. *WCWDF* #3. (279)

Day, Charles. Hokes Bluff. Unknown. Photo. "Here are some of the witnesses." *The New Orleans Item* April 13, 1914. (273)

DeVerges, Lucille. Unknown. Photo. *WCWDF* #5. (284)

Donald, G. M. Affidavit. *WCWDF* #72. (105, 287)

Habeas Corpus transcript. *WCWDF* #200. (135-137)

The Trial. Document. Trial notes. *WCWDF* #320. Articles. *The New*

Orleans Item April 15-28, 1914. *The Times-Picayune* [New Orleans, LA] April 15-28, 1914. *The New Orleans Daily States* April 15-28, 1914. (197-225)

Dubuisson, E. B. Opelousas, LA. Attorney. The Trial. Document. Trial notes. *WCWDF #320.* Document. Motion for a new trial. *WCWDF #350.* Articles. *The New Orleans Item* April 15-28, 1914. *The Times-Picayune* [New Orleans, LA] April 15-28, 1914. *The New Orleans Daily States* April 15-28, 1914. (197-225)
Document. *WCWDF #350.* (231)
Document. Motion in arrest of judgment. *WCWDF #352.* (237)
Documents. Bills of Exception. *WCWDF #'s* 353, 354, 355, and 356. (237)
Appeal. *WCWDF #396.* (240)
Letter. *WCWDF #475.* (249)
Letter. *WCWDF #477.* (250)
Unknown. Photo. "Attorneys in the Walters-Dunbar case." *The New Orleans Item* April 12, 1914. (267)

Dunbar, Alonzo. H. J. Harvey. Photo. "This Picture." *The New Orleans Item* April 12, 1914. (169)
Unknown. Photo. "Can these eyes solve Walters-Dunbar case?" *The New Orleans Item* April 15, 1914. (269)
Unknown. Photo. "Can you pick the boy by his nose?" *The New Orleans Item* April 16, 1914. (270)
Unknown. Photo. "Their mouths." *The New Orleans Item* April 17, 1914. (270)
Unknown. Photo. "Compare the full faces now." *The New Orleans Item* April 19, 1914. (271)
Unknown. Photo. "Four of the stars in the Dunbar-Walters case: Mr. and Mrs. C. P. Dunbar." *The New Orleans Daily States* April 15, 1914. (272)
Unknown. Photo. "Bruce and Alonzo." Courtesy of Sharon Bond. (320)

Dunbar, Archie. Article. "Uncle Did Not Claim Boy." *The Times-Democrat* [New Orleans, Louisiana] April 24, 1913. (10, 15)
Unknown. Photo. "Latest picture." *The New Orleans Item* June 9, 1913. (261)

Dunbar, C. Percy. Opelousas, LA. Realtor. Bobby's father. Interview. Margaret Dunbar Cutright. 2002. (XVIII)
Quote. Unknown. Article. "We found only the boy's little straw hat."

The New Orleans Item April 22, 1913. Unknown. Article. "Where Is The Other Boy?: As if Goblin had Whisked Him Away: Only a little hat." *The New Orleans Item* April 9, 1914. Unknown. Article. "Are These Pictures: Robert Disappears: His cap was found." *The New Orleans Item* February 13, 1914. (9)

Quote. "If I do not find that child." Jack F. Storm. Affidavit. *WCWDF* #153. June 14, 1913. (19)

Article. Ray, S. W. "Father Of Bobbie Is First Witness: Asks For Photos: ...I couldn't find the scar then." *The Times-Picayune* [New Orleans, LA] April 16, 1914. (21)

Quote. "Those toes are exactly like Bobby's!" *The Times-Democrat* [New Orleans, LA] April 24, 1913. (21)

Unknown. Article. "Dunbars Bring 'Stolen Son' Here: Trip from Columbia: Walters would be lynched." *The New Orleans Item* April 23, 1913. (23)

Receipt. April 22, 1913. Courtesy of Jarvis Lowe and the Marion County Historical Society. [Columbia, MS]. (24, 279)

Quote. "My wife and I found whip marks." Interview. Margaret Dunbar Cutright. 2002. (30)

Article. Minion Hall. "Don't Hang Him: Three Witnesses for Walters: I immediately told Mr. Dunbar that a mistake had been made: Mr. Dunbar promised." *The New Orleans Item* April 12, 1914. (32-34)

Unknown. Article. Theater Manager Says Dunbar Asked $1,000." *The New Orleans Daily States* June 6, 1913. *WCWDF* #328. (43, 292)

Unknown. Article. "Asks Brewer To Act: In a spirit of fairness." *The Times-Democrat* [New Orleans, LA] April 24, 1913. (53)

Coded message. *The New Orleans Item* Want ads. July 29, 1913: Document. *WCWDF* #221. (159, 300)

The Trial. Trial notes. Document. *WCWDF* #320. Document. Motion for new trial. *WCWDF* #350. Articles. *The New Orleans Item* April 15-28, 1914. *The Times-Picayune* [New Orleans, LA] April 15-28, 1914. *The New Orleans Daily States* April 15-28, 1914. (197-225)

Harvey, H. J. Photo. "This Picture." *The New Orleans Item* April 12, 1914. (268)

Unknown. Photo. "Can these eyes solve Walters-Dunbar case?" *The New Orleans Item* April 15, 1914. (269)

Unknown. Photo. "Can you pick the boy by his nose?" *The New*

Orleans Item April 16, 1914. (270)

Unknown. Photo. "Their mouths." *The New Orleans Item* April 17, 1914. (270)

Unknown. Photo. "Compare the full faces now." *The New Orleans Item* April 19, 1914. (271)

Unknown. Photo. "Four of the stars in the Dunbar-Walters case: Mr. and Mrs. C. P. Dunbar." *The New Orleans Daily States* April 15, 1914. (272)

Dunbar, F. M. Unknown. Photo. "Latest picture." *The New Orleans Item* June 9, 1913. (261)

Dunbar Investigation, The. Transcript. *WCWDF* #115. (117-125)

Dunbar, John. Bruce's son. "The Famous Case of Bobby Dunbar." *The Morning Advocate* [Baton Rouge, LA.] October 10, 1948. (XXVII)

Unknown. Photo. *The Morning Advocate* [Baton Rouge, LA] October 10, 1948. (321)

Dunbar, Katie. Quote. "If you do, the ugly old man will get you." *The New Orleans Item* June 7, 1913. (116)

The Trial. Document. Trial notes. *WCWDF* #320. Articles. *The New Orleans Item* April 15-28, 1914. *The Times-Picayune* [New Orleans, LA] April 15-28, 1914. *The New Orleans Daily States* April 15-28, 1914. (197-225)

Dunbar, Lessie. Opelousas, LA. Bobby's mother. Interview. Margaret Dunbar Cutright. 2002. (XVIII)

Prayer. Memorare. "Remember O Most Gracious Virgin Mary." http://www.ourladyswarriors.org/prayer/memorare.htm. (9)

Unknown. Article. "Father Tells Of Long Search: Don't Lynch Him: Please Don't Lynch Walters" *The New Orleans Item* April 22, 1913.

Unknown. Article. "Tinker in Opelousas: I do not want Walters hanged for this crime, as I know that he was not cruel to my child." *The New Orleans Item* May 9, 1913. (23)

Quote. "Asks Item To Thank Ladies of Hub, Miss.: To the good ladies of Hub." *The New Orleans Item* April 23, 1913. (42)

Unknown. Article. "Says Bilbo Test Means Nothing: No Fear for Walters. Mrs. Dunbar was ill." *The New Orleans Item* June 6, 1913. (116)

Quote. "Don't Hang Him." Minion Hall. Article. *The New Orleans Item* April 12, 1914. (195)

The Trial. Document. Trial notes. *WCWDF* #320. Document. Motion for new trial. *WCWDF* #350. Articles. *The New Orleans Item*

April 15-28, 1914. *The Times-Picayune* [New Orleans, LA] April 15-28, 1914. *The New Orleans Daily States* April 15-28, 1914. (197-225)

Unknown. Photo. "Latest picture." *The New Orleans Item* June 9, 1913. (261)

Unknown. Photo. "Which is the mother of this boy?" *The New Orleans Item* April 9, 1914. (263)

Morel, V. Sketch. "Justice weighs pleas in fight of mothers." *The New Orleans Item* April 14, 1914. (267)

Harvey, H. J. Photo. "This Picture." *The New Orleans Item* April 12, 1914. (268)

Unknown. Photo. "Can these eyes solve Walters-Dunbar case?" *The New Orleans Item* April 15, 1914. (269)

Unknown. Photo. "Can you pick the boy by his nose?" *The New Orleans Item* April 16, 1914. (270)

Unknown. Photo. "Their mouths." *The New Orleans Item* April 17, 1914. (270)

Unknown. Photo. "Compare the full faces now." *The New Orleans Item* April 19, 1914. (271)

Unknown. Photo. "Four of the stars in the Dunbar-Walters case: Mr. and Mrs. C. P. Dunbar." *The New Orleans Daily States* April 15, 1914. (272)

Harvey, H. J. Photo. *The New Orleans Item* April 23, 1913. (319)

Dunbar, Marjorie Byers. Bruce's wife. (XXVII)

Unknown. Photo. *The Morning Advocate* [Baton Rouge, LA] October 10, 1948. (321)

Dunbar, Mary. Bruce's daughter. "The Famous Case of Bobby Dunbar." *The Morning Advocate* [Baton Rouge, LA.] October 10,1948. (XXVII)

Unknown. Photo. *The Morning Advocate* [Baton Rouge, Louisiana] October 10, 1948. (321)

Dunbar, Mrs. F. M. Unknown. Photo. "Latest picture." *The New Orleans Item* June 9, 1913. (261)

Dunbar, Robert (Bobby). Opelousas, LA. Interview. Margaret Dunbar Cutright. 2002. (XVII)

"The Famous Case of Bobby Dunbar." *The Morning Advocate* [Baton Rouge, LA.] October 10,1948. (XXVII)

Burn treatment. Mölnlycke Health Care. Article. December 28, 2011. "Burn care: a historical perspective." http://www.molnlycke.com/com/Knowledge/Burn-care/Burn-care-a-historical-perspective/. (7)

Unknown. Photo. "Can these eyes solve Walters-Dunbar case?" *The New Orleans Item* April 15, 1914. (269)

Unknown. Photo. "Can you pick the boy by his nose?" *The New Orleans Item* April 16, 1914. (270)

Unknown. Photo. "Their mouths." *The New Orleans Item* April 17, 1914. (270)

Unknown. Photo. "Compare the full faces now." *The New Orleans Item* April 19, 1914. (271)

Unknown. Photo. *WCWDF #2*. (278)

Dunbar, Robert. Percy's father. The Trial. Document. Trial notes. *WCWDF #320*. Articles. *The New Orleans Item* April 15-28, 1914. *The Times-Picayune* [New Orleans, LA] April 15-28, 1914. *The New Orleans Daily States* April 15-28, 1914. (197-225)

Dunbar, Robert Jr. (Bob Jr.) Bruce's son. (XIX)
"The Famous Case of Bobby Dunbar." *The Morning Advocate* [Baton Rouge, LA.] October 10,1948. (XXVII)

Unknown. Photo. *The Morning Advocate* [Baton Rouge, LA] October 10, 1948. (321)

Unknown. Photo. *The Columbian Progress* [Columbia, MS] August 10, 2002. (321)

Dunbar, Mrs. Robert. Percy's mother. The Trial. Document. Trial notes. *WCWDF #320*. Articles. *The New Orleans Item* April 15-28, 1914. *The Times-Picayune* [New Orleans, LA] April 15-28, 1914. *The New Orleans Daily States* April 15-28, 1914. (197-225)

Dunbar, Wallace. Percy's cousin. Document. Trial notes. *WCWDF #320*. Articles. *The New Orleans Item* April 15-28, 1914. *The Times-Picayune* [New Orleans, LA] April 15-28, 1914. *The New Orleans Daily States* April 15-28, 1914. (4, 197-225)

Dupree, Leon. The Trial. Articles. *The New Orleans Item* April 15-28, 1914. *The Times-Picayune* [New Orleans, LA] April 15-28, 1914. *The New Orleans Daily States* April 15-28, 1914. (80, 197-225)

Dupree, Mrs. Jack. Lessie's sister. The Trial. Document. Trial notes. *WCWDF #320*. Articles. *The New Orleans Item* April 15-28, 1914. *The Times-Picayune* [New Orleans, LA] April 15-28, 1914. *The New Orleans Daily States* April 15-28, 1914. (197-225)

Eastham, Mr. The Trial. Document. Trial notes. *WCWDF #320*. Articles. *The New Orleans Item* April 15-28, 1914. *The Times-Picayune* [New Orleans, LA] April 15-28, 1914. *The New Orleans Daily States* April 15-28, 1914. (197-225)

Edwards, Alex. The Trial. Articles. *The New Orleans Item* April 15-28, 1914. *The Times-Picayune* [New Orleans, LA] April 15-28, 1914. *The New Orleans Daily States* April 15-28, 1914. (197-225)

Edwards, John. Affidavit. *WCWDF* #18. (63, 280)

Estorage, Henry. Opelousas, LA. Habeas Corpus transcript. *WCWDF* #200. (24, 149)
  The Trial. Articles. *The New Orleans Item* April 15-28, 1914. *The Times-Picayune* [New Orleans, LA] April 15-28, 1914. *The New Orleans Daily States* April 15-28, 1914. (197-225)

Fortenberry, John. The Trial. Document. Trial notes. *WCWDF* #320. Articles. *The New Orleans Item* April 15-28, 1914. *The Times-Picayune* [New Orleans, LA] April 15-28, 1914. *The New Orleans Daily States* April 15-28, 1914. (197-225)

Fortenberry, Otto. Columbia, MS. Jailer. The Trial. Document. Trial notes. *WCWDF* #320. Articles. *The New Orleans Item* April 15-28, 1914. *The Times-Picayune* [New Orleans, LA] April 15-28, 1914. *The New Orleans Daily States* April 15-28, 1914. (197-225)

Fox, Harold. Quotes. Unknown. Article. "Search For Bruce Nears End: S. H. Fox…trying to build up a chain of circumstantial evidence. The Anderson boy was swapped: The Bilbo's…say that the boy…had a web foot." *The New Orleans Item* May 13, 1913. (102)
  The Trial. Articles. *The New Orleans Item* April 15-28, 1914. *The Times-Picayune* [New Orleans, LA] April 15-28, 1914. *The New Orleans Daily States* April 15-28, 1914. (197-225)
  Unknown. Photo. "Latest picture." *The New Orleans Item* June 9, 1913. (261)

Fox, Mrs. Harold. Unknown. Photo. "Latest picture." *The New Orleans Item* June 9, 1913. (261)
  Harvey. Photo. "This Picture." *The New Orleans Item* April 12, 1914. (268)

Frank, Mr. Louisiana agent. (115)

Galloway, Joseph. Letter. *WCWDF* #31. (64, 281)

Gar. Article. http://en.wikipedia.org//wiki/gar. (1, 2)

Garland, R. Lee. Attorney. Letter. *WCWDF* #88. (105)
  Transcript. "The Dunbar Investigation." *WCWDF* #115. (117-125)
  Habeas Corpus transcript. *WCWDF* #200. (136-154)
  The Trial. Document. Motion for new trial. *WCWDF* #350. Articles. *The New Orleans Item* April 15-28, 1914. *The Times-Picayune* [New Orleans, LA] April 15-28, 1914. *The New Orleans Daily States* April

15-28, 1914. (197-225)

Goleman, J. Allen. Spanking. Quote. "He whipped the child, but under circumstances which I thought were justifiable." *The Times Democrat* [New Orleans, Louisiana] April 26, 1913. (30)

Transcript. "The Dunbar Investigation." *WCWDF* #115. (124)

The Trial. Document. Trial notes. *WCWDF* #320. Articles. *The New Orleans Item* April 15-28, 1914. *The Times-Picayune* [New Orleans, LA] April 15-28, 1914. *The New Orleans Daily States* April 15-28, 1914. (197-225)

Unknown. Photo. "Here are some of the witnesses." *The New Orleans Item* April 13, 1914. (273) Affidavit. *WCWDF* #139. (295)

Goleman, Mrs. J. A. (Sarah). "The Dunbar Investigation." *WCWDF* #115. (117, 124)

Affidavit. *WCWDF* #139. (295)

Haas, J. A. Physician. The Trial. Articles. *The New Orleans Item* April 15-28, 1914. *The Times-Picayune* [New Orleans, LA] April 15-28, 1914. *The New Orleans Daily States* April 15-28, 1914. (80) (197-225)

Habeas Corpus transcript. *WCWDF* #200. (131, 135-154)

Unknown. Photo. "Here are some of the witnesses." *The New Orleans Item* April 13, 1914. (273)

Hall, Luther. Louisiana Governor. *WCWDF* #200. (24)

Hall, Mignon. Article. "Biggest Event In Bobbie's Life When He Meets Grandpa." *The New Orleans Item* April 22, 1914. (10)

"Don't Hang Him: Three Witnesses for Walters: I immediately told Mr. Dunbar that a mistake had been made." *The New Orleans Item* April 11, 1914. (32-34)

Article. "Vision of Death Comes to the Tinker." *The New Orleans Item* April 12, 1914. (193)

Article. "Hug and Kiss Seal Greeting of Walters and Julia Anderson." *The New Orleans Item* April 14, 1914. (194)

Article. "Don't Hang Him." *The New Orleans Item* April 12, 1914. Unknown. Article. "2 Fakers and The Facts: The first count they made." *The New Orleans Item* April 14,1914. (195)

The Trial. Articles. *The New Orleans Item* April 15-28, 1914. (197-225)

Article. "Half delirious, Julia Anderson pleads she may get her boy Bruce." *The New Orleans Item* April 20, 1914. (213)

Hall, Toxey. District Attorney. Columbia, MS. Habeas Corpus transcript. *WCWDF* #200. (147-149)

Hamlin. Item staff. *The New Orleans Daily States* June 6, 1913. *WCWDF* #328. (292)

Hammond, A. A. Attorney. Letter. *WCWDF* #155. (133)

Hargroter, Ogee. The Trial. Document. Trial notes. *WCWDF* #320. Articles. *The New Orleans Item* April 15-28, 1914. *The Times-Picayune* [New Orleans, LA] April 15-28, 1914. *The New Orleans Daily States* April 15-28, 1914. (197-225)

Harvey, H. J. Photographer. Photo. "This picture shows Mr. and Mrs. Dunbar." *The New Orleans Item* April 12, 1914. (268)
Photo. *The New Orleans Item* April 23, 1913. (319)

Hathorn, S. J. Sheriff. Quote. "If that kid is Bobby Dunbar." *The New Orleans Item* April 23, 1913. (23)
The Trial. Document. Trial notes. *WCWDF* #320. Articles. *The New Orleans Item* April 15-28, 1914. *The Times-Picayune* [New Orleans, LA] April 15-28, 1914. *The New Orleans Daily States* April 15-28, 1914. (197-225)
Letter. *WCWDF* #331. (220, 309)
Unknown. Photo. "Hero, 'Villian,' And Other Characters." *The New Orleans Item* June 8, 1913. (262)

Hawes, Lee. Reporter for Item. Article. "Search For Bruce Nears End: S. H. Fox…trying to build up a chain of circumstantial evidence. The Anderson boy was swapped: The Bilbo's…say that the boy…had a web foot." *The New Orleans Item* May 13, 1913. (102)
Articles. *The New Orleans Item* April 15-28, 1914. (197-225)

Hawkins, Dr. Palmetto, LA. The Trial. Document. Trial notes. *WCWDF* #320. Articles. *The New Orleans Item* April 15-28, 1914. *The Times-Picayune* [New Orleans, LA] April 15-28, 1914. *The New Orleans Daily States* April 15-28, 1914. (197-225)

Hodges, Mrs. The Trial. Document. Trial notes. *WCWDF* #320. Articles. *The New Orleans Item* April 15-28, 1914. *The Times-Picayune* [New Orleans, LA] April 15-28, 1914. *The New Orleans Daily States* April 15-28, 1914. (197-225)

Holcomb, G. W. Reverend. Letter. *WCWDF* #'s 34 and 87. (66, 283)
Habeas Corpus transcript. *WCWDF* #200. (140)
The Trial. Document. Trial notes. *WCWDF* #320. Articles. *The New Orleans Item* April 15-28, 1914. *The Times-Picayune* [New Orleans, LA] April 15-28, 1914. *The New Orleans Daily States* April 15-28, 1914. (197-225)
Trist. Sketch. "Walters witnesses as seen by Trist." *The New Orleans*

Item April 25, 1914. (176)

Hollimen, Levi N. Affidavit. *WCWDF* #79. Documents. *WCWDF* #'s 64 & 87. (39, 105)

Document. Habeas Corpus transcript. *WCWDF* #200. (137, 145)

The Trial. Document. Trial notes. *WCWDF* #320. Articles. *The New Orleans Item* April 15-28, 1914. *The Times-Picayune* [New Orleans, LA] April 15-28, 1914. *The New Orleans Daily States* April 15-28, 1914. (197-225)

Trist. Sketch. "Walters witnesses as seen by Trist." *The New Orleans Item* April 25, 1914. (275)

Hutson, Ethel. Item reporter. Article. "Julia Anderson, By No Means Unintelligent: Julia Says Bible Always Guides Her." *The New Orleans Item* April 30, 1913. (78)

Jacobs News Depot Co. Opelousas, LA. Photo. *WCWDF* #6. (284)

Jarrell, Mrs. S. J. Document. *WCWDF* #317. (306)

Johnson, Joe. The Trial. Document. Trial notes. *WCWDF* #320. Articles. *The New Orleans Item* April 15-28, 1914. *The Times-Picayune* [New Orleans, LA] April 15-28, 1914. *The New Orleans Daily States* April 15-28, 1914. (197-225)

King, Preston. Percy's Uncle. Habeas Corpus transcript. *WCWDF* #200. (153)

Cantwell's letter. *WCWDF* #204. (155)

The Trial. Document. Trial notes. *WCWDF* #320. Articles. *The New Orleans Item* April 15-28, 1914. *The Times-Picayune* [New Orleans, LA] April 15-28, 1914. *The New Orleans Daily States* April 15-28, 1914. (197-225)

Trist. Sketch. "Principal Witnesses for State." *The New Orleans Item* April 18, 1914. (274)

Kinlaw, W. H. Notary Public. George and Beedie Anderson's affidavit. *WCWDF* #242. (302)

Kleinpeter, Thomas. Attorney. Letter. *WCWDF* #207. (155, 299)

Letter. *WCWDF* #306. (187)

Letter. *WCWDF* #307. (187)

Koenig, A. New Orleans, LA. Umbrella maker. Unknown. Article. "Bruce Anderson Is Being Hidden." *The New Orleans Item* February 21, 1914. (132)

Lampton, William. Unknown. Article. "He's My Boy: Eyes Didn't Look Right." *The New Orleans Daily States* April 22, 1913. (23-25)

Unknown. Photo. *WCWDF* #3. (279)

Lass, Miss. The Trial. Document. Trial notes. *WCWDF* #320. Articles. *The New Orleans Item* April 15-28, 1914. *The Times-Picayune* [New Orleans, LA] April 15-28, 1914. *The New Orleans Daily States* April 15-28, 1914. (197-225)

Lawrence, R. C. Attorney. Letter. *WCWDF* #48. (99)

Lawson, J. R. Justice of Peace. *WCWDF* #18. (280)

Leader Print. [Brookhaven, MS] Flyer. *WCWDF* #122. (293)

Lehon, Dan. Article. "Burns Men Help Him." *The New Orleans Item* April 25, 1913. (48)

Lewis, John W. Opelousas, LA. Article. "Recognizes Playmates: Lawyer Makes Address: The successful politician." *The Times-Democrat* [New Orleans, LA] April 26, 1913. (51)
Quote. "She has failed to recognize him!" May 1, 1913. *WCWDF* #350. (80)
Document. The Dunbar Investigation. *WCWDF* #115. (117-125)
The Trial. Document. Motion for new trial. *WCWDF* #350. Articles. *The New Orleans Item* April 15-28, 1914. *The Times-Picayune* [New Orleans, LA] April 15-28, 1914. *The New Orleans Daily States* April 15-28, 1914. (197-225)

Lewis, Mrs. John. The Trial. Document. Trial notes. *WCWDF* #320. Articles. *The New Orleans Item* April 15-28, 1914. *The Times-Picayune* [New Orleans, LA] April 15-28, 1914. *The New Orleans Daily States* April 15-28, 1914. (197-225)

Linder, J. L. Alexandria, LA. Stove-mender. The Trial. Document. Trial notes. *WCWDF* #320. Document. Motion for new trial. *WCWDF* #350. Articles. *The New Orleans Item* April 15-28, 1914. *The Times-Picayune* [New Orleans, LA] April 15-28, 1914. *The New Orleans Daily States* April 15-28, 1914. (197-225)
Letter. *WCWDF* #387. (238)
Unknown. Photo. "Latest picture." *The New Orleans Item* June 9, 1913. (261)

Loeb, T. L. Mayor of Opelousas. Telegram. *WCWDF* #311. (15, 278)
The Trial. Document. Trial notes. *WCWDF* #320. Articles. *The New Orleans Item* April 15-28, 1914. *The Times-Picayune* [New Orleans, LA] April 15-28, 1914. *The New Orleans Daily States* April 15-28, 1914. (197-225)

Lott, W. W. Sheriff. Document. The Dunbar Investigation. *WCWDF* #115. (118)
Affidavits. *WCWDF* #'s 132 through 143. (130)

Louisiana Lady. Letter. *WCWDF* #335. (226)

Loveless, Miss. McNeill, MS. Nurse. The Trial. Document. Trial notes. *WCWDF* #320. Articles. *The New Orleans Item* April 15-28, 1914. *The Times-Picayune* [New Orleans, LA] April 15-28, 1914. *The New Orleans Daily States* April 15-28, 1914. (197-225)
Trist. Sketch. "Principal Witnesses for State." *The New Orleans Item* April 18, 1914. (175)

Lumpkin, Thomas. Affidavit. *WCWDF* #75. (105)
The Trial. Document. Trial notes. *WCWDF* #320. Articles. *The New Orleans Item* April 15-28, 1914. *The Times-Picayune* [New Orleans, LA] April 15-28, 1914. *The New Orleans Daily States* April 15-28, 1914. (197-225)

M. Letter. "My very dear friend." *Lexington Advisor* [Lexington, MS] May 5, 1913. *WCWDF* #47. (90)

Mallet, William. Forrest Hill, LA. Constable and Sheriff. Habeas Corpus transcript. *WCWDF* #200. (146, 149, 150)
The Trial. Document. Trial notes. *WCWDF* #320. Articles. *The New Orleans Item* April 15-28, 1914. *The Times-Picayune* [New Orleans, LA] April 15-28, 1914. *The New Orleans Daily States* April 15-28, 1914. (197-225)

Maxwell. Photo. "Bobbie now is camera man." *The New Orleans Daily States* April 10, 1914. (272)

Mayson, O. L. Judge. The Trial. Document. Trial notes. *WCWDF* #320. Articles. *The New Orleans Item* April 15-28, 1914. *The Times-Picayune* [New Orleans, LA] April 15-28, 1914. *The New Orleans Daily States* April 15-28, 1914. (197-225)

McGill, A. Notary Public. Document. *WCWDF* #72. (287)

McIntyre, Lawrence & Proctor. Attorneys. Letter. *WCWDF* #48. (99)

McKinley, J. A. Columbia, MS. Justice of Peace. Habeas Corpus transcript. *WCWDF* #200. (147,148)

McManus, Mrs. Pineville, MS. Habeas Corpus transcript. *WCWDF* #200. (146, 151,154)
The Trial. Document. Trial notes. *WCWDF* #320. Articles. *The New Orleans Item* April 15-28, 1914. *The Times-Picayune* [New Orleans, LA] April 15-28, 1914. *The New Orleans Daily States* April 15-28, 1914. (197-225)
Trist. Sketch. "Principal Witnesses for State." *The New Orleans Item* April 18, 1914. (274)

McMullen, Albert J. Letter. "Late tonight I was instructed." *WCWDF*

#44. (89)

Article. "Real Dunbar child drowned." *Lexington Advertiser* [Lexington, MS] May 5, 1913. Document. *WCWDF* #47. (90)

"Tinker retraces his wanderings with the boy." *The New Orleans Daily States* May 4, 1913. (96)

McThenia, Tal. Broadcast. "The Ghost of Bobby Dunbar." *This American Life WBEZ Chicago, Public Radio International* March 14, 2008. (328)

Publication. "A Case for Solomon." *Free Press Simon & Schuster, Inc.* [New York] 2012. (328)

Mitchell, J. P. Justice of Peace. Affidavit. *WCWDF* #78. (288)

Affidavit. *WCWDF* #76. (290)

Affidavit. *WCWDF* #312. (189, 305)

Mizzie, Paul. Opelousas, LA. Butcher. The Trial. Document. Trial notes. *WCWDF* #320. Articles. *The New Orleans Item* April 15-28, 1914. *The Times-Picayune* [New Orleans, LA] April 15-28, 1914. *The New Orleans Daily States* April 15-28, 1914. (2, 197-225)

Monroe, Marion B. Preacher. Letter. *WCWDF* #329. (308)

Moody, Edna. Transcript. The Dunbar Investigation. *WCWDF* #115. (125)

Moody, Homer. Transcript. The Dunbar Investigation. *WCWDF* #115. (120, 124)

Moody, J. A. Sheriff. Transcript. The Dunbar Investigation. *WCWDF* #115. (124)

Moody, S. J. Justice of Peace. Affidavit. *WCWDF* #316. (306)

Morel, V. Sketch. "Justice weighs pleas in fight of mothers." *The New Orleans Item* April 14, 1914. (267)

Morgan, D. L. Brother of Dee. The Trial. Document. Trial notes. *WCWDF* #320. Articles. *The New Orleans Item* April 15-28, 1914. *The Times-Picayune* [New Orleans, LA] April 15-28, 1914. *The New Orleans Daily States* April 15-28, 1914. (197-225)

Morgan, Dee. Brother of D. L. The Trial. Document. Trial notes. *WCWDF* #320. Articles. *The New Orleans Item* April 15-28, 1914. *The Times-Picayune* [New Orleans, LA] April 15-28, 1914. *The New Orleans Daily States* April 15-28, 1914. (197-225)

Mornhinveg, Mrs. R. Opelousas, LA. The Trial. Document. Trial notes. *WCWDF* #320. Articles. *The New Orleans Item* April 15-28, 1914. *The Times-Picayune* [New Orleans, LA] April 15-28, 1914. *The New Orleans Daily States* April 15-28, 1914. (197-225)

Mounger, William Harris (Harry). Attorney. "He would be ashamed." *The New Orleans Item* April 23, 1913. (34)

Murray, William H. (Bill). Barnesville, NC. Mailman. Unknown. Article. "Saw Letter Opened." *The New Orleans Daily States* April 28, 1913. (58, 69)

The Trial. Document. Trial notes. *WCWDF* #320. Articles. *The New Orleans Item* April 15-28, 1914. *The Times-Picayune* [New Orleans, LA] April 15-28, 1914. *The New Orleans Daily States* April 15-28, 1914. (197-225)

Trist. Sketch. "Walters witnesses as seen by Trist." *The New Orleans Item* April 25, 1914. (275)

Myers, Sol. Manager Hippodrome. Article. "Theater Manager Says Dunbar Asked $1,000." *The New Orleans Daily States* June 6, 1913. *WCWDF* #328. (33, 292)

Myley, Charlie. Transcript. The Dunbar Investigation. *WCWDF* #115. (123)

Letter. *WCWDF* #125. Document. #126. (129, 294)

Letter. *WCWDF* #129. (129)

Myley, Mrs. Charlie (Ella). Document. The Dunbar Investigation. *WCWDF* #115. (123)

The Trial. Document. Trial notes. *WCWDF* #320. Articles. *The New Orleans Item* April 15-28, 1914. *The Times-Picayune* [New Orleans, LA] April 15-28, 1914. *The New Orleans Daily States* April 15-28, 1914. (197-225)

Unknown. Photo. "Hero, 'Villian,' And Other Characters." *The New Orleans Item* June 8, 1913. (262)

Nix, Mrs. The Trial. Document. Trial notes. *WCWDF* #320. Articles. *The New Orleans Item* April 15-28, 1914. *The Times-Picayune* [New Orleans, LA] April 15-28, 1914. *The New Orleans Daily States* April 15-28, 1914. (197-225)

Trist. Sketch. "Principal Witnesses for State." *The New Orleans Item* April 18, 1914. (175)

Oge, John. The Trial. Document. Trial notes. *WCWDF* #320. Articles. *The New Orleans Item* April 15-28, 1914. *The Times-Picayune* [New Orleans, LA] April 15-28, 1914. *The New Orleans Daily States* April 15-28, 1914. (197-225)

Oh! Susanna. Song. Stephen Foster. 1848. http://en.wikipedia.org/wiki/Oh!_Susanna. (14)

Owens, Mrs. S. R. Iron City, GA. Affidavit. *WCWDF* #17. (280)

Padgett & Watson. Attorneys. Letter. *WCWDF* #222. (172)
  Letter. *WCWDF* #251. (178)
  Letter. *WCWDF* #259. (179)
  Quote. *WCWDF* #271. (185)
Panic of 1873. Article. "Long Depression." Wikipedia. http://en.wikipedia.org/wiki/Long_Depression. (13)
Parker, John M. Cotton Broker. Transcript. The Dunbar Investigation. *WCWDF* #115. (117-125)
  Unknown. Article. "He's Bobbie: It Is Little Robert: In my opinion." *The New Orleans Item* June 8, 1913. (125)
  Quote. Unknown. Article. "Victory Is On Walters' Side: 'Don't Care A Rap,' Parker: …he doesn't care a rap." *The New Orleans Item* June 10, 1913. (128)
  Unknown. Photo. "Hero, 'Villian,' And Other Characters." *The New Orleans Item* June 8, 1913. (262)
Pavy, B. H. District Judge. Telegram. *WCWDF* #281. (187, 304)
  The Trial. Articles. *The New Orleans Item* April 15-28, 1914. *The Times-Picayune* [New Orleans, LA] April 15-28, 1914. *The New Orleans Daily States* April 15-28, 1914. (197-225)
Picto Theatre. Flyer. *Leader Print* [Brookhaven, MS] *WCWDF* #122. (293)
Piggford, Mr. The Trial. Document. Trial notes. *WCWDF* #320. Articles. *The New Orleans Item* April 15-28, 1914. *The Times-Picayune* [New Orleans, LA] April 15-28, 1914. *The New Orleans Daily States* April 15-28, 1914. (197-225)
Pool, Ott. Receipt. Courtesy of Jarvis Lowe and the Marion County Historical Society. Columbia, MS. (24, 279)
Pulford, Mr. M. The Trial. Document. Trial notes. *WCWDF* #320. Articles. *The New Orleans Item* April 15-28, 1914. *The Times-Picayune* [New Orleans, LA] April 15-28, 1914. *The New Orleans Daily States* April 15-28, 1914. (197-225)
Rabon, Mrs. J. H. Iron City, GA. Affidavit. *WCWDF* #17. (280)
Rabon, Mae. Iron City, GA. Affidavit. *WCWDF* #17. (280)
Rawls, Adele Mounger. Hollis's wife and author's grandmother. Interview. Adele (Dell) Rawls Crisler. 2002 to 2008. (XVI)
Rawls, Ben M. Attorney and Banker. Hollis's son and author's father. (XV)
  Interview. "Walter immediately petitioned for custody of his grandson." 1984. (29)

Rawls, Carol Newsom. Aunt of author. Interview. 2002. (XVIII)

Rawls, Hollis C. Columbia, MS. Attorney. Author's grandfather. Interview. Ben M. Rawls. 1984. (XV)

Article. Minion Hall. "Don't Hang Him: Three Witnesses for Walters: I immediately told Mr. Dunbar that a mistake had been made." *The New Orleans Item* April 11, 1914. (32-34)

Letter. *WCWDF* #13. (49)

Letter. *WCWDF* #90. (43)

Letter. *WCWDF* #41. (88, 99)

Letter. *WCWDF* #250. (95)

Letter. *WCWDF* #46. (99)

Letter. *WCWDF* #54. (100)

Letter. *WCWDF* #56. (101)

Letter. *WCWDF* #68. (102)

Quote. Letter. *WCWDF* #85. (104)

Letter. *WCWDF* #99. (110)

Transcript. The Dunbar Investigation. *WCWDF* #115. (117-125)

Unknown. Article. "Parker misunderstood." *The New Orleans Item* June 9, 1913. (126)

Letter. *WCWDF* #123. (129)

Letter. *WCWDF* #163. (132)

Document. Habeas Corpus transcript. *WCWDF* #200. (135-154)

Letter. *WCWDF* #212. (155)

Letter. *WCWDF* #229. (162)

Letter. *WCWDF* #243. (172)

Letter. *WCWDF* #244. (174)

Letter. *WCWDF* #250. (176)

Quote. Letter. *WCWDF* #252. (179)

Letter. *WCWDF* #276. (185)

Letters. *WCWDF* #'s 272 & 274. (187)

Letter. *WCWDF* #279. (187)

Letter. *WCWDF* #284. (187)

Letter. *WCWDF* #292. (187)

The Trial. Document. Trial Notes. *WCWDF* #320. Document. Application for a new trial. *WCWDF* #350. Articles. *The New Orleans Item* April 15-28, 1914. *The Times-Picayune* [New Orleans, LA] April 15-28, 1914. *The New Orleans Daily States* April 15-28, 1914. (197-225)

Appeal. *WCWDF* #396. (240)

15-28, 1914. *The New Orleans Daily States* April 15-28, 1914. (197-225)

Roberts, Mrs. W. B. Opelousas, LA. The Trial. Document. Trial notes. *WCWDF* #320. Articles. *The New Orleans Item* April 15-28, 1914. *The Times-Picayune* [New Orleans, LA] April 15-28, 1914. *The New Orleans Daily States* April 15-28, 1914. (197-225)

Robertson, Alex. Letter. *WCWDF* #387. (238)

Robertson, Mr. Civil Engineer. The Trial. Document. Trial notes. *WCWDF* #320. Articles. *The New Orleans Item* April 15-28, 1914. *The Times-Picayune* [New Orleans, LA] April 15-28, 1914. *The New Orleans Daily States* April 15-28, 1914. (197-225)

Roderick. Unknown. Photo. *The New Orleans Item* April 24, 1913 and July 3,1913. *WCWDF* #206. (28, 298)

Rose, Lou (Lew). Manager Hippodrome. Unknown. Article. "Theater Manager Says Dunbar Asked $1,000." *The New Orleans Daily States* June 6, 1913. Document. *WCWDF* #328. (33, 292)

Rouse, H. K. Chancery Clerk. *WCWDF* #139. (295)

Rushing, W. L. Receipt. *WCWDF* #130. (129, 130)

Rutherfurd, Edward. Author. "London." *Ballantine Books* [USA] 2002.

Saizan, Dr. The Trial. Articles. *The New Orleans Item* April 15-28, 1914. *The Times-Picayune* [New Orleans, LA] April 15-28, 1914. *The New Orleans Daily States* April 15-28, 1914. (80, 197-225)

Scarborough, J. J. Postmaster. Affidavit. Document. *WCWDF* #'s 132 and 322. (130, 307)
 Document. Habeas Corpus transcript. *WCWDF* #200. (141)
 Trist. Sketch. "Walters witnesses as seen by Trist." *The New Orleans Item* April 25, 1914. (275)

Scarborough, Mr. DeRidder, LA. The Trial. Document. Trial notes. *WCWDF* #320. Articles. *The New Orleans Item* April 15-28, 1914. *The Times-Picayune* [New Orleans, LA] April 15-28, 1914. *The New Orleans Daily States* April 15-28, 1914. (197-225)

Sears, Roebuck and Co., Chicago. Manual—Organ Repair. "The Reed Organ, How to Give it the Proper Care." *Sears, Roebuck and Co., Chicago* 1910. http://www.archive.org/stream/reedorganhowtogi-ooseariala/reedorganhowtogiooseariala_djvu.txt. (12)

Seiferth, Herman J. Article. "Bobbie Dunbar Tells Of The Death Of Bruce: Walters was inside." *The Times-Picayune* [New Orleans, LA] April 18, 1914. (156)

Sherrouse, B. F. Unknown. Photo. "Latest picture." *The New Orleans*

Item June 9, 1913. (261)

Shute, F. C. Physician. Unknown. Article. "Kidnapped Robert: Physical Deformities Are Same: Dr. Shute treated the boy." *The New Orleans Item* April 26, 1913. (53)

The Trial. Document. Trial notes. *WCWDF* #320. Articles. *The New Orleans Item* April 15-28, 1914. *The Times-Picayune* [New Orleans, LA] April 15-28, 1914. *The New Orleans Daily States* April 15-28, 1914. (197-225)

Shute, Mrs. F. C. The Trial. Document. Trial notes. *WCWDF* #320. Articles. *The New Orleans Item* April 15-28, 1914. *The Times-Picayune* [New Orleans, LA] April 15-28, 1914. *The New Orleans Daily States* April 15-28, 1914. (197-225)

Silent Night, Holy Night. Song. Joseph Mohr and Franz Gruber. 1816. http://en.wikipedia.org/wiki/Silent_Night. (13)

Skipper, C. B. Clerk. George and Beddie Anderson's affidavit. *WCWDF* #242. (302)

Sloan, Mrs. M. E. New Roads, LA. The Trial. Document. Motion for new trial. *WCWDF* #350. Articles. *The New Orleans Item* April 15-28, 1914. *The Times-Picayune* [New Orleans, LA] April 15-28, 1914. *The New Orleans Daily States* April 15-28, 1914. (197-225)

Smith, D. F. Postmaster. Telegram. *WCWDF* #310. (15, 278)
Affidavit. "They decided that it was not C. P. Dunbar's child." *WCWDF* #312. (190, 305)
Letter. *WCWDF* #344. (229)
Letter. *WCWDF* #412. (312)

Smith, J. D. Postmaster. Document. *WCWDF* #322. (307)

Sones, B. J. Sr. Affidavit. *WCWDF* #78. (105, 142, 288)
Document. Habeas Corpus transcript. *WCWDF* #200. (142,144,147)

Sones, J. Q. Affidavit. *WCWDF* #81. (105)
Document. Habeas Corpus transcript. *WCWDF* #200. (139, 143)

Spiers, S. Affidavit. *WCWDF* #73. (105)

Stanley, L. W. Clerk. Julia Anderson's affidavit. *WCWDF* #104. (291)

Stephens, F. M. Cantwell's nephew. The Trial. Document. Trial notes. *WCWDF* #320. Articles. *The New Orleans Item* April 15-28, 1914. *The Times-Picayune* [New Orleans, LA] April 15-28, 1914. *The New Orleans Daily States* April 15-28, 1914. (197-225)
Trist. Sketch. "Walters witnesses as seen by Trist." *The New Orleans Item* April 25, 1914. (275)

Stephens, M. A. Letter. Evergreen, NC. "A Plea For The Innocent." *WCWDF* #489. (246)

Stetly, Mr. The Trial. Document. Trial notes. *WCWDF* #320. Articles. *The New Orleans Item* April 15-28, 1914. *The Times-Picayune* [New Orleans, LA] April 15-28, 1914. *The New Orleans Daily States* April 15-28, 1914. (197-225)

Stogner, W. A. Tylertown, MS. Document. Habeas Corpus transcript. *WCWDF* #200. (150, 154)
  The Trial. Document. Trial notes. *WCWDF* #320. Articles. *The New Orleans Item* April 15-28, 1914. *The Times-Picayune* [New Orleans, LA] April 15-28, 1914. *The New Orleans Daily States* April 15-28, 1914. (197-225)

Storm, Jack F. Affidavit. "If I do not find that child." *WCWDF* #153. June 14, 1913. (19)

Strange, A. J. Physician. Letter and map. *WCWDF* #42. (8, 92, 285)

Sweeney, Jobie. Document. Quote. "No, my name is Bruce." *WCWDF* #151. (32)

Swords, Marion. Opelousas, LA. Sheriff. Document. Habeas Corpus transcript. *WCWDF* #200. (24,132,148,149)

Sylverstein, B. A. County Attorney. Columbia, MS. Document. Habeas Corpus transcript. *WCWDF* #200. (148)

Take Me Out to the Ball Game. Song. Jack Norworth and Albert Von Tilzer. 1908. (14)

Tarver, Jewel Rawls. Julia and Ollie's daughter. Interviews. 2002 to 2008. (XIX, 239)
  Unknown. Photo. *The Columbian Progress* [Columbia, MS] August 10, 2002. (321)
  Interviews. Julia and Ollie's family. 2002 to 2008. (323, 324)

Thigpen, Emille. The Trial. Document. Trial notes. *WCWDF* #320. Articles. *The New Orleans Item* April 15-28, 1914. *The Times-Picayune* [New Orleans, LA] April 15-28, 1914. *The New Orleans Daily States* April 15-28, 1914. (197-225)

Thigpen, J. S. Affidavit. *WCWDF* #74. (105, 289)
  Document. Habeas Corpus transcript. *WCWDF* #200. (139)
  The Trial. Document. Trial notes. *WCWDF* #320. Articles. *The New Orleans Item* April 15-28, 1914. *The Times-Picayune* [New Orleans, LA] April 15-28, 1914. *The New Orleans Daily States* April 15-28, 1914. (197-225)

Thigpen, L. A. (Lloyd) (Old Man) *WCWDF* #'s 64 & 87. (40)

Document. Habeas Corpus transcript. *WCWDF* #200. (140)

Thigpen, Mrs. L. A. Affidavit. *WCWDF* #'s 76 & 87. (105,147, 290)

Tinker, Tailor, Soldier, Sailor. Lyric. http://en.wikipedia.org/wiki/Tinker,_Tailor.

Tisdale, F. S. Article. "Mysterious Trunk Is Seized By Officials." *The New Orleans Daily States* April 28, 1913. (47)

Article. "Only Close Friends Of Dunbars Admitted When Woman Sees Boy: Julia To Be Held: In a panting red automobile." *The New Orleans Daily States* May 1, 1913. (79)

Article. "Only Close Friends Of Dunbars Admitted When Woman Sees Boy: Governor Brewer To Grant: E. P. Veazie and Mr. Lewis." *The New Orleans Daily States* May 1, 1913. (82)

Article. "Only Close Friends Of Dunbars Admitted When Woman Sees Boy: Julia To Be Held: The woman is almost a nervous wreck." *The New Orleans Daily States* May 1, 1913. (82)

Article. "Only Close Friends of Dunbars Admitted When Woman Sees Boy: Lawyers Not to Oppose Extradition: Julia Anderson was asked to pick." *The New Orleans Daily States* May 1, 1913. (82)

Article. "Woman quits Opelousas: After Good Night's Rest." *The New Orleans Daily States* May 2, 1913. (82)

Sketch. "Sketched in Opelousas During The Excitement." *The New Orleans Daily States* May 4, 1913. (260)

Touchstone, Mr. Quote. Unknown. Article. "Walters Notorious Criminal, Says This Man." *The New Orleans Daily States* April 27, 1913. (48)

(Tutstone Woodville). Document. Motion for a new trial. *WCWDF* #350. (235)

(Tutstone). Affidavit. R. B. Davis. *WCWDF* #352. (236)

Trist. Sketch. "Trist has here portrayed Walters." *The New Orleans Item* April 20, 1914. (271)

Sketch. "Principal Witnesses for State." *The New Orleans Item* April 18, 1914. (274)

Sketch. "Walters Witnesses as Seen by Trist." *The New Orleans Item* April 25, 1914. (275)

Tulane University. Howard-Tilton Memorial Library. New Orleans, LA. Author's research. (XXV)

Tynes, J. M. Document. Habeas Corpus transcript. *WCWDF* #200. (142)

Yates, A. L. Columbia, MS. Attorney. Unknown. Article. "Witnesses

Insist Dunbars Have the Wrong Boy: Another Important Witness: …A. L. Yates." *The New Orleans Item* June 7, 1913. Unknown. Articles. "Parker Misunderstood: Thinks Parker Misunderstood: A. L. Yates." & "Says He Didn't Send Yates." *The New Orleans Item* June 7, 1913. (117)

Unknown. Article. "Father Tells Of Long Search. We found only the boy's little straw hat." *The New Orleans Item* April 22, 1913. Unknown. Article. "Where Is The Other Boy?: As if Goblin had Whisked Him Away: Only a little hat." Unknown. *The New Orleans Item* April 9, 1914. (9)

Unknown. Article. "Dunbar Has Enemies." *The Times-Democrat* [New Orleans, LA] April 27, 1913. (10)

Unknown. Article. "Boy's Identity Doubted: Uncle Did Not Claim Boy." *The Times-Democrat* [New Orleans, LA] April 24, 1913. (10, 15)

Unknown. Article. "Walters, Divorcee, Once A Prominent Georgia Merchant." *The New Orleans Item* April 14, 1914. (13)

Unknown. Article. "Which Walters Is Guilty One: How The Child Was Found." *The Daily Clarion-Ledger* [Jackson, MS] April 27, 1913. (18)

Unknown. Article. "Dunbars Arrive Here: The Reward Question." *The Daily Picayune* [Picayune, MS] April 24, 1913. (22)

Unknown. Article. "Wallace Takes 'Receipt' for Baby: He would not hand over the boy." *The New Orleans Item* April 23, 1913. (24)

Unknown. Article. "He's My Boy: She again looked into the little boy's eyes—and was not sure." *The New Orleans Daily States* April 22, 1913. (24)

Unknown. Article. "He's My Boy: Eyes Didn't Look Right: Lampton." *The New Orleans Daily States* April 22, 1913. (24)

Unknown. Article. Quote. "Dunbars Bring 'Stolen Son' Here. Trip from Columbia: Walters would be lynched." *The New Orleans Item* April 23, 1913. (23)

Unknown. Article. "Give Me Time Pleads Walters: Yes, I whipped him: I never hurt him so much that welts showed." *The New Orleans Item* April 23, 1913. Unknown. Article. "Tinker in Opelousas: I do not want Walters hanged for this crime, as I know that he was not cruel to my child." *The New Orleans Item* May 9, 1913. (30)

Unknown. Article. "He's My Boy: Then He Called Her Mamma." *The New Orleans Daily States* April 22, 1913. (32)

Unknown. Article. "Theater Manager Says Dunbar Asked $1,000." *The*

New Orleans Daily States June 6, 1913. *WCWDF* #328. (33, 43)

Unknown. Article. "Asks Item To Thank Ladies of Hub, Miss.: To the good ladies of Hub." *The New Orleans Item* April 23, 1913. (42)

Unknown. Article. "Offers From Showmen: Mr. and Mrs. Dunbar are the guests." *The Times-Democrat* [New Orleans, LA] April 24, 1913. (43)

Unknown. Article. "Robbie Knows Just What Kind Of Suit He Likes." *The New Orleans Daily States* April 24, 1913. (45)

Unknown. Article. "Not One In Opelousas Doubts It Is Robert: In fact not one person." *The New Orleans Item* April 26, 1913. (48)

Unknown. Articles. "Remember Tinker As Evil Scoundrel." "Sheriff To Say If Walters Was Felon." *The New Orleans Daily States* April 26, 1913. (48)

Unknown. Article. "Walters Had Three Boys." *The Times-Democrat* [New Orleans, LA] April 25, 1913. (48)

Unknown. Article. "Recognizes Playmates: Pulls Bell Cord, Stops Train." *The Times-Democrat* [New Orleans, LA] April 26, 1913. (50)

Unknown. Article. "Recognizes Playmates: Many Greet Dunbars: At The Hotel" *The Times-Democrat* [New Orleans, LA] April 26, 1913. (50)

Unknown. Article. "Is Not Bruce Anderson: Not Carolina Boy." *The Times –Democrat* [New Orleans, LA] April 26, 1913. (50)

Unknown. Article. "Not One In Opelousas Doubts It Is Robert: Sound of His Weeping: Raised her umbrella and it struck the child in the eye." *The New Orleans Item* April 26, 1913. (51)

Unknown. Article. "Recognizes Playmates: Procession To Home: There was applause." *The Times-Democrat* [New Orleans, LA] April 26, 1913. (51)

Unknown. Article. "Asks Brewer To Act: In a spirit of fairness." *The Times-Democrat* [New Orleans, LA] April 24, 1913. (53)

Unknown. Article. "Robert Quits His Throne To Ride On New Velocipede: Bobbie Deserts Hosts." *The New Orleans Item* April 27, 1913. (54)

Unknown. Article. "New Joy Disperses All Gloom Once in Home of Dunbars." *The New Orleans Item* April 26, 1913. (55)

Unknown. Article. "R. F. D. Carrier Makes Affidavit: Saw Letter Opened." *The New Orleans Daily States* April 28, 1913. (58)

Unknown. Article. "Saw Walters and Boy: McComb Men Encountered Pair." *The Times-Democrat* [New Orleans, LA] April 28, 1913. (60)

Unknown. Article. "Opelousas Awaits Arrival Of Woman: Encouragement: You Is So Got Rong Man: I is ritin you dis leter." *The Daily Picayune* [Picayune, MS] May 1, 1913. (65)

Unknown. Article. "Proves Anderson Child Is Not One Held By Dunbars: Drummer Is Father." *The New Orleans Item* April 26, 1913. (71)

Unknown. Article. "He's Brother's Boy." *The New Orleans Item* April 23, 1913. (72)

Unknown. Article. "Proves Anderson Child Is Not One Held By Dunbars: Suspected Murder." *The New Orleans Item* April 26, 1913. (78)

Unknown. Article. "Bruce's mother to see if she can identify boy." *The New Orleans Daily States* April 29, 1913. (75)

Unknown. Article. "Opelousas Half Frenzied: Sleeps Fitfully." *The New Orleans Item* May 1, 1913. (78)

Unknown. Article. "Dunbar Boy Not Hers: First Test Made: Ringed along the other side of the room." *The Times-Democrat* [New Orleans, LA] May 2, 1913. (80)

Unknown. Article. "Dunbar Boy Not Hers: My Child's Hair Lighter: District Attorney Garland, With Judge Pavy arrived at this Juncture." *The Times-Democrat* [New Orleans, LA] May 2, 1913. (81)

Unknown. Article. "Dunbar Boy Not Hers: Climax of Drama." *The Times-Democrat* [New Orleans, LA] May 2, 1913. (81)

Unknown. Article. Wellwisher. "Gov. Earl Brewer, It is certainly a relief." *The New Orleans Daily States* April 30, 1913. (87)

Unknown. Article. "Bobbie Fell In As Usual: There's no question." *The Times-Democrat* [New Orleans, LA] May 2, 1913. (87)

Unknown. Article. "Was Picked Up On High Bridge: Recalls Details: He said he had been picked up." *The New Orleans Item* May 5, 1913. (96)

Unknown. Article. "Dunbar Lawyers To See Bilbo: Plea for Requisition: Men brought here from McComb City." *The New Orleans Item* May 13, 1913. (102)

Unknown. Article. "Theater Manager Says Dunbar Asked $1000." *The New Orleans Daily States* June 6, 1913. WCWDF #328. (111)

Unknown. Article. "Father Denies Alleged Report: Mr. Dunbar stated... his physician advised that he must find some child to replace his own." *The New Orleans Times-Democrat* May 15, 1913. (116)

Unknown. Article. "We're Keeping Hands Off: C. P. Dunbar Doesn't Attend Test." *The New Orleans Item* June 7, 1913. (116)

Unknown. Article. "Says Bilbo Test Means Nothing: No Fear for Walters: Mrs. Dunbar was ill." *The New Orleans Item* June 6, 1913. (116)

Unknown. Article. "I Can't Understand Her." *The New Orleans Item* June 6, 1913. (116)

Unknown. Article. "He's Bobbie: It Is Little Robert: In my opinion." *The New Orleans Item* June 8, 1913. (125)

Unknown. Article. "Parker Misunderstood." *The New Orleans Item* June 9, 1913. (126)

Unknown. Article. "Victory Is On Walters' Side: 'Don't Care A Rap,' Parker." *The New Orleans Item* June 10, 1913. (128)

Unknown. Article. "A Revelation." *Marion County Progress* [Columbia, MS] November 22, 1913. (181)

Unknown. Article. "Brother of Walters leaves mysteriously as he had arrived." *The New Orleans Item* April 15, 1914. (196)

Unknown. Article. "Julia Anderson longs to look upon 'Bobbie' in court." *The New Orleans Item* April 16, 1914. (204)

Unknown. Letter. "A Christian Woman." *WCWDF* #91. (106)

Unknown. Article. "Bruce Anderson Is Being Hidden." *The New Orleans Item* February 21, 1914. (132)

Unknown. Letter. "Bruce Baby." *WCWDF* #184. (135)

Unknown. Article. "Says Bilbo Test Means Nothing: The father of the little fellow." *The New Orleans Item* June 6, 1913. (135)

Unknown. Letter. "TJK" *WCWDF* #223. (160, 301)

Unknown. Article. Julia to Savannah. *The New Orleans Item* September 12, 1913. (175)

Unknown. Article. "Tinker in Opelousas: I do not want Walters hanged for this crime, as I know that he was not cruel to my child." *The New Orleans Item* May 9, 1913. (195)

Unknown. Article. "Jury Selected." *The New Orleans Item* April 15, 1914. (196)

Unknown. Article. "Carolinians Hold A Mass Meeting For Walters." *The New Orleans Daily States* June 7, 1914. (241, 313)

Unknown. Article. "Walter's Released." *The Daily Clarion-Ledger* [Jackson, MS] February 19, 1915. (255)

Unknown. Article. "The following is the opening statement." *The Marion County Progress* [Columbia, MS] *WCWDF* #185. (296)

Unknown. Letter. "Congratulations." *WCWDF* #335. (226)

Unknown. Photo. Roderick. "William Walters. Is He A Kidnapper?" *The New Orleans Item* April 24, 1913 and July 2, 1913. *WCWDF* #206. (47, 155, 298)

Unknown. Photo. "Dunbar Boy, Columbia Crowd." *The New Orleans Item* April 23, 1913. (40)

Unknown. Photo. "Mrs. Robert Dunbar And Her Child, Posing Exclusively For The Item." *The New Orleans Item* April 23, 1913. (42)

Unknown. Photo. "Julia Anderson." *The Times-Democrat* [New Orleans, LA] May 1, 1913. (261)

Unknown. Photo. "Latest picture." *The New Orleans Item* June 9, 1913. (261)

Unknown. Photo. "Hero, 'Villian,' And Other Characters." *The New Orleans Item* June 8, 1913. (262)

Unknown. Photo. "Which is the mother of this boy?" *The New Orleans Item* April 9, 1914. (263)

Unknown. Photo. "Is this Bobbie Dunbar or Bruce Anderson?" *The New Orleans Item* April 11, 1914. (264)

Unknown. Photo. "On his thousand-string handmade harp." *The New Orleans Daily States* April 12, 1914. (264)

Unknown. Photo. "This is my best photo." *The New Orleans Daily States* April 13, 1914. (265)

Unknown. Photo. "W. C. Walters addressing crowd from jail." *The New Orleans Item* April 13, 1914. (266)

Unknown. Photo. "Attorneys in the Walters-Dunbar case." *The New Orleans Item* April 12, 1914. (267)

Unknown. Photo. "Can these eyes solve Walters-Dunbar case?" *The New Orleans Item* April 15, 1914. (269)

Unknown. Photo. "Can you pick the boy by his nose?" *The New Orleans Item* April 16, 1914. (270)

Unknown. Photo. "Their mouths." *The New Orleans Item* April 17, 1914. (270)

Unknown. Photo. "Compare the full faces now." *The New Orleans Item* April 19, 1914. (271)

Unknown. Photo. "Four of the stars in the Dunbar-Walters case: Mr. and Mrs. C. P. Dunbar." *The New Orleans Daily States* April 15, 1914. (272)

Unknown. Photo. "The boy called Bobbie." *The New Orleans Item* April 21, 1914. (272)

Unknown. Photo. "Latest photographs." *The New Orleans Item* April 15, 1914. (272)

Unknown. Photo. "Here are some of the witnesses." *The New Orleans Item* April 13, 1914. (273)

Unknown. Photo. William Cantwell Walters. *WCWDF* #205. (297)

Unknown. Photo. "The Bobby Dunbar family." *The Morning Advocate* [Baton Rouge, Louisiana] October 10, 1948. (321)

Unknown. Photo. "What matters is way one chooses to live." *The Columbian Progress* [Columbia, Mississippi] August 10, 2002. (321)

Unknown. Song. "Away in a Manger." http://en.wikisource.org/wiki/Away_in_a_Manger. (11)

Veazie, E. P. Document "The Dunbar Investigation." *WCWDF* #115. (117-125)

Document. Habeas Corpus transcript. *WCWDF* #200. (151,152)

Wainwright, Mrs. Document. Habeas Corpus transcript. *WCWDF* #200. (146)

Wallace, Jeff. Deputy. Receipt. April 22, 1913. Courtesy of Jarvis Lowe and the Marion County Historical Society. [Columbia, MS]. (24, 279)

Unknown Article. "Wallace Takes 'Receipt' for Baby: He would not hand over the boy." *The New Orleans Item* April 23, 1913. (24)

Walters, D. B. (Bunt) Unknown. Article. "Brother of Walters Leaves Mysteriously." *The New Orleans Item* April 15, 1914. (196)

Walters, J. M. Letter. *WCWDF* #109. (114)

Letter. *WCWDF* #195. (133)

Quote. Letter. *WCWDF* #249. (175)

Walters, Michael. Robeson County, NC. Author's interviews. 2005 & 2007. (XXII)

Author's interviews. 2005 & 2007. (11-13)

Author's interviews. 2005 & 2007. (323)

Walters, William and Celia. Robeson County, NC. Cantwell's grandparents. Michael Walters. Author's interviews. 2005 & 2007. (XXIII)

Walters, William Cantwell. Robeson County, NC. Organ repairman. Bruce's foster father. Accused of kidnapping Bobby Dunbar. *WCWDF*. (XVII)

"The Famous Case of Bobby Dunbar." *The Morning Advocate* [Baton Rouge, LA.] October 10,1948. (XXVII)

Document. *WCWDF* #'s 65 and 87. (11-14)

Quote. Unknown. Article. "Give Me Time Pleads Walters: Yes, I whipped him: I never hurt him so much that welts showed." *The New Orleans Item* April 23, 1913. (30)

Quote. "My own sister asked me to leave him with her." Iradell Williamson's affidavit. *WCWDF* #33. (31)

Quote. "Well, I've heard stories." Margaret Dunbar Cutright Interview. 2002. (30)

Quote. "…I have also heard rumors." Margaret Dunbar Cutright Interview. 2002. (31)

Letter. "I see that you Got Bruce." *WCWDF* #7. (35)

Document. *WCWDF* #63. (38)

Document. *WCWDF* #'s 64 and 87. (40)

Unknown. Article. Letter. William Murray. "R. F. D. Carrier Makes Affidavit: Saw Letter Opened." *The New Orleans Daily States* April 28, 1913. (58)

Document. *WCWDF* #'s 65 and 87. (61)

Article. A. J. McMullen. "Tinker Retraces His Wanderings With Boy." *The New Orleans Daily States* May 4, 1913. Unknown. Article. "Did Walters Hide in Charity Hospital?: Other attaches interviewed at the hospital." *The New Orleans Item* April 12, 1914. (96)

Letter. J. M. Walters. *WCWDF* #39. (99)

Document. Habeas Corpus transcript. *WCWDF* #200. (143-146)

Letter. *WCWDF* #204. (155, 298)

Unknown. Photo. William Cantwell Walters. *WCWDF* #205. (155, 297)

Letter. *WCWDF* #228. (161)

Letter. *WCWDF* #233. (164)

Letter. *WCWDF* #236. (165)

Letter. *WCWDF* #237. (166)

Letter. *WCWDF* #238. (168)

Letter. *WCWDF* #239. (170)

Letter. *WCWDF* #240. (171)

Letter. "A Revelation." *Marion County Progress* [Columbia, MS] November 22, 1913. (113)

Letter. *WCWDF* #264. (183)

Letter. *WCWDF* #299. (188)

The Trial. Document. Trial notes. *WCWDF* #320. Document. Motion for new trial. *WCWDF* # 350. Articles. *The New Orleans Item* April 15-28, 1914. *The Times-Picayune* [New Orleans, LA] April 15-28, 1914. *The New Orleans Daily States* April 15-28, 1914. (197-225)

Letter. *WCWDF* #410. (241)

Letter. *WCWDF* #500. (256, 313)

Unknown. Photo. "Hero, 'Villian,' And Other Characters." *The New Orleans Item* June 8, 1913. (262)

Unknown. Photo. "On his thousand-string handmade harp." *The New Orleans Daily States* April 12, 1914. (264)

Unknown. Photo. "This is my best photo." *The New Orleans Daily States* April 13, 1914. (265)

Unknown. Photo. "W. C. Walters addressing crowd from jail." *The New Orleans Item* April 13, 1914. (266)

Letter. *WCWDF* #400. (311)

Waxter, H. L. The Trial. Document. Trial notes. *WCWDF* #320. Articles. *The New Orleans Item* April 15-28, 1914. *The Times-Picayune* [New Orleans, LA] April 15-28, 1914. *The New Orleans Daily States* April 15-28, 1914. (197-225)

Weathersby, A. E. Mississippi Circuit Judge. William Cantwell Walters' application for writ of Habeas Corpus. *WCWDF* #157. (131) Document. Habeas Corpus transcript. *WCWDF* #200. (135-154) Appeal to the MS Supreme Court. *WCWDF* #202. (154)

Wellborne, L. C. Chancery Clerk. Receipt. April 22, 1913. Courtesy of Jarvis Lowe and the Marion County Historical Society. [Columbia, MS]. (24, 279)

Wellwisher. Letter. *The New Orleans Daily States* April 30. 1913. (87) Article. *The New Orleans Item* July 29, 1913. William Cantwell Walters. Letter. *WCWDF* #221. (158)

White, Mr. The Trial. Document. Trial notes. *WCWDF* #320. Articles. *The New Orleans Item* April 15-28, 1914. *The Times-Picayune* [New Orleans, LA] April 15-28, 1914. *The New Orleans Daily States* April 15-28, 1914. (197-225)

Whitley, Douce. Lessie's sister. The Trial. Document. Trial notes. *WCWDF* #320. Articles. *The New Orleans Item* April 15-28, 1914. *The Times-Picayune* [New Orleans, LA] April 15-28, 1914. *The New Orleans Daily States* April 15-28, 1914. (197-225)

Whitley, Lorena. Lessie's sister. The Trial. Document. Trial notes. *WCWDF* #320. Articles. *The New Orleans Item* April 15-28, 1914. *The Times-Picayune* [New Orleans, LA] April 15-28, 1914. *The New Orleans Daily States* April 15-28, 1914. (197-225)

Whitley, Mrs. Lessie's mother. The Trial. Document. Trial notes. *WCWDF* #320. Articles. *The New Orleans Item* April 15-28, 1914. *The Times-Picayune* [New Orleans, LA] April 15-28, 1914. *The New Orleans Daily States* April 15-28, 1914. (197-225)

Williams, Bobby Joe. Article. "Mid-South Views the Floods of 1912 and 1913." 2008. http://tn-roots.com/tnshelby/history/Floods.htm. (3, 4)

Williams, Mr. The Trial. Document. Trial notes. *WCWDF* #320. Articles. *The New Orleans Item* April 15-28, 1914. *The Times-Picayune* [New Orleans, LA] April 15-28, 1914. *The New Orleans Daily States* April 15-28, 1914. (197-225)

Williamson, Iradell Walters. Affidavit. "Came very near to adopting the child." *WCWDF* #33. (31, 65)

Winningham, William. Affidavit. *WCWDF* #366. (235)

Willoughby, T. R. (Doc). Document. Jobie Sweeney's affidavit. *WCWDF* #151. (32)

Quote. "Mr. Dunbar stated…his physician advised that he must find some child to replace his own." *The New Orleans Times-Democrat* May 15, 1913. (116)

Document. The Dunbar Investigation. *WCWDF* #115. (117-125)

Winberry, Mr. Reverend. The Trial. Document. Trial notes. *WCWDF* #320. Articles. *The New Orleans Item* April 15-28, 1914. *The Times-Picayune* [New Orleans, LA] April 15-28, 1914. *The New Orleans Daily States* April 15-28, 1914. (197-225)

Zernott, Christine. Lessie's cousin. The Trial. Document. Trial notes. *WCWDF* #320. Articles. *The New Orleans Item* April 15-28, 1914. *The Times-Picayune* [New Orleans, LA] April 15-28, 1914. *The New Orleans Daily States* April 15-28, 1914. (197-225)

Unknown. Photo. "Latest picture." *The New Orleans Item* June 9, 1913. (261)

About the Author

Allison Rawls Bullock attended Columbia High School and the University of Southern Mississippi. In 1991, she found a folder that her grandfather, Attorney Hollis C. Rawls, had put away seventy-six years earlier. Thus began her search for the truth in the Bobby Dunbar kidnapping mystery. *Mizpah* is the product of her twelve-year journey to finish her grandfather's mission. This is her first venture into writing.

Printed in the USA
CPSIA information can be obtained
at www.ICGtesting.com
LVHW062254031023
759759LV00108B/909